The Human Spirit

The
HUMAN
SPIRIT

BEGINNINGS FROM GENESIS TO SCIENCE

Marjorie O'Rourke Boyle

The Pennsylvania State University Press
University Park, Pennsylvania

Library of Congress Cataloging-in-Publication Data

Names: Boyle, Marjorie O'Rourke, 1943– author.
Title: The human spirit : beginnings from Genesis to science / Marjorie O'Rourke Boyle.
Description: University Park, Pennsylvania : The Pennsylvania State University Press, [2018] | Includes bibliographical references and index.
Summary: "Explores significant interpretations of the human spirit in Western culture, with sources ranging from the Hebrew Bible and the apostle Paul to the theologians Augustine, Aquinas, and Calvin and the natural philosopher and physician William Harvey"— Provided by publisher.
Identifiers: LCCN 2018030802 | ISBN 9780271082042 (cloth : alk. paper)
Subjects: LCSH: Spirit.
Classification: LCC B105.S64 B69 2018 | DDC 128—dc23
LC record available at https://lccn.loc.gov/2018030802

Copyright © 2018 Marjorie O'Rourke Boyle
All rights reserved
Printed in the United States of America
Published by The Pennsylvania State University Press,
University Park, PA 16802–1003

The Pennsylvania State University Press is a member of the Association of American University Presses.

It is the policy of The Pennsylvania State University Press to use acid-free paper. Publications on uncoated stock satisfy the minimum requirements of American National Standard for Information Sciences—Permanence of Paper for Printed Library Material, ANSI Z39.48–1992.

Frontispiece: Frontispiece to the first edition of William Harvey's *De generatione animalium*. London: Octavian Pulleyn, 1651. Courtesy of the Thomas Fisher Rare Book Library, University of Toronto.

*To my friend Louis Dupré,
philosopher of religion*

CONTENTS

Acknowledgments (ix)

Introduction (1)

PART I ANCIENT REALITIES
1 Genesis (15)
2 Paul (59)

PART II MEDIEVAL THOUGHTS
3 Augustine (107)
4 Aquinas (151)

PART III EARLY MODERN DISCOVERIES
5 Calvin (195)
6 Science (237)

Notes (285)
Index (331)

ACKNOWLEDGMENTS

I would like to thank my distinguished colleagues for their learned and appreciative readings of chapters of this book in manuscript: †Jerome Murphy-O'Connor, Brian Stock, Marcia Colish, Bruce Gordon, and Vivian Nutton.

I also extend my appreciation to the University of Toronto Library, especially the Library of the Pontifical Institute of Mediaeval Studies; Caven Library at Knox College; and the Thomas Fisher Rare Book Library, which at my request for after-hours access to its first edition of William Harvey's *Exercitationes de generatione animalium* generously posted it online at Internet Archive. The frontispiece for this book, *The Human Spirit,* is reproduced from that library's volume.

Introduction

The modern human spirit is defined by courage. Its awesome character envisions a worthy aim and dares its achievement, often by perseverance in adversity. Yet the human spirit did not always denote virtue, not before science identified the liquid spirit, blood, whose hot circulation in the body inspired courage. *The Human Spirit: Beginnings from Genesis to Science* treats significant interpretations of human nature as religious, in political, philosophical, and physical aspects. It searches its historical subject, in a long duration, through major sources: the Priestly tradition of the Hebrew Bible; the apostle Paul among the Corinthians; the innovative theologians Augustine and Aquinas; the reformatory theologian Calvin; and the natural philosopher and physician William Harvey.

These writers are renowned for their importance and influence. They do not, in this book, represent eras or schools; they present themselves. Their presentations were not necessarily personal, however, as in the modern genre of autobiography. As intellectuals, they could develop abstract and even speculative thinking about the human spirit. Their thoughts about it were not staged on a progressive continuum, however, but displayed the continuities and discontinuities usual to history. Their methods varied, whether traditional or theoretical, scholarly or scientific. This book endeavors to quicken those authors to speak in their distinctive voices from their special experiences and particular notions. It also contextualizes them in their communities.

The biblical source on the creation of humans by the divine Spirit was not the invention of an individual author but the legacy of some Priestly tradents. Chapter 1 of Genesis originated in a communal belief in the Spirit soaring like an eagle to find and choose Israel from the foundation of heaven and earth. A communal context for understanding the human spirit continued in the letters of Paul to the Christian church he founded at Corinth; in the writing and preaching of Augustine, from his commune at Cassaciacum to his bishopric at Carthage; in the lectures and commentaries of Thomas Aquinas to his fellow friars in the Order of Preachers; in the texts and sermons of Jean Calvin as pastor of the reformed church at Geneva; and in the demonstrations and publications of William Harvey as the Lumleian lecturer in anatomy for the College of Physicians, London. A communal context was fitting because the human spirit was universal to all humans, in distinction to animal spirit or divine Spirit. Yet those authors did disclose to their communities personal situations from which they came to their individual convictions about humans as created by God "in our image, after our likeness" (Genesis 1:26). Those were all perilous places: for the Priestly tradents, in the desolate wilderness; for the apostle Paul, on horseback in a storm; for the wayward Augustine, in a whirling abyss; for the disobedient Aquinas, in a family kidnapping; for the perplexed and fatigued Calvin and Harvey, in labyrinths mental or bodily. Whether historical or rhetorical places, they marked beginnings on a thoughtful path from isolation and danger to belonging and security, in God, the divine Spirit, as the beginning and end of the human spirit. The Christian theologians Augustine, Aquinas, and Calvin shared a vocation of interpreting the human spirit in Scripture, as introduced in Genesis and witnessed in Paul's apostolic letters. The philosopher and physician Harvey was different in his empirical investigations of animal nature. Yet, when his anatomical research failed to discover the efficient cause of generation, he, too, acknowledged the biblical Creator. The long, sturdy thread that stitches and binds the pages of this book is a cultural conviction that the human spirit originated in the divine Spirit, from which it derived its identity. The book reveals through its authors, among their distinctive ideas, a shared belief in the human spirit as endowed or designed by a divine source of everything animate.

The method of the book for this challenging subject is broadly interdisciplinary in the arts and sciences. Its research discovers an origin of the human spirit in Western culture in the politics of the biblical Creator Spirit finding and choosing Israel for its own portion among the nations. It interprets in the apostle Paul's biblical first letter to the Corinthians an extraordinary personal witness to the creational bond of the divine

Spirit to the human spirit. It details in the theology of Augustine, then of Aquinas, their speculative transformations of the biblical human spirit into an imaginative or an intellectual soul. It interprets Calvin's theology as an intended restoration of the biblical human spirit in the Spirit's new creation of humans through faith in Christ. It finally documents Harvey's respect for a numen of nature as mind and soul, or for the biblical Creator and Father, as an inference to a final cause from his identification of the human spirit with the vital blood flow in its body.

ANCIENT REALITIES

The origin of the human spirit in Western culture is obscure. Who or what was the controversial agent *rûaḥ 'ĕlōhîm*—polysemous spirit-wind-breath—in or at the beginning of the biblical creation story? Its identity was fundamental because it was in its image and likeness that the Bible introduced humans.

Genesis

The first chapter, on Genesis, accesses the history of the human spirit through comparative linguistic evidence from archaeological excavations. It researches the precise meaning of the controversial agent *rûaḥ 'ĕlōhîm*—polysemous Hebrew spirit-wind-breath—in or at the beginning of creation (Genesis 1:2). It identifies that agent *rûaḥ 'ĕlōhîm* from its action *měraḥepet* by studying its Ugaritic root *rhp* in the *Story of Aqhat*, where its agent is always an eagle. The chapter applies ornithology as a heuristic to understand by science what philology cannot resolve about avian phenomena that have endured relatively stable throughout the millennia. From the aerodynamics of avian flight it recognizes biblical *měraḥepet* as the rare mode of "soaring." From the species of birds that soar it identifies the biblical agent as a metaphorical golden eagle (*Aquila chrysaetos*).

The biblical divine action *měraḥepet* in Genesis 1:2 occurs also only in the Song of Moses in Deuteronomy 32:11, where God *měraḥepet* is designated like a *nešer*, an "eagle." Since both biblical texts belonged to the Priestly tradition, the earlier Song, with its simile of God soaring like an eagle over the Israelites, was the source in Genesis for the metaphor of the Spirit soaring like an eagle over creation. This chapter researches the natural behaviors of eagle flight and parenting to retranslate the astonishing behavior of the Song's eagle toward the Israelites wandering in the desert. It understands the Golden Eagle as a definitive model for the finder of Israel and for the Creator of humans for the same reason. Its soaring involves a magnificent display over its breeding ground to mark and call its territory. That aquiline spectacle in the sky inspired the two Priestly images. Just as the God of the Song in Deuteronomy soared to encircle Israel as its portion among the nations, so did the Spirit God of Genesis soar to create humans for a deputized care of the earth. The relation of the human spirit to the divine Spirit was from the beginning a political belonging.

Genesis 1 was projected about the national origins of Israel, not the natural origins of the cosmos. The generations of the heavens and the earth in Genesis were derived from the generations of Israel in the Song of Moses. Genesis 1 was not directly and explicitly a narrative—not even a mythological or religious one—of the creation of the universe. It was the Priestly location of Israel in a universal order before metaphysics. The Spirit God soared like an eagle to mark his created territory for the increase and multiplication of its creatures. The relation of the Spirit God to the human spirit, as Creator to creature, was political ownership as formalized in Israelite covenant and cult. This interpretation strengthens a modern exegetical consensus about God's image and likeness in v. 26 as historically a political association of sovereign and vassal.

Paul
The biblical New Testament affirmed the human spirit created in God's image and likeness from its earliest writings, the apostle Paul's letters to Christian churches. As with the fortune of Genesis, his situational meanings became erased in later interpretations that cited his verses as theological prooftexts. The second chapter recovers Paul's historical meanings about the relationship of the human spirit to the divine Spirit. The evidence matters because Paul is the prime historical source for knowledge of the first Christians, with his church at Corinth its best documented community. The chapter interprets his reflections on the human spirit not as abstract theological dissertations but as directed pastoral instructions to the Corinthians in their quarrels about its meaning. Who were the truly "spiritual" humans, the "psychics" or the "pneumatics"? Paul confronted their rival boasts of spiritual authenticity and

authority by evaluating the Spirit's manifestation among them in gifts that were diverse yet from the same giver.

The chapter interprets Paul's extraordinary contribution on the human spirit by his own boasting of a personal experience of spiritual rapture. This analysis differs from the interpretation of his rapture as merkabah mysticism since those apocalyptic texts were both anachronistic and incongruous with Paul's verses. Beyond conduct, the chapter discusses Paul's distinction about the human spirit, whether from Adam or from Christ, by interpreting Genesis on creation. It unearths from archaeology the Corinthian artifacts, terracotta lamps, that were Paul's model for the Spirit indwelling in Christians as his new creation. It differs basically from the standard translation and exegesis of Paul's relation of the human and divine spirits. Their premise has assumed a privacy of human thought as arguing for the inaccessibility of divine thought. This chapter explains that Paul wrote a classical a fortiori argument that coordinated and transcended the insights of either analogy or antithesis. At issue was not private epistemology but social experience, as based on the common sympathy of types, like-to-like. Paul inferred a mysterious Spirit God; he did not define human nature.

MEDIEVAL THOUGHTS

Paul, as a learned and devout Jew converted to Jesus the Christ, was faithful to Genesis 1 on the human spirit as a creature of the divine Spirit. Yet he wrote not systematically but situationally to a local church in crisis about its "spiritual" identity. As Christianity continued beyond the biblical era, ecclesiastics still revered his words as authoritative. But their meaning became vague, even opaque. Theologians were temporally and culturally removed by experience from Paul's historical situation. They lacked a historical method for its recovery, a method only developed later in Renaissance humanism from philological science. They were further disabled by their ignorance of the biblical languages, Hebrew and Greek, and by their lack of consultation with their remnant scholars. At that juncture the understanding of the human spirit turned theoretical, although *theōria* was not a biblical word or concept. Gaps in experience and skill for interpreting the biblical human spirit occasioned hermeneutical and exegetical ingenuity.

Without the disciplinary resources to research the biblical texts for their linguistic and historical meanings, theologians unwittingly lost the biblical origins of the human spirit—save, of course, to affirm the Creator. They dedicated their energy toward understanding the human spirit from what they did possess naturally, their experience and a mind to analyze it. Their intellectual efforts exhibited a basic tendency and yearning of the mind itself to insert its human part into the divine whole. Metaphors of a journey from mind to God were common. The medieval thinkers Augustine and Aquinas are still studied for their powerful speculations, which some admirers consider universal and permanent truths. Both theologians meant to interpret the human spirit in fidelity to the biblical text. However, lacking the later developments of historical method, they unwittingly transformed its original meaning. They psychologized about humanity by converting spirit to soul, as either its imaginative or its intellectual faculty of the mind.

Augustine

A justification for such psychology was Augustine's apologetics of pabulum, Scripture as divine baby talk needing philosophical maturation. The third chapter studies Augustine, the most influential Christian author, whether for the acceptance or the rejection of his ideas. Without the resources of historical method or linguistic knowledge for biblical exegesis, Augustine resorted to his own personal experience to understand the human spirit. This chapter presents his celebrated *Confessions* not as autobiographical, a modern genre, but as epideictic, a classical genre for praise or blame of persons. It interprets Augustine as beholding in the pages of Genesis 1 a prophetic mirror of his own creation from gross matter to contemplative mind. Although he identified the human spirit as mind, Augustine relegated that spirit to the faculty of imagination, which he then subordinated to the faculty of intellect. Augustine's identification of spirit with imagination derived from his own terrible struggles with carnal images, both sexual and Manichaean.

The chapter explains how Augustine theorized Paul's metaphor of the mirror, his pastoral exemplar upheld to the Corinthians for their spiritual maturation through charitable regard of one another. It discovers Paul's historical "enigma" in the mirror as the "riddle" of the sphinx about the ages of man. For the most famous Corinthian was Oedipus, who solved that riddle. And archaeological finds establish that the Corinthians were the principal manufacturers of mirrors, which they decorated with sphinxes. Augustine interpreted Paul's down-to-earth lesson as an eschatological norm about the different visions of God, in this life and in the next. He fashioned Paul's communal mirror of behavior into own personal speculation about mentation. The chapter details how Augustine projected the operations of his own mind onto the Trinity as their paradigm, although the creative *'ĕlōhîm* of Genesis was in usage a singular noun. He further converted Paul's spiritual rapture to a philosophical model for a body-soul relationship. By a useful accommodation of philosophy, Augustine's personalized theology achieved beneficial insights into human nature. Yet his translation of biblical spirit to philosophical soul converted the existential Spirit-to-spirit bond to an epistemological mind-to-Mind act. Knowledge subjugated love to the motivation and beautification, but not the essence, of human spiritual union with God.

Aquinas
The fourth chapter studies the spirit of Thomas Aquinas, the thirteenth-century theologian who was six centuries later papally decreed the Roman Catholic Church's normative philosopher. His writings deliberately intended a universality in abstraction from the situations that preoccupied Paul as a missionary and Augustine as a bishop. Although he respected Augustine's theology as his principal source, he dropped his mirror of introspection. Aquinas was quiet personally, and in the end he abruptly quit theology. As a Dominican friar, he was not a freelance thinker but an obedient teacher of the juniors in his religious order, for whom he composed his *Summa theologiae* as a remedial guide for pastoral ministry. Although he believed that God revealed himself in Scripture, Aquinas lacked its languages and even a reliable Latin translation. His writings thus displayed uncritical assumptions and omissions inherited from traditions about the human spirit. He revered Paul as the supreme systematic theologian of the Bible, who syllogized as an Aristotelian logician in propositions and proofs. Aquinas interpreted philosophically Paul's ensouled human as animal sensation and Paul's spiritual human as distinctly intellectual.

Aquinas's norm for defining the spiritual was materiality versus immateriality. He assumed that, because both spirit and soul were immaterial, spirit was soul. In his hierarchy of human powers only the intellective part of the soul was spiritual because it acted without the operation of any bodily organ. Humans were a marginal composite of spiritual creatures, the unbodily angels and the bodily creatures from light to animals. The human spirit was capable of enlightenment by the divine Spirit because of its compatible immateriality, rather than because of an essential Creator-creature relationship. Aquinas rendered Paul's a fortiori comparison of the human spirit with the divine spirit as privacy, heartfelt human secrets on the model of profound divine mysteries. Humans participated in the divine form by their soulful existence from it as the first and universal principle. The eternal vision of God was required to perfect the human intellect by circling back from the mind to its origin. Aquinas assumed that the divine Spirit was mind by projecting the human mind to God as its cause. Yet his treatment of charity as the soul's life intimated a line of argument toward vitality rather than mentality.

EARLY MODERN DISCOVERIES

It remained for scholars and researchers, not speculators, to begin the recovery of the historical biblical meaning of the human spirit. Humanists explored the concept of the human spirit with a literate interpretation of texts, and scientists investigated human bodies for it empirically.

Calvin
The fifth chapter analyzes the spiritual beliefs of Jean Calvin, a magisterial Protestant reformer. Calvin believed the human mirror of divinity had been shattered by Adam's fall in the original sin, and so declined to speculate further. Because the soul was dysfunctional for salvation, Calvin was dismissive of a traditional facultative psychology and preferred a simpler biblical anthropology of spirit and body. Spirit was its primary term. It included soul as the immortal yet created essence that was the nobler part of humans indwelling their bodies. As a Renaissance humanist, Calvin was educated in the biblical languages for scholarly exegesis. He decided that the agent *rûaḥ 'ĕlōhîm* in Genesis 1:2 was not the Trinity, thus rejecting Augustine's philosophical meditation on its image in the human mind with its triune operations. Calvin tolerated the interpretation of *mĕraḥepet* in that verse as either the Spirit's extension

over or incubation of creation, providing that the Creator's power was acknowledged in utter human dependency. In the pulpit Calvin inclined toward pastoral effect over philological accuracy, and he transformed the flying eagle of the Song of Moses for divine majesty into the flightless hen of Matthew's gospel for divine accommodation.

Calvin emphasized theological conformity with the biblical human spirit, which he interpreted as vital. In contrast with the intellectualism of Augustine or Aquinas, he ordered their ideal of contemplation to a model of social relations. Calvin based that society on civil ownership of property, which he knew professionally as a lawyer. The final human end in heaven was less to contemplate God's true reality than to believe his paternal favor. Calvin vitalized the human spirit by asserting the Spirit's perpetual creative sovereignty over existence itself. Life was more essential than thought, and affect was superior to knowledge. The Spirit's new sanctification of humans through faith in Christ was a new and better creation than the original creation told in Genesis. It reformed humans as sons of God through Christ's indwelling image as conferred by the Spirit at baptism. Calvin's relation of the human spirit to the divine Spirit was not antithetical, however, as in rigid readings of his theology. His accomplished rhetorical argumentation was chiaroscuro, a method he derived from classical forensic oratory and contemporary artistic technique. As an appeal to pathos, Calvin's chiaroscuro deliberately magnified the divine Spirit's vivification by debasing the human spirit's depravity, so as to elicit gratitude for the Spirit's re-creation of a fallen human nature. As in the biblical Priestly and Pauline writings, Calvin's bond of the recreated human spirit to the divine creative Spirit was social.

Science
The final chapter treats the English physician and natural philosopher William Harvey, who in the seventeenth century occasioned theoretically the modern identification of the human spirit with courage. His famous deliberation and discovery of the circulation of the blood ultimately mattered to the understanding of the human spirit because that is precisely where he situated it, in the blood flow. Toward understanding that conclusion, this chapter examines his important but scarcely studied *Exercitationes de generatione animalium* (Exercises on the generation of animals). As a scientist of demonstrable causes, Harvey sought to know more than physiological acts, functions, and ends. He sought to know

their creative origins in the absolute act and end of the natural universe. Harvey probed animal nature with a sure conviction of its divine origin. To a natural Aristotelian teleology he grafted the numinous realm, for he believed that a divine principle of life inhered in all nature. His contribution on the human spirit was not theological argument, however, for he did not deduce it from Scripture but induce it from science. His teleology, climaxing in an ultimate divine design, was not religious belief toward worship but scientific investigation toward knowledge. He argued inductively from the functional physical movement of real hens and chicks to their designer as a greater mind, soul, or numen, or, appropriately for Christians, the biblical Creator who made them.

Harvey investigated the vital spirit common to blooded animals by modeling the numinous efficient cause of their generation on the Spirit's creative anaphora in Genesis 1 "let there be." Departing from a medieval philosophical idea, he ascribed the human image of God not to the rational soul but to the vegetative soul, which made and conserved animality. The Creator-creature bond was existential, with the divine imprint on humans being in their births, not in their thoughts. Harvey's deliberation and discovery of the blood's circulation defined the origin and function of animal spirit. Spirit coursed in the arteries and veins of the body as blood, its vital animation. That identification of spirit with blood occasioned theoretically the modern meaning of the human spirit as courageous. For Harvey capitalized on the medical extension of spirit to the sanguine temperament. In humoral theory, as developed in psychology, blood possessed the quality and virtue of heat. Blood, as hot and moist, typically produced in animal bodies the generous passion of courage. In Harvey's conclusion a spirited human was a spirituous animal as vitally blooded. Its optimal expression in the sanguine temperament exhibited courage. And that is how the human spirit finally got courage.

That human spirit was not yet wholly secular, despite Harvey's methods of empirical observation and mental reason. He inferred the human spirit from the divine Creator or the numen of nature as the principle of animal generation. He believed that the efficient cause of life, by any reverent name, imprinted its image supremely in the generation of animals. Humans expressed their divine image in the sexual act of procreation. The biblical Creator's mandate to Adam, the first man, was to govern animals as his steward. As an anatomist, Harvey was a latter-day

Adam investigating animals, after the divine blessing and mandate of Genesis, for their increase and multiplication. Such was a making of the human spirit from biblical creation to scientific procreation. The modern sense of a spirited human derived historically and theoretically from a spirituous animal, whose vitality Harvey traced from a universal sense of divinity as a numinous cause.

The bookends are the Priestly *tôledôt* formula of Genesis about the human generations of the particular Israelite tribes and Harvey's anatomical exercises about the generation of all animals. In between those bookends are other volumes with other ideas about the human spirit, some important tomes of which are opened here. The authors all shared a conviction, albeit distinctly understood, of the human spirit as endowed by or designed by a divine source of everything animate. Harvey's anatomical exercises predated the discoveries of the respiratory function of the lungs and of the element oxygen. That science would disprove his bloody innate heat as the spirituous animating principle of humans. Yet the popular meaning of the human spirit as courageous still endures.

Part I

ANCIENT REALITIES

CHAPTER 1

Genesis

The origin of the human spirit in Western culture is lost in translation. Biblical exegesis debates whether in or at the beginning a divine Spirit created a human spirit "in our image, after our likeness." As Genesis 1:2 told, "The earth was without form and void, and darkness was upon the face of the deep, and *rûaḥ 'ĕlōhîm* was moving over the face of the waters."[1] Translations of *rûaḥ 'ĕlōhîm* differ, from "Spirit," to "breath," to "wind."[2] Who or what was that creative agent? Its identity correlates with and determines the identity of humans in verse 26 as created "in our image, after our likeness." The essential meaning of the polysemous subject—Spirit, breath, wind—depends on its activity, *měraḥepet*. What, then, was happening over the primordial deep? Although *měraḥepet* has been translated variously, philology established in science as a heuristic for aerial movement identifies its one essential meaning. And that action embodying the divine Spirit identifies the controversial agent in whose image and likeness humans were created spirits. Here begins an interdisciplinary study of ideas of the human spirit in some important thinkers, from its beginnings in the Bible to its beginnings in the scientific revolution.

CONTROVERSY

Among Jewish scholars, their customary translation of *rûaḥ 'ĕlōhîm* in traditional sources and also their modern preference is "wind."[3] The rabbinical "wind" arose around the fifth century C.E. in the Babylonian Talmud, an oral Torah that complemented the written Torah of biblical

Genesis to Deuteronomy. The Talmudic tractate Hagiga, about the duty of pilgrimage to Jerusalem, taught, "Ten things were created the first day, and they are as follows: heaven and earth, *Tohu* [chaos], *Bohu* [desolation], light and darkness, wind and water, the measure of day and the measure of night." It explicated, "Wind and water, for it is written: 'And the wind of God hovered over the face of the waters.'"[4] That exegesis rendered *rûaḥ 'ĕlōhîm*, the agent in Genesis 1:2 over the deep, as the creature wind, not a creator Spirit. It respected the Talmudic injunction not to pry into the mystery of God "before" that creation. A speculator about the above, below, before, or after of creation was severely condemned. "Better for him if he had not come into the world."[5] Yet even the modern champion of that Talmud as a rigorous rational system has confessed bewilderment at the intrusion of Genesis into a logical argument about the festival obligations. For the Talmudic topic of the works of creation was miscellaneous, lacking an organizational proposition or an orderly rationale for its varied statements and juxtapositions.[6] Yet, with Talmudic authority, *rûaḥ 'ĕlōhîm* became in Jewish tradition not the spirit of God as a personal identity or a possessed quality but the wind as his creature. Only the Renaissance exegete and philosopher Isaac Abravanel is said to have dissented,[7] although so had Solomon ben Isaac, or Rashi, the medieval paragon of Talmudic commentary.

Once "wind" was established as the authoritative Jewish translation of *rûaḥ* at creation, the alteration of *'ĕlōhîm* from a nounal subject to an adjectival modifier ensued. Biblical Hebrew expressed comparison by applying *'ĕlōhîm*, its usual designation for a god or God, as an aggrandizer to create the superlative degree. Thus, trees plus *'ĕlōhîm* became "mighty cedars" (Ps. 80:10). By that construct some translations erased a spirit, rendering *'ĕlōhîm* a superlative adjective modifying *rûaḥ*. There was "an awesome wind sweeping over the water" or "a terrible storm."[8] The Talmudic reading, "wind," was augmented by the modern archaeological discovery of ancient Near Eastern myths with cosmogonic winds, which the Hebrew Scriptures purportedly adapted but altered for its God as unique.[9] The idols of the other nations evaporated to non-gods, vain puffs[10] whose mouths were breathless.[11] From his throne crowning the skies[12] the God of the Israelites became the true creator[13] and master of the winds. In early Hebrew poetry God mounted and rode the winds and thunderclouds;[14] then he careened by earth prophetically on the winged wheels of a glorious throne.[15] He snorted the winds from their four points to smash and scatter his foreign enemies or to threaten an idolatrous Israel.¹⁶ God's visitations were frequently stormy. The ten commandments were uttered from within a fire to an assembly at Mount Sinai "while the mountain burned with fire to the heart of heaven, wrapped in darkness, cloud, and gloom" (Deut. 4:10–13; 5:22–26). God's ominous footfall tracking the original humans, Adam and Eve hiding shamefully in paradise, was not pleasantly "in the cool of the day," as in the standard translation. He tracked them down fiercely "in the wind of the storm" (Gen. 3:8).¹⁷ The Jewish preference for "wind" as rûaḥ 'ĕlōhîm is shared by those modern Christians who translate it naturalistically as a bad storm.¹⁸

Yet the creation stories in Genesis 1 and 2 lack any role for the wind. It did not even stir to gather or to separate the primordial waters in 1:8, as in the most ancient biblical poem, Exodus 15:8, where the wind churned waves to drown the pharaoh's charioteers. Biblical prose applied God's names as constructs for the superlative degree, not to natural phenomena, such as a strong wind, or even to definite objects, but only to human states. Since 'ĕlōhîm occurs in verses 1 and 3 of Genesis 1 as "God," why would it intervene so very differently in verse 2 as "wind"?¹⁹ For a modern Hebraist, crying against the headwind of Talmudic interpretation, rûaḥ 'ĕlōhîm was indeed the "Spirit of God." That Spirit was the Creator, as in Job's testimony, "The spirit of God (rûaḥ 'l) has made me, / and the breath of the Almighty gives me life" (Job 33:4).²⁰ Biblical "wind" was rûaḥ, but rûaḥ was not always "wind." Not every Jewish scholar has agreed with the Talmudic gloss, "wind," while some Christian philologists have affirmed it. The variety of interpretation allows for an investigation of its historical biblical meaning.

Christian translations—from the Itala, to the Authorized Version of King James, to modern bibles—altered Talmudic "wind" to "spirit" and "breath."²¹ The Revised Standard Version in current scholarly usage translated inclusively. "And the spirit of God was moving over the face of the waters," with "spirit" uncapitalized and "wind" footnoted as another reading. The eminent church father Jerome intended a grammatical Vulgate translation. However, he interpreted his Hebrew codices as a Christian who equated "scriptural knowledge" with "the riches of Christ" and who regarded "those transcripts truer that agreed with the authority of the New Testament." He identified the Creator by annotating his creative action, rendering Latin *ferebatur* for Hebrew *mrhph*. He fleshed out that participle as avian incubation of an egg, a very popular metaphor for a cosmic creation. Jerome believed the verse was "not said about the spirit of the world, as so many think, but about the Holy Spirit, and the very one said to be the vivifier of everything from the beginning." He reasoned, "If, moreover, he is the vivifier, consequently he is the maker; and because the maker, also God."[22]

In translation *rûaḥ 'ĕlōhîm* was personal as the divine "Spirit," or attributed personally to the Creator as a spiritual quality or animate breath. Or *rûaḥ 'ĕlōhîm* was natural as the "wind," either a creature or a phenomenon. Amid this semantic diversity, the essential meaning of the noun *rûaḥ* must be determined, as Jerome understood, by its activation. The Hebrew *měraḥepet* is a participle, in the Piel stem. A major group of intransitive verbs in the basic Qal stem that occur also in the Piel is the verb of movement. In the Piel these are frequentative, either as repeated temporally or as multiplied spatially. A simple example of the progression from Qal to Piel is from "went" to "go about." Moreover, the participle of the Piel stem was very frequent in Scripture for designating professional and other habitual practices.[23] Thus, as a participle in the Piel stem, *měraḥepet* was both motional and habitual, so that its subject, spirit-wind-breath, was moving customarily.

Translations have agreed that *rûaḥ 'ĕlōhîm* was acting *měraḥepet*, while disagreeing on the precise maneuver. The Septuagint translation of the Hebrew Scriptures into Greek in the mid–third century B.C.E. wrote *kai pneuma theou epephereto epanō tou hudatos*, "The breath of God was floating above/upon the water."[24] Yet that bible attested to the dissipation of breath, so that lingering to create everything was incongruous. The transience of breath defined idols, carried off like a "breath," blown away like the wind.[25] Its transience also defined humans, whose thoughts were but a "breath."[26] Both idols and humans in their impotence or their mortality contrasted with the creative and everlasting God. Beyond the Septuagint's "breath," a modern translation of Rashi's medieval translation was also "breath." Rashi annotated his model differently, as dovelike brooding, a Talmudic interpretation.[27] Among Christian translations, the earliest bible, the Itala, had *superferebatur super*, "was carried over above."[28] The Vulgate, the most influential version for patristic and medieval theology, simplified it to *ferebatur super*.[29] The fourteenth-century English translations by John Wycliffe and his followers offered "borne," "borun."[30] Myles Coverdale's translation in the fifteenth century, and the Geneva Bible and Douay-Rheims Bible in the sixteenth century, all published "moved."[31] The Authorized Version in English, or King James Bible, established "moved."

PARTICIPLE

Modern translations of the participle *měraḥepet* for the agent *rûaḥ 'ĕlōhîm* in Genesis 1:2 diverge from broad "sweeping"[32] to poised "hovering."[33] However, the only biblical match to the participle *měraḥepet* occurs in Deuteronomy 32:11 about an eagle (*nešer*). Research in ornithology is needed to recover the meaning familiar to the ancients. Comparative philology and religion benefit from scientific research for those natural phenomena that are relatively stable through the millennia. As a heuristic, ornithology identifies for *měraḥepet* a distinct movement, the flight mode of soaring. It also identifies the few birds that can soar, supremely the eagle. The ancient Israelites were not scientists with demonstrable causal knowledge. But they were keen observers of their natural environment. Modern descriptions of avian behavior corroborate biblical observations and flesh out their meager words. Scientific research on aquiline flight for territorial display, for predation and provision, interprets ancient observations that underlay the figurative language of Scripture about the Spirit's creative activity. Although the concept of the Hebrew root *rḥp* has been declared "movement,"[34] avian movement differs essentially as either active or passive. Only the initial Latin versions "was carried" and the Vulgate rendered by the Wycliffite "borne/borun" copied the passivity of the Hebrew participle. The Vulgate's editor, Jerome, lived as an eremite in a Syrian desert while pioneering the Christian study of Hebrew. He could have observed eagles soaring passively on the desert thermals or the updrafts from the cliffs of his arid habitat.[35] He was well situated to understand the passivity of the Spirit in Genesis 1:2 above the deserted (*inanis et vacua*) earth. And indeed, the ornithological evidence supports a singular, wondrous role for a creative Spirit of the Israelites as looking and behaving at creation like an extraordinary eagle.

Exegetes confronted with unique and rare Hebrew words such as *měraḥepet* have resorted to comparative linguistics. The alphabetic cuneiform texts from 1550–1200 B.C.E. excavated at Ugarit in a singular but related Semitic language have proved valuable for deciphering the development of Hebrew as a language.[36] Yet there is no assurance that the lexicons for cognate languages captured their archaic meanings. The philological notation that the rare Hebrew root *rhp* for *mĕraḥepet* had occurred in Ugaritic poetry as *rhp* for the "fluttering" or "hovering" of a bird[37] assumed a common flapping flight for all birds. Although feathers were generic to biblical fowls,[38] not all biblical birds flew.[39] And ornithology informs that, for those birds that do fly, there are two aerodynamically distinct methods: powered, flapping flight by active exertion; and gliding or soaring flight by passive dependence on the air. Motion as a basic common meaning for avian flight, *rhp*, is not factual, and biblical writers knew the difference between the two methods.

What, then, was the energy *rhp* of Ugaritic birds? And what species was comparative for Hebrew *mĕraḥepet?* Ugaritic *nšr* precedent to Hebrew *nšr* has been identified inclusively as either an "eagle" or a "vulture."[40] But those species are hostile to the match. The biblical conflation of the eagle and vulture originated with the Septuagint version of Hebrew *nešer* as Greek *gyps*, for *Gyps fulvus*, the Griffon Vulture. That vulture set the precedent for Hebrew lexicons to assign *nešer* to both the eagle and the vulture, then to apportion the biblical verses some to this bird, some to that.[41] Theological reference works spread the confusion.[42] The basic study identified the Imperial Eagle as the commonest eagle in Israel, whereas it is not native there. It reasoned that eagles nest both in trees and cliffs, while vultures usually nest in cliffs; therefore the biblical bird must be a vulture. Yet eagles avoid wooded areas, preferring open spaces conducive to hunting. The regions relevant to the biblical texts—the deserts of North Africa, the Middle East, the Arabian Peninsula, and the mountains of Israel—are treeless landscapes largely devoid of vegetation. There eagles inhabit cliffs, as in Scripture. The study also proposed that a vulture's larger wingspan better supported carrying the Israelites on it. Yet the biblical verse about human transport on avian wings was misconstrued as locational "on," rather than causal "by the power of." The study supposed that a simile of balding compared the white patch on a vulture's head, whereas it compared an eagle's molt. The study inferred that avian devouring of spoil must mean a vulture. But all raptors feed on carrion. The study concluded, "The ancient Hebrew is no more likely than the modern Arab to have distinguished a vulture from an eagle flying at a high speed overhead." Therefore, "*nešer* may designate both birds," depending on the context, although "*nešer* is without doubt primarily the vulture, in all probability the griffon-vulture, rather than the eagle." It added that, if an eagle was meant, the golden eagle was the probable referent because of its swift flight.[43]

An insistence on "vulture" exclusively for biblical *nešer* reiterated the alleged difficulty of distinguishing raptors in midair and so chose the commoner vulture.[44] Such a difficulty is not substantiated by the field guide to Near Eastern raptors. In size, shape, and silhouette in flight, and also in coloration, the eagle and the vulture are distinguishable even from a far distance. Any risk of confusion is not between different species of birds but between birds within the same family. Because the plumage of raptors varies extensively, coloration is the most reliable factor for identification long-distance.[45] Scripture noted them as "rich in plumage with many colors" (Ezek. 17:3; Jer. 12:9), as if dyed. The golden eagle is the raptor most commonly sighted in flight.[46] Spied from the ground, the usual vantage, its shape is distinguished from all other raptors by its proportionately longer head and tail and its long broad wings with an S-curve at the edge. The designation "golden" derives from the tawny feathers on its crown and hind neck. In the field guide that classifying gold coloration is "usually visible" long-distance, as sharply delineated by the eagle's dark brown face and belly for camouflage while hunting. That raptor's shape, wing, and entire bearing are also "obvious" from a long distance. The golden eagle conveys a "majestic appearance."[47]

Ornithology confirms the *nšr* of Hebrew texts as behaviorally like an eagle, not a vulture. The identification matters because the avian metaphor of the Spirit in Genesis 1:2 is foundational for the creation of humans "in our image, after our likeness" (v. 26). The Golden Eagle (*Aquila chrysaetos*) best matches the text. It belongs taxonomically to the order *Falconiformes*, the family *Accipitridae*, genus *Aquila*, the most evolved.[48] The golden eagle is universal in distribution from latitudes 70 degrees north to 20 degrees south, with dispersal even farther south. Although its migrations can be "spectacular," its normative behavior in the temperate zone is sedentary. Its broad environment is open landscape generally devoid of human population, but it principally inhabits mountains. Eagles resident or wintering in Israel inhabit mountainous slopes and ledges and also the clefted wadis of its deserts.[49]

For ornithologists, the golden eagle is a "complete individualist" that is "supremely aerial" and "arguably the most impressive flier of all." As "a supreme artist" of "unrivalled powers of flight," it is the "king of birds."⁵⁰ The eagle was thus a compatible metaphor for divine sovereignty in Israelite religion, which revered its God as utterly incomparable with other gods. In repudiation of polytheistic idolatry, its prophets and priests proclaimed him singular and solitary. By association, Israel as his chosen people was unlike any other nation.⁵¹ When the psalmist posed, "For who in the skies can be compared to the Lord?" (Ps. 89:6), the appropriate response was not an ordinary and gregarious vulture. The ornithological evidence supports a singular, wondrous role for a creative Spirit of the Israelites as looking and behaving like an extraordinary eagle. The comparative rarity of the eagle to the vulture commended it as a metaphor or simile for Israel's unique God.

Observers in the field of the vast and unobstructed desert sky would not have confused or conflated an eagle and a vulture. Israelite bird watching was not optional and recreational, but necessary and serious for protection of the flocks from predators. Although the two species belong to the same Linnaean order, *Falconiformes*, they are neither interchangeable nor compatible. The physique of those two raptors is distinct in size, in wingspread, and in color. The identification of the griffon vulture is "unmistakable" as the only large, pale bird of the species.⁵² Behaviorally the eagle and the vulture are also distinct. Eagles in habitat are solitary. Vultures are sociable, even roosting in rows, while more than a hundred may converge on a hunk of carrion. Eagles are hunters, while vultures are scavengers. Because the feet of vultures are too weak to attack or kill prey, they eat opportunistically the kill of other species on the ground.⁵³ Genesis attested to birds of prey (*'ayim*)—screamers—descending on the carcasses of sacrificed animals. When the patriarch Abraham shooed them away, the Lord covenanted with him for Canaan and promised many other foreign lands for his descendants.⁵⁴

AQHAT

Biblical *nšr* as a divine agent had a precedent Ugaritic *nsr* in the *Story of Aqhat* as the goddess Anat's predator. She retaliated against Aqhat's refusal to exchange his divinely wrought bow for immortality by transforming the mercenary Yatipan into an eagle to hunt and kill him. Perching that hooded bird on her glove, Anat merged into a flight of eagles and sent Yatipan for the kill. "He po[ured out] his blood [like] a murderer, / like a slaughter[er] (he brought him) to his knees]. [His] lifebreath went out like the wind, / [like spittle] his vitality, / as (his) dying breath from [his nostrils]." A flight of eagles portended Aqhat's death to his family. Eagles recurred when his father, Danel, cursed his son's murderer, imploring the god Baal to fell them for inspection. Danel then slit the belly of the father of all eagles, to failure; but he slit the belly of the mother of all eagles, to success. He extracted his son's fat and bones, buried them, and cursed any eagle that might fly over Aqhat's grave to disturb his repose.[55] In the Ugaritic *Baal and Anat Cycle* the *nsr* was again an agent of divine destruction. Baal, "rider of the clouds," battled with Yam, the sea, by releasing an eagle from his hand to strike his adversary's skull and brow fatally.[56] The association of the eagle's flight with Baal's fingers alluded to an eagle's deeply slotted pinions, which when spread in flight resemble splayed human fingers. Ornithologists even term such wingtips "fingers."[57] The flight to kill was a vertical descent, a "stoop." That ornithological term designates a raptor's bolt from an altitude of 3,300 feet / 1,000 meters to plunge at lightning speeds of 99 to 273 miles per hour.[58]

Details in the *Story of Aqhat* confirmed accurate observations of eagles hunting and eating prey. Anat hooded the eagle to blindfold its keen vision lest it instinctively seek its natural prey. She pursued human prey, Aqhat, as she tethered her hunter on her wrist for release as a precision weapon. Her merger into a flight of other eagles implied her takeoff from a high altitude, as befitting a goddess acting with El's consent. A high altitude was also aerodynamically necessary for avian soaring.[59] Anat's merger into a migration hid her presence, lest Aqhat on the ground spy her flying vengefully and duck or run for cover. The literary surveillance of the eagles by other birds copied their actual behavior at the appearance of a raptor: strategic convergence in close formation to maneuver effectively out of danger.[60] The goddess Anat then released the eagle directly over Aqhat so that he could not foresee its lethal stoop. In search of his son's corpse, Aqhat's father approached Hargab and Sumul, the father and mother of all eagles,[61] as consistent with hunting by a mated pair.[62] Their conspiracy with Anat premised Danel's discovery of his son's remains inside Sumul. Anat herself viciously bit Aqhat's skin, halved and dismembered his corpse, and ate its entrails.[63] The remains of his son that Danel found in the eagle mother's belly reversed Aqhat's conception and gestation in his human mother's belly. Danel slit Sumul open in a violent reversal of Aqhat's natural birth. The fertile mother of all eagles counteracted Aqhat's infertile mother, who had conceived him only at the blessing of the gods. The raw feasting of the female goddess, then the mother eagle, on Aqhat's corpse grimly reversed the ritual feasting of the gods with his human family at his birth and coming of age.

The original translation of the *Story of Aqhat* correctly identified Ugaritic *nsr* as an "eagle."[64] However, the notion that Semitic *nšr* originally designated "any carnivorous bird belonging to the hawk or falconid family"[65] has since prevailed. Translations have flown a variety of birds into the scenes.[66] That avian miscellany has disregarded the observational powers of the ancients, who would not have confused the species. The most recent translation declared, "Hebrew *nešer* is undoubtedly a falcon."[67] An analysis of Aqhat's hunt as a coming-of-age ritual agreed.[68] An argument for "falcon," a peregrine falcon, rejected "eagle" as impossible to bag live, as Anat did in the story.[69] Yet modern tribesmen in the mountains of central Asia and of Iran regularly bag and release golden eagles for hunting valuable pelts.[70] The argument for "falcon" further contended that eagles do not flock, as the birds in Aqhat's tale do.[71] Yet eagles do flock in migration. Phenomenal intercontinental migration of tens of thousands of *Aquila* eagles occurs over Israel for several weeks every fall and spring to and from their wintering grounds in Africa. Those diurnal migrations by eagles soaring and gliding on main, specific overland routes have been classified as "heavy" and "abundant," "widespread" and "very common."[72] They have been judged not merely "dramatic" but "one of the finest spectacles in all ornithology." Indeed, "Migration is probably the most awe-inspiring natural phenomenon. What it lacks compared with the enormous power of the weather, an earthquake or a volcano, it makes up for in romance—a small bird pits its wings against the elements and accomplishes, as routine, a journey that is truly superhuman."[73] Historical migrations of *Aquila* eagles may well have grounded the *Story of Aqhat* in the turn of the seasons. Just as Aqhat's dining was interrupted by his murder, so too the crops that provided his food died with the withering of the harvest as marked by the autumnal migrations of eagles.[74]

Although the peregrine falcon as the current choice for Ugaritic *nsr* is a predator, all species of falcon kill differently from all other raptors.

A falcon's usual prey is a bird in flight, which it strikes distinctively on the neck and eats midair.⁷⁵ That detail differs from the point of kill for Anat's command, "Hit him twice on the skull, three times above the ear." So, "He hit him twice on [the skull], three times above the ear."⁷⁶ The coloration of falcons, multipatterned and mottled all over, is also distinct from all other raptors.⁷⁷ Falcons fly unexceptionally by the majority mode, flapping, an infelicitous model for the activity of Israel's God as rare.⁷⁸ Their habitat is not even native to Israel.⁷⁹

The golden eagle is superior to any falcon for achieving the goddess Anat's vengeful bloodshed. Its much greater size and weight increase its lethal impact. The golden eagle adroitly employs multiple strategies for hunting, at high and low altitudes, from stooping to walking, by grip and by grab—all adapted primarily to the escape response of its prey, from quadrupeds to reptiles. Its usual method is to stoop vertically from high soaring or gliding to prey on the ground or just above it. It kills with unique speed and accuracy. Its techniques "combine acute vision with power, speed and a surprising degree of aerial agility and dexterity." Its stoop at awesome speed, its abrupt leveling off close to ground, and its snatching of prey are flawless. Its stoop to kill, at well over two hundred miles per hour, doubles the speed of most raptors. Its common prey worldwide is medium-sized birds in the air or mammals on the ground. It preys also on the young of larger hoofed animals, especially lambs—a reason for Israelite shepherds to guard their flocks. It catches moderately large sheep by flying low over the herd, isolating its quarry, and then landing on its back or neck. It grips the victim with its talons, driving them into its flesh, and exerts a pressure that either knocks it forcibly to the ground or effects an internal collapse. Large prey is usually halved, then dismembered, and a manageable portion carried off to the nest.⁸⁰ As if she were an eagle, the goddess Anat accurately halved the cadaver of Aqhat the human mammal and consumed it. "Like a chisel was her mouth: / her teeth seized (him) and she devoured his [en]trails. / She cleft him like the heart of a terebinth, / she cut the cadaver in two. / She divided the cadaver, / She dismembered Aqhat."⁸¹ That behavior corresponded to an eagle's behavior as the Ugaritic ancestor of Hebrew *nešer*.⁸²

The *Story of Aqhat* was the Ugaritic poem with the most affinities to the Hebrew Scriptures, including the Song of Moses in Deuteronomy 32 with its Priestly simile of the eagle.⁸³ The *Story of Aqhat* was not a creational myth. But it was a generational story about familial survival against the ambiguity of the gods who both crafted and gave Aqhat's hunting bow, then coveted and grabbed it back. Its plot celebrated fertility, birth, and growth, and it grieved the death of progeny, for its premise was a father's anguish at his lack of offspring. The tale narrated his prayer to the gods for fertility, his intercourse with his wife, and finally the celebrations of the gods at Aqhat's birth and later at maturity, when he was presented the divinely crafted bow.[84] A generational theme would have resonated with the biblical recounting of generations. With the special *tôledôt* ("generation") formula of the Priestly writing,[85] Genesis 2:4 announced "the generations of the heavens and the earth," fulfilling the injunction to all creatures to be fertile and multiply (Gen. 1:11–12, 20–22, 24–28). The Song of Moses in Deuteronomy 32, another Priestly composition, boasted of an eagle as a simile for God, whose benefactions Moses ordered retold "to your children" (vv. 11, 45–46). That biblical poem reversed the Ugaritic plots from death to life. In the foreign tales the eagle as a divine agent soared then stooped to kill and consume the god's enemy. In the biblical Song of Moses an aquiline God soared then stooped to save and feed his own people. When the God of Israel sent a metaphorical eagle as a weapon against foreign nations, his resort was to protect the territory he established for his own people. When he released an eagle prophetically against an idolatrous Israel, he summoned it to repentance for sin and to renewal of their covenant with him. When in the Song of Moses the eagle roused its nestlings, God roused Israel to attack its enemies rather than collude with their idolatry.

FLIGHT

The identification of biblical *nešer* as an eagle, supremely the golden eagle, distinguishes its rare flight mode from ordinary birds. Its aerial movement interprets the metaphorical Spirit's movement *mĕraḥepet* in Genesis 1:2 over the wasteland. The Ugaritic root *rhp* for biblical *mĕraḥepet* occurred twenty-one times, fifteen in the *Story of Aqhat*. Its original translation, "soars," corresponded to its eagle's mythological flight.[86] Translations since have flown in a miscellany of birds.[87] The comparative rarity of Semitic *rhp* argues for its identification of the rarest mode of flight, soaring. The common mode of flight for almost all birds is flapping with some interspersed gliding. The definition "fly, soar" for the frequent Ugaritic *d'y*[88] is logically invalid because soaring is a mode of flight, but not all flight is soaring—most is not. That verb logically denoted only flapping or only soaring. The favored peregrine falcon, for example, is a typical flapper, exerting five or six short wingbeats per second, relieved by brief glides.[89] A large raptor (*Accipitridae*)—eagle, vulture, condor—can only soar or glide; it scarcely flaps and it never hovers. Avian flight does not denote movement with synonymous empirical or aesthetic values. Soaring and hovering are the opposite ends of the spectrum of effortless versus energetic flight. The distinction matters for understanding the presence of *rûaḥ 'ĕlōhîm* at creation. What in Genesis 1:2 was *rûaḥ 'ĕlōhîm* doing *mĕraḥepet* over the wasteland? The rarity of *rhp* compared to common *d'y* argues for the supreme Spirit the rarest mode of flight over Israel's deserts, soaring. Israelite observations of eagles soaring to hunt prey for provision—but above all to mark their territories by spectacular display—based biblical comparisons of the Spirit with an eagle. The activity of the creative Spirit as a metaphorical eagle was hunting and marking, for finding and choosing Israel.

That natural metaphor for the divine Spirit in Genesis 1:2 related to the command "let birds fly above the earth across the firmament of the heaven" (v. 20). The phenomenon of flying was inherently mysterious. Flight is locomotion for four groups of animals: among invertebrates, insects—the first fliers; among vertebrates, pterosaurs from the fossil record and also birds and bats.[90] Flight is the characteristic of birds, a challenging natural adaptation because of the difficulty of movement in air. The most advanced research in the interdisciplinary science of avian flight confesses fascination with it primarily because "we don't fully understand how birds actually do it." Features of that behavior, from takeoff to landing and flight in between, remain even to zoologists "enigmatic," under "a veil of mystery." By simple observation, birds go both up and forward in the air. But advanced science acknowledges that "the overall conclusion must be that we do not know exactly how birds fly." Ornithologists only estimate the factors of energies and powers, and judge their relative importance very roughly.[91]

The avian norm is straightforward level flight, achieved by flapping the wings up and down, rotating them front and back, and folding and stretching them, all at changing speeds.[92] In that elementary method birds fly by generating two forces—lift to counteract gravity and thrust to overcome drag—by accelerating masses of air downward or backward. Yet the aerodynamics of even ordinary flapping flight remains "enigmatic," with its science "still in its infancy,"[93] a natural mystery that biblical writers observed as a sign of divine powers. Flapping flight allows efficient coverage of distance, but only by great exertion. The maximum flapping flight is hovering, an intense flight without speed. A hovering bird sustains its airlift without forward momentum purely by beating its wings to create the airflow that supports its weight. The power invested in overcoming atmospheric drag and supporting bodily weight demands enormous energy, much more energy than forward flight. The normative hoverer is the Hummingbird (*Trochilidae*). Its morphological and kinematic adaptations allow its unique ability, with 60-hertz wingbeats, or up to 80 times a second, to lift twice its bodily mass while stationary in midair. The metabolic cost is so strenuous that figures in the aerodynamic models approach infinity. Only the hummingbird can sustain this mode of flight, and only for several minutes.[94] Hummingbirds are only native and migrant in the Americas, thus they were unknown to Semitic writers. None of the birds of the comparative Ugaritic and Hebrew texts whose flight has been translated as "hovering"—eagles, vultures, falcons, hawks, or kites—hover.

Hovering like a hummingbird and soaring like an eagle represent the extremes of avian flight in energy. Metabolic cost proportionate to the size of the bird determines a soaring flight for the giant birds—eagles, condors, and albatrosses.[95] Of these, only the eagle is native to Israel; and it is also migrant there. An eagle can flap only instantly in alteration with glides: to ascend to its characteristic undulating display, to maintain its balance when alighted on hoofed prey, and to lift that kill to its sites.[96] Its wing loading, or the ratio of body mass to wing expanse, and its aspect ratio, or the wing area divided by wing breadth, necessitate an eagle's flight as soaring or gliding.[97] Soaring differs from gliding because it occurs without any loss of altitude.[98] An eagle depends for soaring on natural aerodynamics external to its body rather than on its own internal physiology. Most birds actively power themselves by flapping their wings. But eagles passively extend their wings to catch updrafts, either wind currents created by topographical obstructions, such as cliffs and mountains, or thermal currents from deserts heated by solar reflection and radiation.

Both the orographic and thermal conditions for soaring are provided by Israel's mountainous and desert terrains. Israel's geographical position at the juncture of three continents and its varied climate and habitats have privileged it with diverse species of native birds. Its site as a bottleneck on major migratory paths has also afforded it unparalleled scientific knowledge.[99] Israel is specifically an international axis for raptors because two main migratory routes cross Israel and the Sinai.[100] The Hebrew Scriptures preserved observations. An eagle's flight was proverbially wonderful. "Three things are too wonderful for me; / four I do not understand: the way of an eagle in the sky, / the way of a serpent on a rock, / the way of a ship on the high seas, / and the way of a man with a maiden" (Prov. 30:18–19). An eagle symbolized speed as it came, hastened, rushed, flew, ascended, and mounted.[101] Its sudden flight heavenward was proverbial for vanishing wealth.[102] Job's archaic poetry attested to an eagle's hunt and stoop. "Thence he spies out the prey; / his eyes behold it afar. His young ones suck up blood; / and where the slain are, there is he" (Job 39:30, 29).[103] Job lamented his fleeting days that pass "like an eagle stooping [not RSV "swooping"] on the prey" (9:25–26). The eagle's velocity was not only a general passage[104] but also a precise movement to kill. The heroes Saul and Jonathan were "swifter than eagles" to slay (1 Sam. 1:23, 25.) An oracle against the Israelites summoned a foreign nation "as swift as the eagle flies" (Deut. 28:49).

The sustained metaphor for the everlasting and effortless Creator who empowered the Israelites like eagles was in the prophet Isaiah's oracle. "Have you not known? Have you not heard? / The Lord is the everlasting God, / the Creator of the ends of the earth. / He does not faint or grow weary, / his understanding is unsearchable. / He gives power to the faint, / and to him who has no might he increases strength. / Even youths shall faint and be weary, / and young men shall fall exhausted; / but they who wait for the Lord shall renew their strength, / they shall mount up with wings like eagles, / they shall run and not be weary, / they shall walk and not faint" (Is. 40:28–31). The comparison was apt because an eagle's lifespan can be more than a century,[105] since it regularly renews its flight feathers in molting.[106] Isaiah compared the tireless Creator with an eagle because an eagle soars passively without actively flapping like ordinary birds. The psalmist also blessed God for forgiving injury, healing disease, redeeming life, crowning with love, and satisfying humans with good "so that your youth is renewed like the eagle's"

(Ps. 103:2–5). The eagle symbolized new beginnings legally, physically, vitally, affectively, and morally.

What did Scripture observe about eagle's wings that ornithology confirms and explains toward understanding the Spirit soaring metaphorically at creation (Gen. 1:2)? It recognized the creation of "every winged bird according to its kind" (vv. 20–21) with a function to fly. It also observed an eagle's wings in soaring flight as extended[107] by the verb *pāraś* for spreading fabric. As God pitched the heavens as a tent over the earth,[108] so an eagle extended its wings in the sky. The prophet Ezekiel described "a great eagle with great wings and long pinions" (Ezek. 17:3). Aerodynamically all wings function the same, with structural variations to accommodate the different modes of flight.[109] There are almost ten thousand species of birds,[110] and each species has a different wing. The basic types are elliptical, high-speed, high-aspect ratio, and slotted high-lift. The eagle has the last type to enable its distinctive soaring. This is a broad wing, with deep U-slotting at the tip, whose expanse allows it to catch the air for spiraling slowly in thermals and updrafts.[111] Birds of prey are the grand soarers, attaining heights up to 14,000 feet / 4267.2 meters above ground. Among them, the golden eagle is the supreme soarer, adapting its altitude to atmospheric conditions. In high thermal soaring it spreads its wings and tail to present the maximum surface to the vertical air current. In orographic soaring, because there is more horizontal airflow, it often bends its wings and lowers its feet, flying lower. In this controlled attitude the bird appears to be poised motionless.[112]

Biblical writers would have observed eagles exploiting the atmospheric conditions over Israel to launch and sustain their flight. Species of birds that are extensively airborne depend on vertical airflow created in the lower atmosphere by orography, convection, or turbulence. The large raptors such as the eagle are masters at coordinating orographic and thermal soaring. Orographic soaring exploits the vertical drafts forced by the ascent of air over high ground.[113] On a windy day a large raptor can launch itself from a lofty perch, such as a bluff or mountain, and create lift just by facing into the wind and extending its wings.[114] In contrast to orographic soaring is thermal soaring. Thermals are upcurrents of varying intensity produced by convection, the solar heating of the ground. They originate over expansive dry sand or soil in a solar-warmed bubble of air at a higher temperature than the surrounding atmosphere. A buoyant bubble rises; a series creates a thermal. Its area may extend 984.252–1640.42 feet / 300–500 meters wide at an altitude of 1640.42–4921.26 feet / 500–1500 meters, but greater at higher levels and in thunderclouds. Thermals provide the lift that reduces the rate of sink, allowing soaring birds to maintain or gain altitude with a minimal consumption of energy.[115]

Israelites in the desert would have seen cumulus clouds, which ideally indicate the formation of thermals beneath them. Uninhibited solar radiation in the desert ensures constant formation of thermals until cooling later in the day. Raptors thus soar most toward midday, when thermal activity peaks, and less from midafternoon, when temperatures cool. Thermals blowing downwind over flat planes such as deserts frequently form streets, which migrating or foraging birds may use as a level flight path.[116] Because hilly and mountainous slopes facing south heat more quickly than those facing north, thermals form there.[117] Raptors face south to exploit them, as in the archaic biblical poem about the hawk that by divine wisdom "spreads its wings toward the south" (Job 39:2). Species of large raptors with long, broad wings slotted at the tips, such as the eagle, exploit thermals to gain altitude, frequently rising to 6000 feet / 1828.8 meters or more above ground. Strategically they circle upward in tight curves around the center of a thermal, then glide down to the next thermal, and then repeat the process by circling up in it. Where thermals are abundant, the circling motion can be forgone for gliding among them. For large raptors, soaring in thermals is common during hunting and migrating. The altitude gained on rising currents enables travel, for the golden eagle up to 13.6702 miles / 22 kilometers when hunting.[118]

SONG

An eagle soaring over the desert was the metaphor in Genesis 1:2 for the Spirit soaring over the wasteland at creation. Its first creature, commanded in the very next verse, was light, as consistent with the heat it generates for thermal soaring. The only match to the Spirit *měraḥepet* in Genesis 1:2 was the eagle *měraḥepet* in Deuteronomy 32:11. On linguistic evidence, both semantic and morphological, the archaic poetry of Deuteronomy 32 predated the exilic or postexilic prose of Genesis 1 by five centuries.[119] Both texts belonged to the Priestly tradition,[120] one of the four sources of the biblical Torah in the modern documentary hypothesis. Despite revisions of that general theory, the identification of the Priestly writing remains intact because it is stylistically and theologically the most distinctive. Although its redaction is usually dated to the exile or later, it incorporated older traditions.[121] It has even been argued that not only its material but also its literature belonged to the pre-exilic Jerusalem temple, not to the postexilic temple.[122] A hallmark of Priestly style was the reduction of plot, dialogue, characterization, and description to a bare minimum.[123] The striking absence of narrative from Priestly passages has been argued to discredit it as an independent source,[124] and most exegesis writes of a tradition. The terse Priestly economy is easily apparent from a comparison of the Priestly creation of nameless humans in the two verses of Genesis 1:26–27 with the descriptive Yahwist story in Genesis 2:7–25 of the creation of Adam and Eve.

Consistent with Priestly minimalism, its story of creation barely identified the Spirit, *rûaḥ 'ĕlōhîm*, in Genesis 1:2. However, the occurrence of biblical *mĕraḥepet* only in Genesis 1:2 and Deuteronomy 32:11 was not coincidental. Both texts belonged to the Priestly tradition, and Deuteronomy 32 was a context for Genesis 1. The Spirit in Genesis 1:2 *mĕraḥepet* at creation over the waste and void earth was acting like God in Deuteronomy 32:11 *mĕraḥepet* over the desert wilderness. As a projection from Deuteronomy 32, the emphasis of Genesis 1 was not abstractly about the divine act of creation itself, but particularly about the Creator's possession of his creatures. It established ownership from origin, as in a psalm that acknowledged the Lord's supremacy over other gods, and thus his ownership of creatures as their Creator.[125] The creation story of Genesis 1 was the primordial model for the election of Israel among the nations—not natural history but political claim.

The ancient Song of Moses was inserted into the later Deuteronomic book (32:1–43), although foreign to its theology. The Song may have once belonged to a cultic collection of the Priestly tradition, whose code retained poetic fragments.[126] For there were Israelite epic poems by sages before the biblical Torah's compositions and redactions.[127] The preservation of the Song of Moses was presented as authorized by Moses himself, whose farewell speech enjoined its memorization for recital from generation to generation.[128] It exhorted the Israelites to perseverance in allegiance to the Lord, who would be militant for them against the nations.[129] Moses's audience comprised Israel's assembled elders and officers. That human assembly imitated the heavenly court that witnessed the Creator's decision to "let us make man in our image, after our likeness" (Gen. 1:26). The Song rebuked the Israelites for repudiating their origin. It commanded them to learn from their ancestors how God had apportioned inheritances to the nations, separating and limiting them, and choosing Israel as his special portion and allotted heritage. The Song then initiated an amplified lawsuit against Israel for breach of covenant.[130] The eagle appeared in the plaintiff's recital of God's benefactions as a premise for his indictment of Israel for idolatry. "You were unmindful of the Rock that begot you, / and you forgot the God who gave you birth" (Deut. 32:18–19).[131] It announced that the Father of the Israelites now disowned his children. They were not simply "foolish" (*nbl*) as imprudent or silly. They committed *něbālâ*, a rare word for a serious, destructive breach of customary law.[132]

Moses ordered the assembly to recount their generations, to ask their fathers and elders about the ancient time when the Most High divided the nations to bestow his inheritance. Genesis 1 abbreviated that narrative. The Creator's collection then separation of the elements by setting bounds to each imitated his establishment of political boundaries by gathering then dividing peoples, especially Israel from all other nations. By a repetition in Genesis 1 of that gathering then separating in Deuteronomy 32, the Priestly tradition projected back to the creation the paradigm for the finding and choosing of Israel.

God created in Genesis 1 by separation or distinction,[133] and the verb *bārā*, "to create," has even been argued to mean "to separate."[134] However, separation is only half the story, for the Priestly creation account was not only about distinctions. Before God divided and separated, he collected. That dynamism, in which collection was fundamental, was explicit for the sea, whose very name meant gathering. "And God said, 'Let the waters under the heavens be gathered together into one place, and let the dry land appear.' And it was so. God called the dry land Earth, and the waters that were gathered together he called Seas" (Gen. 1:9–10). That collection of the seas repeated their agency in the oldest biblical poem, the Song of the Sea at Exodus 15:8–10. There the sea acted tautologically. The sea as a "gathering" gathered its waves to drown by their violent movements the pharaoh's charioteers in pursuit of the Hebrews fleeing Egyptian bondage. The sea collected itself so that God could collect Israel by saving it in that exemplary Exodus from enslavement by a foreign nation.[135]

The Priestly story in Genesis 1 summarized creation as "these are the generations of the heavens and the earth when they were created" (v. 2:4a). Implicit in those generations were the human generations of Israel invoked in the Song of Moses. "Remember the days of old, / consider the years of many generations; / ask your father, and he will show you; your elders, and they will tell you." What was that story? "When the Most High gave to the nations their inheritance, / when he separated the sons of men, / he fixed the bounds of the peoples / according to the number of the sons of God. / For the Lord's portion is his people, / Jacob his allotted heritage" (Deut. 32:7–9). Implicit in the creation in Genesis 1 of various matter, ultimately humans, was the choosing of the people Israel. The standard exegetical division of Genesis into primeval history (1–11) and patriarchal history (12–50)[136] is not plausible historiographically for its motive of composition. The Priestly creational story was compiled from traditional and contemporary sources many centuries after the election and establishment of Israel.[137] Its story reminded Israel of its foundation in or at the very beginning, before it was summoned in the call of Abraham,[138] as if it was gestating as God's favorite forever. The tradents, composers, and redactors of Genesis were already covenanted Israelites. They were not disinterested chroniclers capable of discerning and articulating a prehistory before historical method. The Priestly story of creation presupposed the choice of Israel as implicit in that creation. As Isaiah understood, the Creator was "calling the generations from the beginning" (Is. 41:4).

The Song of Moses in Deuteronomy 32 was original in beginning Israel's history in the primeval era, before the patriarchs.[139] In that Priestly writing Moses summoned the Israelite assembly to remember the olden days by questioning their fathers and elders. "When the Most High gave to the nations their inheritance, / when he separated the sons of men, / he fixed the bounds of the peoples / according to the number of the sons of God" (Deut. 32:7–8). That unique perspective underlay Genesis 1, the Priestly creation account. God appeared in both Deuteronomy 32:10–11 and Genesis 1:2 as a figurative eagle, and appeared in the same place, in the sky over a wasteland. The desert in Deuteronomy where the Israelites marched in their Exodus toward their land was projected back in Genesis to a primordial wasted earth. The Song of Moses in the standard modern translation declares of God's chosen people and inheritance, "He found him in a desert land, and in the howling waste of the wilderness; / he encircled him, he cared for him, he kept him as the apple of his eye" (Deut. 32:10). The rare action of the Spirit *mĕraḥepet* in Genesis 1:2 imitated *mĕraḥepet* in Deuteronomy 32:11. In the standard translation, "Like an eagle that stirs up its nest, that flutters (*mĕraḥepet*) over its young, spreading out its wings, catching them, bearing them on its pinions, / the Lord alone did lead him, and there was no foreign god with him" (vv. 11–13). That translation of *mĕraḥepet* as "flutters" was inconsistent with the flight mode of soaring for its simile for the Spirit, the eagle.

RESCUE

The wasteland of the Song of Moses in which God found Israel recurred in the Priestly story of creation at Genesis 1:2, where "the earth was without form and void." The Song, as poetry inset in prose,[140] was typically replete with novel and rare archaic language, such as the "howling" in the desert. A unique noun, *yll* vocalizes as *yĕlêyl*, sounding like the English "yowl" or "howl." Early biblical translations into English rendered "yowl" and "howl" about dogs for the different Hebrew root *hmh*. The "howling" desert of Deuteronomy. 32:10 in the Authorized Version (King James Bible) of 1611 introduced that word into the English language. Its translators did not mean a stormy wind, however. Howling was not predicated of inanimate subjects before very late in the seventeenth century.[141] That bible cleverly translated the novel *yĕlêyl* as an onomatopoeia, "howling," but misattributed it to the desert. Subsequent versions echoed it. The related noun *yĕlālāḥ* was always predicated of humans—foreigners—screaming in distress at God's destruction of their nation.[142] Its verb *yālāl* cried out humanly in oracles of doom for both the nations and Israel.[143] The "howling" in the desert of the Song was human, not animal or demonic. It was the wailing of the Israelites, to whose piteous cries for deliverance God responded.

As the Deuteronomic recital for the liturgy of the first fruits recalled, "Then we cried to the Lord the God of our fathers, and the Lord heard our voice, and saw our affliction, our toil, and our oppression; and the Lord brought us out of Egypt with a mighty hand and an outstretched arm, with great terror, with signs and wonders; and he brought us into this place and gave us this land, a land flowing with milk and honey"

(Deut. 26:7–9). That liturgical cry epitomized their historical cry for the right to worship, for relief from plague, for safe passage at the Sea of Reeds, for water in the desert, and for Moses's rescue from a rioting crowd about to stone him, as divinely promised.[144] A psalm of thanksgiving for God's steadfast covenant recited the desert experience first. "Some wandered in desert wastes, / finding no way to a city to dwell in; / hungry and thirsty, their soul fainted within them. / Then they cried to the Lord in their trouble, / and he delivered them from their distress" (Ps. 107:4–6). The Song of Moses in the standard translation has "He found him in a desert land, / and in the howling waste of the wilderness" (Deut. 32:7). Rather, God, like the eagle of that Song, found Israel "howling in the waste wilderness." The simile was consistent with a bird's keen sense of hearing, which enables it to judge distance and range,[145] so as to locate the source of a sound.

God rescued those howling Israelites first by sound then by sight, as also consistent with aquiline behavior. Birds have the best vision among vertebrates, and birds of prey probably the sharpest resolving vision of all creatures due to their large, dense retina. The acuity of eagles exceeds human vision from two to eight times in value and that of all other animal species.[146] Eagles are bifoveate, allowing not only the sharpest vision[147] but also dual modes to vary binocular fixation for depth perception in negotiating space while hunting.[148] In the open expanse of the desert, where prey is scattered, an eagle depends on its vision over long sight lines to hunt by a stoop from a long range. With its extraordinary vision an eagle can spot a rabbit running, its common prey, from more than 1 mile /1.60934 kilometers distant.[149] That extraordinary vision for hunting prey compared well in poetic imagination with God enthroned above the sky, spotting the wandering Israelites in the desert far below.

A psalm praised their divine deliverance "with a strong hand and an outstretched arm, for his steadfast love endures forever" (Ps. 136:12). The human hand and arm as metonyms for power were matched in the Song of Moses by an avian wing and pinion. Like an eagle soaring over the desert God heard, sought, found, and rescued the Israelites, as if grabbing them with its talons. God's aerial intervention "like an eagle" in Deuteronomy 32:11 imagined an eagle's natural advance from 164.042 feet /50 meters / or more up in the air, or in thermal soaring even much higher. Once a golden eagle detects its prey, it partly retracts its wingspread to begin gliding at a low angle for a distance of 1 mile

/ 1.60934 kilometers or more. As it approaches its quarry, it retracts its wings further to increase its speed for the final stoop. Just before its attack the eagle opens its wings again, fans its tail, and thrusts its talons forward to grab its prey.[150]

The Song of Moses in the standard translation has God "guards" Israel "like the apple of his eye" (Deut. 32:10; see also Ps. 17:8). No eye is stated or implied in that Hebrew verse, however. Hebrew *ayšwn* was twice a biblical simile for preciousness, and twice for the middle of the night and deep darkness.[151] The associations were transferred to the precious pupil as both in the middle of the eye and as dark. It was the Vulgate translation that interpreted *ayšwn* as "the pupil of his eye." Bibles since the Wycliffite converted the Latin "pupil" into an English "apple" from their similar rotundity. The Authorized Version planted its apple in the Renaissance conceit of mutual amatory gazing, in which the lover spied his image reflected in the pupil of his beloved.[152] But gazing is only affiliative in humans and primates; in other animals, including birds, it is an aggressive signal.[153] The golden eagle's hazel-brown eye with a yellow iris is an adaptation that intimidates both enemies and prey.[154] The diameter of the pupil in raptors is greater than in human eyes, as their muscular iris widens the pupil to accommodate more light for their superior long-distance vision.[155]

The Song of Moses did not mean at verse 11 that God guarded Israel like the apple of his eye. It meant literally that God "kept him in his midst," reinforcing his encirclement of Israel in the same verse. The verb *sābab* means "turn about, go around, surround." God encircled Israel to create its boundaries within his special provision. He then deposited Israel in the middle of his circle, within the boundaries he drew for his own portion, when he allotted and established limited territories to all the nations.[156] God's keeping (*nāṣar*) of Israel connoted a special fidelity because it remembered his covenantal keeping. The only prior mention of God's "keeping" was his forgiving replacement of the broken tables of ten commandments, when he proclaimed himself to Moses as "keeping *ḥesed*," covenantal fidelity.[157] Just as *ḥesed* was not "guarded" but maintained and fulfilled, so was the settling of Israel in the midst of the divine circle not principally about guarding or watching it. The standard translation of the Song has "he encircled him, he cared for him, he kept him as the apple of his eye."[158] Rather, "He encircled him, he established him, he kept him in his midst." God encircled Israel because that is exactly how eagles soar in thermals over the desert, by spiraling. But God did not care for it; he established (*kwn*) it. And he kept Israel in the middle of the circle he had drawn. The verbs progressively advanced God's choice of Israel as his own people: find, encircle, establish, keep. The keeping of Israel in the Song of Moses was introduced in verse 11 by the parallel verb *kwn*, which did not mean "to care for" but to "constitute, make" a people.[159] The verse developed the premise "Is not he your father, who created you, / who made you and established you?" The actions to find, encircle, establish, and keep were territorial, with religious connotations. They were political acts of divine sovereignty over Israel. "The Lord alone did lead him, / and there was no foreign god with him" (Deut. 32:6, 12). The verb "lead" (*nḥh*) can also mean to ally with, as in a covenant.[160]

The Song then introduced in verses 11–12 the simile of an eagle. In the standard translation, "Like an eagle that stirs up its nest, / that flutters over its young, /spreading out its wings, catching them, / bearing them on its pinions, / the Lord alone did lead him, and there was no foreign god with him." The aquiline simile has been interpreted by exegetical consensus as God's parental nurturing of Israel. However, this familiar anthropomorphism has missed the astonishing character of the finding of Israel in the desert as if by an eagle. The biblical Torah—Genesis to Deuteronomy—was the written Jewish law. The primary fact about the eagle in that law was its uncleanness. The eagle had first place in the lists of unclean birds in the Priestly insertion of dietary regulations into the Deuteronomist law and its supplement.[161] The Priestly creation story told that on the fifth day God created, judged, and blessed all birds as "very good," and on the sixth day gave Adam charge "over the birds of the air ... and to every bird of the air" (Gen. 1:20–23, 28–31). The survival of the ritually unclean birds, eagles first, during the later flood was ensured by their entry into Noah's ark for preservation and their exit for breeding.[162] Although the Israelites hunted birds with snares and nets,[163] in biblical law birds of prey were forbidden food. "You may eat all clean birds. But these are the ones which you shall not eat: the eagle, the vulture, the osprey, the buzzard, the kite, and their kinds, and so on" (Deut. 14:11–13). In the Levitical list, "And these you shall have in abomination among the birds, they shall not be eaten, they are an abomination: the eagle, the vulture, the osprey, the kite, the falcon according to its kind" (Lev. 11:13–14). That classification of ritually unclean birds encompassed in the scientific Linnaean taxonomy the natural order *Accipitridae*, the largest family of birds of prey: the eagle, the vulture, the osprey, the buzzard, and the hawk.[164] Although those biblical texts did not state the reason for their uncleanness, their exclusion probably obeyed priestly sanctions against consuming live blood or touching a corpse.[165]

Birds of prey are all carnivores, characterized by strong talons for attacking and killing flesh and by hooked bills for tearing prey.[166] They are also carrion feeders, wholly so for the vulture and partly so for the eagle. The eagle was first among the unclean birds of biblical law as the king of raptors in hunting and eating flesh. In the deserts it not only hunts live prey but also scavenges the carcasses of wild and domestic ungulates. Golden eagles eat carrion they have located while soaring, landing near the carcass and walking to it with a presence that scares off other scavengers that would themselves be up for grabs.[167] Scripture told of even generic birds (*'op*) scavenging, in the baker's dream that portended them pecking his carcass hung from a tree.[168] Rizpah protected the hung corpses of her sons and others from birds.[169] Eagles even fed on the flesh of the Israelites conquered by invading heathens who abandoned their corpses unburied.[170] Deuteronomy cursed the Israelites with eagles "pursuing and overtaking you until you are destroyed, because you did not obey the Lord your God, by observing the commandments and the decrees that he commanded you" (Deut. 28:45). For their ingratitude God would force them to serve their enemies in destitution and slavery. "The Lord will bring a nation from far away, from the end of the earth, to stoop [not RSV "swoop"] down on you like an eagle" (v. 49). The ruthless enemy would be unsparing of elders and babes, consuming livestock and harvest, and destroying the land and towns. A gruesome detail foretold that the desperate Israelites would cannibalize to survive, with even dainty women eating their afterbirth.[171]

PREDATION

It is incoherent that the Deuteronomist tradition would legislate the eagle ritually unclean for Israel, then upset that normative status by proposing the eagle as a nice theological simile for God's finding of Israel. The eagle, *nešer*, approximates the Hebrew for military weapons, *nešeq*, and its biblical reputation as a killer continued in the name of the first native fighter jet for Israel's modern Air Force.¹⁷² The identification of a ruler in a military attack with a raptor was a metaphor of ancient Near Eastern texts that the Bible shared.¹⁷³ Israel became like a bird of prey surrounded by other raptors.¹⁷⁴ The natural observation of biblical writers would have been the spread-eagle display that threatens enemies by aggrandizing appearance. The feathers of the head and neck are erected, the head with its ferocious eyes is stretched up or forward, the wings are partly or wholly opened, and the talons are thrust forward.¹⁷⁵ Jeremiah's oracle, which adapted older conventions and language,¹⁷⁶ pronounced against the foreign nations of Moab and Edom, "'Behold, one shall fly swiftly like an eagle, and spread his wings . . . the cities shall be taken and the stronghold seized'" (Jer. 48:40–42; 49:22).¹⁷⁷

The prophetic doom oracles also staged the avian predation of humans as eagle-to-eagle. Their imagery replicated inimical eagles with their talons locked in aerial display to claim and settle their territorial rights for breeding and hunting. Oracles symbolically accused Edom of becoming an eagle to supplant God's nesting of Israel on the high ground. As Jeremiah previewed the divine destruction of that foreign nation, "You who live in the clefts of the rock, / who hold the height of the hill. / Though you make your nest as high as the eagle's, / I will bring you down from there, says the Lord" (Jer. 49:16). In Obadiah's version, "You who live in the clefts of the rock, / whose dwelling is high, / who say in your heart, / 'Who will bring me down to the ground?' / Though you soar aloft like the eagle, / though your nest is among the stars, / thence I will bring you down, says the Lord" (Obad. 1:3–4). Although the altitude of aeries varies with the topography, eagles rarely nest on or even near the pinnacle of a mountain. They are deterred by the severe weather at extreme altitudes as potentially destructive of the nest and chick. Their nesting site is also selected for inaccessibility to predators and balanced by the need to transport their own prey from their hunting grounds up to it.¹⁷⁸ The Edomites' construction of a "nest among the stars" (v. 4)¹⁷⁹ was not a natural site but an *adynaton*, a rhetorical figure for hyperbolic impossibility. Obadiah prophesied that, even at a stellar altitude, an enemy ascendant over Israel was still within God's crushing grasp.

Edom's offense was its military occupation of the heights that God appointed to Israel in the Song of Moses "to ride on the high places of the earth" (Deut. 32:13).¹⁸⁰ He "set it to straddle the high ground" politically for territorial advantage over the other nations. Obadiah's oracle of doom especially accused Edom of usurping the altitude that God chose for Moses's exclusive prerogative of seeing his divine glory, the cleft on Mount Sinai in the wilderness.[181] What was properly "high, uppermost, most high" was *elyon*, the name for God in whose shadow Israel lived.[182] Edom's offense in settling in a high cleft exceeded presumption. It was fraud, just as its idols were fraudulent. Its army was an imposter and an intruder on the heights that were divinely ordained for Israel. Edom ascended toward the heavens from its apportioned land below, among the other nations. The prophets proclaimed that God would drag it back down to earth. Edom's fault was deceit—double deceit—for it had deceived itself into being a deceiver. Isaiah's oracle against Edom prophesied its utter desolation as inhabited only by predatory animals and birds.[183] The Song of Moses in contrast praised God as the perfect and just Rock "without deceit" (Deut. 32:4). But God's attack and kill of Israel's enemies was turned against Israel in other oracles. Prophesying a foreign conqueror, Micah ordered the faithless Israelites to symbolize the impending loss of their children as an eagle molted its feathers. "Make yourselves as bald as the eagle, / for they shall go from you into exile" (Mic. 1:15–16; and Dan. 4:33). In Habbakuk's prophecy God roused and commissioned the Chaldean army to "fly like an eagle swift to devour" Israel as its preying (Hab. 1:4, 6–8, 9–11; and see Deut. 32:35).

An eagle in flight over a desert hunts for prey to consume,[184] not for people to save. The appropriation in the Song of Moses (Deuteronomy 32) of natural predation for God's finding of Israel in the desert was astonishing.[185] It praised God for lifting the Israelites as his select "portion" (v. 9) from the desert to his nest. But, instead of eating them there like an eagle consuming its prey, he reversed and exceeded the natural order by providing Israel with abundant food. The Song recited how "He made him ride on the high places of the earth, / and he ate the produce of the field; and he made him such honey out the rock, / and oil out of the flinty rock. Curds from the herd, and milk from the flock, / with fat of lambs and rams, / herds of Bashan and goats, / with the finest of the wheat— / and of the blood of the grape you drank wine" (vv. 13–14). Honey and oil from flinty rock surpassed the miracle for Moses in the wilderness of water gushing from flinty rock (8:15; and see Is. 41:18–20). Those feats were again an adynaton, a hyperbolic impossibility. The

Song did not align God's nurture with ordinary nature. It proclaimed God's choice and care of Israel as extraordinary, a singular beneficence, as its premise for his indictment of Israel for breach of covenant.[186]

The Song recalled that, after God found, encircled, established, and kept Israel as its portion, it lifted it from the desert to his nest. There it performed the rare *měraḥepet* over its young that the Spirit in Genesis 1:2 performed at creation over the deep and the wasteland. In the standard translation of Deuteronomy 32:11, "Like an eagle that stirs up its nest, / that flutters (*měraḥepet*) over its young, / spreading out its wings, catching them, / bearing them on its pinions." However, ornithology establishes scientifically that an eagle cannot flutter, and the biblical writers would have observed naturally the difference between regular flapping birds and exceptional soaring birds. The rarity of *rḥp* argues philologically for the rarity of "soaring," although that translation has itself been rare.[187] What was happening by the participle *měraḥepet* in the poetic simile of the eagle above its nest? The Vulgate Bible inserted influentially into verse 11 an unauthorized explanation that is not in the text: "*Sicut aquila provocans ad volandum pullos suos, / Et super eos volitans . . .* ('Like an eagle provoking its chicks for the purpose of flying')." That translation differed from Jerome's rendition of *mrḥpḥ* at creation in Genesis 1:2 as past continuous passivity, *ferebatur*, "was being carried." The Vulgate altered the past passive participle *měraḥepet* in Genesis 1:2 to the active present *volitans* in Deuteronomy 32:11, "flying." That translation with its unwarranted addition to the text has produced a fantastical exegetical commonplace. God became like a parent eagle that shoved its babies out of the nest for flight lessons, then swooped strategically below the fledglings to catch them safely on its back if their wings faltered and they fell. The moral was supposedly that God nurtured Israel tenderly.

Certain facts about nests were available to ancient explorers or travelers, even from the chance discovery of abandoned nests, discarded eggshells, ejected or fallen chicks, and other debris. A Deuteronomic law spared a mother brooding her nest in a tree or on the ground by allowing only the removal of her eggs or chicks.[188] The psalmist witnessed nests protected at God's altar.[189] Birds construct nests as a principal care to enhance the survival of egg and chick.[190] The golden eagle, the shared biblical model for the Spirit in Genesis 1:2 and Deuteronomy. 32:11, in nature constructs several aeries and sometimes more than a dozen. Those eagles are skillful architects, and their nests are huge, at

4.92126 feet / 1.5 meters in diameter and 1.64042 to 3.28084 feet /0.5 to 1 meter / high, but as high as almost 16.4052 feet / 5 meters.[191] Their nests are prominent in the open landscape they favor as hunting grounds. For golden eagles, orientation is influenced by weather and climate since incessant exposure to the sun can cause overheating and death. In arid regions of Israel most of their aeries face north.[192] The biblical image of the Israelites sheltering under the divine wings for shade was consistent with that natural habit. "He who dwells in the shelter of the Most High, / who abides in the shadow of the Almighty, / will say to the Lord, 'My refuge and my fortress; / my God, in whom I trust.' / For he will deliver you from the snare of the fowler / and from the deadly pestilence; / he will cover you with his pinions, and under his wings you will find refuge." That refuge and habitation prevented death from "the destruction that wastes at noonday" (Ps. 91:1–4, 6, 9). Shelter under the shadow of God's wings referred not only to brooding in the nest but also to soaring overhead to shade creatures in the desert below from the scorching sun and sand.[193] Scripture thus imitated an eagle's natural flight at the hottest hours, when the sun forms thermals, with its promise of God's shady protection to the Israelites in the desert below.

The Vulgate's insertion into Deuteronomy 32:11 about the parent eagle's behavior toward its brood was a fanciful invention. In nature, avian parental care is exercised in brooding the egg, sanitizing the nest, and feeding the chick. Those behaviors principally originate not as adult initiatives but as responses to solicitation by the chick, even vocalizations from the embryo.[194] Initially the chicks are not fed. Unless by aggressive cheeping they stimulate the mother to shred the food in the nest and present it to them on the cere of her beak, they starve to death.[195] An eagle was not a natural model for God's initiative in feeding the Israelites either in its lofty nest or on the heights of the land. An eagle does not "rouse" or "stir" its nestlings, as in translations of verse 11, although jarring the nest upon landing may stimulate the chick to beg.[196] In the political context of that Song, rousing Israel as God's choice referenced military action against the nations, with the eagle as a figurative weapon.

An eagle was also not a natural model for God's parental nurturing of Israel because it only tolerates plural nestlings briefly. Brood reduction by starvation is extensive among large raptors and invariable in nine species of *Accipitridae*.[197] The golden eagle among them exemplifies the fatality of "Cainism." That ornithological term derives from the notorious fratricide in Genesis 4:1–8, when the elder Cain murdered the younger Abel after losing the competition for the Lord's favor on their offerings, agricultural versus animal. The aggression of the golden eagle begins at birth with violent sibling competition in the nest for parental investment. The firstborn chick, which has the advantage of size for dominance over the brood,[198] frequently kills any sibling, by wounding it with its sharply pointed beak, by forcing its starvation, or by ejecting it from the nest.[199] The tiny predator pecks and stabs with its bill at the head and back of its sibling with grabs, twists, and tears; and it squats on it. If its victim dies in the nest, the parent consumes it or feeds it to the aggressive sibling.[200] Although an adult golden eagle will bark with alarm at a foreign predator threatening its nest,[201] it does nothing to protect a lesser chick from a sibling's attack. The Song of Moses at verse 11 uniquely designated God's nestlings *gôzālim*, "little raptors," from *gāzal*, "tear" and "seize," as related to "robbery" (*gāzēl*) and its "plunder" (*gĕzēlāh*). However, avian parental tolerance of natural Cainism would have been a horrific model for God's nurture of Israel. The biblical message was different: that God not only transcended but even reversed natural avian behavior by extraordinary divine behavior. In the biblical story of fratricide God missed Abel and sought Cain to inquire about his brother. The God of Genesis then marked and banished the human murderer.

NATURE

Parental behavior in the nest responds to the stimuli of the young; it does not control their development.[202] The eagle of the Song of Moses was not giving its young flying lessons as in the Vulgate's translation, "Just like an eagle provoking its chicks toward flying, / And flying over them, / It extended its wings, and it took him up, / And it carried him on its shoulders" (Deut. 32:11). The interpolation into the text of "provoking them toward flying" and the rest of that translation was anthropomorphic. The still mysterious origin of avian flight may in evolutionary ecology devolve to the parental preadaptation of protobirds.[203] But adult eagles do not coach their nestlings to fly. By the time the fledgling has developed wings strong enough to support flight, the parents are usually long since gone from the nest.[204] The chick progresses on its own from preening its feathers and stretching its wings, to flapping windward, then jumping in the nest or hopping from it locally. But its decision to fly is solo and sudden.[205] Although ancient observers were not likely privy to activity within its lofty nest, they would have observed in the sky that eaglets left it in solo flight.

The Vulgate's translation remembered an earlier verse in Deuteronomy about God bearing Israel like a father carrying his child across the desert.[206] Its eagle "shoulders" imitated Aeneas's classical rescue of Anchises from burning Troy by lifting him onto his shoulders.[207] The Vulgate's translation was repeated in the Wycliffite versions, where the eagle "forthclepynge" or "stirynge" his birdies to fly, spread its wings to take Israel on his "shuldres/schuldris."[208] On that premise of flying lessons hung the Vulgate's next translation, "spreading out its wings, catching them, / bearing them on its pinions" (v. 11). But no avian species transports anything on its wings. The wings of birds are airfoils, convex above and concave below, tapering at the rear edges.[209] The notion of Israelites transported atop an eagle's wings neglected the complexity of the Hebrew particle *al*, which is like the English "on." It can be positional, meaning "atop," or functional, meaning "on the basis or ground of which something is done." The biblical eagle was not carrying its young on top of its wings but lifting them by virtue of its wings. Its *al* was a metonym for power, a marker of place. The verb *nāśā'* in the standard translation is "carry" or "bear," but in that verse it denotes "lift up." The parallel verb *lāqaḥ* is rendered "catch," but in that verse it denotes "take," "bring," or "lift." The translation of chicks atop parental wings determined the notion of a parent catching them if they fell off. Rather, in the biblical simile God uplifted Israel to his nest as an eagle lifts its prey to its nest. The prominent deep U-slotting of eagles' wings allows for the carriage of heavy prey.[210] An eagle holds its prey either tight to its body or in its talons with the legs extended,[211] and it lifts it by the power of its wings, not on them.

Birds are quadrupeds whose forelegs have modified to wings, suppressing the functions of arms and hands. Although the wing of each species differs, the wings of all flying birds consist in scientific terms of "arm" and "hand" portions,[212] with a "wrist" as their joint.[213] Ornithologists compare a soaring golden eagle's deeply notched outermost primaries to splayed human fingers.[214] The biblical vision of God's throne by Ezekiel, a priest in the Priestly tradition of Genesis 1 and Deuteronomy 32,[215] recognized the similarity of an eagle's wingtips to human hands. His visionary creatures composing God's throne had feathers stretching from an eagle at the rear. Under the wings were human hands that clasped at the tips, the flight feathers.[216] The biblical comparison of avian wings and pinions for human arms and hands was evident from Deuteronomy's very first chapter. Moses reminded the Israelites of their sojourn "in the wilderness, where you have seen how the Lord your God bore you, as a man bears his son, in all the way that you went until you came to this place" (Deut. 31:29–31).[217] The simile recalled their Exodus from Egyptian slavery as the premise for the divine commandments. "You have seen what I did to the Egyptians, and how I bore you by the power of [not RSV "on"] eagles' wings and brought you to myself. Now therefore, if you will obey my voice and keep my covenant, you shall be my own possession among all peoples; for all the earth is mine, and you shall be to me a kingdom of priests and a holy nation" (Ex. 19:4–6).[218]

Genesis 1:2 on creation did not propose that God was an eagle, like the mythological gods of the ancient Near East who metamorphosed into birds[219] flying majestically with extended wings.[220] What, then, was the meaning of the Priestly tradition's metaphor of the Spirit at creation *měraḥepet* over the primordial deep like the eagle in its Song of Moses *měraḥepet* over the Israelite nest? As the Spirit's metaphor, the biblical eagle overshadowed the foreign celestial gods whose assembly witnessed his creation.[221] Ornithology establishes the golden eagle as the supreme master of the skies, achieving the highest altitudes. Its flight is distinctively effortless compared to the energetic flapping of ordinary birds. It is native to Israel. It is in habitat solitary, not flocking. It appears in the sky at the solar zenith, thus visible to observers on the ground. These behaviors all commended it as a biblical metaphor for divine activity.

Most significantly, the golden eagle was an excellent figure for both the Spirit's creation of humans and for finding of Israel for the same reason: its soaring *měraḥepet* includes magnificent territorial display. Most species of large raptors (*Accipitridae*) are territorial[222] and display to attract other birds.[223] The golden eagle's display[224] is renowned for its grandiose show while soaring aloft at more than 100 miles / 160.93 kilometers per hour. Over its breeding ground the eagle, usually the male, commonly displays by soaring in wide circles and calling out to announce its territory. In its characteristic undulating display the golden eagle then stoops dramatically. It plunges headfirst from 1000 feet / 304.8 meters to 50 feet / 15.24 meters, then levels off before rising up steeply and swiftly. It repeats the performance serially.[225] With the "spectacular manoeuvres" of its undulating display, the golden eagle can soar in an upcurrent with extended wings, fold them to dive rapidly below, then suddenly extend them and soar up again.[226] If another bird intrudes on its space, the golden eagle aggressively turns over and presents its talons to the occupier for locking and whirling in combat.[227] A mutual display of the eagle pair—eagles are monogamous—may also occur in mating or bonding.[228] Since eagles usually display in thermals and updrafts only in fair sunny weather,[229] their behavior was observable to Israelites below. That avian spectacle in the skies inspired the Priestly image of the creative Spirit in Genesis 1:2 soaring to mark its ownership of all its creatures, as it had in Deuteronomy 32:10 found and selected Israel as its own portion among the nations.

Genesis 1:2 positioned the soaring Spirit directly over its creation. "The earth was without form and void, and darkness was upon the face of the deep, and the Spirit of God was moving over the face of the waters (*mayim pěnēy*)." The Spirit soaring (*měraḥepet*) as a figurative eagle in the sky was circling because that is how an eagle naturally soars. The biblical proverb about Wisdom personified attested, "When he established the heavens, I was there, / when he drew a circle on the face of the deep" (Prov. 8:27). The Spirit's metaphorical soaring as an eagle indicated the marking and advertising of his territory. That image coincided with Job's archaic verse about the territorial marking at creation. "He has described a circle upon the face of the waters (*mayim pěnēy*) / at the boundary between light and darkness" (Job. 26:10). Job's phrase "face of the waters" (*mayim pěnēy*) was identical with Genesis 1:2, where the Spirit "was moving over the face of the waters (*mayim pěnēy*)." Job's poetic exaltation of God's majesty imagined his breath (*nišěmaḥ*) making ice and solidifying those expansive waters. He "spread out the skies, / hard as a molten mirror" (37:10, 18). Genesis 1:2 imaginatively projected the Spirit to an extraordinary altitude—far above the earth, as yet without land separated from sea, up where an eagle could not naturally survive. Although that altitude was again an adynaton to assert God's sovereignty, the circular pattern imitated an accurate natural observation of an eagle soaring. The creative act relating the divine Spirit to the human spirit "in our image, after our likeness" (Gen. 1:26) was a territorial claim. The Priestly story was not about the Spirit's creation abstractly but possessively. His territorial marking of creation continued in the gathering and separating of creatures and their apportioning specific places: birds to the air, beasts to the land, fish to the sea, and humans on land over all the animals. Humans especially belonged to God, spirit-to-Spirit, as made "in our image, after our likeness." Creation was projected in the Priestly version of Genesis 1 from its archaic Song of Moses in Deuteronomy 32 about God like a soaring eagle encircling Israel as its own portion. The Priestly writing was not a historiographical record first of all humans, later of Israel, as in the standard exegetical division of Genesis into primordial and patriarchal histories. Israel as the Spirit's own portion was its profound center point.

CREATION

The remarkable coherence of the story of creation in Genesis 1 derived from poetic orality, which required a topical density for memorization toward recital. The origins of creation were consistent with its metaphor for the Spirit as an eagle. In poetic imagination the Spirit's appearance in or at the beginning over the waste earth and dark waters happened in a thunderstorm. Because eagles, like all raptors, are diurnal birds,[230] they need solar light to see and to navigate.[231] The diffused elemental light before the biblical creation of the discrete luminaries—sun, moon, stars—was imagined as lightning,[232] with God's commanding voice as thunder.[233] "And God said, 'Let there be light,' and there was light" (Gen. 1:3). The Hebrew Scriptures frequently ascribed those meteorological phenomena to God's power as master of the atmosphere, lord of the storm.[234] Since a thunderstorm over the desert kicks up dust, the Priestly redaction of Genesis 1 incorporated the Yahwist version of creation in Genesis 2. There dust coherently became the matter from which God made Adam. "Then the Lord God formed man of dust from the ground, and breathed into his nostrils the breath of life; and man became a living being" (Gen. 2:7).[235] In the Priestly story of Genesis 1 the earth began as "waste and void" like the desert in Deuteronomy 32:10 where God found Israel crying out. The Yahwist story of Genesis 2 reversed the Priestly order of Genesis 1 by forming Adam from dust as the first, not last, of creatures. Adam originated before the barren earth was vegetated or watered, "when no plant of the field was yet in the earth and no herb of the field had yet sprung up" (Gen. 2:5). He was made from its dust. Dust is the erosion of surface matter when the soil in any environment, but mainly deserts, is blown by wind.[236] The Yahwist placement of Adam emerging dusty from the ground was consistent with natural observation of a desert. It cohered with its Creator as a blower of the desert's dust into the shape of Adam, then of his own air into Adam's nostrils. And it recalled biblical stories of the finding and choosing of Israel in the desert.[237] Dust belonged also to the Yahwist source of Exodus 14, where God's guiding presence to the Israelites in the desert by the pillar of cloud by day and of fire by night may have been modeled on a dust storm[238] with lightning. The Lord clogged the wheels of the chariots of the pharaoh's pursuing army, so that they drove sluggishly into the dried-up Sea of Reeds.[239] A dust storm, which can occur in dry lakebeds,[240] may have been their natural hindrance.

Despite the apparent fluffiness of dust, as particulate matter it coheres. Dust collects ordinarily in piles on surfaces, but especially in the atmosphere so thickly as to impair or impede visibility. Air, as wind, blows up dust in contact with bare soil. Dust storms are a constant and extensive phenomenon of arid and semiarid regions of the earth. They originate in major deserts, particularly the Sahara, but also in the southern coast of the Mediterranean, in northeast Sudan, and in the Arabian Peninsula. A particular atmospheric phenomenon, the dust devil, forms when air converging at the base of a thermal exaggerates the horizontal rotation of eddies in the airflow. Its vortex sucks up loose material to whirl and transport silt and clay particles from the surface of the desert 98.4352–328.083 feet / 30–100 meters above ground. When its force rivals a tornado, a vortex can spew dust up to 3280.84 feet / a kilometer high.[241] It was from such a whirlwind that God eloquently addressed Job about the divine knowledge and power to lay the foundations of heaven and earth and to design all of their creatures. God's catalogue of rhetorical questions emphasizing his sovereignty climaxed in the eagle. As he interrogated Job, "Is it at your command that the eagle mounts up / and makes his nest on high? / On the rock he dwells and makes his home / in the fastness of the rocky crag. / Thence he spies out the prey; / his eyes behold it afar off. / His young ones suck up blood; / and where the slain are, there is he" (Job 38:1; 39:27–30). Job's climax about divine sovereignty was exemplified by an eagle because only raptors can exploit a whirlwind.[242] The Creator of Adam from dust was *Yahweh 'ĕlōhîm* as the lord of thunderstorms who stirred up that dust. Creation from that dust implied lightning with thunder, for not only clouds but also dust can generate electrical discharges of lightning.[243] As electrically active, the blowing matter of dust storms generates friction. Electrification is intense in dust devils, which are great bursts or whirls raised from ground level into the lower atmosphere by gusting winds. Those strong electrical disturbances are frequent in deserts worldwide.[244]

The Creator's mastery of a thunderstorm as the metaphorical eagle was exceptional. Turbulent weather obscures the sun and the stars, which are birds' celestial compasses. It distorts with infrasound the geomagnetic field, which is their terrestrial compass. Avian flight would be doubly disoriented in a storm, so a storm is avoided.[245] The psalmist thus longs like a dove to find "a shelter from the raging wind and tempest."[246] However, eagles do fly in gales,[247] so they remain a consistent metaphor for the Spirit soaring. God frequently stormed to humans, thundering after the primordial pair hiding in the Garden of Eden, flashing to the Hebrews assembled at Mount Sinai for his commandments, tearing open the heavens before the prophets Isaiah and Ezekiel for visions of his turbulent throne. The flight of the creative Spirit preceded and governed the creation of birds. The noun *nešer* has been suggested onomatopoeia based on *šr*, a "gleaming flash or rushing sound," because a vulture "drops rushing like flashing light through the air."[248] Ancient Near Eastern texts associated lightning with the eagle, not the vulture, however.[249] A meteorologist has described lightning bolts that strike a few hundred yards or meters away from an observer as sounding like tearing cloth,[250] while an ornithologist has described the rushed stoop of a golden eagle about to contact its prey as "like the sound of ripping cloth."[251] A lightning strike to ground and an eagle's attack on prey are associated aerodynamically. The orographic effect enabling an eagle to soar on updrafts contributes to the upward convection of air that causes a thunderstorm.[252]

In the Priestly story of Genesis 1 the human was spoken into existence by God's breath. In the Yahwist version of Genesis 2, the male was shaped from dust, then inspired by breath; the female was then fashioned from his rib. Together the stories told of dual human origins: from the sky and from the earth, belonging to air and belonging to dust. In the

Yahwist story human matter was blown into a dust pile, then scooped up by divine handfuls. But before a human was ever separated from the earth in that Yahwist story, he was in the Priestly story gathered by God to himself. Genesis 1:26 designated humans universally alone among all creatures created in God's image and likeness. That image has been proposed as the rationale for the Priestly code of holiness,[253] which delineated boundaries. Yet holiness presupposed an obligation on humans as based in a relationship to a God sovereign over them.[254] The fundamental Priestly message of creation was not the philosophical definition of human nature, but the social identification of humans as their Creator's possession. That privileged identity justified the divine commandments since humans were claimed by God's decision, even before their creation, to make them. That divine claim on humans was the reason for the biblical first commandment, which forbade idolatry. "You shall not make for yourself a graven image, or any likeness of anything that is in heaven above, or that is in the earth beneath, or that is in the water under the earth; you shall not bow down to them or serve them" (Ex. 20:4–6). Hebrew "image" denoted physicality, especially that of idols.[255] Genesis depicted humans as God's physical image not by their bodies, as if God were anthropomorphic. He expressed his image physically by blowing elemental air to speak and by grasping elemental earth to make. The importance of the human image physically made by the Creator was the displacement of the image of idols humanly fashioned. Humans were thus forbidden by the first commandment to make idols of foreign gods, not only because God was superior to his rivals but also because humans were God's own chosen image and likeness of himself.

The climax in Genesis 1:26, "'Let us make man in our image, after our likeness,'" has generated a full history of readings, from semantics to clones.[256] The modern exegetical consensus reads the creation of humans in the divine image and likeness in its context. "Then God said, 'Let us make man in our image, after our likeness; and let them have dominion over the fish of the sea, and over the birds of the air, and over the cattle, and over all the earth, and over every creeping thing that creeps upon the earth.'" The exegetical emphasis on human dominion was occasioned by a chance discovery in 1979 by a Syrian farmer bulldozing his field. He uncovered a life-sized basalt statue of a male, whose skirt was engraved with the oldest extant Aramaic-Akkadian inscription. Its terms "image" and "likeness," parallel to Genesis 1:26, identified the king's delegation of authority to the provincial official whom the statue represented.²⁵⁷ However, the biblical God as Hebrew ’elōhîm was not a local suzerain, hiring Adam and Eve as the groundskeepers of the Garden of Eden. What or who finally was the rûaḥ ’ĕlōhîm in whose image and likeness humans were made?

It was the Spirit God, in whose image and likeness humans were created as also spirits. Before their creation the Spirit appeared metaphorically in the rare avian event of a soaring display. Because the original agent soaring (mĕraḥepet) in the Song of Moses at Deuteronomy 32:11 was animate, specifically "an eagle," the consequent agent soaring (mĕraḥepet) in Genesis 1:2 was cogently animate, the Spirit. The alternative translations of rûaḥ, "wind" and "breath," are not flatly mistaken because they are implicit as natural to soaring and speaking. They connote intuitively, rather than denote precisely, the Spirit's presence. Wind was necessary in Genesis 1:2 as the physical element on which the Spirit was imagined to soar like an eagle. Unlike other birds, large raptors fly comfortably in winds of force 8 to 9, and the golden eagle exceeds that measure beyond force 10, above 91.8635 feet / 28 meters per second.²⁵⁸ Breath was also necessary because the Spirit spoke creatures into existence. Scripture knew that speech drew air from within the body and then dispelled it.²⁵⁹ The Hebrew divine name YHWH was rooted in the Ugaritic verb "blow." It designated "the Blower," the storm god who imparted life by blowing.²⁶⁰ Biblical belief was in the animation of humans by breath, with the nostrils as metonyms. The Priestly association of the Spirit with breath in speaking creatures in Genesis 1 was explicated by the Yahwist making of Adam in Genesis 2. "Then the Lord God formed man of dust from the ground, and breathed into his nostrils the breath of life (ḥayiyim); and man became a living being (nĕpĕsh)" (Gen. 2:7).²⁶¹ Isaiah celebrated the Lord "who created the heavens and stretched them out, / who spread forth the earth and what comes from it, / who gives breath to the people upon it / and spirit to those who walk in it" (Is. 42:5). Job defined his lifespan, "as long as my breath is in me, / and the spirit of God is in my nostrils" (Job 27:3).²⁶² Although Scripture told that many animals breathed through their noses,²⁶³ God's breath making Adam "a living being" was unique.

Historiographically that divine inspiration of Adam justified the Davidic monarchy as obligated to Yahweh's covenant. The Yahwist story of Genesis 2 modified Near Eastern mythologies of kingship as a likeness exhaled by a divine breath into human nostrils.[264] Adam's breathy nose complemented his creation from dust, the metaphorical ground from which God uplifted humans to enthronement.[265] The collective variant *rûaḥ 'ap* for "breath of our nostrils" designated "the Lord's anointed" (Lam. 4:20), the king under whose brief shadow the Israelites would live among the nations even as they sheltered under God's long shadow. The Priestly account of God's enthronement among the foreign gods introduced humans in the divine "image" as their royal designation and dignity.[266] The anthropology in the redaction of Genesis was coherently political. The nose for breathing symbolized ownership and leadership. Adam was entrusted with care of other animals, by their symbolic hook in the nose.[267] God threatened to remove the nose rings of wanton women who violated his covenant with them, for he no longer owned them.[268] Cutting off the nose of an enemy punitively was a sign of possession.[269]

The focus on Adam's nostrils at creation in Genesis 2:7 was repeated in the biblical story of the flood in 7:22, when everything on earth with the same "breath of life" (*nišĕmah ḥayiyim*) in its nostrils died under divine wrath. But the word *rûaḥ* interrupted that phrase to add "the breath *the spirit* of life." Both *nišĕmah* and *rûaḥ* can mean the "breath" of living creatures in their nostrils. Just as the Creator quickened life by conferring breath, so he ended life by withdrawing breath. Human vanity was deprecated as "but a breath" that dissipated when weighed in the balance of divine judgment.[270] Evil was destroyed by divine *rûaḥ*, as it perished at the blast of his nostrils.[271] In the Song of the Sea, a blast from God's nose whipped up the Sea of Reeds into a tempest that drowned the pharaoh's inimical charioteers.[272] In another archaic poem God's nose snorted a thunderstorm.[273] In contrast to his potency, idols had dysfunctional noses unable even to smell.[274] Idolaters who burned incense to those gods blew smoke in God's nose.[275] Idolaters who had breath in their own nostrils were of no account.[276] God promised to impart his Spirit on Moses also to the seventy elders in the tent, but the rebellious people would have meat coming out of their noses.[277] There was little biblical interest in nasal physiology other than to remark a nosebleed.[278] Like throaty sounds gurgling through the mouth, the final gasp for breath ended in deathly silence.[279] The stench of rotting men and horses felled in camp by the plagues assaulted the nostrils of the living.[280] An angry God "remembered that they were but flesh, / a wind that passes and comes not again" (Ps. 78:39).

NAMES

Yet the basic meaning of *rûaḥ 'ĕlōhîm* at creation was not breath but the divine Spirit as the source of the human spirit made "in our image, after our likeness." The phrase *rûaḥ 'ĕlōhîm* in Genesis 1:2 has been translated as a grammatical construct, two terms that produce a possessive compound, the "Spirit/wind/breath *of* God."[281] Parallels in the same verse have been translated as a construct, "face *of* the abyss . . . face *of* the water." The subject *rûaḥ 'ĕlōhîm* has also been translated possessively with respect to the Septuagint's *pneuma theou*. Greek *pneuma* replicates Hebrew *rûaḥ* as spirit-wind-breath, and *theou* is a possessive genitive, "*of* God." However, the Septuagint was inconsistent in translating *'ĕlōhîm*. Although *ho theos* predominated, *kyrios* and *kyrios ho theos* were offered, and the word was thrice omitted.[282] The premise of the translations was "God" as substance to whom "spirit" was attributed as an accident, either a quality or a relation, as in the Aristotelian categorical distinctions.[283] Even grammars of Hebrew biblical apposition have resorted anachronistically to Aristotelian logic.[284] However, as a subject, *rûaḥ 'ĕlōhîm* is grammatically translatable not only as a construct, "Spirit *of* God," but also as an apposition, "Spirit God," which grammar is consistent with the other divine names.

Apposition in Hebrew grammar is the juxtaposition of a noun or nounal phrase with another to which it is coordinate, not subordinate. Apposition expresses an identical or equal relationship between distinct words or phrases with the same syntactic function and agreement. Yet the second noun usually serves to determine the first more precisely. More broadly and variously used in Hebrew than in English, apposition conforms to the Semitic tendency to juxtapose elements where English prefers an attributive adjective or a possessive noun. Apposition includes the designation of persons, collectively such as "my people Israel" and individually such as "Isaiah the prophet." When an appositive follows a personal name, it identifies its bearer simply. The phrase "Isaiah the prophet" means that Isaiah is a prophet among other prophets. However, when the name and the identification coincide uniquely, the name is the apposition, as in "the King, David." That distinctive usage denotes only one king, who is David. Biblical apposition also named God, although that usage has instead been translated as a construct, "God *of* hosts." Strict apposition can be repetitive. Genesis had "I am God, the God of your father." Its Priestly creational story had "the two great lights, the greater light . . . and the lesser light."[285]

The grammatical formation of the construct state, which translated *rûaḥ 'ĕlōhîm* as "the Spirit *of* God," was a later development, from syndetic parataxis to parallelism.[286] It designated *rûaḥ* as God's quality or relation, "the spirit" as personally attributed to him. The translation contradicted the earlier Priestly affirmation that God does not possess personal attributes but simply is. "I am I and there is no other God than I" (Deut. 32:39; and Ex. 3:14). However, a coherent translation of *rûaḥ 'ĕlōhîm* is the apposition Spirit God. By its *regens-rectum* order, it belongs to the type where the name itself is in apposition, as in "the King, David," rather than "David the King." Thus, *rûaḥ 'ĕlōhîm* in Genesis 1:2 announced that this particular *'ĕlōhîm*, the God among the gods *'ĕlōhîm* assembled at creation, was uniquely Spirit. That declaration was consistent with the Hebrew Scriptures before monotheism, in the exaltation of the God of Israel as incomparable with foreign gods. The order of apposition was reversed in the renewal story at Genesis 8:1 as *'ĕlōhîm rûaḥ*, when God abated the flood by the wind. That apposition was of the other type, as in "David the King" among other kings. That usage meant that over the flood the *rûaḥ* of God was his agent among other agents, just as David was not the only king. There *rûaḥ* was indeed the wind. "And God made the wind (*'ĕlōhîm rûaḥ*) blow over the waters, and the waters subsided" (Gen. 8:1). The apposition *'ĕlōhîm rûaḥ* was not a variant of the apposition *rûaḥ 'ĕlōhîm*. The apposition in Genesis 1:2 was exclusive; in Genesis 8:1, inclusive.

Although the noun *'ĕlōhîm* for the Spirit at Genesis 1:2 is semantically plural, it functions syntactically as a collective singular in most biblical texts, except when referring to foreign gods.[287] Genesis introduced the Creator in its very first verse as *'ĕlōhîm*, the common biblical designation for God. It amplified and specified God in verse 2 as *rûaḥ 'ĕlōhîm*, "Spirit God," who was not anthropomorphic like the gods assembled to witness his creation. The redaction of Genesis that integrated the Priestly and the Yahwist creational stories in chapters 1 and 2 elevated *rûaḥ 'ĕlōhîm* in 1:2 to *Yahweh 'ĕlōhîm* in 2:4b. That phrase introduced retroactively the name "Yahweh," which was only ages later revealed to Moses for the Israelites as the God of their fathers.[288] The Israelite name *Yahweh 'ĕlōhîm* was normative in Genesis 2–3, occurring nineteen times as the maker, commander, and punisher of Adam and Eve, the human pair.

The significance of *Yahweh 'ĕlōhîm* was emphasized by the deviation four times to simply *'ĕlōhîm*.

The simpler name *'ĕlōhîm* disrupted the narrative solely in the conversation between the serpent and Eve. The serpent insinuated itself into the Garden of Eden not as a free actor but as the moral product of the Yahwist tradition. "Now the serpent was more subtle than any other wild creature that the Lord God (*Yahweh 'ĕlōhîm*) had made. He said to the woman, 'Did God (*'ĕlōhîm*) say, "You shall not eat of any tree of the garden?"'" (Gen. 3:1–2). The subtlety of the serpent was precisely not to acknowledge its own Creator, *Yahweh 'ĕlōhîm*, as Eve's Creator also. He altered her Creator by a semantic shift from the *Yahweh 'ĕlōhîm* of the narrative to *'ĕlōhîm* alone. And that was its plot. The serpent exploited the ambiguity of *'ĕlōhîm* as the designation for both God and gods. Eve responded in kind without correcting its error, thus either really or tacitly accepting the serpent's demotion of the God of Israel to any god. The serpent's deception was "'God/gods (*'ĕlōhîm*) said, "You shall not eat of the fruit of the tree which is in the midst of the garden, neither shall you touch it, lest you die"'" (v. 3). Eve responded with the name *'ĕlōhîm*. She spoke as if the command were that of any some *'ĕlōhîm* whoever not to eat the forbidden fruit, whereas it was the command of her Creator, *Yahweh 'ĕlōhîm*. Translations of their conversation that render *'ĕlōhîm* as "God" miss the serpent's semantic duplicity with that word also meaning the collective gods and any god among them. The exchange between the serpent and Eve continued notoriously with both speakers referring only to *'ĕlōhîm* generically. After disobeying the true divine command of *Yahweh 'ĕlōhîm* by eating the fruit, Eve and Adam heard that Lord God who created them thundering after them in hiding. Eve admitted that she had been beguiled by the serpent into disobeying their Creator, the God above other gods.[289] The story asserted the sovereignty of *Yahweh 'ĕlōhîm*, the God of Israel, over *'ĕlōhîm*, the gods of other nations assembled to witness his creation of humans.

The apposition for that divine name *Yahweh 'ĕlōhîm* has been rendered a double name, "Lord God."[290] A major example was the Shema of Deuteronomy 6:4, which devout Jews pray twice daily: "The Lord our God is one Lord."[291] Although that liturgical formula respectfully substitutes *'ādon*, "Lord," for *Yahweh*, no translation, biblical or liturgical, offers for *Yahweh 'ĕlōhîm* the possessive construct "the Lord *of* God" in parallel to *rûaḥ 'ĕlōhîm* as "the Spirit *of* God." The exemplar of "Lord

God" at Genesis 2:4 allows for "Spirit God" at Genesis 1:2. The name "Lord God" in the Yahwist story at 2:4 advanced beyond *ʾĕlōhîm* and *rûaḥ ʾĕlōhîm* in the Priestly story of Genesis 1:1–2 to acknowledge the Creator's sovereignty as *Yahweh ʾĕlōhîm* over that just-told creation. The redaction of Genesis progressed from God in general *ʾĕlōhîm*, to Spirit God in particular *rûaḥ ʾĕlōhîm*, to Lord God of Israel *Yahweh ʾĕlōhîm*. The appositions conformed to the parallelism characteristic of Hebrew biblical literature. Such intensification was essential for its poetic parallelism, which progressed from a common noun in the first colon to a literary noun in the second. In that dynamic, parallelism was not synonymity but interpretation. Moreover, all Hebrew biblical syntax was characteristically "additive." Literally it was hooked by a *waw*, a particle meaning "and" prefixed to the first word of a clause.[292] The Priestly naming of God in Genesis demarcated a covenantal sequence: a generally designated *ʾĕlōhîm* for the first, universal covenant with Noah; a more intimately and precisely designated *ʾēl šadday* for the covenant with Abraham; an absolutely and uniquely designated *Yahweh* for the covenant with Moses and Israel.[293] The model for the developmental narrative was the consecutive naming of God at creation.

Biblical Hebrew lacked a concept of universality. Everything was literally particular: heaven and earth, not universe; male and female, not humanity; Israel with its God, and the nations with their gods. Genesis expressed totality by merism, a Semitic figure to designate the universal by the connection of such opposites.[294] A distinguished Jewish philosopher has stated "the most profound of all human questions: What is my true place in the universal order of things? That is *the* ontological existential question."[295] The creation story of the Priestly tradition in Genesis 1 projected the historical foundation and formation of Israel onto a primal scene of the making of "heaven and earth." It was not directly and explicitly a narrative, even mythological or religious, of the creation of the universe. It was the special location of Israel in a general order before metaphysics. The Spirit God soared at creation to mark his territory for the human spirit made "in our image, after our likeness" (Genesis 1:26), which he deputized with the care of the earth. That Priestly story in Genesis 1 remembered the Priestly tradition in Deuteronomy 32 of God soaring possessively like an eagle to mark Israel as his special portion. It was not a confession about a cosmological beginning but about a Spirit-to-spirit relationship. The political relation of the human spirit to the Spirit God would change over the centuries in semantic and cultural translations. Yet a sense of human spiritual belonging to the Spirit God who created it would endure.

CHAPTER 2

Paul

The human spirit as created in the divine image and likeness in Genesis 1:26 endured as a biblical belief in the beginning Christian Church. The earliest writings of its New Testament affirmed it in the letters of the apostle Paul (d. 67 C.E.), the prime source for knowledge of the first Christians. Corinth is the best documented of their communities through Paul's two extant letters to the Corinthians and through the later secondhand account in the Acts of the Apostles about his missionary activity there. Paul's words to the Corinthians about the human and divine spirits were urgent because factions there were arguing—and not theoretically so. Who personally among them was authentically "spiritual"? Paul's responses about the human spirit were pastoral rebukes to the boasting of the spiritualist faction, for he wrote situationally, not systematically, to a church in crisis about its spiritual identity. That crisis he hoped to resolve by a practical discernment of the manifest gifts of the Spirit among them, with his famous climax "and the greatest of these is love" (1 Cor. 13:1–13).[1]

SPIRITS

Paul was an authoritative Christian writer on the human spirit for his exploration of the Spirit's charismatic gifts in the early Church.[2] He also reflected theologically on the relation of the human spirit and the divine Spirit in an a fortiori argument that later became interpreted divisively as either analogical or antithetical. Paul believed that the Spirit's creativity continued beyond the original creation of humans told in Genesis

1:26. He claimed its divine presence within him as authorizing his own spirit to teach spiritual truths to others spiritually.[3] His pastoral mission was to discern the Spirit's creativity. Who was the Spirit active in Paul and in the Corinthians? and what was the human spirit in relation to the divine Spirit he preached? Paul wrote his letters in Greek, and for biblical interpretation he usually favored the Septuagint translation of the Hebrew Scriptures into Greek.[4] That was the bible the Corinthian church, as composed diversely of converted Gentiles and Jews, possessed for a common knowledge of biblical spirit. Paul either cited the Septuagint obviously or alluded to it sufficiently. His own word *pneuma* occurred there more than three hundred times, an abundant resource. The Hebrew *rûa 'ĕlōhim* of Genesis 1:2, for the Spirit God soaring, was in Paul's usage the Greek *pneuma theou*, the Spirit of God floating.[5]

Paul's first letter to the Corinthians addressed their controversy about the human and the divine spirits. In the standard translation, "What person knows a man's thoughts except the spirit of the man which is in him? So also no one comprehends the thoughts of God except the Spirit of God." With that comparison Paul taught the Christians at Corinth an exalted spirituality. It was a mature wisdom, "a secret and hidden wisdom of God, which God decreed before the ages for our glorification." Before the ages meant before the creation, when God was only designing the human spirit in his own image, before he spoke his intention to create it or breathed life into Adam's nostrils. If the civil and religious authorities had understood God's wisdom, Paul thought, "they would not have crucified the Lord of glory," Jesus. But Scripture told that humans could not humanly understand the divine purpose. As Paul remembered the prophet Isaiah's testimony, "What no eye has seen, nor ear heard, nor the heart of man conceived, what God has prepared for those who love him." That mystery was only revealed through the Spirit, who "searches everything, even the depths of God" (1 Cor. 2:11–12, 7–10).[6]

Paul's argument about the human and divine spirits seems lost in that standard translation. His meaning has been restricted exegetically to either an analogy or an antithesis. Those interpretations either compared or contrasted the privacy of a person's thought, unless expressed to others, with the privacy of God's thought, unless revealed to others. Such privacy referenced the "inmost self."[7] Paul's "human spirit (*pneuma tou anthrōpou*)" has been defined as "the basic interior component of the human personality," but the biblical texts elicited as evidence[8] are not psychological. And although the human spirit as related to the divine Spirit has been affirmed as Paul's central anthropological concept,[9] the interpretation of the knowledge of God by and through God alone has prevailed.[10] That conviction has prevailed although the creation of humans in the divine image in Genesis 1:26 was about resemblance, not about knowledge. Instead, the translated notion that only an individual's spirit knows his own thoughts has been defended: only the individual man knows his own mind, thus only God knows God's mind.[11] That translation "the spirit of a man that is in him" referenced an individual, with an assumed privacy of thought that argued for the inaccessibility of God's thought.

Paul's argument did not define the human spirit, however, since it was a presupposition of common understanding. He offered a simple persuasion from ordinary experience, not a formal philosophical or theological premise for rational development. At most his was a sociological observation about humanity. Its rhetorical topic was sympathy. In classical sources the human spirit based socialization, from friendship in Aristotle's *Ethica Eudemia* to politics in Cicero's *De officiis*.[12] Although both personal and social alliances were important in Paul's letters to the conflicted Corinthians, he was not philosophical in his application to the human spirit of the topic of sympathy. The human spirit devolved to kinship amity[13] as ordinarily and commonly observable. The Hebrew Scriptures evidenced the social cohesion of the Israelite tribes against the foreign nations. By extending God's promise from Israel to those other nations, Paul, as an apostle to the Gentiles, related the human spirit to a commonality. That belief developed in his first letter to the Corinthians from the original creation of Adam in Genesis to a new creation in the second Adam, Jesus as the Christ, the promised Messiah. Paul's argument about human and divine spirits was based on the proverbial compatibility of a type—like to like. It appealed to an appropriate human knowledge of humanity from human experience. Who understands what it is to be human better than a human? Certainly not an animal or an angel.

Paul developed that common experiential premise into neither an analogy nor an antithesis. He constructed an a fortiori argument, a rhetorical inference by stronger reason from a lesser fact to a greater probability.[14] Paul's rhetorical argument was, Who would question that the human spirit, being of social cohesion and kinship amity, knew humanity? If the human spirit knew humans, then the more so (a fortiori) God's Spirit knew God. Paul's argument was neither analogical nor antithetical; it acknowledged both similarity and difference. His emphasis was not anthropological but theological. He was inferring a mysterious God, not defining an observable man. The human spirit was only considered in relation to the divine Spirit, not in itself. As a relational concept, spirit was both similar and different, comparative and contrasting. It derived from the biblical verses in Genesis 1:26 and 2:7 about the spiritual creation of humans, of Adam. Paul then stated that what knew God was his own Spirit. Therefore, as Paul's argument progressed, that divine Spirit revealed to the human spirit the mystery of Christ hidden since before the creation. Paul's lesson was that the human spirit, as a creature, could be made receptive to the divine Spirit, as its Creator. That preaching was Paul's mission.

Paul's parallel was not between one human and God, but between humanity and God. That was the parallel of *anthrōpos to theos* since Homeric epic, the primary lexical definition of *anthrōpos* as humanity.[15] The distinction was epitomized in the Delphic oracle *gnōthi seauton*, "know thyself," which meant not analytical introspection but pious reverence for the difference between mortal humans and immortal gods.[16] Paul's proclamation of the resurrection of the dead in Christ altered that distinction. The parallel of humanity and God was also common in the Hebrew Scriptures.[17] As the psalmist praised, "The sons of gods and humans take refuge in the shadow of thy wings" (Ps. 36:7).[18] Paul's verse was not a theological abstraction but a personal confession of God's revelation about Christ crucified. That revelation surpassed ordinary human perceptions, such as those of his crucifiers. What Paul wrote was, "For who of humans knows humanity if not the spirit of the human that is in him; so, the godhood of God no one perceives if not the Spirit of God" (1 Cor. 2:11).[19] The Vulgate translation of Paul's letters into Latin was not by Jerome, who was learned in the Greek language and its rhetoric. It was the contribution of an unknown Roman editor working from the old Latin (Itala, or Vetus Latina) version of the Bible.[20] In the Vulgate translation of Paul's verse Greek *mē*, "if not," was rendered as *nisi*, "except."[21] Greek *mē* means here "if not" to express exemplarity, not exceptionality. Paul did not state that only humans knew humans and only God knew God. He argued the comparison that humans essentially and appropriately knew humanity, just as God essentially and appropriately knew God. His question was rhetorical: Who knew humanity better than the human spirit? By a fortiori inference, who knew divinity better than God's Spirit? But those parallels were only the prime and middle terms of his argument toward his conclusion that the divine Spirit revealed Jesus the Christ to the human spirit. At issue was common experience, not abstract ontology, toward understanding that the Creator Spirit's revelation to created spirits was compatibly spiritual.

Paul deliberately alternated the verbs for "know," *oida* and *gignōskō*, which may have classically connoted reflective or observational knowledge. Their semantic variance should not be exaggerated, however, for *oida* derives from sight and *gignōskō* is progressive.[22] Paul's diction emphasized that the human confession of the crucified Christ as God conformed to the Spirit's own comprehension of God. Paul stated that he came among the Corinthians to know (*eidenai*) only Christ crucified, whom the worldly authorities did not perceive (*egnōsan*) as God. For, if they had so perceived (*egnōsan*) him, they would not have crucified him. A new knowledge had intervened, not human but divine, a revelation (*apekalupsen*). Its standard translation reads "for the Spirit searches everything, even the depths of God" (1 Cor. 2:10). The search was investigative to reveal what was hidden, as in the Septuagint's proverbial use of *erauvaō*. "The breath of men (*pron anthrōpon*) is the light of God, which searches the chambers, the cavities" (Prov. 20:27 LXX), in Greek medicine the thoracic venter.[23] The proverb repeated the Septuagint version of Greek *pron* for Hebrew *nišĕmaḥ* in Genesis 2:7 for the Creator's breath that inspired Adam's life.

The Spirit in Paul's verse did not search the "depths" of God, however. The word *bathē* serves for full vertical dimensionality, both height and depth, depending on the viewer's perspective.[24] Paul would measure in other epistles the full dimensionality of God as merism for his universality and plenitude.[25] Yet, as points of reference for viewers, depth was proverbial for earth, height for heaven.[26] The prophet Isaiah declared the God of the Israelites as "the high and lofty One / who inhabits eternity, whose name is Holy" (Is. 57:15). Fittingly, he dwelled "in the high and holy place" above the visible heavens (63:15). As the psalmist confessed, "The Lord is high above all nations, and his glory above the heavens! / Who is like the Lord our God, who is seated on high, / who looks far down upon the heavens and the earth?" In contrast, "He raises the poor from the dust" (Ps. 113:4–7)[27] as he had in Genesis 2:7 raised

Adam from the dust. The depths were positioned opposite to God in heaven, outside him not inside him. The Spirit at creation in Genesis 1:2 soared above the deep, not dove into it. The traditional translation "depths" has conveyed divine interiority against superficiality on a biological model of innards versus skin. The only surface of the creative Spirit in the archaic metaphor of Genesis, however, was his extended wingspan like an eagle aloft on air currents. Paul wrote, "For the Spirit of God searches everything, even the heights of God," not his depths. Further, the modern translation contrasting human "thoughts" with divine "thoughts" has intellectualized Paul's a fortiori argument into an antithesis. It has recalled Isaiah's verse as if its meaning were similar, "For my thoughts are not your thoughts, / neither are your ways my ways, says the Lord. / For as the heavens are higher than the earth, / so are my ways higher than your ways / and my thoughts than your thoughts" (Is. 55:8–9).[28] However, Paul's verse paralleled, not distinguished, the neuter *ta*, "the matters," that were proper to humans and proper to God. Those matters did not mean metaphysical essences. By inference from the conclusion of Paul's a fortiori argument in an act of divine revelation, his "matters" referenced his deliberations toward action.[29]

REVELATION

Paul's meaning was neither intellectual profundity nor moral baseness. He intimated that humans could be raised on high with the Spirit. There they would approach his divine perspective before the act of creation, "his secret and hidden wisdom, which God decreed before the ages for our glorification." That wisdom was the divine knowledge from eternity of the purpose of Jesus the Christ. Paul will confess in his second letter to the Corinthians that such an elevation in the Spirit happened to him. But his message in this first letter already denied the divine ineffability, by which the standard translation guards the privacy of God from humans. Paul declared, "we impart a secret and hidden wisdom" (1 Cor. 2:7)—not that we keep it to ourselves. Paul proclaimed Christ crucified, whose identity his crucifiers did not perceive. Isaiah had pronounced the Creator's understanding "unsearchable," in empowering the weak who waited for him, just as the eagle stretched its wings to soar effortlessly, outstripping the wearied youths racing on the ground below.[30]

Paul revised God's inscrutability by asserting that God was no longer unsearchable. The Spirit searched the heights of God, and the Spirit had made God known to the human spirit as Christ crucified. The waiting of the prophet Isaiah for God's presence to humans was ended. As that oracle of God in his high and holy dwelling had promised, he would temper his anger and dwell also with the lowly, "for from me proceeds the spirit, / and I have made the breath of life" (Is. 57:15–16).

Paul wrote the Corinthians that the revelation of the divine wisdom before the creation as Christ crucified rendered philosophical speculation foolish. Paul's defense of his mission among them forcibly rejected Greek wisdom for Christ's folly as he played his own inverted role as a fool among the wise.[31] The biblical "man of the spirit (*anthrōpos 'o pneumatophoros*)" (Hos. 9:7; and see Zeph. 3:4), who was deemed mad like a foolish prophet, was suggestive for Paul's characterization of himself as bearing the Spirit among them as a fool. His announcement of the Spirit's revelation of Christ followed immediately upon his paraphrase of Isaiah's verse, "What no eye has seen, nor ear heard, nor the heart of man conceived, what God has prepared for those who love him" (1 Cor. 2:9).[32] His model Isaiah wrote, "From of old no one has heard / or perceived by the ear, / no eye has seen a God besides thee, / who works for those who wait for him" (Is. 64:4). Waiting belonged to the vocabulary of Israel's lamentation for idolatry and its expectation of divine deliverance.[33] In Second Temple Judaism waiting was a hopeful longing for a swift Lord's day, when he would reveal his glory and salvation.[34] Isaiah's waiters upon God reappeared from his oracle of their renewed strength, when they would share God's extraordinary energy and "mount up with wings like eagles" (Is. 40:31).

Paul's paraphrase of Isaiah was not a theological abstraction. It recalled the prophet's communal lament at the invasion of Jerusalem by Nebuchadnezzar's army, the razing of the temple, the capture of people, and their Babylonian exile.[35] The prophet Daniel, as a youth among the exiles, had debased their captor, Nebuchadnezzar, from human to beast. His "body was wet with the dew of heaven till his hair grew as long as eagles' feathers, and his nails were like birds' claws" (Dan. 4:13).[36] Once freed from that predator, the exiles, upon their return to Jerusalem, demanded that God restore their ruined temple. Isaiah's communal lament begged God not merely to "look down from heaven and see, / from thy holy and glorious habitation," his pitiful people. The prophet pleaded, "O that thou wouldst rend the heavens and come down, / that the mountains might quake at thy presence." That plea remembered ancient theophanies, as at Mount Sinai, where divine thunder and lightning shook that mountain. Isaiah's historical recollection praised God's incomparable deeds, which had formed and delivered his people in the Exodus, in the wilderness, and at the Sea of Reeds.[37] His recollection revered the Spirit with a very rare modifier, the "holy Spirit." The people's rebellion had "grieved his holy Spirit" until he remembered his deliverances. So Isaiah asked anew, "Where is he who put in the midst of them / his holy Spirit, / who caused his glorious arm to go at the right hand of Moses, / who divided the waters before them / to make for himself an everlasting name, / who led them through the depths?" (Is. 63:11–13; Ps. 51:13).

Upon that recital of God's beneficence Isaiah confessed the peoples' sins and questioned their salvation. "We have all become like one who is unclean, / and all our righteous deeds are like a polluted garment." And, "We all fade like a leaf, / and our iniquities, like the wind, / take us away" (Is. 64:6). Without *rûaḥ* as the Spirit active among his creatures in blessings, *rûaḥ* had become the agent of his anger, the wind that destroyed and scattered his enemies. God hid his face and delivered up his chosen people to the power of their sins. Isaiah begged God to abate his anger in compassion for the desolation of Jerusalem with its burned temple. He reminded him that, before historical events constituted Israel as his chosen people, there was at or in the beginning the fundamental Creator-creature relationship. "Yet, O Lord, thou art our Father; / we are the clay, and thou art our potter; / we are all the work of thy hand" (Is. 64:8, 9–12). That verse recalled the creation of Adam in Genesis 2:7 when he was fashioned from the dust. The asserted continuity of the Israelites with Adam asked for Yahweh to refashion them in the new wilderness of Zion and to breathe into them new life. Indeed, the prophet did announce in God's forgiveness a new creation. "For behold, I create new heavens and a new earth" (66:22).

Isaiah lamented the destruction of Jerusalem in 586 B.C.E., which finalized the Jewish diaspora when people of Judah, the southern kingdom, were deported.[38] His similes for sinners, polluted garments and withered leaves, were unequaled in biblical literature. "There is no more poignant expression of abandonment and godforsakenness induced by the disaster." Isaiah's lament and also the book of Lamentations directed a universal penitence characteristic of Judaism in the Second Temple period.[39] That was the era and the piety in which Paul flourished during the first century C.E. as a Pharisee in the reconstructed Jerusalem.[40] But he was unexpectedly converted to another mission. As he identified himself in the salutation of his letters to the Corinthians, he was "Paul, called by the will of God to be an apostle of Jesus Christ" (1 Cor. 1:1; 2 Cor. 2:1). As an apostle to the nations beyond Israel, he remembered Isaiah's metaphor of the Creator as a potter shaping clay in the original formation of Adam from dust.[41] Paul argued momentously from pottery making in his letter to the Romans about divine freedom of choice to elect peoples beyond Israel,[42] the premise for his own mission to those nations.

Paul's paraphrase to the Corinthians of Isaiah's communal lament was specific. As the prophet wrote, the Spirit had revealed what no eye has seen, nor ear heard. For Isaiah, the eyes that did not see and the ears that did not hear the God of Israel were graven on the breathless idols of the foreign nations. Their idols could not compare with the uniquely omniscient God of the Israelites.[43] Like idols with dysfunctional eyes and ears, all idolaters lost their own senses in worshipping such empty winds. They were eyed but blind, eared but deaf.[44] Paul's introduction of Isaiah's verse to the Corinthians was not about divine ineffability beyond human intelligence, but about divine holiness beyond human sinfulness. Isaiah had beseeched God to penetrate through a rift in the clouds that barrier between God's lofty and holy dwelling and Israel's low and impure situation. He prayed for God to appear in a stupendous, thunderous flash of lightning, to shake even the stability of the mountains. Paul proclaimed the fulfillment of Isaiah's plea in the Spirit's revelation of Jesus the Christ of what no human senses could perceive. That was the earth-shattering manifestation of the divine wisdom before creation, Jesus the Christ as the lord of glory, who was crucified toward human glorification.

Paul's initial witness to that glory was narrated as perverse, as happening during his consent to the stoning of Stephen, the first Christian martyr. The episode was not in Paul's own letters, which only generalized his violently destructive persecution of Christians in his zeal for the Jewish traditions.[45] His witness to Stephen's witness was told in the Acts of the Apostles, a canonical biblical book attributed to Luke, also the ascribed author of a synoptic gospel. Acts dated to several decades after Paul's letters, to about 80 C.E., and it served distinct purposes from them.⁴⁶ Since it differed from Paul's own writings in essential aspects, it is not judged historiographically reliable to interpret their accounts mutually.⁴⁷ Acts emphasized Paul's assumption of Isaiah's vocation by concluding with the apostle's citation of that prophet on disbelief as being like sensory dysfunction. Acts had Paul interpret Isaiah's verses as an endorsement by the Holy Spirit to justify his own mission to the nations. As Paul echoed Isaiah, "'Go to this people, and say, / You shall indeed hear but never understand, / and you shall indeed see but never perceive. / For this people's heart has grown dull, / and their ears are heavy of hearing, / and their eyes they have closed; / lest they should perceive with their eyes, / and hear with their ears, / and understand with their heart, / and turn for me to heal them.'" Paul in Acts concluded that doom oracle with "Let it be known to you that this salvation of God has been sent to the Gentiles; they will listen" (Acts 28:25–28; cf. Is. 57:15). Isaiah's same doom oracle for the Israelites was the foundation of Paul's historical announcement to the Corinthians of the Spirit's revelation of Christ as "'what no eye has seen, nor ear heard, nor the heart of man conceived, what God has prepared for those who love him'" (1 Cor. 2:9).

Acts would introduce Paul by his Jewish name, Saul, in allusion to the simile of polluted clothing in Isaiah's communal lament.⁴⁸ The prophet Isaiah in his plea for a theophany had confessed of the Israelites "all our righteous deeds are like a polluted garment" (Is. 64:6). So did Paul learn of his own zealous obduracy as the keeper of the filthy garments that false witnesses against Stephen the martyr dropped at his feet in the dirt. For Paul was among the Sanhedrin of Jerusalem, whose fury at Stephen's denunciation of the Temple incited a mob to stone him. Stephen, a Christian, exclaimed a vision in the Holy Spirit of the heavenly glory of God, with Jesus as the Son of Man at his right hand; whereupon Jewish perjurers stoned him. "And Saul was consenting to his death." The narrative implied that Paul heard Stephen's exclaimed vision and his dying prayer, "Lord Jesus, receive my spirit." A persecution ensued in Jerusalem in which "Saul was ravaging the church, and entering house after house, he dragged off men and women and committed them to prison" (Acts 7:54–8:3). He was en route to Damascus, "still breathing threats and murder against the disciples of the Lord," when "suddenly a light from heaven flashed about him" that felled him to the ground. A voice demanded, "'Saul, Saul, why do you persecute me?' And he said,

'Who are you, Lord?' And he said, 'I am Jesus, whom you are persecuting; but rise and enter the city, and you will be told what you are to do'" (Acts 9:1–8). Saul's travel companions were astounded, for they heard the voice but saw no speaker, just as Paul had heard Stephen's voice but did not see the glory of God with Jesus in the opened sky. Not only did Paul not see Jesus, but also he was temporarily blinded.[49] Acts ascribed Paul's cure to a laying on of hands by Ananias, Jesus's disciple. That narrative device allowed for an explanation of Saul's evil reputation as a persecutor of the church and the Lord's intention to reverse his role, "for he is a chosen instrument of mine to carry my name before the Gentiles and kings and the sons of Israel." In Damascus after his baptism, Paul proclaimed Jesus in the local synagogues as the Son of God, so the local Jews plotted to kill him. When he learned of their watch for him at the city gates, lest he escape, he was lowered over the wall in a basket at night (vv. 10–23).

EXPERIENCE

That escape Paul himself related to the Corinthians in boasting feebly of his apostolic labors as his glorious folly. His dramatic catalogue—of imprisonments; punishments to near death by beating, whipping, and stoning; drifting at sea, and even shipwreck; threats on land by robbers, by Jews and Gentiles alike, and by false Christians, whether in the city or in the wild; deprivation of sleep, food and drink, and clothing—was from personal experience. As Paul concluded it, "At Damascus, the governor under King Aretas guarded the city of Damascus in order to seize me, but I was let down in a basket through a window in the wall, and escaped his hands" (2 Cor. 11:22–33). After reciting his general difficulties, Paul concluded emphatically with that particular detail about evading capture in Damascus. The detail was coherent because that escape allowed him to continue his mission, which eventually landed him in Corinth to preach the gospel there. Damascus was the catchword for his climactic boast to the Corinthians, the most celebrated Christian account of personal revelation. "I know a man in Christ who fourteen years ago was caught up to the third heaven—whether in the body or out of the body I do not know, God knows. And I know that this man was caught up into Paradise—whether in the body or out of the body

I do not know, God knows—and he heard things that cannot be told, which man may not utter" (12:1–4).

Paul dated his experience precisely by "fourteen years (*pro etōn dekatessarōn*)." But from what date did he calculate? Exegesis has reckoned backwards from the composition of this second letter, dated around 56–57 C.E., thus to about 41–42 C.E. That calculation located Paul in no-man's land, lost in the unknown years between his residences at Damascus and at Antioch.[50] A vague date, without any decisive motive to preach from that revelation, discredited its importance for authenticating Paul to the Corinthians as a spiritual person. It undermined his mission. Paul's adverb *pro* does not mean "ago," however, as in the standard translation, which favors the composition of the letter as the point for dating Paul's personal experience. For time, however, *pro* means "earlier."[51] Earlier than when? At issue among the Corinthians was the legitimacy of his apostolate, which was challenged by other leaders in their church. Paul's logical point of reference for dating his rapture was his evangelization among the Corinthians, to whom he wrote about it. He was wont to emphasize his mission "from the first day" of his preaching to a community, and to marking its end time as the ultimate day of Christ or the Lord.[52] As he wrote in his first letter to the Corinthians, he reckoned his mission there from "when I came to you." He declared how he initially "laid a foundation" and became their "father," although others would build upon his foundation and become their guides (1 Cor. 2:1; 3:10; 4:15). Paul stated in his second letter to the Corinthians two—and only two—markers of time with place that are verifiable by historical records. He did so precisely because they dated his Corinthian apostolate, regarding the contested question of his authority in that church.

Paul arrived in Corinth in the spring of 50 C.E., when the treacherous road there from Athens was again passable, and he stayed for eighteen months. He departed in 51 C.E. late in the summer, or in the early autumn before the close of the sailing season.[53] Acts later told independently that Paul converted both Jews and Gentiles by preaching in the synagogue at Corinth until its Jews ousted him. He then began an exclusive mission to the Gentiles by going door-to-door.[54] That more public presence may have coincided with the Isthmian Games, which were held in the locale of Corinth in the spring, in April or early May, of 51 C.E. The Games, as major athletic and cultural events sanctioned by religious ceremonies, drew large, leisurely crowds. The Panhellenic festivities would have afforded Paul a prime opportunity for declamation about this new god, Jesus the Christ, in the open air or in a tent such as he stitched and sold for the comfort of the spectators. Indeed, he offered Corinthian converts to Christ an imperishable crown surpassing the prize for victory at those Games, which was merely a wreath of wilted celery leaves.[55] But some Corinthian converts were agitating against Paul's apostolate. In that same spring of 51 C.E., some Judaizers—Jewish Christians who insisted that Gentile Christians observe their Jewish circumcision and diet—hauled him for a hearing before M. Annaeus Gallio, the proconsul. Gallio's tenure in Corinth for only one year began on July 1, 51 C.E.,[56] thus establishing Paul's chronology there.

Fourteen years retrospective from that spring of 51 C.E. was the spring of 37 C.E. As Paul wrote the Corinthians about that earlier date, "At Damascus, the governor under King Aretas guarded the city of Damascus in order to seize me, but I was let down in a basket through a window in the wall, and escaped his hands." That fact, climaxing Paul's boasts of the dangers he survived, immediately and cogently directed his account of a personal rapture. As he continued, "I must boast: there is nothing to be gained by it, but I will go on to visions and revelations of the Lord. I know a man in Christ who fourteen years earlier . . . [not RSV "ago"]" (2 Cor. 11:32–12:2). His reference did not mean earlier than the composition of that letter but, rather, earlier than 51 C.E., the year of the legal hearing before the proconsul Gallio about his Corinthian apostolate. The rule of the governor at Damascus dated from late in 36 C.E to 37 C.E., not long after Passover, in May or June. His term afforded a brief period of six months for Paul's furtive escape from that city.[57] His activity in Corinth was early to mid-51 C.E., as dated from the Isthmian Games and his hearing before Gallio, the proconsul.[58] Paul's calculation was perfect, disregarding an inclusive calendrical count. Fourteen years "earlier" than his Corinthian mission, which was legally challenged by Judaizers in the spring of 51 C.E., was his escape from Damascus in the spring of 37 C.E. Paul deliberately ordered his catalogue of his missionary perils to emphasize his escape from Damascus last. Why? Because it premised the spiritual experience he was about to reveal to the Corinthians of his validation by Christ fourteen years earlier. Although translations insist on the utterances Paul heard as unlawful to divulge,[59] the word *exesesti* means not only "is lawful" but equally "is possible." Paul did not mean that his revelation of his experience noted to the Corinthians was forbidden—a contradiction to his very mission to preach—but ineffable. He told them that his exalted spirit experienced a divine mystery whose transcendence of human ability could not be verbally expressed. By that measure Paul acknowledged his preaching to the Corinthians as weak,[60] not because he was a poor orator but because his speech was inadequate to his experience. Speech, as the intentional and intelligible expulsion of breath (*pneuma*), became a norm for Paul's discernment of the Spirit's activity or absence in the Corinthian church.

Although Paul's experience has commonly identified him as a "merkabah mystic," that was a figure of later Jewish apocalypticism. His privileged visions on the road to Damascus of the risen and glorified Messiah as Lord[61] have been supposed a reward for his practiced meditation as a Pharisee on Ezekiel's prophetic visions of God's glorious throne with a human form.[62] However, the account in Acts about Paul on the road to Damascus told of no Christophany, only of the persecuted Jesus's voice.[63] Paul in the secondhand narrative of Acts saw no vision, only a flash of light, which blinded him. Moreover, there is no evidence of Jewish meditation on God's throne, such as Paul supposedly practiced, until a century later. It will occur then in the story of the Babylonian Talmud about the four rabbis who ventured into *parĕdēs*, the Hebrew paradise. That was only a story, however, a cautionary tale against breaching God's holiness. It was elaborated from the very same rabbinic injunction that forbade speculation about the above, below, before, or after of creation, lest some dire end befall the curious. Three of those curious rabbis did meet horrible ends—death, madness, heresy; none achieved any vision of God's throne; one survived to warn prospective adventurers.[64]

The term "merkabah mysticism" is macaronic. It derives from the biblical Hebrew *merĕkābāh*, "chariot," although it never occurs in the biblical book of Ezekiel, the visionary of God's chariot,[65] and the English "mysticism," which only dates to the eighteenth century C.E.[66] In Christian literature the noun "mystic" was not applied to a person before the seventeenth century C.E. Before then the adjective "mystical" modified Scripture, Church, or theology.[67] The term "merkabah mysticism" is a modern academic convention for disparate Jewish texts about human ascents to heaven that converged on an authenticating vision of God's throne of glory. The imaginative journey there was fantastic, even bizarre, demanding the aspirant's theurgic adjuration of angels in order to progress through the halls of the divine palace to its sanctuary for worship. Whether interpreted as experiential or literary, "merkabah mysticism" depended on deliberate techniques toward perfect knowledge of the Torah.[68]

Its future narratives would be elaborate, whereas Paul's verses were meager, lacking dialogue or description—and lacking God's definitive throne. His were not self-aggrandizing accounts of privilege but self-effacing expectations toward service. Paul introduced his personal experience with rhetorical modesty, obliquely in the third person, "I know a man who . . ." And he twice dismissed any phenomenological knowledge, "whether in the body or out of the body I do not know, God knows" (2 Cor. 12:2). That admission of ignorance referenced the quarrel among those Corinthians who boasted of being "spiritual" about the bodily resurrection of the dead.[69] Paul indicated in his asides that his personal experience of rapture was not informative for that issue. Only belief in the revealed resurrection of Jesus from the dead would resolve their quarrel.[70] Moreover, unlike the future Jewish heroes of "merkabah mysticism," Paul faced no formidable task or ferocious opponent. His disclosure to the Corinthians of his extraordinary experience was preceded by a catalogue of the perils from which he had suffered grievously. But all of those perils were natural or human; none was angelic.[71] The Corinthians would have understood his dangers at sea and on land. Their city, on an isthmus flanked by two major ports, was a haven from that perilous sea and a refuge from the infamous robberies on the Scironian Road skirting its cliffs.[72] Paul's reality was remote from the fantasy of "merkabah mysticism," about the daring Jewish visionary with spinning eyeballs whose passwords and seals magically outwitted or defeated the menacing angels who guarded their heavenly chambers with shooting flames.

The modern notion of "merkabah mysticism" departs speculatively from Paul's association with the simplicity of God's revelation to Moses in Exodus 3:14, "I am who am," and from the clarity of his divine commandments.[73] Paul introduced his rapture by naming himself a descendant of Abraham,[74] a legitimization by the patriarchal tradition, which predated by many centuries any "merkabah mysticism." And, although that future practice was inspired by Ezekiel's vision of the divine enthronement, Paul's letters to the Corinthians only cited that prophet's visions from his later chapters about a new temple, not from his early chapters about the throne of glory. Paul's letter referenced Ezekiel in a miscellany with other biblical books, among multiple sources. Its first citation of Ezekiel promised a new covenant, "and I will be their God and they shall be my people." Its second citation paraphrased Ezekiel on the contingency of the Israelite covenant upon Israel's separation from the nations, "then I will welcome you" (2 Cor. 6:18; Ez. 37:26; 20:34, 41). By those two appeals Paul affirmed God's presence in a nonidolatrous Christian community at Corinth as the fulfillment of that promise of God's welcome. Paul transcended Ezekiel's imaginary vision of the temple with apostolic labor, as he laid the foundation of the Corinthians as the Spirit's new temple.[75]

VOCATION

Jesus called his disciples, principally Peter the fisherman, in their occupations, not their meditations. Paul was later called as a Pharisee. Any technique for the attainment of God and coercion of his will, as in "merkabah mysticism," contradicted Paul's experience. He was not identified as a practitioner or advocate of merkabah method. In Acts' first story toward his conversion, Paul's experience of Jesus en route to Damascus was sudden and unexpected, not methodical and conclusive. There was visually a lightning flash, not a revelation of God's throne. The event was not a prize for Paul's religious behavior, but a correction of his irreligious behavior. It reversed his self-righteous persecution of Christians. It did not confer angelic status but required spiritual baptism.[76] That version of his experience was a narrative. Acts further told of Paul's reported self-defense to King Agrippa against Jewish charges. It corroborated the version about how, while riding to Damascus to arrest Christians, Paul only saw a light brighter than the sun, which unhorsed him, and about how he heard Jesus rebuke his persecution. In that further story Jesus by name uniquely commissioned Paul to evangelize the nations.[77] The first story was an impersonal narrative; the second, personal oratory. The flash and the voice around Paul reverberated from the lighting and thunder in the Hebrew Scriptures as signs of Yahweh's powerful presence resounding in speech.[78] The attribution to Jesus of a flash and a voice identified him with that divine power.

Paul's own account of his call in his first letter to the Corinthians ascribed to God the Father the revelation of Jesus the Christ and Son. It also identified the Father's choice, even before Paul's birth, of the mission to evangelize the nations.[79] Unlike the stories in Acts, Paul himself did not describe or date his conversion. He simply acknowledged his past, when he had "persecuted the church of God." He did not distinguish as events his experience of conversion from his commission as an apostle. Yet, just as he ascribed the origin of his conversion to the Father's revelation of Jesus, he emphasized his divine commission as jointly given by them. As he introduced himself to the Galatians, "Paul an apostle—not from men nor through man, but through Jesus Christ and God the Father, who raised him from the dead." He affirmed that the gospel he preached he did not learn from the other apostles. "For I did not receive it from man, nor was I taught it, but it came through a revelation of Jesus Christ." He acknowledged his reputation as a Jew who zealously and violently persecuted the church until God manifested to him his plan. "But when he who had set me apart before I was born, and had called me through his grace, was pleased to reveal his Son to me, in order that I might preach him among the Gentiles, I did not confer with flesh and blood." Paul specified that he did not consult the other apostles in Jerusalem but traveled independently on his own mission (Gal. 1:1, 11–23). As he commended his mission to the Corinthians, "Am I not an apostle? Have I not seen Jesus our Lord? Are you not my workmanship in the Lord?" (1 Cor. 9:1). The argument had a certain illogic in confirming apostolate by vision since they were not equatable. Vision alone did not confer an apostolic mission because many brethren were reported to have seen Jesus, yet they were not apostles. Paul knew the difference, for he continued by distinguishing between the brethren who had seen the Lord and the apostles who had seen him. Paul's emphasis in his commendation to the Corinthians was on his last rhetorical question, his activity among them. "Are you not my workmanship in the Lord?" From that final evidence his Corinthian readers were expected to infer its divine origin. Paul's authentication of his commission was his good acts among them. His next verse reinforced that end. "If to others I am not an apostle, at least I am to you; for you are the seal of my apostleship in the Lord" (v. 2.) Paul declared his liberation from "human authority," an authority he then questioned. He declared himself "free from all men." Paul concluded with himself as "entrusted with a commission" (v. 17). He meant by his designation "apostle" a messenger sent to the Corinthians not by another local church but by the Lord himself, who alone chose his apostles.

Paul's exposition of the authentic spiritual gifts among the Corinthians insisted that those who regarded themselves as prophetic or spiritual "acknowledge that what I am writing to you is a command of the Lord." Paul reminded them of his preaching of the gospel that "delivered to you as of first importance what I have also received." That gospel was, in accordance with Scripture, Christ's death for sinners, his burial, and his resurrection. Beyond that essential proclamation, Paul acknowledged Christ's appearances as confirmations of his resurrection. "He appeared to Cephas [Peter], then to the twelve. Then he appeared to more than five hundred brethren at one time, most of who are still alive, though some have fallen asleep. Then he appeared to James, then to all the apostles." Finally, in turn, to Paul. "Last of all, as to one untimely born, he appeared also to me. For I am the least of the apostles, unfit to be called an apostle, because I persecuted the church of God. But by the grace of God I am what I am, and his grace toward me was not in vain" (1 Cor. 14:37–15:10). Thus, Paul told of his conversion from a persecutor to a preacher of Christ. That conversion inferentially involved Christ's appearance to him, but it was not equatable with Acts' story of the light on the road to Damascus. Again, Paul himself did not describe or date his conversion. The Acts of the Apostles was by definition about the apostolate. It began by reviewing Luke's gospel of "all that Jesus began to do and teach, until the day when he was taken up, after he had given commandment because of the Holy Spirit to the apostles whom he had chosen."[80] As it continued, "To them he presented himself alive after his passion by many proofs, appearing to them during forty days, and speaking of the kingdom of God." Jesus distinguished the baptism by water from John from the baptism with the Holy Spirit that his disciples would soon receive at Pentecost. Acts later explained that the interception of Saul on the road to Damascus was as his chosen "instrument" (Acts 1:1–5; 9:15).

Paul's second letter to the Corinthians told of an extraordinary spiritual experience. In the standard translation, "I know a man in Christ who fourteen years ago was caught up in the third heaven—whether in the body or out of the body I do not know, God knows. And I know that this man was caught up into Paradise—whether in the body or out of the body I do not know, God knows—and he heard things that cannot be told, which man may not utter" (2 Cor. 12:2–4). Paul's verbal austerity was not from indifference but from propriety. He wrote pastorally to the Corinthians as children squabbling about their personal charismata. His discernment of their conflicts determined him not to elaborate on his own spiritual authenticity. His conviction of charity as the greatest gift in his hymn to love was governed by prudence. Paul counseled against self-indulgent boasting without communal love. He admonished the Corinthians not to exude proud enthusiasm for personal charismata but to subject them to the service of others. Grace was personal, but not exclusively private. Paul accommodated his own revelation charitably to the Corinthian quarrelers. His writing presented a model for behavior within the Corinthian community.

Paul's boasting of his own spiritual experience was incited by the boasting of certain Corinthians about their spiritual experiences. His response was necessarily brief, however, since his rapture had left him speechless, as he stated. That silence was a succinct rejoinder to the noisy boasters. Paul modestly adopted the rhetorical third, not first, person. He explained that what he heard in rapture was not in the auditory-oral spectrum. His was an ironic boast—even an antiboast. His rapture led directly to his puncture by "a thorn in the flesh, a messenger of Satan" (2 Cor. 12:7–10). That thorn was a certain opposition to his apostolate, which exacerbated his weakness. It did not enhance his glorification.[81] Paul's admission to the Corinthians that he asked the Lord three times to pluck the thorn from him suggested that it grew provocatively among them. Immediately he stated, "Here for the third time I am ready to come to you." Toward the end of his letter he repeated "this is the third time I am coming to you." He warned the Corinthians that he would not spare those dissenters who demanded proof of Christ's power speaking through him and acting among them. He reminded them that, although Christ was crucified in weakness, they now lived by God's power. As for his personal authority, Paul affirmed, "We are also weak, in union with him, but in our dealings with you we shall be fully alive, along with him, because of God's power." That message reflected the Lord's answer to Paul's plea three times that he pluck out the thorn. "But he said to me, 'My grace is sufficient for you, for my power is made perfect in weakness.'" Paul responded with obedient acceptance by informing the Corinthians, "Here for the third time I am ready to come to you" (12:14,

13:1, 12:8–9). That resolved tension of divine power and human weakness characterized Paul's mission among them.[82] In his second letter to the Corinthians he elaborated that defense. Paul disclosed his extraordinary experience to the Corinthians in response to intensified challenges to his apostolate there from internal factions and Judaizing intruders. He had already upbraided them for aligning with various disciples—Paul, Apollos, Cephas—divisively.[83] Now he passionately rebuked their disturbing defection from his preaching. He accused them of accepting "a different spirit from the one you received," that is, from him (11:4).

RAPTURE

Identification of Paul's experience as an "ecstasy"[84] has ignored the phenomenological distinction between ecstasy and rapture. An ecstasy is a mental abstraction; a rapture is a spiritual possession. Paul was not ecstatic but enraptured. It was the encounter of "a man in Christ . . . fourteen years earlier" that he offered his doubting congregation about his spiritual authentication. He presented it not as theologically informative but as spiritually confirmative. Paul wrote the Corinthians that he had been "seized" (*harpazo*), the Greek verb that invented the Harpies, mythological winged creatures who abducted humans into the air. Originally they were winds.[85] Paul was not "taken up" (*meatithenai*), as in the Septuagint translation, to die like Enoch, the prototype in Genesis for heavenly journeys.[86] Nor was he "taken up" (*anelambanō*) like Ezekiel, the exemplary visionary of God's heavenly throne, although the Septuagint employed *harpazo* appropriately for his prophecies about human robbery and animal prey.[87] Nor was Paul "taken up" (*anelambanō . . . epairō*) into heaven like Jesus himself.[88] The Septuagint employed *harpazo* and its cognates for "seizure, robbery, rape" about spoils of battle or injustice against the poor. It also denoted the act of wild animals tearing the flesh of their prey.[89] The verb of Paul's seizure was matched by the Spirit's seizure of Philip in the Acts of the Apostles. The Spirit instructed the disciple Philip to approach an Ethiopian eunuch on the road from Jerusalem to Gaza. Philip was to interpret to him Isaiah's prophecy for his baptism. Then the Spirit snatched (*harpazo*) Philip out of sight, only to set him down further on the road for evangelism.[90] That episode in Acts directly preceded the call on the Damascus road of Saul, who would later as Paul be snatched up (*harpazo*) for a mission. The violence of Paul's seizure for an apostolate matched the violence with which he had seized Christians for imprisonment.[91]

In the account in Acts, Paul escaped in Damascus from capture by political hands through the intervention of ecclesiastical hands, which eased him in a basket through the city wall. That escape led to his eventual capture by divine hands. Paul, the "man in Christ" that his letter to the Corinthians about his rapture referenced, was not abstractly "caught up" to heaven as in the standard translation. His verb *harpazo* means to "take up," particularly into the hands with the intention of carrying.[92] Hands were the biblical metonym for power. Paul's diction remembered the historical recollection of Isaiah's communal lament, how "the angel of his presence saved them; / in his love and in his pity he redeemed them; / he lifted them up and carried them all the days of old" (Is. 63:9). That verse recalled the lessons of Deuteronomy on how Yahweh "took up" Israel from the desert to carry it, like a father his child or an eagle its catch. Ultimately, Paul's memory circled back to its archaic Song of Moses, where Yahweh lifted Israel from the hostile open desert to his secure enclosed place, like an eagle gripping its prey in its talons for carriage to its nest. The Septuagint euphemized the eagle's actions with *anelambanō*,[93] thus inventing an image of paternal care that erased the unnatural violence by which Yahweh seized Israel for his own portion from among all his creatures.[94] The Song of Moses was important to Paul's mission and theology for a universal extension of the choice of Israel to the nations.[95]

However, his destination was not a metaphorical nest but a spiritual paradise. Although Western culture imagined paradise as a garden, like Eden in Genesis 2–3, his Greek word, *paradeisos*, originated in the Old Persian *pairidaēza*, meaning any "enclosure," from *pariri* "around" with *diz*, "mold, form."[96] Thus was Paul lifted from one walled enclosure, the city of Damascus, to another walled enclosure, the paradise of God. As he wrote to the Corinthians, "We know that if the earthly tent we live in is destroyed, we have a building from God, a house not made with hands, eternal in the heavens" (2 Cor. 5:1).

Paul claimed to be an apostle, although the last and the least of them. He retold the Corinthians the gospel of Jesus's death and resurrection, about his appearance to Peter, then to the twelve, then to more than five hundred brethren, to James, and to all the apostles. "Last of all, as to one untimely born, he appeared also to me. For I am the least of the apostles, unfit to be called an apostle, because I persecuted the church of God. But by the grace of God I am what I am, and his grace toward me was not in vain." Indeed, he worked harder than the others, he averred; or rather, grace worked harder in him (1 Cor. 15:3–10). And, just as the Creator had no counselor for his acts, so Paul refused to be judged by anyone, for "we have the purpose [not RSV "mind"] of Christ." His was an extraordinarily bold claim. "The spiritual man judges all things, but is himself to be judged by no one." Paul's designated authority was to proclaim the crucified Lord of glory, but not sophistically, "for I decided to know nothing among you except Jesus Christ and him crucified." His was not an arrogant, but an abject, authority that survived among them "in weakness and in much fear and trembling" (2:3). It was meant to demonstrate that any spiritual power was from God alone as the foundation of their faith.[97]

Paul's metaphor for his apostolate among the Corinthians was the construction of a temple. It was an appealing metaphor, for the Corinthians were proud of their civic architecture. Their cult of Athena, the Greek goddess of craftsmen, was prominent in Corinth, and craftsmanship itself was more valued there than in any other Greek city.[98] Paul wrote exclusively to them how "according to the grace of God given to me, like a skilled master builder I laid a foundation . . . Jesus Christ." Although other builders might add to it with various materials, from straw to gold, their work would be finally tested by the Lord's judgment. "Do you not know," Paul concluded, "that you are God's temple and that God's Spirit dwells in you?" (1 Cor. 3:9–17).[99] His message summoned them communally and personally to holiness against idolatry and to purity against immorality.[100] Beyond his pastoral concern with the manifestation of that indwelling Spirit in their virtues, or powers, he offered metaphors of Christians as bearers of that Spirit. The temple was one such metaphor, conceived as an external structure with an inner sanctuary. Paul taught in prohibition of sexual immorality that bodily flesh was sanctified. He posed rhetorically, "Do you not know that your body is a temple of the Holy Spirit within you, which you have from God?" The temple was the sturdiest of Paul's spiritual metaphors, for he associated it with the heavenly building awaiting the reception of the faithful Corinthians into glory. As he instructed, "We know that if the earthly tent we live in is destroyed, we have a building from God, a house not made with hands, eternal in the heavens" (1 Cor. 6:19; 2 Cor. 5:1). The Corinthians understood that even a temple was perishable. For they built with the unstable local sandstone, a lightweight material quarried from the overlay to the lowest stratum of marl. Their temples would not withstand the devastating earthquake of 77 C.E., after which they were protectively rebuilt in imported marble.[101]

Christians bore the Spirit while living in an earthly tent, of whose final collapse Paul was certain. His metaphor did not mean that the body was a tent for the spirit, but that humans lived on earth, under the sky. In a verse Paul cited, Isaiah had affirmed that God's Spirit could not be instructed or counseled. The prophet then recalled the creation, how God "stretches out the heavens like a curtain, / spreads them like a tent to dwell in" (Is. 40:13; 1 Cor. 2:16; Is. 40:22). To live in an earthly tent was Paul's redundancy for being on earth, under heaven. He referred not to the death of an individual body but to the end of the whole world at Christ's coming, which they expected to be imminent. A tent was not "destroyed," however, as in the standard translation. As a temporary and portable shelter, it was "taken down," dismantled, folded up, and carried away by its inhabitants on the move. Paul knew the utility but temporality of tents firsthand, for he sewed them as his livelihood.[102] In Corinth he dwelled and worked in the shop of his hosts, Aquila and Prisca, who were tentmakers. Acts related that Paul found them upon his arrival there, for tentmaking was his trade too.[103] He personally denigrated himself to the Corinthians as a manual laborer, and he mentioned those artisan hosts.[104] Corinth was a great city, expanding in commerce and trade to its apex at the end of Paul's century as Greece's largest city. It was an opportune site to make and sell tents, although they were usually the necessity of nomads, rather than citizens. Tents were in special demand to shelter visitors to its Isthmian Games that coming spring. But tents and awnings were always needed in that most mercantile of all Greek cities for the shopkeepers' stalls in its center and forum. The numerous postholes for tents and awnings in the archaeological excavations of Corinth[105] may attest to some trace of Paul's craft.

Paul's model in his role as master builder of the Corinthian church was biblical Bezalel, for they shared an endowment by the Spirit to construct. Bezalel was not the architect of the contemporary urban Jerusalem temple but the craftsman of the ancient wilderness tent of meeting. The Hebrew Scriptures recorded extensive instructions for Yahweh's cult, recited to Moses over forty days, when he was summoned up Mount Sinai by the glory of God burning at its summit. Toward the conclusion of that recital in the Sabbath law and covenantal tablets, Bezalel was called to accomplish the work of constructing the tent of meeting. The Lord told Moses, "See, I have called by name Bezalel the son of Uri, son of Hur, of the tribe of Judah: and I have filled him with the Spirit of God (*rûaḥ ... 'ĕlōhîm*), with ability and intelligence, with knowledge and all craftsmanship, to devise artistic designs, to work in gold, silver, and bronze, in cutting stones for setting, and in carving wood for work in every craft" (Ex. 24:15–31:5). Bezalel was given a spirited companion in Oholiab and able workmen to fulfill the commands for the tent of meeting with its ark of the covenant and elaborate furnishings. Moses repeated to the Israelites the Lord's words about Bezalel's endowment with the Spirit of God for the task. And Moses summoned Bezalel to that task, whose accomplishment was detailed for Moses's blessing.[106] Although that tent has been judged a fiction retrospective from the actuality of the Jerusalem temple and the legend of the Shiloh temple, its construct centered the biblical Priestly tradition of the wilderness.[107]

Bezalel was "filled with the Spirit of God (*rûaḥ ... 'ĕlōhîm*)" (Ex. 31:3). That was the *rûaḥ 'ĕlōhîm* that soared at creation, although the Septuagint translation lessened its *pneuma theou* in Genesis 1:2 to *pneuma theion* for Bezalel's possession. Both the first chapter of Genesis and the story in the book of Exodus about Bezalel's commission for and construction of the tent were Priestly writings. Indeed, Bezalel's tent, although a splendid fictitious projection from the ancient theophanies, has been identified as "the central phenomenon of the priestly Utopia."[108] Allusions associating the Priestly accounts of the divine work of creation and the human building of the temple have been theorized as a probable model of world and sanctuary.[109] Like the Creator who stretched out the heavens like a tent,[110] Bezalel was commissioned to construct its earthly imitation of that heavenly dwelling. It was coherent that God's first man-made dwelling should be constructed by one specially summoned by name and empowered by his creative Spirit. It was by such an endowment with the Holy Spirit that Paul justified his own architectural role in the Corinthian community. And it was thus that he admonished them, "Do you not know that you are God's temple and that God's Spirit (*pneuma theou*) dwells in you?" (1 Cor. 3:16). The Spirit invested Paul with the pastoral skills to build the Corinthians into a temple for divine worship.

They also became that constructed temple in which the Spirit dwelled. Bezalel's spiritual possession continued the activity of the Spirit (*rûaḥ 'ĕlōhîm*) in Genesis 1:2 at creation. By inference from Bezalel's spiritual possession, Paul believed his own spiritual possession was an empowerment toward creating and enhancing the Corinthian worship. The only biblical exemplar of spiritual possession before Bezalel was Joseph, whose interpretations of the pharaoh's dreams excited a singular admiration of his gift. As the pharaoh marveled, "Can we find such a man as this, in whom is the Spirit God (*rûaḥ . . . 'ĕlōhîm, pneuma theou*)?" (Gen. 41:37). That endowment elevated Joseph to power as the overseer of Egypt under the pharaoh's throne. Joseph's divine gift for management fulfilled the creation of humans "in our image, after our likeness" (Gen. 1:26) as divine deputies to maintain the created earth.

CONSTRUCTION

It was as a lowly tentmaker, rather than a prestigious architect, that Paul imitated God's instructions to Bezalel. The wilderness tent of meeting that Bezalel constructed was the very tent of witness that the martyr Stephen recalled in his speech in Acts that inaugurated Paul's persecution of Christians. As Acts related, "Our fathers had the tent of witness in the wilderness, even as he who spoke to Moses directed him to make it, according to the pattern that he had seen" (Acts 7:44). In his radical denunciation of the Jerusalem temple cult, Stephen asserted that "the Most High does not dwell in houses made with hands" (v. 48.) Although Paul's letter to the Corinthians did not explicate his personal consent to Stephen's death by stoning, he echoed his speech in his own promise to them of "a building from God, a house not made with hands, eternal in the heavens" (2 Cor. 5:1). The Jerusalem temple was Israel's primary cultic institution, retaining symbolic prominence even for Jews in diaspora.[111] Paul among the Corinthians had no need to reject it, however, as Stephen the martyr did. For Jews in diaspora, that temple was inaccessible because most of them could hardly afford the thrice-annual pilgrimages there for worship. A local synagogue probably served as their religious center,[112] and Paul was plausibly associated with one.[113] Moreover, the Corinthian church was composed primarily of non-Jews, or Gentiles. They had their own experiences of the impressive local temples to pagan deities, from whose cults they had been converted to Jesus the Christ.[114] Further, Paul's theology did not establish the Corinthians as a temple to rival or substitute for the Jerusalem temple. His pastoral concern was for a holiness exceeding ordinary behavior.[115]

A tent afforded Paul from his Jewish heritage an attractive model for his trade. A tent, not a temple as for other gods, had been the dwelling of the supreme Canaanite god, El, in the Ugaritic myths.[116] It was to his tent that the vengeful goddess Anat went to extort his blessing to steal back, by her mercenary eagle, Aqhat's marvelous bow.[117] The Israelite tent of meeting that Belzale erected in the wilderness for God was prominent in the Priestly code for the oracular choice of political leaders during the wanderings. The presence of the tent affirmed the universality of Yahweh as God but the particularity of Yahweh as the God of the Israelites, to whom he descended at its flap. There in the tent of meeting his name dwelled, enthroned on the ark in the innermost chamber, where the high priest ministered each New Year's day.[118] It was with that tent that God's glory was intrinsically identified in Priestly theology, for there it was manifest to all Israel, not only to Moses or privileged elders on the mountain. In the Priestly tradition God only appeared once outside of the tent, and that was before its erection. In the tent of meeting he remained veiled from visitors and secluded by a screen whose flames consumed the sacrificial offerings. God sat between the cherubim, with the ark for his footstool, in an earthly dwelling as an anthropomorphic deity. The priest supplied his bodily needs as if God were human: food and drink for taste, lamps for sight, incense for smell. Those anthropomorphic features were schematized and dogmatized,[119] but they were present. Thus, a tent was a traditional holy site for Paul to encounter God, and the traditional anthropomorphism of the Priestly story prepared him for faith in God's human presence as Jesus. As Paul announced to the Corinthians, the ancient God of glory became manifest toward their own glorification in Christ—yet scandalously so in Christ crucified.

The tent that Bezalel made was of the ethnographic type "black," so named for its fabrication from dark goat's wool, which was woven on a loom into cloth. God's instructions specified that material, and Bezalel complied in using it. He also fashioned a cover from the skins of rams and goats.[120] However, although the Septuagint translated his Hebrew *'hl* as Greek *skēnē*, a Greek tent was unknown until centuries later. Even then it was pitched neither for worship nor for habitation, but for entertainment in festivals and theaters. In Paul's native Cilicia black tents were similarly made of goats' hair.[121] Since he returned there after his baptism, he may have learned its native trade for his financial support while a Christian missionary.[122] In Corinth he would have made a Roman tent, the type used by soldiers and travelers, which was not woven of hairs but stitched from skins.[123] Since he identified himself as already a tentmaker upon his arrival in Corinth, the particular skill for sewing leather goods he may have acquired there from Aquila and Prisca, his hosts. Yet, for either type of tent, the basic components were the same, a pole and a cover. And all tents served the common purpose of shelter from the natural effects of sun, wind, and rain.

The name *běṣalĕ'ĕl* for Bezalel, the spirited tentmaker, means "the shadow of God." It recalled God's role of sheltering Israel, as if in a tent, from those natural elements.[124] And it recalled God acting like an eagle that spread its wings over the desert to shade Israelites from its scorching sun.[125] A psalm paralleled the similes longingly. "Let me dwell in thy tent for ever! / Oh to be safe under the shelter of thy wings!" (Ps. 61:4). Aquila, the name of Paul's host and coworker, means "eagle," specifically the family of *Aquila* eagles, among which the golden eagle was supreme. Aquila was a Latin surname, not a personal name; its modern Hebrew equivalent, Nesher, is also a surname meaning "eagle." Aquila the tentmaker, as a Jewish laborer in Rome, may have been surnamed Nesher, translated as Aquila, or he may have adopted Aquila as a moniker. Perhaps he was a tentmaker there for the Roman army, whose standard was the *Aquila* eagle.[126] At Corinth he embodied his name by sheltering Paul there in his own lodging and workshop. Paul's mission was to enlarge his apostolic tent, after Isaiah's prophecy for the inclusion of the nations. "Enlarge the place of your tent, / and let the curtains of your habitations be stretched out; / hold not back, lengthen your cords / and strengthen your stakes. / For you will spread abroad to the right and to the left, / and your descendants will possess the nations / and will people the desolate cities" (Is. 54:2–3).

As the artisan of the metaphorical tent in which the Corinthians communally bore the Spirit, Paul was inclined to discern the Spirit's manifestation pastorally, rather than to define its nature theologically. He elaborated the Spirit's gifts cogently in addressing the quarrel among the Corinthians about who was spiritual.[127] His catalogue of spiritual gifts climaxed in his frequently cited verse "the greatest of these is love" (1 Cor. 13:1–13). But, as that church became more quarrelsome, he addressed it in a second letter beginning with the same apostolic salutation, "Paul, an apostle of Christ Jesus by the will of God." Eschewing sophistry for grace, Paul sought plain speech. "For we write you nothing but what you can read and understand: I hope you will understand fully, as you have understood in part, that you can be proud of us as we can be of you, on the day of the Lord Jesus." Again he declared about his spiritual knowledge that "in every way we have made this plain to you in all things." Paul considered the moral integrity of the Corinthian church bound to its trust in his own spiritual authority. "But it is God who establishes us with you in Christ, and has commissioned us; he has put his seal upon us and given us his Spirit in our hearts as a guarantee" (2 Cor. 1:12–13; see also 11:6; 1:21–22). The church was his "letter of recommendation" from Christ, visible and legible by everyone, "written not with ink but with the Spirit of the living God, not on tablets of stone but on tablets of human hearts" (3:1–3). That verse remembered Ezekiel's oracle of the new covenant for Israel. "A new heart I will give you, and a new spirit I will put within you; and I will take out of your flesh the heart of stone and give you a heart of flesh. And I will put my spirit within you, and cause you to walk in my statutes and be careful to observe my ordinances. You shall dwell in the land which I gave to your fathers; and you shall be my people, and I will be your God." And, "I will not hide my face any more from them, when I pour out my Spirit upon the house of Israel, says the Lord God" (Ezek. 36:26–28, 39:29).

Paul's imitation of Ezekiel was apposite because that biblical prophet and priest was the divider between the Hebraism of communal salvation and the Judaism of individual salvation. As the concept of salvation developed into an otherworldly reality, an individual was transformed from the limitations of his mortal birth into an eternal possibility. Ezekiel inaugurated that hope when the heavens opened for him; for no other canonical prophet, nor even Moses before them, had seen a rift in the clouds.[128] Ezekiel's frequent use of the word *rûaḥ/pneuma* as polysemous "spirit, breath, and wind" commended his book a resource for Paul's examination of the Spirit's activity among Christians. Although Paul allied his teaching somewhat with Ezekiel's prophecy, that was not through any practice of the future "merkabah mysticism." Indeed, Paul's teaching fulfilled Ezekiel's prophecy only by destroying its hope for

God's new covenant with Israel exclusively among the nations. Paul was the Christian apostle to the nations. He built the new spiritual temple, which Ezekiel only envisioned, in the Corinthians, who were mostly not Jews. Christ was its cornerstone and the apostles were its foundation.

Beyond Paul's architectural metaphor of the Spirit indwelling the Corinthians in a temple was his artisanal metaphor of bearing the gospel of Jesus the Christ in a clay vessel. In defense of his ministry Paul affirmed a splendid new dispensation of the Spirit. It outdazzled Moses's glimpse of God's back that was reflected to the Israelites in the fading glory on his veiled face. Paul wrote that through Christ that veil was lifted, although unbelievers still remained veiled or blinded from "seeing the light of the gospel of the glory of Christ, who is the likeness of God." Paul proclaimed that the veil was removed by Christians, who faced toward the Spirit. "Now the Lord is the Spirit, and where the Spirit of the Lord is, there is freedom. And we all, with unveiled face, beholding the glory of the Lord, are being changed into his likeness from one degree of glory to another; for this comes through the Lord who is the Spirit" (2 Cor. 3:7–18). That introduction of Christ as the likeness of God, and of Christians as transformed into his likeness, implied their new creation in Christ as a second Adam. For in the beginning God had said, "Let us make man in our image, after our likeness" (Gen. 1:26).[129] Paul announced a new creation through the same Spirit who primordially created humans. The crucial difference, he stated, was that humans created in the likeness of God through the first Adam were subject to death. However, through their new creation in the second Adam, or Christ, they could be incorporated into his resurrected life. Paul's lesson intended to refute the disbelief of some Corinthians in the resurrection of the body because they regarded themselves as already fully spiritual beings while on earth.

CREATION

Paul intimately related the gospel of Jesus to the creation story in Genesis 1 by a paraphrase. "For it is the God who said, 'Let light shine out of darkness,' who has shone in our hearts to give the light of the knowledge of the glory of God in the face of Christ." That revelation of Christ fulfilled the original creation. Paul's context of light and dark, vision and blindness, climaxed in the divine illumination of humans refashioned from Adamic clay into Christian vessel. As he taught, "We have this treasure in earthen vessels, to show that the transcendent power belongs to God and not to us." Paul described overcoming the afflictions of his ministry to the Corinthians as "carrying in the body the death of Jesus, so that the life of Jesus may also be manifested in our bodies" (2 Cor. 4:6–7, 10). His metaphor of "earthen vessels" conveyed human fragility and breakage. A psalm acknowledged potter's ware dashed to pieces under God's wrathful iron.[130] Jeremiah's oracle threatened the divine destruction of disobedient Israel just as a potter's clay was ruined at the wheel. "'O house of Israel, can I not do with you as this potter has done? says the Lord. Behold, like the clay in the potter's hand, so are you in my hand, O house of Israel" (Jer. 18:1–6). Isaiah's oracle warned the Israelites against striving against the Creator's fashioning of his children, as the work of his hands. That dispute was like the clay questioning and complaining to its potter.[131] Paul's metaphor of clay vessels remembered Isaiah's verses about the expectation of things beyond sensory perception that were promised to those lamenting Israelites who waited for God. Paul proclaimed that they were fulfilled for Christians who loved God. The prophet's prayer had addressed an ancient God of terrible unsought deeds, imploring him to "rend the heavens and come down" as in the lightning strikes of old that shook the very mountains. Despite the people's iniquity, the prophet begged God not to boil over in anger. He reminded him "thou art our Father, / we are the clay, and thou art our potter; / we are all the work of thy hand" (Is. 64:1–5, 8–9). Isaiah's metaphor of the divine potter of human clay interpreted the story of the creation of Adam from earthen matter. After God caused a mist to seep from the earth to water it, he then "formed man of dust from the ground, and breathed into his nostrils the breath of life; and man became a living being" (Gen. 2:6–7).

Paul had explained in his first letter to the Corinthians how "the first human (*prōtos anthrōpos*) Adam became an ensouled [not RSV "living"] being (*psychēn zōsan*)." He amplified it that "the last man Adam became a life-making spirit (*pneuma zōopoioun*)." Christ's designation, *zōopoioun*, meant not "life-giving," as in the standard translation, but "life-making," from the same root as *poieō*, "to make." A live human, as ensouled, preceded the possibility of a spiritual human. "The first man was from the earth, a man of dust; the second man is from heaven." All humans bore the dusty image; Christians also bore the celestial image (1 Cor. 15:45–49). Paul believed this participation in the mystery of Christ's resurrection not only from catechetical instruction but also from personal commission. As he offered his credentials in the salutation of his letter, "Paul, called by the will of God to be an apostle of Christ Jesus." And as he asserted defensively, "Am I not an apostle? Have I not seen Jesus our Lord? Are you not my workmanship in the Lord? If to others I am not an apostle, at least I am to you; for you are the seal of my apostleship in the Lord" (1 Cor. 1:1, see 2 Cor. 1:1; 1 Cor. 9:1–2).

Paul's metaphor of bearing the gospel in an earthenware vessel[132] illuminated the Corinthians with the light of divine glory. For he did not reference any container whatsoever that a potter might throw but the clay artifacts that were Corinth's best-documented industry. Those were unglazed terracotta lamps, produced on wheels and sold cheaply to compete with more expensive Italian imports they copied. The vast deposit of marl that formed the lower stratum of central Corinthia guaranteed a generous supply of clay for the manufacture of pottery, tiles, and other terracotta ware. Corinthian production of lamps increased during the first century C.E., during Paul's visitations there, so that he invoked an item of local pride and profit. Since the manufactories employed many Corinthians to make the lamps, both for local consumption and for trade with merchant ships in their two ports, the basis for Paul's metaphor could not have been missed.[133] Corinthian lamps were visible religiously at its Isthmian Games during Paul's visit in 51 C.E., when hundreds of them lit the shrine to Palaimon, its hero. Worshippers carried the ordinary, small lamps cupped in their hands. Another type, unique to Corinth, consisted of large open bowls centered with wicks. Those were set on the ground or on pedestals for the nocturnal mystery rites in Palaimon's honor.[134] Beyond the rites for the Games, worshippers at the city's shrines also frequently left dedications of terracotta objects made by local craftsmen.[135]

Paul's "earthen vessels" may also have alluded to another popular Corinthian ware. In his first letter to the Corinthians he introduced a comparison with athletic games, by which he urged them to self-control to run the moral race competitively so as to win the imperishable wreath.[136] His reference was the *hippios*, a footrace of four stadia, or about 874.9 yards / 800 meters, that was particular to the local Isthmian Games but not run in the Olympic or Pythian Games.[137] Paul maintained that he himself strove against disqualification in athletic contest. He did not shadow box, jabbing at the air, but bruised his own body in discipline.[138] In that athletic context Paul's metaphor of "earthenware vessels" for the indwelling Spirit may have alluded to the aryballos. That was a small clay bottle or flask, usually of globular shape, that contained oil. It has been defined as common Corinthian ware,[139] with examples excavated at the sanctuary of Poseidon at Isthmia, the site of the local Panhellenic Games.[140] Although the aryballos itself was rare among Attic ware, depictions of it on Attic vases and sculpture were a conventional attribute of the public palaestra, or wrestling school. Male athletes either held the aryballos in hand while pouring its oil onto their skin or they carried the aryballos suspended from their wrist by a string attached to its neck or handle. In sports olive oil was used for the anointing.[141] The commonality at the Isthmian Games in Corinth of that pot for sports with the lamp for the sanctuary was that both earthenware vessels were containers for oil. Paul may have recalled the pure pressed olive oil that God specified for the lamp burning in the Israelite tent of meeting.[142] His second letter to the Corinthians, which described the glory of Christ as a treasure in "earthen vessels," presented himself as divinely "anointed" for his mission to them. "But it is God who establishes us with you in Christ (*Christou*), and having anointed us (*chrisas*) [not RSV "commissioned"] . . ." (2 Cor. 1:21). That parallelism literally associated Paul, as anointed, with Christ, which title meant "the anointed one." Paul remembered the anointing of the prophet Isaiah, whom he invoked for his own mission beyond Israel to the nations. "The Spirit of the Lord God is upon me / because the Lord has anointed me" (Is. 61:1). Jesus had in Luke's gospel begun his public ministry by reading in the synagogue that same verse of Isaiah's about spiritual anointing. Paul affirmed his own anointing and immediately continued "he has put his stamp [not RSV "seal"] upon us and given us his Spirit in his hearts as a guarantee" (2 Cor. 1:22).

Paul named (*sphragizō*) the authenticating mark that an artisan stamped on his earthenware, a general practice in the factories and workshops of Roman Empire. Such "signed" lamps have survived from their distribution in the tens of thousands.[143] A type of ancient Roman pottery, a red glazed ware, was decisively called *terra sigillata*, "stamped earth."[144] Numerous stamped lamps have been excavated near Corinth, even from a prehistoric settlement.[145] Imitations of the Italian type of fineware began at Corinth early in the first century C.E. By the middle of that century, when Paul visited, local products including lamps dominated imports.¹⁴⁶ The terracotta lamps of Paul's era continued to be stamped with the names of their individual makers. The Latin initials of the origin of manufacture could also be added: COL(onia) L(aus) IVL(ia) COR(inthiensis).¹⁴⁷ Paul's term *sphragizō* meant the maker's stamp on his artifact. A stamp on pottery was a mark of authentication, precedent to a modern legal trademark. The divine stamp on Paul and the Corinthians marked his creation, or better, through Christ his new creation. That creative stamp was the image of the heavenly man through whom Christians would share in the resurrection of their earthen bodies. That was a belief some Corinthians doubted or denied because they regarded themselves already "spiritual" on earth. Again, as Paul wrote, "The first man was from the earth, a man of dust; the second man is from heaven. As was the man of dust, so are those who are of the dust; and as is the man of heaven, so are those who are of heaven. Just as we have borne the image of the man of dust, we shall also bear the image of the man of heaven" (1 Cor. 15:47–49).

A local context for the biblical image of earthen humans was Corinth's fame for terracotta statuary, of which some fragments of life-sized human heads have been excavated. As Pliny's *Historia naturalis* told, it was a potter at Corinth who invented terracotta sculpture by modeling from clay. Making a memento for his daughter of her beloved, "He drew in outline on the wall the shadow of his face thrown by a lamp. He pressed clay on this and made a relief, which he hardened by exposure to the fire with the rest of his pottery." Such was the legendary origin of the decorated pediments on classical temples.¹⁴⁸ The Corinthian industry for handmade terracotta figurines was historically impelled by the local cults, whose rituals needed such votives for maturation, fertility, and good health. The industry was strongly revived in the refounded Roman colony just at the time of Paul's visitation.¹⁴⁹ By comparison with that industry, Paul meant the spiritual stamp as the Creator's guarantee of the full redemption in Christ of his own newly fashioned works. Paul's metaphor of the divine Spirit lighting Christians as terracotta lamps illuminated God's glory in Christ. As Paul explained, that was the same light spoken into existence in Genesis 1:3, which shone in the darkness at the primordial creation. The new creation in Christ outdazzled the radiance on Moses's face, which reflected the fires burning at Mount Sinai's summit. It also outrivaled the lightning storm that electrified

Ezekiel's vision of Yahweh's throne of glory in its hybrid image of his sovereignty over humans and other animals.

That creational context clarified Paul's introductory parallel between the human spirit and the divine Spirit. "Who of humans knows humanity if not the spirit of the human that is in him; so the godhood of God no one perceives if not the Spirit of God. For the Spirit searches everything, even the heights of God." The Spirit's investigation was a revelation of a hidden mystery, like the proverbial equation of human breath with the divine light that searched darkened chambers.[150] Thus did Paul imagine the Corinthians as terracotta lamps illumined by the Spirit who created both their human breath and their Christian spirit. The Spirit's stamp upon them was their assurance of their resurrection in Christ, whose heavenly image they bore. Paul's demonstration of the Spirit's empowerment of himself extended to the Corinthians through his apostolate. It was that spiritual empowerment of Christians that his scant discussion of the human spirit remarked. The same Spirit who searched the heights of God revealed to humans Jesus crucified as the Christ, the promised Messiah.

DISTINCTIONS

Paul distinguished between the spirit from the world and the Spirit from God, who was received "that we might understand the gifts bestowed on us by God." Its articulation was given in words the Spirit taught rather than in wisdom that humans acquired, so that the apostle Paul might "interpret spiritual truths to those who possess the Spirit." He distinguished between the "ensouled human (*psychikos anthrōpos*)" and the "spiritual human (*pneumatikos*)." The ensouled human, who was already breathing as alive, was not a receptor of the Spirit's gifts from Christ's new creation. Rather, the simply ensouled human spurned them as folly and could not understand them because they were only recognized spiritually. The spiritual human, however, judged everything but was himself beyond judgment. In response to the biblical question "But who can know the mind of the Lord?," Paul affirmed, "But we have the purpose of Christ" (1 Cor. 2:4, 10–15). Paul's reflections on the human spirit were not an abstract philosophical dissertation but a directed pastoral rebuke to the Corinthians in conflict. He blamed them for being not "spiritual (*pneumatikoi*)" but "fleshly (*sarkinoi*)" (3:1) because of their lapse into ordinary human squabbling about the church leadership. The Spirit acted to sanctify and justify sinners so as to unite them with the Lord.[151] To this end it conferred diverse spiritual gifts, but always as a manifestation of the same Spirit who gave them. Paul enumerated those gifts as: manifestation for the common good, utterance of wisdom, utterance of knowledge, faith, miracle-working, prophecy, discernment of spirits, varieties of tongues, and interpretation of tongues. All gifts were inspired by the same Spirit who apportioned them to individuals as he willed. But all Christians were baptized into one body by one Spirit and they confessed Jesus as Lord only in same Spirit.[152]

In discussing the charism of speaking in tongues versus the charism of interpreting them, Paul made a distinction that has been translated misleadingly. Because he believed the manifestations of the Spirit should build up the church, he evaluated speaking as good but interpretation as better. He reasoned that in speaking in tongues "the spirit (*pneuma*) prays but not the mind (*nous*)."[153] That standard translation, which assumes a facultative psychology,[154] is imprecise. Paul wrote that *nous* was *akarpos*, literally "fruitless, barren." Its futility clarified that his *nous* in his ecclesiastical context revealed the "purpose, design" of Christ. Similar was Paul's response about having of the "mind (*nous*)" of Christ as knowing his "purpose, design." Christians knew the purpose of Christ, not his mind. That purpose was in Paul's announcement the secret wisdom before the creation of the ultimate revelation of God's glory in Christ.[155] For Paul, speaking in tongues, because it was an individual charism, was "unmindful" of the community, who could listen to but not learn from such unintelligible utterances. Speaking in tongues evidenced a neglect or disregard of the entire church. Paul's solution was to pray with both the spirit and the mind—or better, with a mindful spirit, to sing with both the spirit and the mind—or better, a mindful spirit, and to bless with both the spirit and the mind—or better, a mindful spirit. That charity would allow the community to join in the final "Amen," he taught. The spirits of pneumatics were subject to prophets, and the spirits of prophets to other prophets for communal intelligibility.[156] Thus, Paul was not distinguishing between human *nous* and *pneuma* as psychic or physiological categories; rather, he integrated their ecclesiastical functions.

Paul's further words to the Corinthians about his being "absent in body but present in spirit" for them was not enthusiastic fellowship.

That spiritual presence actively manifested Jesus's power in judgment on a certain notorious sinner in the community. Paul identified "my spirit (*tou emou pneumatos*)." Absent at a distance from that church, he could only commit his condemnation of the sinner to a letter. It was delivered in ink, rather than by breath, so that the sinner's "spirit" might be saved on the day when the Lord himself would be present.[157] In further discussing sexual morality, with the legitimate options of marriage versus celibacy, Paul supposed that the widow who did not remarry was happier than she who did. His opinion on that choice does not deserve the strong standard translation "I think (*dokō*) I have the Spirit of God" (1 Cor. 7:40). Yet Paul's opposition between "spiritual" and "fleshly" humans did not exclude the body from divine service. Having established that the Spirit dwelled in the Corinthians as his temple, Paul specified that "your body is a temple of the Holy Spirit within you, which you have from God.... So glorify God in your body" (3:16; 6:19, 20). Again, in parallelism, he proposed the ideal of being "holy in body and in spirit" (7:34). A lesson was an integrated spirituality of the whole Christian that avoided the sexual immorality of the flagrant sinner he condemned in writing.

Toward the end of his first letter to the Corinthians, Paul circled back to his parallel near its beginning about the spirit of humans and the Spirit of God as both essentially self-knowing. He then addressed a mystery revealed spiritually to humans by the Spirit, the resurrection of the dead. Paul differentiated from Genesis 1 the fleshly (*sarx*) bodies—human, animal, bird, and fish as terrestrial; then the unfleshly (*somata*) bodies—sun, moon, and stars as celestial. Human flesh had unique potential for change: sown perishable, dishonored, and weak; raised imperishable, glorious, powerful, and spiritual. He argued that "if there is an ensouled [not RSV "living"] body (*psychikon*), there is also a spiritual body (*pneumatikon*)" (1 Cor. 15:44). Paul made this a fortiori argument because the resurrection (*epairō*) of the body did not correspond to own his experience as "a man in Christ" (2 Cor. 12:2) who was snatched up (*harpazo*) to paradise, whether in or out of the body he did not know. His word-pair *psychikon-pneumatikon* was unique. Paul's diction has been attributed to contemporary Jewish exegesis of Genesis 2:7, especially the distinction between the earthly man and the heavenly man in the writing of Philo, a philosopher.[158] Yet that word-pair *psychikon-pneumatikon* does not appear there.[159]

Paul's diction has been further translated by opposing the "physical" and the "spiritual" (1 Cor. 2:14; 15:44). However, he did not write *physikon*, for "physical" or "natural"; he wrote *psychikon*, for "ensouled." Paul defined his meaning of "ensouled (*psychikon*)" in contrast to "unsouled (*apsycha*)." His example of something unsouled was a flute.[160] A flute was not merely inert, like a rock, but also potentially meaningful. A flute was an intelligently crafted instrument into which an ensouled human could intentionally blow his breath to emit sounds for communication with others. Paul added the examples of another wind instrument, the bugle, and also the harp, which was stroked and plucked with human fingers. To be ensouled, rather than unsouled, was not simply to be alive physically, as evident from breathing. To be ensouled was to breathe life from a creative source with the power of communication, as Adam in Genesis 2 obeyed the Creator in naming the animals and in speaking to Eve. So did a flute emit sound by a musician's breath. It was not coincidental that Paul clarified the meaning of "unsouled" in his lesson about speaking in tongues. That charism was unintelligible, therefore uncharitable for its lack of communication to others in the church. As Paul argued, just as a flute must emit distinctive sounds for listeners to know the music, so prayer must emit intelligible words for listeners to know the message.

His polemical language was biblically inspired. Paul appealed to the creation in Genesis 2 of Adam as the first human. Although he usually depended on the Septuagint translation, Paul also improvised with omissions and interpretations, as was consistent with the contemporary practice of citation.[161] As he cited Genesis 2:7, "'Thus it is written, 'The first man Adam became a living being (*Egeneto ho prōtos anthrōpos Adam eis psychēn zōsan*).'" The Septuagint text is "Then the Lord God formed man of dust from the ground, and breathed into his nostrils the breath of life; and man became a living being (*kai enephusēsen eis to prosōpon autou pnoēn zōēs*)." Only the prototypical human, Adam, among all creatures received God's direct exhalation as the breath of life (*pnoēn zōēs*). The other animals were simply formed from the ground, and a human woman was fashioned from the man's rib. In Paul's interpretation the first man became an ensouled being (*psychēn zōsan*), not a physical being (*physikon zōsan*).

Paul then compared the first and second Adams. "'Thus it is written, 'The first man Adam became an ensouled [not RSV "living"] being'; the last Adam became a life-making [not RSV "life-giving"] spirit (*pneuma zōopoioun*)." Paul ordered the soulful (*psychikon*) first, then the spiritual (*pneumatikon*). As he elaborated, "The first man was from the earth, a man of dust; the second man is from heaven." Dusty humans resembled that dusty man, Adam; heavenly humans, the heavenly man, Christ. Paul reasoned that at the resurrection of the dead, "just as we have borne the image of the man of dust, we shall also bear the image of the man of heaven" (1 Cor. 15:45–49). Paul's reflection on Genesis 2:7 was somewhat consistent with contemporary Judaic writings.[162] However, he did not dismiss the created human being (*psychikos*) as merely physical, as in the standard translation. For, since there was no divine "image" in Genesis 2:7 but, rather, a shaping of Adam from dust and a blowing into his nostrils, Paul's phrase "the image of the man of dust" was redacted in continuity with the prior chapter. There humanity was made by God "in our image, after our likeness" (Gen. 1:26). The second image of the heavenly man, to be conferred on Christians at their resurrection, did not negate but fulfill the first image conferred at creation. For Paul, the resurrection of the body was not a denial of or an exemption from death. It was a "victory" over its fatality, given through Jesus Christ the Lord, the second Adam and the heavenly man.

Creation in Genesis 1 happened by breathing for speech, by the inhalation and exhalation of the air that bore the Spirit over the deep. Then God said, "Let us make man in our image, after our likeness" (Gen. 1:26) as a bond. That account of the creation foreshadowed God's choice of Israel from among the nations by circling it and gathering it to himself as his special portion in social alliance. The subsequent account in Genesis 2 emphasized that solidarity by God's breathing directly into the nostrils of the first human to impart life. That inspiration of breath was again a bond. But the bond extended beyond God to Adam's naming with his own breath the other animals, as a deputy, with Eve the helper, the earth from which he was formed. When the Spirit entered into particular persons, its agency was unitive to bind Israel to God in covenantal obedience. Bezalel was specially endowed with the Spirit, beyond his basic life, to construct the Israelite tent of meeting for worship. Spirit in the Hebrew Scriptures was unitive, with the Israelites as its special portion of the creation.

Paul's distinction between the ensouled (*psychikos*) human and the spiritual (*pneumatikos*) human has been interpreted to distinguish humans without the Spirit of God from Christians with it. That exegesis has divided nonbelievers from believers, or even natural persons from supernatural persons. The Spirit thus became the criterion for division: the ensouled human did not belong to him, but the spiritual human did.[163] Such exegesis by division was not Paul's argument, however. His distinction of ensouled versus spiritual humans was unique to that Corinthian letter, and it have may have repeated some local usage. If it was the claim of certain Corinthian dissenters to boast of themselves as spiritual and denigrate others as ensouled, then they relegated those other Christians to ordinary human existence. Paul, however, was intent on correcting the meaning of "spiritual" in that church. He wrote that the Spirit was conferred on all Christians by their baptism. Spiritual authenticity was discerned by the exercise of the Spirit's charismatic gifts, culminating in love. After all, he argued, those boastful "spiritual" Corinthians ironically committed or condoned grave immorality (*porneia*) within their church. Paul chastised them as "puffed up" (1 Cor. 4:18), airy blowers rather than solid builders of the community. With puffery he defined them as mortal, like idols.[164] Paul affirmed that all Christians, as truly spiritual humans, would share in Christ's resurrected life. But his terms "ensouled" and "spiritual" did not deprive non-Christians of the Spirit. They were gifted by the Spirit essentially as created humans. All humans were ensouled by virtue of their creation in God's image and likeness as in Genesis 1:26, and by his inbreathing of life as in Genesis 2:7. There were, nevertheless, two bestowals of the Spirit: creational in the first Adam and re-creational in the second Adam. That re-creation in Christ was foreshadowed in the renewal of the earth after the flood, as evident in Noahide laws subjecting all nations to God, and in prophetic oracles of a renewed covenant but one inclusive beyond Israel of all nations.

SCRIPTURE

The creation told in Genesis 1 and 2 was consistent with God's choice of Israel from among the nations as his special portion. Humans were created in his divine image and likeness (1:26), not in that of the assembly of foreign gods. God lifted Adam from the dust as a metaphor for enthronement and breathed into his nostrils as a likeness for kingship.

Paul did not read those biblical texts as a report of God's abstract making of parts of the universe into which humans were inserted. His apostolic mission was to expand the original exclusive covenant with Israel to the other nations. He did so by proclaiming the Spirit's new creation, meaning his new choice of all nations. Only one other biblical phrase matched Paul's introduction to the Corinthians of the "human spirit (*pneuma tou anthrōpou to en autō*)" of common experiential knowledge. "For who of humans knows humanity if not the spirit of the human that is in him; so, the godhood of God no one perceives if not the Spirit of God" (1 Cor. 2:11). That verse related the human spirit of humans, not of an individual man, to the divine Spirit. Paul's precise message was not about human interiority but about the Spirit's revelation of Christ as God's wisdom before the creation. His phrase "the human spirit" had only occurred biblically in the prophet Zechariah's oracle of Jerusalem's victory over the nations. "The word of the Lord concerning Israel: Thus says the Lord, who stretched out the heavens and founded the earth and formed the spirit of man within him (*pneuma anthrōpou en autō*)" (Zech. 12:1).[165] That human spirit was created by the divine Spirit, who declared it to be in its image and likeness by breathing his creative words, or who formed it by breathing life into Adam's nostrils.[166] Paul's mission to the nations extended Zechariah's oracle of the divine victory of a restored Jerusalem to the defeated nations as also sharing in the Spirit of God as created human. That original human spirit known to all living humans provided Paul's comparison with the Spirit who searched the heights of God. His creative Spirit, who knew God's wisdom even before the creation, had now revealed its hidden mystery to be the second Adam, who was Jesus the Christ as Messiah and Lord.

The significance of Jesus, as Paul instructed the Corinthians, devolved to the creation. Christ, as a "life-making spirit" for humans, was God's mysterious purpose since before creation to reveal his glory in Jesus. He completed Adam's potential and promise, while his crucifixion was the error of worldly spirits who failed or refused to recognize that glorious Lord. The gospels would generously affirm the presence to Jesus of the Spirit, from his very conception to his baptism for a mission.[167] However, the gospels were not yet composed. Paul's testimony through his letters was the earliest record of that Christian belief. The re-creative indwelling of the Spirit in the Corinthian church continued its creative indwelling in the Israelite community. The Spirit of God had formed Israel by empowering the charismatic leadership of Moses, then of Joshua, the early judges, and the kings, and by promising the Messiah. The Spirit's manifest presence to or in the prophets inspired their speech toward Israel's observance of the covenant.[168] Paul claimed to have inherited those spiritual traditions; indeed, he claimed that all Christians exceeded them. Paul's letters to the Corinthians were preoccupied with similar issues in the Hebrew Scriptures of leadership—his own spiritual authority versus others' spiritual claims—and of prophecy, whose intelligible speech he exalted above unintelligible tongues. At question among the Corinthians was who possessed the authentic Spirit to lead and to prophesy. Paul established its discernment in the exercise of its spiritual gifts, above all the love that bound community. That was consistent with the Spirit's biblical role among the Israelites. However, he came to believe that the Spirit was newly conferred on Christians by baptism into the mystery of Christ for a new creation. "He who is united to the Lord becomes one spirit with him." Paul's comparison was with the creation in Genesis of Eve from Adam as "bone of my bones and flesh of my flesh" and with the consequent socialization of a man leaving his family for a woman so that "they become one flesh" (Gen. 2:23–24; 1 Cor. 6:16–17).

Paul's social context for that teaching was incest and prostitution in the Corinthian church. To condemn its immorality authoritatively, he identified his own extraordinary experience as "a man in Christ" who participated in Spirit's new creation. As Paul instructed the Corinthians, they should not judge from a simply human perspective as Jesus's crucifiers judged. "Therefore, if any one is in Christ, he is a new creation; the old has passed away, behold, the new has come" (2 Cor. 5:16–17).[169] That statement announced a new spiritual order not only according to the flesh, as with the creation of the first Adam. The prophetic oracle of a new covenant Paul converted into the prophetic reality of a new creation. God had no longer hidden his face, as he had from Moses, but revealed his glory shining on the face of Christ. "For it is the God who said, 'Let light shine out of darkness,' who has shone in our hearts to give the light of the knowledge of the glory of God on the face of Christ" (2 Cor. 4:6).[170]

As a receptor of the divine Spirit, the human spirit created in Adam and re-created in Christ was a receptacle, like the metaphorical earthenware lamp. The human spirit was created and gifted. It was acted upon, not active except to manifest the activity of the Spirit or to betray its absence. The human spirit as a creature was, as Paul introduced it, the human spirit that knew itself as human, just as the divine Spirit knew God as divine. "For who of humans knows humanity if not the spirit of the human that is in him; so, the godhood of God no one perceives if not the Spirit of God" (1 Cor. 2:11). Paul's writings on spirits operated in parallels, but not all were antitheses; some were analogies. That particular statement to the Corinthians was neither antithetical nor analogical but an a fortiori argument inclusive of both. Paul affirmed a similarity between the human spirit and the divine Spirit because of the creation of humans in God's image and likeness. Yet even his apparent antitheses between the spirit from God and the spirit from the world, and between the spirit and the flesh, were not predicated absolutely. They were only human constructs, not divine abstractions, for world and flesh were capable of transformation by the Spirit into a new creation.

The traditions of creation in Genesis 1 and 2 agreed in an expression of God's creative agency as breath, whether spoken or exhaled. Biblical translations of *pneuma* as "spirit" could compare with natural air, a pervasive and necessary element commonly observed through the effects of its movement as physical wind or animal sound. The church at Corinth would have also inherited various notions of animal air from Greek culture and medicine. The theories ranged from the ancient belief in air as a material and visible substance whose penetration of the body caused pain and disease, to the Hippocratic theory of air mixed with blood as the source of life. The physiology of animal breathing was believed to be the activity of the entire body, through the pores of the skin into the inner vessels. The function of the lungs as the respiratory organ was as yet undiscovered, however. Lungs were imagined as sponges that absorbed the essential mixture of air and blood, or as fans that cooled the heart as the organ of vitality.[171] Biblical spirit, as *pneuma* in the Septuagint translation of creation, could be compatible with the concept of spirit (*pneuma*) in *Peri physeōn*, where, as internal spirit (*phusa*), it was breath for life and health. Although that text was included among the Hippocratic writings, it was not a medical treatise but a sophistical exercise on the popular understanding of breath as elemental air. It acknowledged wind as the most powerful and pervasive manifestation of such spirit (*pneuma*), as observable in the tossing of ships at sea. "For mortals too this is the cause of life, and the cause of disease in the sick." Indeed, "So great is the need of wind (*pneuma*) for all bodies that while a man can be deprived of everything else, both food and drink, for two, three, or more days, and live, yet if the wind passages into the body be cut off he will die in a brief part of a day, showing that the greatest need for a body is wind (*pneuma*)." Although all other human actions were brief and interrupted, alternate breathing between inspiration and expiration continued until death.[172] Such was an opinion the Corinthians might have shared with classical writings before Paul's preaching about the divine and human spirits. But his preaching was distinctively spiritual, not commonly natural, and he derived it from the Hebrew Scriptures, not Greek culture.

Paul was pastorally concerned about the manner in which the quarrelsome Corinthians expressed the Creator Spirit by the exhalation of breath in speech to others. His attention to speaking in tongues among them did not reflect an essential objection to tongues since he claimed to surpass them in that very charism.[173] His priority for intelligible speech imitated the Creator Spirit, who spoke humans into being in the divine image and likeness. The essential commonality of humans as creatures based Paul's argument for the revealed commonality of Christians as new spiritual creatures. Paul taught that the divine activity was discernible in unity, the bond of love, which he judged lacking in the divided and divisive Corinthian church. Paul's referent was the Spirit; his purpose was spiritual community. He consistently taught that the exhalation of the Spirit's charism in speech should be prayer that edified by building up the community on the apostolic foundation he had laid.

Paul's letters to the Corinthians emphasized the ecclesiastical community of the human spirit. However, he did not dismiss an individual human possession of God, except for ethical misconduct, in favor of a corporate indwelling.[174] The distinction between God and humanity did not logically contradict the divine indwelling in individual persons. Paul did not deny that each human being had a created spirit or that each Christian was endowed with the Spirit at his baptism into the Church as Christ's body. He identified himself as a spiritual man, and he testified to his own extraordinary possession by the Spirit as a "man in Christ" snatched to paradise. Yet he only confessed his personal rapture toward resolving a communal conflict. His message to the Corinthians was unity in community, with an appreciation that their diverse gifts were all from the one Spirit, with love as the greatest gift. That church was fractured by partisan allegiances and personal claims to spiritual authority and authenticity. Paul concluded his second letter to the Corinthians with the blessing of "the fellowship of the Holy Spirit" (13:14), the unitive presence in the community.

That blessing foreshadowed the Christian doctrine of the Holy Spirit as the union of the Father and the Son in one God. The interpretation of that doctrine on a model of the human mind would radically develop but alter the biblical meaning of the human spirit. Paul, as a learned and devout Jew converted to Jesus the Christ, was faithful to Genesis on the human spirit as created by the divine Spirit. Yet he wrote not systematically but situationally to a local church in crisis about its "spiritual" identity. Centuries later his words were revered as authoritative by the universal Church, but their meaning had become vague, even opaque. Temporal and cultural removal from his historical situation, and a lack of historical method for its recovery, were further disabled by ignorance of the biblical languages and want of consultation with their remnant scholars. Paul's a fortiori argument about spirits, toward the divine Spirit's knowledge to reveal Christ to human spirits, was lost in the Vulgate translation. Gaps in both skill and experience occasioned hermeneutical ingenuity. At this juncture the theological understanding of the human spirit became theoretical, although *theōria* was not a biblical word or concept. The theorizing of the biblical text was powered by an apologetics of pabulum, which judged Scripture to be divine baby talk that demanded human philosophical maturation. Without the historical method or linguistic knowledge to understand Paul's meaning in its Corinthian context, theologians speculated toward universal applications.

Spirit was converted to soul, with the contemplation of God as its proper end. Paul's rapture, which commended him to the Corinthians as spiritual, became the philosophical model for the body-soul relationship, although he explicitly rejected such usage. Exegesis of his revelatory verses deliberated in detail the faculties of the soul, whether imaginative or intellectual. By a useful accommodation of philosophy, theology achieved beneficial insights into human existence. But it unknowingly suppressed the biblical sense of the human spirit by translating its vitality to the soul. The existential relation spirit-to-Spirit became epistemological. Love, which Paul extolled as the greatest spiritual gift, was reduced to the motivation for and the beautification of knowledge. The alteration of text to theory clouded Paul's pastoral mirror. Paul upheld a metaphorical mirror to the Corinthians, the principal manufacturers of mirrors, not about a theological "enigma" but about a commonplace "riddle," the riddle of the sphinx. After all, the most famous Corinthian was Oedipus, who solved it: a human in the developing ages from child, to adult, to elder. Paul presented himself as a model of spiritual progress from childhood to adulthood. He summoned the Corinthian church to a similar maturation in its charismatic gifts: from the privileged viewpoint of one's own face to a communal perspective face-to-face. The apostle's moral lesson would become theorized into a distinction between the obscure knowledge of God in this life and the beatific vision of him in the next. That theory would be cited to promote and justify a medieval ideal of contemplation.

Part II

MEDIEVAL THOUGHTS

CHAPTER 3

Augustine

"The grace of the Lord Jesus Christ and the love of God and the fellowship of the Holy Spirit be with you all" (2 Cor. 13:14). Paul's parting blessing on the Corinthians foreshadowed a patristic development of Trinitarian doctrine that the writings of the bishop Augustine (354–430 C.E.) would crown.[1] Theologians had articulated a Christian belief in Father, Son, and Spirit as three Persons in one God.[2] Augustine's meditation on that Trinity was his mature reflection on humans created in Genesis 1:26 in the image and likeness of God. Convinced of the superiority of philosophy to the rhetoric he had practiced professionally before his conversion to the Catholic faith,[3] Augustine philosophized the biblical human spirit. For his translation of Scripture to his Latin culture, he did not know Hebrew, although he cited some words[4] and his native Punic was a Semitic language. As for Greek, he admitted in *De trinitate* (On the Trinity) that "we are not so familiar with the Greek language as to be capable in any way to discover by reading and understanding the books on such matters."[5] His study of the Trinity was from Latin patristic texts, which he found insufficient to the subject, although he cited Hilary's treatise with hesitant approval.[6] Augustine's biblical citations were in Latin translation from mixed manuscripts. The first book of *De trinitate* cited from the Itala (Vetus Latina) Bible, his stated preference for its close literalness.[7] Despite some controversy with Jerome, editor of the later Vulgate Bible, its subsequent books cited that version.[8] Augustine relied in *De trinitate* on Paul's letters to the Corinthians more than any other New Testament book, save for John's gospel.[9] His preferred Itala version was his source for all Pauline citations.[10]

EXEMPLAR

Emboldened to defend Catholicism from the heresies that occasioned his treatise, Augustine burned with admiration for Paul's steadfast ministry so eloquently boasted to the Corinthian church.[11] The motive for Augustine's *De trinitate* was not speculative any more than Paul's letters to it had been. It was a polemic provoked, Augustine wrote, by the stupidity and sophistry of carnal minds that invented errors about God, who was truly one and triune.[12] Yet Augustine's book became speculative as he gazed into an innate mirror at himself. That introspection envisioned the human spirit in the mind.

Like Paul, he deprecated his knowledge and eloquence, he appealed to divine guidance, and he pleaded for human charity. Augustine immediately cited Paul's apology to the Corinthians, how he had known only Christ crucified and had come quaking among them to address them as fleshly infants, not spiritual adults. Augustine was comforted by Jesus's response to Paul's thorn in the flesh, that divine grace was sufficient and perfect in human weakness. Augustine the brilliant theologian willingly cast himself in the apostle's shadow. Paul was so vivid an exemplar that Augustine imagined him a personal proof of his own Trinitarian argument. Augustine considered that the rational soul (*animus*) must invent the bodily objects it has read about or heard of but not seen, just as it invents bodily outlines and shapes when it thinks. "For who reading or hearing what the apostle Paul wrote or those things written about him does not invent with his rational soul the face of the very apostle . . . ?" The multitudes who knew the literature thought of Paul's outlines and shapes variously, although their accuracy was unverifiable because the image might differ from the reality. Faith did not concern those imagined faces, however, but their actual lives and deeds. "For we have, as if according to rule, an impressed notion of human nature whereby when we see such an object we immediately know it to be a man or the form of a man."[13] Augustine's invention of Paul became his model for the process of the human mind in understanding the Trinity reflected in the mind itself. "How do we love by believing that Trinity that we do not know?" asked Augustine. "Is it according to a special or a general knowledge, according to which we love the apostle Paul?" He probed the question. Was it by the intimately known human species by which Christians believed Paul to have been a man that they loved him? No, he responded, because Paul was no longer a man since his soul had separated from his body in death. Augustine decided that what he loved in loving Paul was his "just rational soul." He theorized that particular inspiration to love Paul's form to argue for the soul's general love of the soul. "Behold," Augustine exclaimed, "there are three: the lover, the beloved, and the love." That trinity existed both in the fleshly body and in the rational soul.[14]

Augustine's admiration for the apostle Paul extended to citing from the biblical Acts of the Apostles the speech of Stephen, whose martyrdom had incited Paul's persecution of Christians before his conversion.[15] Both men were Christian converts, Paul from Judaism, Augustine from Manichaeism, an Oriental dualist heresy. It was Augustine's reading from Paul's letter to the Romans that prompted his famous moral conversion from concupiscence to chastity. That scene in his *Confessiones* was stormy, as the penitent tears flooding Augustine's face streamed his soul back to God.[16] But there was no thunder and lightning overhead, although Augustine cited them in *De trinitate* among examples of natural phenomena. He thought thunder and lightning were not a direct manifestation of God himself—as they had been for Paul on the road to Damascus—but only his creatures in the control of angels. Even the biblical storms on Mount Sinai that flashed about the divine presence Augustine reduced philosophically to transitory signs necessary to human sensation.[17] The smoky tent of meeting to whose open flap God descended to receive the ministry of the Israelite priest[18] was packed away in history. Augustine the Christian bishop sought refuge in another "tent" from "the confusion of tongues," that is, from "the chicaneries of heretics." That "tent" was "the correct faith of the Catholic Church."[19]

The flash that arrested Augustine's attention was not an extraordinary theophany but an ordinary intellection of truth. He summoned his soul, burdened by the body and even by thought, to try to see that "God is truth." The light of that truth was not perceived by eyesight, however. Augustine forbade asking for the nature of truth since misty images and cloudy phantasms would disturb the serenity of enlightenment "at the first blink when I said to you, 'truth.'" He admonished, "Look, remain if you can in that first blink by which like a flash you saw when 'truth' was spoken to you."[20] That epistemology remembered Augustine's initial exercise in his *Confessiones* toward contemplation as inspired by some Platonist manuscripts. His reading of Scripture would convince him that Platonism was not the sure and saving method; only Christ was. Augustine nevertheless related how initially his youthful reasoning progressed gradually "from bodily matters" to the sentient soul, to its reason, to its judgment, to its intelligence, to "that which is." He approached that ontological end, he wrote, "in a blink of blurry sight." Although the frailty of his soul rebuffed the contemplation of pure existence, he learned that God existed, as eternal, unchanging, and the source of all existence. Augustine identified that supreme being as the biblical God by citing his voice to Moses from the burning bush, "I am who I am" (Ex. 3:14).[21] He significantly identified Moses's experience by citing Paul's metaphor for the Corinthians of a mirror. Augustine interpreted it as a glimpse of God's eternity "'in an enigma through a mirror.'"[22]

Augustine in *De trinitate* rehearsed many topics from the Corinthian letters that bore on Paul's association of the human and divine spirits. To admonish his own readers against idolatry, for example, Augustine similarly reminded them that the body was a "temple of the Holy Spirit." But exceedingly he yearned for the dissolution of bodily restraints, when God would be seen not as a reflected likeness in a burnished mirror but in a "face-to-face" encounter. The standard translation of Paul's verse 1 Corinthians 13:12 is not historically literal but theologically dependent on Augustine's influential exegesis, "For now we see in a mirror dimly, but then face to face." That interpretation about a puzzling comprehension in a mirror prompted Augustine to pray for help with his Trinitarian topic and for forgiveness for his inadequacy to it.[23]

Yet their pastoral purposes greatly differed. Paul had endeavored to discern practically the authentic charismatic activity of the Spirit in the Corinthian church as its bond of love. Augustine acknowledged those spiritual gifts and the need for their discernment.[24] But he employed Paul's articulation of the gifted utterances of wisdom and knowledge to distinguish between wisdom as the knowledge of divine truths for contemplation and science as the knowledge of human affairs for action.[25] Augustine's precise intention was to identify that same Spirit, bestower of gifts on the Church, as a Person in the triune God equal with the Persons of the Father and the Son, who bestowed that personified Gift on humans. Augustine's emphasis was on the shared equality of the Spirit with the Father and the Son as their bond of love. His topic of divine triune unity differed from Paul's topic of human ecclesiastical unification. Augustine's appropriation of the Pauline verses in abstraction from their historical practical context for the Corinthians altered their meaning in Christian theology.

Augustine's major composition *De trinitate* was probably late,[26] during his episcopacy at Hippo in North Africa, his native Roman province. His ministry to its Catholic Church was challenged by Manichaean, Donatist, Pelagian, and Arian heretics, the refutation of whose errors consumed his writings. Augustine announced the orthodox purpose of *De trinitate* as to "reason, as much as we can, that the Trinity is the one and only and true God, and that rightly the Father and Son and Holy Spirit are said to be of one and the same substance or essence."[27] He professed to teach "according to the Scriptures that the Father and the Son and the Holy Spirit of one substance in an inseparable equality attain a divine unity."[28]

TRINITY

Augustine revered the biblical verse of Genesis 1:26 about the creation of humans in the divine image.[29] But he believed that image was of the Trinity, not of the one God *'ĕlōhîm*. Despite the plurality of its form, biblical Hebrew *'ĕlōhîm* was used as a singular noun that referenced "the gods," "a god," or "God,"[30] as in Genesis 1:2, where *'ĕlōhîm* meant the one God. Augustine thought preferable to the Hebrew biblical manuscripts their translation into Greek in the Septuagint Bible. He respected the Septuagint as a unanimous collaboration of seventy Jewish men guided by the Holy Spirit, perhaps so for the future use of those Jewish books by Gentiles.[31] It translated Hebrew *'ĕlōhîm* customarily as Greek *theos*, one God.[32] However, Augustine premised the Trinity not on that exemplar of Genesis 1:2 but on the later verse 26. As he argued, "For, if the Father only without the Son had made man, it would not have been written 'Let *us* make man to our image and likeness.'" The plurality of "let us (*faciamus*)" and "our (*nostrum*)" was latent language for the Trinity, he thought.[33] Augustine had already presented that interpretation in his commentary *De Genesi ad litteram* (On Genesis grammatically). There he stated that Genesis 1:26 insinuated a triune Creator God: the Father, the Son as the Word, and the Spirit as the pleasure of goodness. The phrase "in our image" implied God's Trinity, while the phrase "to the image of God" designated God's unity.³⁴

Augustine's grammatical reading was different from the ancient biblical context of the divine council, in which Israel's God was superior to the gods of other nations.³⁵ The biblical verse originally denoted the subsequent creation of humans in a Godlike image of Israelites, not a Trinitarian image of Christians. Reflecting on the verse "Let us make man to our image and likeness," Augustine argued retrospectively in *De trinitate* from his Trinitarian belief. "Certainly because 'our (*nostram*)' is plural in number it would not be said correctly if humanity were made to the image of one person, either the Father, or the Son, or the Spirit." The phrase "to our (*nostram*) image" thus indicated "to the image of the Trinity." He explained further that, to obviate a false belief in three gods in that Trinity, the next verse affirmed the divine unity by adding "and God made man to the image of God." Genesis 1:26 became the premise of Augustine's reflection on the Trinity as the divine Creator of the human image. "And truly that image of which it is said, 'Let us' make man to our (*nostram*) image and likeness,' because it is not said 'to my (*ad meam*)' or 'thy (*tuam*)' we believe that man was made to the image of the Trinity." Augustine intended to comprehend that truth as much as possible by his investigation.³⁶

Augustine's interpretive principle for the Trinity, as derived from the Persons of the Nicene Creed, was that "through the many modes of divine expressions what is said of one is said of all because of the inseparable operation of the one and same substance."³⁷ Thus, the particular biblical role of a Creator Spirit in Genesis 1:2 was subsumed into the Trinity of Christian faith. Augustine had inquired in his *Confessiones* whether in that verse the Spirit, but not the Father and the Son, moved above the waters. He decided that, if the movement was by the unchangeable Godhood above every changeable reality, then the Trinity acted. Asking why only the Spirit was named, he considered that the verse was written as if the Spirit above creation was in a place, although the Spirit was placeless. The Holy Spirit of the Trinity, as Gift, was the place of repose for humans who were borne aloft there by divine charity.³⁸ As Augustine argued further in *De trinitate*, the Holy Spirit was not alone in the Trinity called "spirit" because the Father and the Son were also spirit. Yet, because the Spirit was "common to both, he himself is properly called that which is common to both."³⁹

Augustine allowed certain activities to be attributed appropriately to the individual Persons of the Trinity—Father, Son, Spirit. But he reasoned from the prologue to John's gospel for the creation happening through the Son, the Word (*Verbum*). "All things were made through him, and without him nothing was made" (John 1:3).[40] Nevertheless, Augustine conceded that God operated by "the steadfast methods of his Word, co-eternal to himself" and also "by the warming of his equally co-eternal Holy Spirit." In comparison with Augustine's emphasis on the role of the Word in creation,[41] he commented briefly on Genesis 1:2 about the Spirit over the waters at creation. He remarked that, while the Latin bible translated the Greek as *superferebatur*, the Syriac version had *fovebat*. That latter choice, he explained, did not refer to the fomenting of diseased bodily tumors or wounds with hot or cold water. Rather, it signified the brooding of eggs by the hen's maternal body so that chicks might be formed by her care.[42] Augustine considered the Holy Spirit relatively to the Father and the Son, as their Gift. And through an examination of the human mind's love of its knowledge he explored the meaning of the Holy Spirit as their mutual love. Just as Paul had instructed the Corinthians that the greatest spiritual gift was love, so Augustine reasoned that love was not only from God but also was God. Properly, love was the Holy Spirit, through whom it was given to humans as an indwelling of the Trinity.[43]

Augustine affirmed all creation as lovable by reiterating the anaphora "good" sixteen times to advance from particular goods to God as the "good of every good." He marveled at creation visibly unfolding from invisible seeds, but he insisted that better than natural philosophy was self-knowledge. For it was roundabout to ascend to the heights of the heavens and descend to the depths of the earth searching for God when he was "with us." Moreover, any human distance from God was not spatial but affective. People strayed externally from themselves, deserting their internal realties, while God was present in their very interior.[44] Augustine knew that deviation from personal experience. His *Confessiones* narrated his own round-trip journey from a Catholic upbringing, to Manichaean stolen waters, to a safe landing in the port of Catholic orthodoxy.

Augustine in *De trinitate* interpreted the Delphic oracle "Know thyself" as meaning that self-knowledge measured and minded the distinction between mortal humans and immortal gods.[45] As in its Christian understanding, he acknowledged that humans should live according to their created nature subject to God.[46] But he followed Cicero's specific interpretation of the oracle, that to know oneself was to know one's mind.[47] Augustine encouraged the mind to perceive itself as present, so to distinguish itself from foreign knowledge. When the mind heard the oracle "Know thyself," it could not take care to heed it if it did not know what "know" or "thyself" were. For Augustine, to know the meaning of both those terms was to know oneself. For self-knowledge was not of the powerful but absent angels. Nor was it of the will of another human, whose intentions were imperceptible and incomprehensible without overt bodily signs—and even then, more believed than understood. As he continued, "Nor is a man told, 'Look at your face' because he cannot do so except in a mirror. For our very face is absent from our sight because it is not where that can be directed. But when it is said to the mind 'Know thyself,' it understands by that beat by which it understands what the saying 'thyself' is, that it knows itself." That knowledge happened simply because the mind was "present to itself."[48]

Augustine persevered to perceive the image of the Trinity in that human act of the mind knowing itself.[49] He cited from the rhetor Quintilian's *Institutio oratoria* a traditional definition, "man is a mortal and rational animal."[50] That definition, however, was merely incidental to Quintilian's example of a rhetorical persuasion of judgment that lacked a strict logical definition of the subject. As he taught, "Even without saying 'Man is a mortal and rational animal,' can I not set out all the properties of mind and body at greater length, and so draw a distinction between man and the gods or the dumb animals?"[51] Quintilian's treatise was composed for the education of schoolboys, a textbook that Augustine as a rhetor would have used as a resource.[52] Augustine's premise for interpreting the biblical image of God in humans at Genesis 1:26 was that extrabiblical commonplace. Among the methods he advocated for the interpretation of difficult verses of Scripture was their judicious comparison with clearer passages. Any resort to reasoning for clarification was a "dangerous usage." Interpreting Scripture by Scripture was much safer, he decided.[53] However, his argument did not search other biblical verses to clarify Genesis 1:26 as if it were a difficult verse to understand. Augustine cited, rather, a philosophical commonplace about humanity because to him that biblical verse of Genesis 1:26 was plain and simple. He indicated that the faculty of human reason as a divine endowment was knowable by reason itself. That interpretation was consistent with Augustine's conviction that not only Scripture but also creation was revelatory. He exhorted that God's substance was to be sought and loved in either and both sources, "for he inspired the one and created the other."[54]

Augustine thus conflated the biblical verse Genesis 1:26 with a philosophical commonplace to determine "that image that the creature is, is the rational soul (*animus*)."[55] It was "the true honor of humanity." He asserted "the perfectly truest reasoning that 'man was made to the image of God' not according to the form of the body but according to the rational mind (*mens*)."[56] As he explicated the Apostles' Creed, "And he made man to his image and likeness in the mind: there is God's image."[57] The image was not by equality but only by a certain similarity because humans did not know God as he knew himself. Self-knowledge by introspection was the definitive norm. Augustine's *De trinitate* reasoned for "a certain image of the Trinity: the very mind; and its knowledge, which is its offspring, and also its word about its very self; and love the third. And this one triad is also one substance."[58] Thus was the divine image reflected in the human mind.

What, then, was the human spirit? Augustine reviewed the semantics of "spirit" exegetically on the New Testament injunction to "be reformed in the spirit of your mind and assume the new man who has been created according to God" (Eph. 4:23–24). Its phrase "according to God" Augustine equivalated to the creation of humans in Genesis 1:26 "to the image of God." He explained that "in the spirit of your mind" did not name two distinct things, spirit and mind. Since every mind was a spirit, but not every spirit was a mind, he assumed that Paul needed to specify "the spirit of your mind." For God was a spirit, but he was not renewable because he was ageless; therefore, God's spirit was not Paul's reference. "Moreover, there is said to be a spirit in man that is not mind, to which pertain the like images of bodies, about which he told the Corinthians when he said, 'If, moreover, I should pray in the tongue, my spirit prays; my mind, however, is barren.'" Augustine interpreted that verse as about spiritual speech, which was not understood. He thought that intelligibility required spiritual thought to produce the images of bodily sounds that preceded the oral sound. Further, "The human soul (*anima*) is also called 'spirit,'" for example in the biblical verse about Jesus's death as the departure of his soul from his body. Augustine thought the spirit of a human was also paralleled with the spirit of a beast in Genesis, in the story of the flood, in which all flesh that had the spirit of life perished. Finally, "Spirit is also 'wind,' a very obviously bodily reality." Augustine concluded his review of Paul's attributed phrase "the spirit of the mind" by deciding it meant "that spirit that is called 'mind.'"[59]

MIND

Augustine's own reflections on the human "spirit" specified "mind." He determined basically that "the mind is not body but spirit." About the body he wrote, "There is doubtless in the human body a certain mass of flesh, and a species of form, and an order and distinction of members, and a balance of well-being. The soul (*anima*) rules the body and the same [soul] is rational. And therefore, however changeable, nevertheless that [soul] can be a partaker of that unchangeable wisdom, so that it may be 'its participation it in the self-same,'" who is God. The soul (*anima*) as "a spiritual creature" was simpler than the body, which was "manifold." The spirit was also preferable to the body because the death of the spirit meant that God had deserted it, while the death of the body meant that the spirit had deserted it. The soul (*anima*) was the life of the body, and again a "spiritual creature."[60] Thus, "soul" and "spirit" were somewhat interchangeable.

Augustine's ruling topic in *De trinitate* was the mind. The mind was rightly called "the principle of a human, that is, as if the head of the human substance, since with the mind a human is a human." For Augustine, that was not an essential anthropological definition. It was the human premise for his a fortiori argument about the divine Word, through whom the human mind was created. His full argument reads, "For *if* the mind is rightly called the principle of a human, that is, as if the head of the human substance, since with the mind a human is a human, why is it not exceedingly more fitting and more true [a fortiori] that the Word that is God with the Father is at the same time the head of Christ, although it is impossible to consider Christ the human unless with the Word that 'was made flesh.'"[61] Augustine thus projected an understanding of the Trinity from humanity, similar to Paul's a fortiori argument to the Corinthians about the propriety of self-knowledge by the human spirit and the divine Spirit. As Paul had argued, "For who of humans knows humanity if not the spirit of the human that is in him; so, the godhood of God no one perceives if not the Spirit of God (1 Cor. 2:11)." Paul and Augustine both employed rhetorical inference, not logical proof, from lesser to greater realities.

Yet Augustine disregarded the import of Paul's a fortiori argument, which was off his own Trinitarian topic. Augustine cited it in *De trinitate* only to criticize subversive thinkers who quoted it as "no one knows the things of God except the Spirit of God" to exclude the Son from that knowledge, and so demote his divine equality with the Spirit. However, the error Augustine censured was occasioned not by heretics but by the Vulgate translation *nisi*, "except." Greek *mē* there means "if not," to express exemplarity, not exceptionality. The biblical argument was a fortiori, "For who of humans knows humanity if not the spirit of the human that is in him; so, the godhood of God no one perceives if not the Spirit of God." Paul reasoned that no one understood humanity better than its spirit; a fortiori, no one understood God better than his Spirit. That was Paul's creational premise for the revelation of the crucified Jesus as Lord by the divine Spirit to the human spirit. Augustine interpreted Paul's a fortiori argument exclusively, "For the animal human cannot perceive the things that are the spirit of God."[62] That understanding differed from Paul's argument, which was in the biblical tradition of the human creature as a spirit related to its creator Spirit. In Paul's theological, rather than logical, argument a human was undefined essentially. It was posited relationally to God. But both spirits, human and divine, were realities.

Augustine assigned the human spirit to the mind. That mind operated in imitation of the Trinity, in the Father's thoughtful begetting of the Word and in their mutual love as the Spirit in that eternal relationship. Considering the human mind as an "imperfect image but nevertheless an image" of the Trinity, Augustine reasoned to a triad of "I myself loving, what is loved, and the love." The mind and its love were not two spirits or two essences but one. "Truly the mind and the spirit are not spoken relatively but demonstrate an essence. For, since mind and spirit exist in some man or other, therefore mind and spirit exist." Even "with the withdrawal of the body from a man, the mind and spirit remain." Paul had witnessed biblically to the human spirit as created by the divine Spirit. Augustine identified their relationship as existent in the mind. He examined the likeness of the mind to the species it knew, "wherefore insofar as we know God we are like him."[63] Augustine thus defined the relationship of the human creature to its Creator epistemologically.

Augustine reviewed his *De trinitate* as an exercise in examining created matters toward a knowledge of their Creator. Finally he ventured, "We arrive at his image, which is man, in that by which he surpasses the other animals, that is, by reason or intelligence, and whatever else can be said of the rational or intellectual soul that pertains to that reality that is called 'mind (*mens*)' or 'rational soul (*animus*).'" Augustine explained that some Latin writers called *animus* what excelled in humans and was missing from other animals, which had *anima*, or "soul." He affirmed, "Not the soul (*anima*) but what excels in humanity is called 'soul (*anima*).'" Augustine did not consider the human soul to be corporeal, however, as was the soul of lesser animals. For humans, he maintained that "the soul (*anima*) is a spiritual substance" because the Word created it. That divine causality did not explain how, since all creation was by the Word, animal souls were not also spiritual substances. Augustine summarized his speculation on the human mind as the principal part of the human soul. "The Trinity appears in the image of God that is man according to the mind, which 'is renewed in the knowledge of God according to the image of him who created' man to his image. Thus it perceives the wisdom where the contemplation of eternal realities is."[64]

Augustine peered into his own mind to perceive its image of the Trinity. His inspiration was Paul's message to the Corinthians, in the standard translation, "But now we see in a mirror dimly; but then face to face" (1 Cor. 13:12).[65] Literally the phrase *di esoptrou en ainigmati* translates "but now we see through a mirror in a riddle." The Authorized Version (1611), or King James Bible, popularized the dim rendering "through a glass darkly." However, Paul's metaphor did not reference a glass mirror of seventeenth-century usage but a metal mirror of the classical type. His term, *esoptron*, was not the standard Greek mirror, *katropton*, of either practicality or philosophy.[66] The Septuagint translated *esoptron* in Solomon's prayer for the gift of wisdom that praised its utility as divine mirror. "For she [wisdom] is a reflection of eternal light, a spotless mirror of the working of God, and an image of his goodness" (Wis. 7:26). Augustine cited the shiny mirror of that hymn to wisdom as "She is the brightness of the eternal light." It prophesied, he thought, the Father's begetting of the Son professed in the Nicene Creed as "light from light."[67] That biblical metaphor of wisdom as a mirror did not intimate Paul's reflection, however. He had come among the Corinthians, he proclaimed, to confound and upset the wisdom of the sages with the oxymoronic folly of Christ crucified.[68]

Just as Paul had referenced the Corinthian industry of terracotta lamps to typify Christians as fragile vessels of the enlightening Spirit,[69] so he upheld another local product, the mirror. Corinth was the classical center for mirror making because it was also the most famous foundry for bronze, its material.[70] By legend a unique Corinthian bronze was accidentally discovered when the Roman army sacked and burned that city, melting ordinary bronze—an alloy of tin and copper—with precious gold and silver. As Pliny related in *Historia naturalis*, the novel bronze, whether silvery or golden in composition and sheen, was an exceedingly admired and collected item.[71] Corinth was historically an important manufactury of ordinary bronze, made from ingots of tin and copper imported through its harbors. During the Roman Empire the city then excelled with a bronze uniquely high in tin.[72] Travelers disembarking at the port of Isthmia could have observed the bronze statue of the oceanic god Poseidon in its sanctuary, which had a foundry on-site tended by highly skilled craftsmen. Bronze statuary in athletic style was displayed in the city's forum.[73] When Paul visited the city, there were also large foundries in the gymnasium and west of the agora. Yet even before his arrival in Corinth, he would have been familiar with that item of civic pride. Corinthian commerce in the first century C.E. was substantial in the bronze trade, with the Jerusalem temple as a beneficiary. Its main entrance, facing the altar, was a splendid gate of Corinthian bronze, which exceeded in value and magnitude the nine lower gates overlaid in gold and silver.[74] It was the "beautiful gate" of the Acts of the Apostles, where Peter and John cured the beggar lame from birth.[75] Paul, as a Pharisaic rabbi, customarily entered the Jerusalem temple through that Corinthian gate. As a Christian convert, he would pass through it finally for his arrest by the Jews in that very temple.[76]

Paul upheld to the Corinthian church a special utilitarian object of local bronze, a mirror. Corinth had been the major factory for mirrors in every period since the sixth century B.C.E.,[77] so his church there would have appreciated his reference. A brazen mirror was a profound choice for Paul's reflection to the Corinthians for several reasons. Their bronzes traditionally had a sacral function in worship, their manufacture was technically imitative and repetitive, and the process began with modeling in clay. That medium was twice used, as the original working model of clay, then as a coarser investment of it applied in layers to each section of the subsequent wax model.[78] Clay was the matter from which the Creator fashioned Adam, and Paul imagined his Corinthian descendants as clay vessels of the enlightening Spirit.[79]

RIDDLE

Paul's *ainigma* in the brazen mirror was in classical Greek a "riddle, obscure saying," or a "problem."[80] The Septuagint translation of the Hebrew Scriptures used the word for unobvious speech, such as a parable or a saying requiring interpretation.[81] Paul's "enigma," his classical "riddle," continued a biblical tradition. The primary episode was the Lord's descent in a pillar of cloud to the flap of the Israelite tent of meeting that Bezalel constructed in the wilderness. As Paul knew, that tent was made with brazen parts and utensils. A particular material resource for Bezalel's craft were bronze mirrors. "And he made the laver of bronze and its base of bronze, from the mirrors of the ministering women who ministered at the door of the tent of meeting" (Ex. 38:1–8 RSV). With its brazen grating and poles, the tent imitated the heavens, for the Creator had "spread out the skies, / hard as a molten mirror" (Job 37:18 RSV). God summoned Moses, Aaron, and Miriam to his presence at that tent to remark that he spoke to prophets "in a vision" or "in a dream." However, God distinguished his speech to Moses. "Not so with Moses; he is entrusted with all my house. With him I speak mouth-to-mouth clearly, and not in dark speech (*ainigma*); and he beholds the form of the Lord" (Num. 12:8 RSV).

God's speech to prophets "in a vision" or "in a dream" recalled the patriarch Joseph as a seer among his Egyptian captors. Joseph interpreted the dreams of the pharaoh's butler and baker, then of the pharaoh himself, by attributing his art to God. As he declared to those servants, "Do not interpretations belong to God?" And then he said to their master, "It is not in me; God will give Pharaoh a favorable answer." In admiration of Joseph's gift of interpretation, "Pharaoh said to his servants, 'Can we find such a man as this in whom is the Spirit of God (*rûaḥ . . . 'ĕlōhîm*)?'

So Pharaoh said to Joseph, 'Since God has shown you all this, there is none so discreet and wise as you are; you shall be over my house, and all my people shall order themselves as you command; only as regards the throne will I be greater than you.' And Pharaoh said to Joseph, 'Behold, I have set you over all the land of Egypt'" (Gen. 40:1–41:43 RSV).

The biblical evidence of Joseph's character was primarily as a wise man who solved dreamed riddles.[82] The pharaoh entrusted Joseph with his Egyptian house because of his indirect interpretation by a divine gift of an obscure dream. However, God entrusted Moses with his Israelite house by his direct revelation in clear speech. The historical comparison between "now" and "then" in Paul's letter to the Corinthians about the riddle in the mirror was not Augustine's theological distinction between the temporal and the eternal knowledge of God. Paul allusively compared Joseph and Moses and their different modes of knowing God on earth—not in heaven—as indirect and direct. Paul cast the Corinthians in the tradition of Joseph, who had a riddle to solve, rather than of Moses, whom God addressed mouth to mouth. The "now" of Paul's contrast was to be like Joseph, the "then" was to become like Moses. Augustine himself was also a Joseph figure, for that is what his role as a "bishop" (*episcopus*) meant, an overseer of a house. His episcopal charge included the correction of heresies within the Church, a polemical purpose of his *De trinitate* and many other writings. Paul as the apostle to the Corinthians had also been concerned for correct belief, to promote the maturation of his foundling community beyond childish squabbling about prerogatives. His solution to their dissension was the practice of charity as the supreme spiritual gift. As he taught, knowledge would perish, while charity endured. Paul's calendar of "now" and "then" did not mark time versus eternity, as in Augustine's interpretation. It advised about what changed and what endured—both as values in time. The lesser charismata in the Corinthian church changed and faded; but faith, hope, and charity were stable and remained. And the greatest of those spiritual gifts was love.[83] No contemporary document survived to report the Corinthians' response. Paul's letters were early collected in the Roman province of Achaia, of which Corinth was the capital. But their meaning became detached from their historical contexts. An apocryphal third letter to the Corinthians in the sensational *Acts of Paul* was uninformative.[84] The fortune of Paul's letters became their selective exploitation as "a quarry of proof-texts ... through all subsequent centuries."[85] Corinth itself was reduced to rubble when seismic activity late in the fourth century devastated the once-thriving city. In the year of Augustine's succession to the bishopric of Hippo in 396 C.E., the Visigoth invaders under Alaric burned the remains of Corinth to the ground.[86] But Augustine's contemplative interpretation of Paul's communal mirror would endure through the centuries. It exemplified a theological transformation of the biblical human spirit.

One earthly material that did endure was Corinthian bronze because it resisted rusting.[87] The valuable material and beautiful craft of Corinthian bronze produced items that were collected with avaricious passion.[88] Their literary exemplar was the figure of a sphinx. Pliny's *Historia naturalis* recorded that type from the trial of Verres, a corrupt Roman governor whose counsel for the defense, Hortensius, owned such a sphinx. Quintilian's *Institutio oratoria* expounded the anecdote in his treatment of jokes. He offered as a historical example of learned jesting the prosecutor Cicero's quip to Hortensius during Verres's trial. During Cicero's examination of a witness Hortensius confessed, "I do not understand these riddles," to which protest Cicero retorted, "But you should, since you have a sphinx at home." Cicero referred to the bronze sphinx of great cost that Verres had given his counsel, probably a bribe from his plundered collection of Corinthian bronzes. Verres was executed for refusing to surrender his hoard.[89] The joke was the famous riddle of the sphinx. Although Augustine early knew and revered that Verrine oration as Cicero's "noblest,"[90] he did not associate its riddle of the sphinx with Paul's same riddle in the Corinthian mirror.

A classical mirror was a polished bronze disk that was usually concave, with a decorative handle, reverse, and rim. The largest class had the handle with a stand on a base for upright placement on a flat surface. The favorite support, of Corinthian design and manufacture, was the human figure of a draped female. Corinth originated most of the engraved mirrors, and among the popular, fanciful subjects for decorating their handles were sphinxes.[91] The Greek name *sphinx* derived from the Theban *sphinge*, a monster that differed from the Egyptian model, notably Giza's colossal sphinx.[92] The Theban sphinx was a hybrid of a woman's face, a lioness's breasted body, and an eagle's wings.[93] Although in art she was always winged, she was grounded, frequently perched on a column or a rock.[94] Her universal literary location was also a high place, a natural mountain or cliff, or the manmade Theban acropolis.[95] That altitude was consistent with her eagle's wings, which required height for takeoff in soaring flight.⁹⁶ Art depicted the sphinx's predation as pursuit, seizure, overpowering, and attack. Although literature did not describe the death she caused the youths who failed to solve her riddle, poets and mythographers employed the verb *harpazein* to intimate her rapacity. The sphinx was the "ravisher of men" for the dramatist Aeschylus, who coined the neologism *harpazanoran*. For Euripides, she was not merely the raptor but even rapture incarnate, who soared onto Theban heads.⁹⁷

The riddle of the sphinx was cited fully in Athenaeus's *Deipnosophistai* (Learned banquet) from Asclepiades' classical anthology, a mythographical source. "There walks on land a creature of two feet and four feet, which has a single voice. / And it also has three feet: alone of the animals on earth it changes its nature. / Of animals on the earth, in the sky, and in the sea. / When it walks propped on the most feet, / Then is the speed of its limbs least."⁹⁸ In legend the sphinx posed her riddle to Theban youths, then killed them for their incorrect answers. It was Oedipus who answered her riddle by native heroic intelligence.⁹⁹ His solution was "a human," who crawled on four limbs as an infant, walked erect on two legs as an adult, and hobbled with a cane on three supports as an elder. The scene of the sphinx with Oedipus, the solver of her riddle, was among the most popular in Greek art for more than three centuries, and it continued on Roman wall painting and stucco relief, sarcophagi, stamped ceramics and lamps, and as bronze statuary such as Verres possessed.¹⁰⁰

For enacting live the myth of Oedipus and the sphinx, Corinth had a classical theater from the late fifth century B.C.E., with a renovated stone stage after the founding of the Roman colony. Its theater was a public site for religious festivals, processions, and rituals, and also for political and social events.¹⁰¹ Corinthians had reason for favoring dramas about Oedipus, as did Paul for allusion to its riddle of the sphinx in his letter to their church. Oedipus, the solver of the riddle, was a Corinthian, the greatest citizen, albeit by the adoption that premised his tragedy. The myth was best told in Sophocles's *Oedipus tyrannus* (Oedipus the tyrant),¹⁰² the most influential drama in the global history of the theater. As the hero who solved the riddle of the sphinx, Oedipus became a model of intellectual achievement who similarly fell on an intellectual error. In the tragic conclusion he embodied with his staff the final stage of the riddle—old age hobbling on three pegs.¹⁰³

In Sophocles's plot Oedipus unknowingly killed with his staff Laius, his true father. Further on his journey he encountered the sphinx, a "cruel singer" with "riddling demands," "the winged maiden," and "the oracle singer with her crooked talon claws."[104] She challenged him as a passerby to solve her riddle, or die. Oedipus's correct answer, "a human," forced her suicide. The grateful citizens of Thebes awarded him their queen, Jocasta, as a wife—unaware that she was his birth mother. Oedipus lamented, "Woe is me! How wretched I am, self-cursed / through my own ignorance!"[105] The theme of the tragedy was self-knowledge as identity by parentage. As the classical paradigm of the tragic hero, Oedipus was himself the answer to the riddle of the sphinx. Sophocles's drama recalled him as an infant unable to walk on his pierced feet, as an active adult journeying to seek his identity, and as a blinded elder with a cane.[106] Such were the stages of human life—the "ages of man"—in which modes of movement changed.[107] The plot depended on the Delphic oracle, who prophesied to a horrified Oedipus his parricide and incest.[108] The tragedy ultimately devolved to the Delphic oracle "Know thyself," the command to honor the distinction between humans and gods.[109] Oedipus's self-knowledge was not Augustine's epistemological analysis but, rather, physical security in biological parentage. Oedipus's search was for "the truth of my birth," meaning his humanity from sexual reproduction, not from created participation in divinity.[110]

MORAL

In Aristotle's poetics Oedipus's tragic flaw, *hamartia*, literally meant "to miss the mark." He echoed Sophocles's prophet Tiresias, who early criticized Oedipus with "I see your words fall wide of the mark and miss their aim."[111] In Paul's letters to the Corinthians *hamartia* was not error but sin, sin from which Jesus's death saved them. Paul's context for the riddle in the mirror was their boasting and contention about the Spirit's varied distribution of charismatic gifts among them. In a Corinthian mirror Paul spied a riddle for that church to solve, the most famous classical puzzle, the riddle of the sphinx. Paul urged the Corinthians to a maturation toward charity as the Spirit's greatest gift. He wrote them that he could not address them as spiritual adults but only as fleshly ones, indeed "Christian babies." Because of their divisiveness, he explained, "I fed you with milk, not solid food; for you were not ready for it; and even yet you are not ready" (1 Cor. 3:1–3 RSV). He exhorted the

Corinthians not to be childish but mature in their thinking. Paul's metaphorical mirror was of moral purpose. It extended his hymn to love as the supremely enduring gift, in comparison with speaking in tongues, which signified to unbelievers, and speaking in prophecy, which signified to believers. Tongues would cease, and knowledge would pass, for both were imperfect.[112] As Paul affirmed, "When I was a child, I spoke like a child, I thought like a child, I reasoned like a child; when I became a man, I gave up childish ways. For now we see through a mirror in a riddle [not RSV "dimly"], but then face to face. Now I know in part; then I shall understand fully, even as I have been fully understood. So faith, hope, love abide, these three; but the greatest of these is love" (1 Cor. 13:8–13). That was a pastoral lesson, not an epistemological thesis.

Paul upheld an exemplary Corinthian mirror to his church members to view themselves in the various stages of life, yet still as one body. The hybrid sphinx of three parts—bird, beast, and human—afforded Paul a model of multiple identities in one body. Oedipus's answer to her riddle, a human by a single name who moved differently in the progressive stages of life—infant, adult, elder—suited Paul's lesson about unity in diversity. Oedipus's issue of true identity by parentage also addressed the ecclesiastical quarreling. Paul's legitimacy as their father in the faith was questioned by Corinthian factions who identified other apostles as their authorities. Admonishing them as his "beloved children," Paul declared, "For though you have countless guides in Christ, you do not have many fathers. For I became your father in Christ Jesus through the gospel. I urge you, then, be imitators of me" (1 Cor. 10:10–17; 4:14–16 RSV). He also taught them the essential difference between being sons of Adam, born for dust, and sons of Christ, reborn for glory. And, as in the Oedipus myth, Paul censured among them the crime of incest. "It is actually reported that there is immorality (*porneia*) among you, and of a kind that is not found even among pagans; for a man is living with his father's wife" (1 Cor. 5:1 RSV). Paul then upbraided the Corinthians for being "arrogant," rather than mournful, about it, and he ordered the banishment of the offender from the church.[113]

Augustine's *De trinitate* theorized universally Paul's local mirror of behavior. Augustine saw the Corinthian mirror's enigma as a rhetorical similitude, not as a puzzle like the riddle of the sphinx. That similitude was the human mind as a reflection of its Creator's divine mind. Augustine praised wisdom as "an incorporeal substance and a light in which we see what is not seen by fleshly eyes." He then relied on Paul's metaphor to substantiate contemplation. "And yet a man so great and also spiritual: 'We see now,' he said, 'through a mirror in an enigma but then by face to face.'" Inquiring into Paul's mirror, Augustine concluded that it surely meant that "in a mirror nothing but an image is perceived." As he explained, "If we seek what sort and what might be this mirror, the fact surely occurs that in a mirror nothing is descried except in an image. Therefore we have tried to do this, so that through this image that we are we might somehow see by whom we are made, just as if through a mirror."[114]

Augustine would have known of Oedipus the riddle solver and also about Boeotian riddles from comedy, where the Oedipus myth first emerged in Roman culture.[115] It was from those plays that Augustine learned Latin, and later as imperial grammarian he taught them to the new boys.[116] Various other sources, notably Seneca's tragedy *Oedipus* and Statius's *Thebaid*, also transmitted the myth.[117] Augustine wrote of the *sphinge* in *De civitate Dei contra paganos* (On the city of God against the pagans) twice. Cataloguing the monsters of classical mythology, he related that "Oedipus, having solved what a certain monster called Sphinge, a quadruped with a human face accustomed to pose a seemingly insoluble question, forced her to perish by her fall."[118] The detail of the toppling of the sphinge by a fall copied Apollodorus's mythographical *Bibliotheca*.[119] Augustine reflected further on the status of deformed humans, as they were portrayed from books on the mosaic in Carthage's seaside street. He decided that those monsters were Adam's descendants, for they were still rational and mortal animals. However, he excluded from Adamic descent the hybrid sphinx, although it bore a human face. "But sphinxes are not humans but beasts."[120]

Augustine's understanding of Paul's "enigma" or any "enigma" was detached from the sphinx's riddle, however. He wrote that what the sphinx posed to Oedipus was "an apparently insoluble question (*velut insolubili quaestione*)." As for the image in Paul's mirror, when Augustine reflected on the quality of the human vision of God in the next life, he quoted the letter to the Corinthians for "enigma."[121] He did not understand Paul's enigma precisely as a riddle. Augustine's *De doctrina christiana* (On Christian teaching), his biblical hermeneutics, concerned "solving the enigmas of the Scriptures." It equated "allegory or enigma," and it classified as tropes "allegory, enigma, parable."[122] In his exegesis

Augustine defined an "enigma" as a "similitude," "an obscure parable that is understood with difficulty." It was "an ununderstood question," "a certain obscure figure of things."[123] He sought to pilgrimage beyond the mirror and enigma to the species where God would be seen face-to-face.[124] Those synonyms for *ainigma* were consistent with classical usage.[125] Augustine's particular example was not classical but biblical, however, "Solomon's enigma." Augustine rued his seduction among the Manicheans by folly personified, who counseled, "Stolen water is sweet and bread eaten in secret is pleasant" (Prov. 9:17).[126] Augustine the rhetor explained Paul's mirror as an obscure allegory called an "enigma." In reviewing *De trinitate*, Augustine stated that he had endeavored to see God through the image of the human creature as "through a mirror." He distinguished both semantically and phonetically between *speculum*, a "mirror," and *specula*, "a watchtower." He explained that Paul's metaphor intended "from an obscure form to a lucid form," when God would be seen "as he is."[127]

Such was Augustine's appropriation of Paul's mirror. He assumed that Paul's reference was personal not communal, theological not behavioral, and eschatological not temporal. Augustine's interpretation has become the exegetical consensus, as reflected in biblical translations of seeing a dim, indistinct, blurred, dark, or obscure image, in sum "a poor reflection."[128] Yet classical literature did not attest that a mirror was an imperfect and unsatisfactory medium for vision. On the contrary, it reported a mirror as clear and reliable.[129] By Augustine's influence, Paul's metaphor of mirrored vision came to signify the imperfect knowledge of God in this life, as compared to the perfect knowledge of God in the next life. Paul never stated, however, that the vision in the mirror now was of God, or that the vision then "face to face" would be of God. When he wrote to another church he founded, the Thessalonians, he desired to see *them*—not God—face to face. "But since we were bereft of you, brethren, for a short time, in person not in heart, we endeavored the more eagerly and with great desire to see you face to face; because we wanted to come to you—I, Paul, again and again." As he explained, "For what is our hope or joy or crown of boasting before our Lord Jesus at his coming? Is it not you? For you are our glory and joy" (1 Thess. 2:17–20 RSV). The glory and joy of the eternal life were already anticipated by the glory and joy of the temporal life of the church in communal love. Paul's mirror was not the only New Testament example. The letter of

James upheld a mirror practically, not theoretically, in advising believers to act against self-deception. "But be doers of the word, and not hearers only, deceiving yourselves. For if anyone is a hearer of the word and not a doer, he is like a man who observes his natural face in a mirror; for he observes himself and goes away and at once forgets what he was like" (James 1:22–24 RSV). James then classed those who presumed themselves to be religious but did not curb their tongues as vain deceivers,[130] much as Paul warned some boastful charismatics about self-deception.

MIRROR

Augustine's vision of Paul's mirror not only theorized its pastoral intention but also misrepresented a mirror's function. A mirrored image displays incorrectly the person looking into the mirror, for it reverses his figure laterally left and right. It thus reflects to the gazer not his accurate self—existentially as he is—but the view another person has of him—socially as he appears. Paul's mirror imaged how others saw oneself, not how someone saw himself. Paul's norm was not personal but social, a metaphor for how the Corinthian church viewed its charismatics and its sinners. His specific topic was the progressive ages from childhood to manhood, whose distinct stages he personally articulated. "When I was a child, I spoke like a child. I thought like a child. I reasoned like a child; when I became a man, I gave up childish ways" (1 Cor. 13:11–12 RSV). Immediately upon that distinction, in the next verse Paul raised the metaphorical mirror. He addressed the behavior proper to the growth of Christian life. His message concerned moral characterization, not intellectual theory. Paul's meaning and purpose was pastoral toward eliciting moral behavior, not meditative toward achieving theological understanding. His riddle in the mirror reflected the human body, as did the riddle of the sphinx, as possessing different powers of movement in different stages of life. His adverbs "now" and "then" were temporal on a trajectory of growth, but the human subject remained single although it grew continuously. Now the body was seen one way, then it would be seen in another way. Yet the reflection in the mirror was consistently human, not divine. Paul's face-to-face vision was the seeing and knowing of oneself as others in the church saw one. It was the true-to-life realization of the Christian self as social.

Paul taught charismatics to be responsible to the community by their spiritual maturation to love.

Paul's riddle in the mirror was consistent with the nature of a riddle, for a riddle was not only a literary genre but also a social contest. It was not, as in Augustine's interpretation of an enigma, a philosophical puzzle for a solitary solution. In the folkloric type of riddle, to which the sphinx's riddle belongs, the setting was public and so was the solution, with its civic consequences. A riddle required a live encounter between at least two persons, the riddler and the tested, and it was often interpreted communally.[131] Augustine changed the social face of Paul's mirror from the perception others had of oneself to one's personal vision of God. He also projected in the mirror an understanding of how a person viewed himself from how God envisioned him. However, a mirror was not an apposite model for Augustine's reference to the human mind. A mind is not visible in a mirror, although bodily gestures may indicate its animated operations. Yet even that reflection is of a physical expression, not a mental idea. A mirror is a physical object, whether its surface is natural (like still water) or manufactured. Its image is also physical, a reflection of the human body. Notably, a mirror reflects the face, which is not otherwise seen, because, as Augustine realized, the eyes are situated there. "The eyes have never seen themselves other than in mirrors." Augustine saw the mind in the mirror by abstraction. Although he classified the mind as "a spiritual substance (*substantia spiritalis*),"[132] he did not explain how a spiritual substance could be glimpsed in a physical mirror, even metaphorically.

For Augustine, what was spirit? His doctrine has been evaluated as the most comprehensive since Christian origins and as a historical turning point from corporeality toward spirituality. His achievement was deemed to be the total disengagement of spirit from matter so to understand the simplicity or indivisibility of the Supreme Being. Toward that theology the Bible has been claimed as his principal source because he derived the meanings of the word *spiritus* from it and because he discovered there its immaterial reality, although Platonism aided his elucidation of it.[133] Augustine declared in *De trinitate* that he would understand "the Holy Spirit according to the holy Scriptures," and he did so dynamically by considering the Church's experience of its gifts.[134] He did not identify the human spirit, with Genesis 1–2, as created life with a political alliance to the Creator Spirit. Augustine's premise was his philosophical determination that what defined God as spirit was immateriality. God was a simple substance. Since humans were not God, he distinguished them as an impure mixture of immateriality and materiality. A human was a dual substance. Augustine then defined the human spirit by its immaterial mind or soul, whose supreme, pure, infallible act was the intellectual vision of the immaterial. Yet he also associated that same mind or soul with materiality by a lesser, impure, fallible activity called spiritual vision. Augustine thus varied the designation "spirit" for humans.

In his commentary *De Genesi ad litteram*, written almost parallel to *De trinitate*, he explored the varied meanings of "spirit" by an interpretation of Paul's Corinthian letters. He inquired of the first verse of Genesis whether heaven was a spiritual creature and earth a material one, or whether both were material and its author had omitted the creation of spiritual beings. Or Augustine wondered whether spiritual life existed in itself, unturned to the Creator. As for a human, Augustine decided that he was "a creature truly spiritual and intellectual and rational." Those equivalences defined the human spirit as intellectual and rational, although neither word or concept was biblical. They were philosophical terms. The biblical story of God's delegation to humans as caretakers of creation Augustine converted to a philosophical distinction. He observed that once God decided in Genesis 1:26 to make humans in his image he immediately in the next verse bestowed on them power over the birds of the air and the other animals devoid of reason. Augustine argued, "Thus we plainly understand by this that humanity was made to the image of God in what surpasses the irrational animals. Moreover, that is reason itself, or mind, or intelligence, or by whatever word it is more properly named." Augustine cited the letter to the Ephesians on renewal "in the spirit of your mind" (Eph. 4:23–24), a verse that *De trinitate* explicated. He thought it demonstrated that a human was created to the divine image not by his bodily shape but as "a certain form of the illuminated intelligible mind." Considering the biblical stories of creation in Genesis, Augustine discredited the interpretation that a human was the preeminent species because God uttered other creatures whereas he fashioned Adam. For Augustine, human excellence consisted in the divine image. "This excels in a human, since God made man to his image on account of this, that he would give him an intellectual mind by which he would surpass the beasts." That image Augustine reiterated as not body but mind.¹³⁵ That appealed to the classical topic of erect bipedality for an indication of human mental dignity surpassing the quadrupeds.¹³⁶

Augustine addressed the biblical creation of Adam as a "living soul (*animam viventem*)" (Gen. 2:7). He explained that God "blew or puffed into his face the breath of life." Augustine refuted the belief that this breath was "part of God's soul or wholly God's substance." There was no divine analogy with human exhalation, in which the very soul expelling breath from the self moved the nature of the body from itself. Augustine identified the attribute of God as self-same as meaning "utterly immutable." He reasoned from it that God could not have transferred part of himself to the human soul when he breathed life into Adam. Even human breathing was the soul's movement of the body but not of the soul. Reciprocal breaths took and returned the surrounding air, yet not from the soul but from the body. Thus, God's breath was not the human soul, although God's breath made the human soul. Therefore, the soul was the breath of God but not from his nature and substance. God's spirit proceeding from him and breathing forth was not his bodily breath but the human soul. God made the soul by breathing not from himself as from a body, but by taking from the air, a creature that was subject to him.¹³⁷

SOUL

Augustine wondered whether God made the soul from nothing or from something spiritual that was not yet a soul. Was the creation of the soul analogous to the creation of Adam's body from dust? What would that spiritual matter be, if it existed? Augustine pondered its name, form, and use; whether it was alive or not; its activity, whether happy or miserable; where it rested in secret leisure; if living, how rational, and how distinct from the life of a beast. He asked whether the spiritual matter was the possibility but not the faculty of reason. Was it like an infantile soul, which was called rational, although not yet functional? Was it a sort of quiet, as in the mode of reasoning? His tenderest question, because it arose from his troubled personal search for God, inquired whether the spiritual life from which the soul was made was happy. Augustine was certain that, if it was happy, then its transfer into a human body was by an inferior flowing. He decided that the material of the human soul was not an irrational soul. Nor was the human soul made by God's breath taken from air. Although breath belonged to that element, only human, not divine, breath was physical.[138]

As he reasoned, the soul was incorporeal, however, so that it was not made from elemental air or fire, although they were the finest elements through which the soul governed the body. In sum, the biblical verse that "the human was made a living soul" (Gen. 2:7) denoted for Augustine the beginning of sensation in the body. That was "the most certain indicator of animate and living flesh." God breathed into Adam's face because only the face had the organs of all five senses. Augustine deliberated further on the soul as a spiritual creature. "Whatever the soul is, it is not of those four very well-known elements, which obviously are bodies, but it is also not what God is. What it may be, moreover, is not better said than 'soul (*anima*)' or 'spirit of life (*spiritus vitae*).' Therefore, 'of life' is added because elemental air itself is often called 'spirit.'" Although before his Catholic conversion Augustine was a professional grammarian, he judged it "difficult to find a noun by which to distinguish properly that nature that is neither body nor God; not life with sensation, which type is credible in trees; nor life without the rational mind, which exists in beasts; but a life now lesser than the angels and in the future that of the angels, if it should live by the commandments of its Creator." Augustine doubted the material origin of the soul, or its emanation from a substance, or its creation from nothing. He concluded that "if it was anything before, it was made by God what it was, and now it is made by God so that it may be a living soul: for either it was nothing, or this which it is was not."[139]

He identified the parent of the human soul as some spiritual creature, so that soul derived from spirit. In that spiritual creature might exist the reasonable cause (*ratio*) of the future soul, which was not then existent unless God made it for the purpose of being inspired into a human. Augustine proposed that the rational cause of the body was created in the works of the six days as the material elements, but the rational cause of the soul was created on the first day. "Created, it lay hidden in the works of God until in its time for breathing it, that is for inspiring it, he would insert it, having formed the body from the mud." The making of the soul "from spiritual matter" was fitting for belief, he thought. Augustine concluded, "About the soul, which God imparted to the human creature by breathing in his face, I confirm nothing, except that it exists thus from God so that it is not the substance of God, yet is incorporeal; that it is not a body but a spirit, nor born from the substance of God nor proceeding from the substance of God, but made by God." The soul was not made by the conversion of a bodily nature or irrational soul, and through that from nothing. The soul was a hybrid of the mortal and the immortal.[140]

But if the human soul was a spiritual creature, as Augustine decided, what was a spirit? and what in particular was the human spirit? Augustine examined the term "spirit" in the final book of *De Genesi ad litteram*. He began by acknowledging that the word "spiritual (*spiritale*)" was polysemous. Although its classical usage pertained to breath, wind, or air, Augustine applied its ecclesiastical usage.[141] That reference had been established by the first Christian Latin writer, Tertullian, and *spiritale* was also the Vulgate translation for the *sōma pneumatikon*, or "spiritual body," of Paul's first letter to the Corinthians.[142] The Corinthian letters were a primary source for Augustine's grammatical commentary on Genesis. The first letter was the most frequently cited of the New Testament books in the initial half of his commentary, and it was cited second only to Romans in its latter half. Augustine noted of Paul's verse that he called "spiritual" even the future body of the resurrected saints. Augustine interpreted that spiritual body to mean a bodily—not unbodily—substance marvelously subject to the spirit and vivified by it alone without bodily food. It was "a body, not a soul, because it is called 'animal.'"[143] Augustine's exegesis conflated Paul's distinction between the ensouled body and the spiritual body. As Paul taught the Corinthians, "What is sown an ensouled body (*sōma psychikon*), is raised a spiritual body (*sōma pneumatikon*)" (1 Cor. 15:44). For Paul, who coordinated the two creation stories of Genesis, about God's speaking humans in the divine image and likeness and about inbreathing life into Adam, no human was a brute physical animal. As animate, a human was already divinely ensouled, unlike the lesser animals under his care.

Augustine continued that "'spirit (*spiritus*)' was called either the air itself or its breath, that is, its movement." He referenced for physical elements the psalm verse "Fire, hail, snow, ice, the spirit of the storm" (Ps. 148:8). Moreover, he wrote, "spirit" is called the soul (*anima*), whether that of beast or human, just as was written, "Who knows whether the spirit of man goes upward and the spirit of the beast goes down to the earth" (Eccl. 3:21).¹⁴⁴ That biblical verse was preceded by an equation of beast and human. "For the fate of the son of men and the fate of beasts is the same: as one dies, so dies the other. They all have the same breath, and man has no advantage over the beasts, for all is vanity. All go to one place; all are from the dust, and all turn to dust again" (vv. 19–20 RSV). Thus was Augustine prompted to equate their breaths and their spirits. However, Paul's belief in the resurrection of the dead had rejected that common fate of the biblical wisdom literature. He taught the Corinthians that humans created from Adam's dust were not ultimately subject to decay as were the other animals. As Christians, they were re-created in the second Adam's glory to be raised with him from the dead. Moreover, human breath was not merely identical to animal breath for physical respiration. It had been imparted by God to Adam for an existence superior to the other animals.¹⁴⁵ Augustine did not disbelieve the resurrection from the dead, and he pondered the meaning of that divine breathing to Adam. But he interpreted Scripture distinctly and significantly by identifying the human spirit as the soul, and the soul as the rational mind.

Augustine defined the human spirit decisively and influentially as mental. "'Spirit' is said of the rational mind itself, where it is as if a certain eye of the soul, to which pertains the image and knowledge of God." As apostolic evidence he cited the biblical letters to the Ephesians and the Colossians, "Be renewed in the spirit of your mind and put on the new human, who is created according to God" (Eph. 4:23–24), since in another passage it is also said about the interior human, "who is renewed in the knowledge of God according to the image of him who created him" (Col. 3:10).¹⁴⁶ Neither of those letters is accepted in modern biblical scholarship as Paul's authentic writing or theology.¹⁴⁷ Augustine, lacking historical method, compiled his arguments from disparate biblical texts. Paul himself had done the same. The method was not illegitimate, for the Bible was a big book, open for fruitful reflection by textual comparison. But such collation of texts allowed for some confusion in composing a line of argumentation.

The biblical phrase "the spirit of your mind" Augustine examined in *De trinitate* as distinct from other uses of the word "spirit."¹⁴⁸ However, that phrase did not equate, as Augustine supposed, the human mind with the human spirit. Its Greek was *tō pneumati tou noos humōn*. Its context in Ephesians was compatible with Paul's authentic message to the Corinthians, for it taught a single source of the various gifts of the Spirit for the edification of the Church. That passage in Ephesians also reinforced Paul's ideal for the Corinthians of maturation from childhood toward adulthood. It counseled spiritual progress "to mature manhood, to the measure of the stature of the fullness of Christ, so that we may no longer be children, tossed to and fro and carried about with every wind of doctrine." Its author compatibly urged the Ephesians to "speak the truth in love," so that "we are to grow up in every way into him who is the head, into Christ, from whom the whole body, joined and knit together by every joint with which it is supplied, when each part is working properly, makes bodily growth and upbuilds itself in love" (Eph. 4:1–16 RSV).

However, it continued by paralleling "in the spirit of your minds (*tō pneumati tou noos humōn*)" with "the futility of their minds (*en mataiotēti tou noos autōn*)" (vv. 17–24 RSV). Those phrases contrasted Christians and Gentiles behaviorally. They did not identify or distinguish psychologically the types of minds the Christians had from those the pagans had. They accused the Gentiles of living with darkened or dizzy purpose, remote from the life of God because of their hard-hearted ignorance. They were eager for licentiousness. Christians, in contrast, were exhorted to be humans renewed to live in holiness. That biblical argument concerned opposite ways of living, moral versus immoral. Augustine altered it to a philosophical dictum about the human spirit as universally mental. He also claimed for support that Paul did not distinguish between mind and spirit in affirming to the Romans that "I myself with the mind serve the law of God, but with the flesh the law of sin." However, that verse did not mention the spirit. Augustine's discussion of spirit noted finally that John's gospel also called God "spirit."[149] He associated the human spirit with that divine spirit mentally, although Scripture did not equate God's spirit with his mind. It introduced the Spirit in Genesis 1:2 soaring over the waters, from which superior vantage over other gods he commanded creatures into existence.

Augustine's review of the meanings of "spiritual" developed from his examination of Paul's extraordinary experience of a rapture revealed to the Corinthians. The apostle's account of how he was seized to paradise, where he heard ineffable words, fascinated Augustine. He pondered how Paul could have protested ignorance of his state, whether in or out of the body. Augustine articulated three kinds of vision: sensual by the eyes of a present physical object, spiritual by the imagination of an absent physical object, and intellectual by the perception of an imageless abstract object. He designated spiritual vision "whatever is not a body and yet is something, is rightly called spiritual." That definition determined his discussion of "spiritual." He argued, however, that none of those meanings of "spiritual" applied to Paul's extraordinary vision of God. Rather, he thought it spiritual in the singular sense of Paul's distinction to the Corinthians between the mind and the spirit. As Augustine cited Paul's hymn to love, "If I should pray in a tongue my spirit prays, but my mind is barren" (1 Cor. 14:14). Augustine interpreted "tongue" as obscure and mystical meanings that, in the absence of the mind's intellect, edified no listener. The tongue presented meanings as if they were the images and likenesses of things that required mental perception for understanding them. The tongue was the bodily member moved in the mouth in speaking, so to produce the signs of things but not the things themselves. Augustine supposed that Paul employed the word "tongue" by transference for any utterance of things before they were understood. Such utterances were exclusively spiritual. Although they happened in the soul, they were not mental. It was the intellectual accession to things, which was proper to the mind, that became revelation, knowledge, prophecy, or teaching. Such understandings were greater than spiritual visions, which were by that distinction not understood.[150]

STATUS

Augustine identified the spirit as the intermediate part of the soul, and he reduced its function to imagination and babble. He judged spiritual vision greater than corporeal vision, but lesser than intellectual vision. Augustine interpreted the biblical "image and likeness" of humans to their Creator in Genesis 1:26 as mentation. Although the stories of the creation in Genesis did not explicate either a divine mind or the human mind in its imitation, Augustine inferred mind from intelligible divine and human actions. Persons to whom signs of bodily things were shown in the spirit, but whose minds did not understand them, were not yet prophets. Moreover, an interpreter was more a prophet than a seer was because prophecy was more mental than spiritual. Augustine meant "spiritual" properly speaking as "a certain power of the soul inferior to the mind where likenesses of bodily things are produced." In his example, the biblical patriarch Joseph, who understood the meaning of the pharaoh's symbols, was more a prophet than the pharaoh who dreamed them. "For his spirit informed him so that he should see; the illuminated mind of the other, so that he should understand." Augustine decided that the pharaoh had the gift of tongues to produce images, but Joseph had the gift of prophecy to understand them. The most gifted person had both; such was Daniel the dreamer and interpreter. Augustine affirmed that his usage of "spirit" corresponded to Paul's distinction of it from the mind in his resolution to the Corinthians, "I shall pray with the spirit, but I shall also pray with the mind" (1 Cor. 14:15). Augustine interpreted that verse as about the production of corporeal images in the spirit but the understanding of them shining in the mind. From that distinction Augustine termed "spiritual" the type of vision that was the thought of bodily images, even when they were absent.[151]

Augustine considered vision the most perfect of the bodily senses. The eyes saw, in the popular extromissive theory, by darting rays to contact external objects. Bodily images began in the spirit and were remembered by the spirit in their physical absence.[152] Augustine distinguished corporeal vision as physical from spiritual vision as imaginative. Spiritual vision, whether awake or asleep, was the same. Augustine explored the phenomena of spiritual vision, including some case studies of altered states in fevered delirium. He concluded, "It is doubtless that there is a certain spiritual nature in us (*spiritalem quandam naturam in nobis*), where the likenesses of bodily realities are formed." He catalogued spiritual activity as

- contact with a body by a bodily sense so that its likeness was immediately formed in the spirit and recalled in the memory
- thought of already known bodies, now absent
- intuition of unknown but undoubted bodies
- thought by will or fancy of unknown or nonexistent bodies
- occupation of the rational mind by various bodily images without personal action or will
- rehearsal in thought of the future performance of a bodily action
- anticipation during a bodily act of the execution of the movement
- dreaming, whether meaningful or not

- disturbance by ill health of sensory communications, so that real and unreal images were indistinguishable or nearly so
- appearance in grave illness or suffering of images, meaningful or not, that obstructed sensation during a state higher than sleep
- seizure of the soul by the spirit, without bodily cause, for seeing bodily likenesses
- assumption and seizure without any bodily cause of the soul by some spirit to see bodily likenesses with a mixture of bodily visions and bodily senses
- deprivation of the taken spirit from all bodily sensation and its direction to only spiritual vision of bodily likenesses.[153]

Augustine summarized that the spiritual nature of humans concerned the formation of bodily likenesses—normal, paranormal, and abnormal. He determined that formation as clearly an operation of the soul, from which the spirit was not distinguished. Augustine then evaluated its worth. This spiritual nature (*natura spiritalis*), which produced bodily images, had a vision inferior to that of the light of the mind and intelligence. That highest vision judged lesser objects and saw unbodily ones, namely, "the very mind itself and every good state of the soul, and God himself, from whom everything, through whom everything, in whom everything existed." The same soul experienced bodily, spiritual, and mental visions in that order of excellence. Augustine interpreted Paul's message to the Corinthians that "the spiritual man judges all things" (1 Cor. 2:15) to mean that the spirit was not distinct from the mind, as in his later verse "I will pray with the spirit and I will pray with the mind also" (14:15). The spirit related, rather, to the attributed verse in Ephesians "be renewed in the spirit of your mind" (4:23). For Augustine, the spirit could be called "mind" because of its judgment of spiritual realities. But spiritual vision occupied a middle state between corporeal and intellectual vision. Spiritual vision could err by deception and confusion in understanding sensory images. Intellectual vision could not err.[154]

Augustine distinguished intellectual vision "through species" from spiritual vision "through enigmas." He identified its supreme experience as Moses's vision, not on the mountain or in the tent, but "in the very substance by which God is . . . through its species, as much as a rational and intellectual creature can receive it." Augustine identified Moses's vision of the clarity of God as not a corporeal substance presented to the fleshly senses but a direct encounter, "'face to face,' one opposite the other." He thought that ineffable, secret, and intimate speech of God to Moses happened in a sort of death, without a complete departure from the body, just as Paul related his experience "whether in the body or out of the body." Augustine designated the "third heaven" of Paul's rapture as Moses's identical vision. Its revelation transpired "not through any bodily or spiritual figured meaning, as through a mirror in an enigma, but 'face to face,' or, as was said about Moses, 'mouth to mouth' (Num. 12:6–8)." That intellection meant "through the species that God is whatever he is, insofar as the mind, which is not what he is—even if cleansed from every earthly stain, separated and detached from every bodily likeness—is able to receive." For Augustine, Paul's vision displayed the soul's eternal life.[155]

Augustine thought that some types of intellectual vision, such as virtue and vices, were seen in the soul itself. Utterly distinct was vision of the divine light itself, by which the soul was enlightened, so that the intellect perceived everything in itself truthfully. "For that light is God himself, but this is a creature, although made rational and intellectual in his image." The human mind fluttered weakly and failed when it tried to observe that divine light. Yet it was from that light that it was helped to understand whatever it understood when it was rapt from the body to see above itself. Augustine believed that the three kinds of vision—bodily, spiritual, and intellectual—would endure in paradise, but without error. He affirmed that "the intellectual, which is proper to the mind, is more excellent than" spiritual apprehensions, as he reviewed them. The word "intellectual" did not range over as many meanings as "spirit" did, but a synonym was "intelligible." Again, in contrast the spiritual was by definition unintelligible. Corporeal vision with the eyes perceived an object, which produced an image in the spirit. But its reality was not discerned unless, with the eyes averted, its image was discovered in the rational mind. In beasts, because their spirit was irrational, bodily vision halted at the spirit. In humans, with a rational spirit, the notification of the image extended to the intellect, which presided over the spirit. The intellect either readily understood the significance of the sign or it searched for it. In sum, "Corporeal vision is referred to the spiritual, and the spiritual to the intellectual."[156]

Augustine devalued spiritual apprehensions because of his terrible personal struggle for truth, from the imagination of to the intellection of God. His conviction that the apprehension of God's spirit required intellection, not imagination, determined his ultimate subordination of the human spirit to the rational and intellectual mind. Augustine confessed that his early spiritual exercises had belied the truth, whereas his mental exercises finally attained it. He concluded that the spiritual part of the soul, which contacted bodies, was a fallible and lesser power than the intellectual. His *Confessiones* told how as a professional rhetor he was influenced by Aristotle's category of substance to think of God as a huge shining body, of which he himself was a piece. He then fell among Manicheans, whom he later despised as carnal. They falsely spoke "truth, truth," while serving up "splendid phantasms" that were only "bodily phantasms, false bodies," untrue even by the physical sight of created objects. Their sect seduced him by "Solomon's enigma," folly personified, who bid him enjoy their occult secrets. With his vision restricted to physical objects, and his mind to stupid phantasms, Augustine confessed his ignorance. "I did not know that God is a spirit, whose members are not through length and breadth, nor is he a heap. . . . And I was absolutely ignorant of what is in us, according to which we exist and rightly in Scripture are named 'to the image of God.'" He dallied with Manichaean fables about the creation that were mindless of the Creator. As he admitted his reluctant heresy, "When I wished to think of my God I did not know to think except for a bodily heap, for it seemed to me that nothing existed that was not that. And that was the greatest and almost only cause of my inevitable error." When he tried to recall the Catholic faith he was taught as a child, he was still immersed in materiality. "For I did not know to think of the mind except as a subtle body, which was nevertheless diffused through local spaces." He even thought of Christ the Savior as a projection from the mass of the dazzling divine heap. He wrote how those bodily heaps pressed on his thoughts to suffocate him so that he could not simply breathe the truth.[157]

IMAGERY

At his physical maturation from adolescence to youth, Augustine confessed that he was still trapped in imagining God as a corporeal substance, although not in the shape of a human body. A flock of phantasms flew circling about his unclean mind. They imagined

God as spatial; either localized or diffused, yet somehow a "nothing." Augustine explicated his spiritual vision, how he used to fix in the sight of his spirit the entire creation, bodily and unbodily, although even the unbodily realities resembled bodies. He imagined a finite creation, "one grand mass" full of infinity, with God "surrounding and penetrating it from every side, but everywhere infinite." He imagined an infinite sea flooding an immense space, with a giant sponge in it that was finite but soaked with the infinite sea. Bodily images rushed at him on all sides so that he could scarcely breathe or rest, and they obstructed his understanding. Providentially, he wrote, he was given some Platonist manuscripts, which he compared with John's gospel about the Word in the beginning, through whom everything was created and enlightened. Admonished by his biblical readings to retreat to his authentic self, Augustine entered by divine guidance into his most intimate parts. As he discovered, "I entered and saw with the eye of my soul whatever it was above that same eye of my soul, above my mind, the immutable light." It was not the common light of physical vision or a special universal light, but the light that was his Creator. Augustine believed that to know it was to know eternity, although his slight glimpse ended, and he realized his own great distance from that strong steady light. And he heard in his heart God's biblical cry, "I am who I am" (Ex. 3:14).[158] That climax was personally compelling. It determined for Augustine the hegemony of intellectual vision, hence his disdain for the swarming mass of bodily imagery that his lesser spiritual vision had fantasized.

Thus Augustine at the very beginning of *De trinitate* criticized those rationalists who immaturely transferred their experience of bodily sensations to the designation of spiritual realities. He denounced theirs as a fleshly knowledge of God.[159] To purge the human rational soul (*animus*) of such falsehood, he rationalized that biblical imagery was a mere adaptation of intellectual truth for childish comprehension. Whereas Augustine might have respected Scripture as normative and elaborated a rhetorical theology in imitation, he judged contemplation as ideal, then developed a theory to explain Scripture as rhetorical. That was the theory of accommodation, although itself a rhetorical principle. In Augustine's pedagogy the divine mystery adapted itself to human misery through sensible images that appealed to its concupiscent nature. From those images the mind might ascend dialectically to ideas, and so rise from the slime to the stars.[160] Augustine taught that Scripture borrowed words from all types of objects, shunning none, to act the wet nurse. But it did so only to coax the immature intellect step by step to contemplation of the divine reality. "Contemplation is surely the payment of faith," he averred. He sought to "inquire about the Trinity, that God is in those very eternal realities, in the perfect contemplation of which is promised to us the blessed life that is none other than eternal."[161] Thus did Augustine turn Scripture philosophically, although contemplation (*theōria*) is not a biblical word or concept.

With intellectualist conviction Augustine deprecated Scripture as divine baby talk. He believed that the paradigm of truth was the creative Word of John's gospel in the beginning. That Word was analogous to intellectual concept, not to oral discourse. In its ideal imitation a theologian was a dialectician, not a rhetorician. Augustine defined dialectic as the exhibition of reason, which knew knowledge itself and had the power to make humans learned. Rhetoric was an accommodation to ordinary feelings and habits through the arousal of affects toward performance of the good. Augustine tolerated the rhetoric of biblical language as a condescension to human nature that was modeled on the humiliation of immaterial God made flesh in Jesus. In his distinction, whereas dialectic discovered truth, rhetoric only expressed it. Dialectic as the discipline of theoretical disputation, and logic as the science of the formal laws of reason, allowed the exegete to treat rigorously the questions that a profound study of Scripture raised, to ensure the coherence of the steps of its thought, and to avoid grave errors.[162]

Augustine juxtaposed continence and concupiscence in an ideology by which rhetoric metaphorically fornicated with images. In vigorously sexual language he blamed the rhetoric he learned as a schoolboy for inciting his personal depravity. He blamed his boyish sins of lust in imitation of Jove's comedic rape, studied in school, on the cultural valuation of rhetoric in the service of social necessity. The figures of rhetoric, as carnal, were suspect even in the service of religion, he judged. Rhetoric postured toward the truth obliquely; if it did not blatantly lie, it elided the truth silently. As a bishop, Augustine necessarily preached in the oratorical mantle he had discarded when he quit the forum. Yet even his ecclesiastical imitation of Jesus's parables was a condescension to the flesh. Augustine the pastor imagined himself as a charitable whale created from the primordial abyss who swam toward drowning persons to offer them a safe ride. Because concupiscent humans could not contemplate the truth, they had to be persuaded by carnal images until they were mentally continent. The archetypal Word that existed eternally without syllables descended in Jesus as God-man as bits of sound spoken imaginatively. Although the eternal Word lacked metaphor, in its descent from eternity to time it became figurative for the sake of human nature. Jesus spoke allegorically to vocalize one thing while signifying another. Scripture spoke "to terrorize the proud, to stir the negligent, to exercise the questioners, and to nourish the intelligent, which it would not do if it did not first bend itself and descend somewhat to those flat on their backs."[163]

In Augustine's salient metaphor of accommodation, Scripture stooped to children as a nursing mother. The eternal Word, which was solid meat or bread, became temporal flesh in Jesus to suckle infants tenderly with his milk. Breastfeeding modeled the purpose of the Incarnation. Just as a mother transferred her bodily milk to her baby, so God, clothed in the flesh as Jesus, adapted his divine wisdom to nourish humans. Just as the solid food of the Word became milk for humans, Augustine argued, so humans should grow up by sucking that milk until they were weaned and strong enough to contemplate the solid food of the Word. That Word was the essence of Christ in reality. Everything else, as created, was only similitude. Images were perceived and formed in the soul, but the types and ineffably beautiful art of the forms were comprehended above the eye of the mind in simple intelligence. Augustine urged the banishment of imaginative conceptions for the cultivation of intellectual ones. That subordination of imagination to intellect continued his deprecation of spiritual vision as the soulful function associated with bodily images. For Augustine, the proper interpretation of Scripture was ultimately philosophical, not rhetorical. The exegete's task was to develop its images into ideas. Augustine interpreted the divine command to humans at creation to "increase and multiply and fill the earth" (Gen. 1:28) as not about sexual reproduction. It meant, rather, the generation of bodily expressed signs and intelligibly thought realities. Those realms symbolized for Augustine rhetoric and dialectic as respectively the dark abyss of whirling words and the enlightened port of firm reality.[164]

A contemplative tradition of abstraction from body to intellectual form influenced Augustine to discourage or deny theological anthropomorphism. He specifically opposed in *De trinitate* the anthropomorphism of Genesis 3, where God in the garden literally spoke to Adam, whom he had fashioned from mud. That divine speech seemed to Augustine to be "in the human species." Although he conceded the idea was not expressed in the verse, he thought it implied by the whole tenor of the passage. The narrative situated God walking and talking in paradise, which activities Augustine decided had to be taken literally as "in the human species." He wondered whether the actor was God the Father, the Son, or the Spirit, or perhaps the Trinity. He considered the Christian exegetical custom of understanding that speaker in continuity with the speaking Creator of Genesis 1, the Father. Yet he thought Genesis 1 might have alluded to the Son, through whom, as the Word in the prologue to John's gospel, everything was created. Augustine determined the question "occult," and he invited sharper minds to solve the mystery of how God in the garden was visible to Adam's eyes and audible to his ears.[165] In *De Genesi ad litteram* he decided that God spoke by means of an intermediate creature because the invisible substance of the Trinity could not have appeared to bodily senses.[166] Augustine also railed against the anthropomorphism of classical religion and myth,[167] disallowing any providential preparation for the recognition and acceptance of Jesus as the God-man.

Augustine's prime example in *De trinitate* of the biblical use of bodily language for God was avian. "For it has used words taken from bodily objects when it says, 'Under the sunshade of thy wings protect me'" (Ps. 17:8). He deprecated the psalmist's metaphorical appeal to divine wings for human shelter and security. Augustine's treatise was also disinterested in birds as a model for the Holy Spirit. The biblical descent of the dove was merely a sign. It was "a creature serving the Creator, at the nod of him who is unchangeable and in himself permanent, to signify and show him." The Holy Spirit "did not beatify the dove" or "join it in the unity and habit of himself in eternity." Augustine conceded that the dove in descent on the apostles at Pentecost was certainly seen with human eyes. But he refused to call the Spirit "dove." Birds were convenient for logical distinctions but inaccurate for spiritual revelations. Augustine proposed the examples of a black swan or a quadruped bird as never seen, thus never recalled, but easily imaginable by superimposing black on white or by adding two extra feet to a flier. The black color of a raven's feather was an example of an inseparable accident, a type called *akorista*, which disappeared with the demise of the bird or its feather.[168] However, his grammatical commentary on Genesis acknowledged the gospel's simile of a chicken, which was not a flier. As an accommodation, divine wisdom gathered human weakness under its wings, like a hen its chicks, so that the faithful might cease being mentally childish.[169] Augustine's *Confessiones* imagined himself a fledgling. He was a nester in the faith, growing feathers for wings of charity, while God flew circling above him. Augustine confessed that he failed at his trial flights in meditation from earth to heaven. But God mercifully picked him up and replaced him in the nest, lest he be trampled to death.[170]

INTERIORITY

The air in which only birds flew Augustine considered a good shared by all animals. As he acknowledged, "Good is the air temperate and healthful." As for the descent of the Holy Spirit as a dove, Augustine belittled the biblical manner of speech borrowed from creatures to invent "toddler toys." It was "degradingly vain" to circumscribe and define God by bodily outlines or to explore him in the human body. "No one doubts that not according to the body or according to any part of the mind whatsoever, but according to the rational mind, where there can be a recognition of God, 'man was made to the image of him who created him.'" That was Augustine's steadfast exegesis of Genesis 1:26 about any Spirit-to-spirit relation as mental. He assumed that Scripture rarely spoke of God properly abstracted from creatures, as in his declaration to Moses, "I am who I am" (Ex. 3:14).[171] Contemplation of that divine reality was Augustine's aspiration. The biblical context for that revelation was Moses's inquiry about the name of the god of the fathers since Abraham, Isaac, and Jacob unto all generations. Its purpose was to solicit divine assurance of Israel's deliverance from Egyptian oppression toward the safety of the promised land.[172] That biblical language was relational between God and humans; it was not about mental processes. For Augustine, however, the human creature related to the divine Creator by the higher rational and intellectual functions of the mind, not by its lesser spiritual functions consorting with materiality. Augustine reasoned that the divine Spirit could not be known by the human spirit because the human spirit involved bodily images, whereas God was an unbodily substance. Therefore, the divine Spirit had to be apprehended by the human intellect, which was similarly unbodily. Augustine did not acknowledge that Genesis did not conceptualize the creative Spirit as mind. He inferred the divine mind from his belief in the Trinity's created image in the human mind.

Paul, on whose letters Augustine relied for his analysis, did not, however, equate the human spirit with the human mind or soul in whole or in part. In an epistolary farewell to the Thessalonians he prayed, "May you all be kept safe and blameless, spirit, soul, and body, for the coming of our Lord Jesus Christ" (1 Thess. 5:23 RSV). Although that was not a philosophical statement, Paul there distinguished spirit from both soul and body. Its Greek was *to pneuma kai ē psychē kai to sōma;* in Latin, *spiritus vester, et anima, et corpus.* Paul did not identify and order epistemological operations in writing about spirit and mind, as Augustine interpreted him. He compared speech in tongues as purposeless for the edification of the church to speech in prophecy as purposeful to it. His was a social distinction of private versus public, individual versus communal speech. Augustine philosophized Paul's moral teaching about personal behavior mindful of the entire Church into a hierarchy of mental operations. That hierarchy subjected the spiritual, with its attachment to bodily images, to the intellectual, with its abstraction from them. That order conformed to Augustine's apologetics of biblical pabulum.

From his very first reading of Scripture, Augustine was offended by its plain language. He disdained it as unworthy of the Ciceronian ideal,[173] both rhetorical and philosophical. Cicero's examination of nature so to understand a human being as "a citizen of the whole universe" fulfilled the Delphic oracle "Know thyself." As Cicero exclaimed, "Ye immortal gods, how well it will know itself, according to the precept of the Pythian Apollo!"[174] Augustine also sought self-knowledge by determining his place in the universe. The final books of his *Confessiones* about the creation in Genesis were not biblical exegesis appended to an autobiography. His genre was not modern autobiography but epideictic rhetoric, the broad classical genre for praise or blame. Augustine's *Confessiones* invented his praise of the Creator from the personal topics of good and evil, as organized by the Ciceronian virtue of prudence, which judged them. The parts of prudence—memory, intelligence, and foresight—structured the work. Its final books interpreted the creation story of Genesis 1 as an allegorical prophecy of Augustine's personal creation. The biblical Priestly writing, before metaphysics, had framed the creation story in Genesis 1 to locate Israel as God's special portion. Augustine did not have the historical method to discern that ancient composition, but he did have metaphysical knowledge to discern his own place. He upheld the pages of Genesis 1 as a mirror of himself. That exegesis in conclusion of the prudential triad of his *Confessiones* was foresight of himself as the deep and dark abyss the Creator formed by enlightenment into a spiritual creature. Genesis 1 became Augustine's paradigm for the interpretation of himself, as the memory and intelligence that composed his rhetorical exercise of praise for his Creator were unified by the normative divine Word that illuminated his relative human words.[175]

Augustine prayed in his *Confessiones* to learn and understand from God himself how in the beginning in Genesis he had created heaven and earth. Although the author Moses was unavailable, "If he were, I would detain him, and beg him, and beseech him through you to unfold those [words] to me, and I would offer my bodily ears to the sounds bursting from his mouth." Augustine acknowledged that if Moses should speak in a Hebrew voice, it would pulse in his ears and impinge on his mind in vain, although in Latin he would understand him. How would he know that Moses was telling the truth? "Inside me, inside in my little domicile of thought, neither Hebrew, nor Greek, nor Latin, nor barbarian, the truth without the organs of mouth and tongue, without the noise of syllables, would say, 'He speaks truly.'"[176] Augustine uplifted the pages of his *Confessiones* to those of Genesis as if to a mirror that might truly reflect his words from the Word at the beginning of creation. The principle of creation, to which he desired to return from his errors by the acquisition of knowledge, was the divine wisdom that shone through him as the primordial light had pierced the darkness. Augustine learned that he himself was in "the depths of the abyss," like the unformed world before the creation. For him, that was the mud of a pigsty, to whose symbolic hogs he flung the ripe fruits of his schooling and his sexuality. It was reading Cicero's exhortation to philosophy that arrested his slippage. That book altered his sensual disposition by inflaming him to yearn for "an immortality of wisdom." Yet the Ciceronian rhetorical standard had taught Augustine to disdain Scripture for its lowly style. For that arrogance, he confessed that he slid from the brief stability of wisdom into a deeper hole, Manichaean mouths feigning truth. In their pit he became stuck, mesmerized by their "splendid phantasms" that tricked his mind. He was lured underground through dark caves into the "depths of hell," where he foolishly drank their cultic secrets, the stolen waters of "Solomon's enigma."[177]

Augustine identified from experience both false phantasms and true fantasies as the objects of spiritual vision, whereas thoughts were the surpassing achievements of intellectual vision.[178] He aspired to realize Paul's end of knowing as one is known,[179] but his gaze in the mirror differed from the apostle's exhortation of knowing oneself as others in the Corinthian church did. Augustine's *Confessiones* intended by intelligence that "I shall know Thee even as I have been known." He meant to know God as God had known him in his personal creation. Augustine studied Genesis 1 to interpret himself as its "formlessness of matter," by foreseeing the providence by which he himself would be formed. Marveling at creation, he acknowledged that, as a spiritual creature by virtue of his soul, he was once the darkness, although alive, because he was turned away from God's light. Although the Spirit over the waters at creation had commanded the light for his conversion, his soul remained ever "a deep," "a dark and flowing inner life" over which the indwelling Spirit moved to animate even his body. Augustine believed in the verity of the creation both of the universe and of himself. He allegorized the biblical story as about his own creation. He was the heaven and the earth as a spiritual and corporeal creature. He was the light and the dark as a just and unjust soul. He was in the firmament as a holy interpreter of Scripture, at sea and on land in the company of bitterness then the congregation of zeal, and in the germinating and fructifying earth as a worker of mercy.[180]

Through that biblical exegesis Augustine sought knowledge of himself as a creature and of the providence of his Creator. By reflecting on the divine purpose he believed was revealed in Genesis 1, he glimpsed through its eternal forms his own future as a creature with a living soul. He awakened from oblivion the memory of his past with God, when he was dark and formless matter preexisting in the divine mind. As he ultimately remembered, he was from eternity with God, in the divine mind through whose wisdom and in whose providence he was in time created. Thus did Augustine answer his introductory question to God, "I know not whence I came here into this mortal life, or whether I should say living death."[181] His personal end was the intellection of God, of that which is, the eternal self-same, which he had glimpsed in the blink of his first contemplation. It became his aspiration to perpetuate that intellection lifelong and enjoy it eternally. His eternal life with God, past and future, is what he saw through his meditation on Genesis 1 as Paul's metaphor "in an enigma and as if through a mirror."[182] Augustine poised, in counterpoint to Paul's view of spiritual growth through the stages of this life, a mirrored image of God in time and the face-to-face vision in eternity.

Augustine gazed tirelessly into that mirror for images of the Trinity reflected in the human creature. He concluded *De trinitate* with his discovery that that "the image of God, which a human is according to the mind," had "a certain trinity." Augustine defined it as "the mind, and the knowledge by which it knows itself, and the love by which it loves its knowledge." Like the Godhood "this trinity is equal among themselves and one." The Spirit was operative in the human mind, and, when the human spirit inhered in the divine spirit, it became one spirit with it through the mind.[183] Augustine's method of meditation from the human mind to the divine reality reasoned by ascent toward contemplation. However, the descent by God to Paul and Israelite prophets before him had been spiritual, not mental. It happened by divine revelation, not by human motive, however graced. The agency and energy of those events differed essentially. When Augustine sought to imitate Paul's apostolate of teaching spiritual things spiritually, he recalled how in Genesis 1:2 the Spirit moved above the waters at the beginning of creation. Its charity, Augustine believed, raised him from the concupiscence that sank his impure spirit to submersion in the abyss. That was the weight of his carnal loves, from which the Holy Spirit bore him safely upward. Augustine thus lifted up his heart to where the Spirit moved above the waters so that he might attain repose there once his soul passed in death through the unsubstantial waters.[184] Augustine's translation of the human image of the Creator to the mind was a beautiful idea. The human spirit was left to the imagination.

CHAPTER 4

Aquinas

"'For who of humans knows those things that are of a human,' that is, those things that are hidden in the heart, 'except the spirit of the human, which is in him,' that is, the intellect?" Thomas Aquinas (1224/25–1274) thus philosophized Paul's a fortiori argument to the Corinthians about the human spirit.[1] Paul wrote differently: "For who of humans knows humanity if not the spirit of the human that is in him; so, the godhood of God no one perceives if not the Spirit of God" (1 Cor. 2:11). Aquinas's philosophical exegesis about human versus divine privacy differed from Paul's biblical premise for divine revelation to humans as Spirit-to-spirit.[2] Although Aquinas's writings were prodigious, his life was self-effacing. He wrote nothing revealing his inner self, unlike Paul and Augustine, who were eminently personal. The repetitious formal arguments sed contra of Aquinas's celebrated *Summa theologiae* proposed refutations of unwanted opinions. "But on the contrary . . . I answer that . . ." That "I" was an intellectual whose personal human spirit remained secreted in his heart. For Aquinas was not a secular thinker but a religious friar vowed to teach Church doctrine. His authorization as a degreed bachelor of theology was to lecture on Scripture as a "master in the sacred page."[3] The very first question of his *Summa theologiae* declared its science as the mysteries beyond human knowledge that God had revealed to the human intellect.[4]

ERASURE

He was born Tommaso d'Aquino in 1224/25 at Roccasecca to Italian parents of the lesser nobility. Being their fourth son, he was donated at the age of five or six as an oblate to the monastic Order of St. Benedict at Monte Cassino, its venerable but then degenerate foundation.⁵ Had he progressed to religious profession as a monk, he would have made the novel and prime Benedictine vow of stability. That vow would have enclosed him until death in that same monastery in its communal life of prayer and of work, notably the copying of manuscripts.⁶ But Aquinas was at age fourteen or fifteen transferred by his parents, on the abbot's advice, to study arts at the university in Naples. There he encountered the new Dominican friars and joined their Order of Preachers, a decision that provoked his parents to kidnap him. Released from his confinement after about a year, he traveled as a mendicant friar to study and teach in various cities—to Paris three times, to Cologne, to Orvieto, and back to Naples—but without any memoirs of his destinations or duties.⁷ His writings intended a universality, in abstraction from the particular situations that preoccupied Paul as a missionary and Augustine as a bishop. Aquinas's scant recognition of the human spirit was deliberately impersonal.

The incomplete text of Aquinas's commentary on Paul's letters to the Corinthians was composed at an uncertain date and place during his career as an esteemed theologian in his religious order.⁸ Aquinas's lack of a mature commentary was not unusual. It was the bane of medieval manuscripts to be fragments for which the intact original was lost, forgotten, or vanished. The authorial culture differed from modern notions of the empirical, individual creator whose writing is self-expressive. Not originality but imitation was the medieval norm of invention from traditional commonplaces, so that textual voices were fundamentally anonymous.⁹ Aquinas's authentic commentary on Paul's first letter to the Corinthians extended only to chapter 7 verse 10. Aquinas's companion, Reginald di Piperno, transcribed from his notes on Aquinas's lectures chapters 11–13:11, and an unidentified scribe or student added his own notes on chapters 11–16,¹⁰ while Peter of Tarentaise supplied the lacuna.¹¹ Aquinas's commentary on the second letter to the Corinthians was entirely from two such reports of his lectures, again not his dictations but auditors' notes.¹²

Aquinas believed in his first commentary that the spiritual gift of wisdom endowed all the faithful to interpret Scripture. He was intent on the revelation of its secrets, for he chose his topical verse from the biblical book of Wisdom. "I will tell you what wisdom is and how she came to be, and I will hide no secrets from you, but I will trace her course from the beginning of creation, and make knowledge of her clear" (Wis. 6:22; Vulg. v. 24).[13] That personified Wisdom was the "spirit," the *rûaḥ*, *pneuma*, *spiritus* introduced in Genesis 1:2 at creation. Aquinas treated it as the mind. He determined from Aristotle's metaphysical hierarchy that wisdom was the principal intellectual virtue because its object, God, was the highest cause.[14] Aquinas thought the "secrets (*sacramenta*)" of the Corinthian letters were the Church's sacraments and their ministry, and he dedicated his biblical exposition to that understanding. But he also pondered the human secrets he supposed only an individual human spirit could know. He did not identify Paul's divine and human affairs, his neutral *ta*, as "thoughts," as the standard translation does. He explicated it as "secrets." Those human secrets paralleled divine mysteries. Aquinas honored the context of Paul's biblical argument, which affirmed revelation as a gift of the divine Spirit, not an achievement of human philosophy or rhetoric. As Paul wrote after Isaiah, the Spirit revealed "what the eye has not seen, nor the ear heard, nor has ascended into the human heart, what God has prepared for those who love him" (1 Cor. 2:9; Is. 64:4). Yet although Aquinas acknowledged Paul's revision of Isaiah's prophecy about "waiters" to "lovers,"[15] he continued Augustine's identification of that promise as the eschatological vision of God.[16]

Aquinas, as a Dominican friar, was assigned by his religious superiors to teach the Bible traditionally to students in his religious order of preachers and confessors. His important source, Augustine, had been differently empowered as a consecrated bishop with magisterial authority. Aquinas respected that higher authority and dutifully followed Augustine's general interpretation of Paul's biblical text by philosophical theory. Aquinas's amplification, through Aristotle's philosophy, of the divine image in humans differed some from Augustine's precise epistemology.[17] But Aquinas did not doubt that the divine image resided in the human mind.[18] Although the power of the mind to know God while still in the body was feeble, Aquinas believed that its knowledge would be fulfilled in the afterlife of resurrection from the dead. He argued from Aristotle's epistemology that "the glory of the vision" was humanly unknown because, as colorless and invisible, it was not presentable to eyesight. Sensation was the essential basis for a progress to cognition. Aquinas cited as evidence of the invisible divine essence Job's verse "The bird has not known the path, nor has the eye of the vulture observed it" (28:7).¹⁹ The Hebrew named generic birds of prey (*'ayim*) in allusion to the vision of raptors as the keenest of all animals.²⁰ Aquinas supposed that birds could not fly above the mines in Job's verse because of their polluted sulfurous atmosphere. But noting that vultures could see intensely at remote distances,²¹ Aquinas emphasized the imperceptibility of the eschatological vision of God to human sight, and he projected it even beyond bird's-eye vision. It was an adynaton, the hyperbolic impossibility. Aquinas disqualified the glorious vision of God as achievable by human intellection alone because the heart was carnal, inferior to the mind and incapable of ascent to it. It was necessary in the proper ordering of lower to higher realities for divine revelation to descend to the heart.²²

Aquinas designated that promised eternal glory as the reward of "lovers," as Paul's letter to the Corinthians had corrected Isaiah's "waiters." He allowed that other virtues might contribute to meriting glory, but only as informed by charity. Aquinas then divided Paul's argument to analyze it scholastically as proposition and proof. The proposition was the Spirit's exclusive revelation of wisdom because the Spirit of truth proceeded from the Son, who was the Father's truth. The proof was Paul's verse in his a fortiori argument to the Corinthians that began "for the Spirit searches" (1 Cor. 2:10–11). Aquinas thought that the Spirit's revelation of divine wisdom to the faithful was possible because "the Spirit searches everything." He then qualified that search. It was not an investigation to learn since the Spirit knew perfectly the intimate facts about everything, even God's depths. Aquinas identified those depths as the things hidden in God himself, not his superficial vestiges knowable through creation.²³

Aquinas explicated Paul's argument. "He then proves what he had said about the Spirit of God through the likeness of the human spirit, saying, 'for who knows the things that are of humans,' that is, those things hidden in the heart, 'except the spirit of the human that is in him,' that is, the intellect?"²⁴ Aquinas copied there the Vulgate Bible, whose Latin translation *nisi*, "except," altered the Greek *mē*, "if not." Paul's verse expressed exemplarity, not exceptionality. His a fortiori argument was "For who of humans knows humanity if not the spirit of the human that is in him; so the godhood of God no one perceives if not the Spirit of God" (1 Cor. 2:10–11). Paul reasoned that no one understood humanity better than a human spirit; a fortiori, no one understood God better than his Spirit. That was Paul's creational premise for the revelation of the crucified Jesus as God, as revealed by the divine Spirit to the human spirit.[25] Aquinas did not recognize Paul's a fortiori argument. He used that term infrequently and never for a rhetorical inference. Aquinas only stated logically the ordinary observation that the weaker was changed or conquered by the stronger.[26] Classical argumentation a fortiori was a rhetorical inference by stronger reason from a lesser fact to a greater probability. Aristotle's *Rhetorica* taught it among the positive proofs. It argued that if the less likely thing was true, then the more likely thing was the more so true.[27] That was Paul's usage in the verse on which Aquinas commented. However, Aquinas did not have Aristotle's *Rhetorica* until late in 1270, only four years before death, when his fellow friar William of Moerbecke, archbishop of Corinth, translated it from Greek to Latin.[28]

Nevertheless, even before the availability of Aristotle's *Rhetorica*, Aquinas generally understood argumentation a fortiori, although the Vulgate translation misled him on Paul's verse. Aquinas wielded its type *multo minus*, "much the less," frequently. He simultaneously compared and contrasted to show that if something greater were true, so much the less was something lesser true. Its initial occurrence in his *Summa theologiae* argued that, because of the broad distinctiveness of certain creatures, nothing univocal could be predicated of them. Therefore, much less could anything have been predicated univocally of God and creatures, but everything was predicated equivocally.[29] However, Aquinas did acknowledge a "similitude" of the divine and human spirits. He did not, therefore, oppose them, as the Vulgate's "except" in its translation of Paul's verse justified their antithesis. Aquinas identified human affairs as heartfelt secrets in parallel to divine affairs as profound mysteries. He focused on interior secrets invisible from one human to another. "And therefore the things that are hidden on the inside cannot be seen."[30]

As he explained the epistemology, "The obvious reason why a human cannot know the things of another that are hidden in the heart is because knowledge of a human is taken by sense. Therefore, those things hidden in the heart of another cannot be known except to the extent that they are communicated by sensible signs." That necessity applied not only to human knowing but also to angelic knowing. Aquinas interpreted Paul as teaching that only a human could know his own thoughts because they were within him, where no angel could pry—only God could perceive. Aquinas thought from the Vulgate translation that Paul "applied that similitude to the Spirit of God, saying 'thus those things which are of God,' that is, that are hidden in God himself, 'no one can know except the Spirit of God.'" He cited Job, "Behold, God is great, surpassing our knowledge" (Job 26:36).[31] Yet the transcendence of God was not Paul's final conclusion, only his intermediate reasoning. Although Paul acknowledged that God surpassed human knowledge, his message to the Corinthians was that God had nevertheless revealed himself as Christ crucified, through his divine Spirit to human spirits. Paul did not write about private human thoughts inaccessible to another human except by direct communication. He reasoned that just as human affairs were known by the human spirit, so the more so were divine affairs known by the divine Spirit. His inference ultimately affirmed the divine Spirit as the agent of revelation to the human spirit.[32]

SPIRIT

Aquinas reached that same conclusion but by a different argument. In precedence Augustine had noted in his search for self-knowledge through the mind as a mirrored image of the Trinity that the intentions of another person were imperceptible and incomprehensible without overt bodily signs.[33] Aquinas did not reference him for that commonsensical observation, however. In his Aristotelian epistemology Aquinas preserved Augustine's essential analysis of human spirit as mind. However, Aquinas specified that the human spirit was the "intellect," not the imagination as Augustine had determined it. Aquinas argued that, just as humans communicated by sensible signs, so God communicated by created effects. "But the Holy Spirit, who is in God himself, as being consubstantial with the Father and the Son, sees the secrets of the divinity through himself." Aquinas cited from the biblical hymn to Wisdom about a "holy spirit of intelligence" (Wis. 7:22–23) possessing every power and overseeing everything. The Spirit that filled Christians he believed was the Holy Spirit who imparted knowledge not from the world but from God.[34]

Aquinas defined spirit. "By the word 'spirit (*spiritus*)' is understood a certain force that is vital and cognitive and affective." That definition broadened his specification of the human spirit as "intellect" because his previous comment concerned only its particular cognitive power.[35] Aquinas then interpreted Paul's distinction between the "ensouled human (*psychikos anthrōpos*)" and the "spiritual human (*pneumatikos*)." That biblical distinction differed from the hierarchical facultative psychology of classical philosophy that Aquinas adapted. Paul identified the ensouled human as all the descendants of Adam, but the spiritual human as the heirs of the second Adam, who was Christ. His context was the apparent disbelief of some Corinthians in the resurrection of the body. His argument contrasted first Adamic humans as destined for burial in the dust with second Adamic humans as destined for resurrection to life in the spirit.[36] Aquinas's commentary on Paul's distinction between the first and second Adams is not extant, although there is an unattributed report of it. He posed that distinction in his *Summa theologiae*, but only to refute an objection to the creation of Adam in grace.[37]

Aquinas philosophized a very different lesson from Paul's letter to the Corinthians about the human spirit. Aquinas commented on the Latin translation of Paul's *psychikos anthrōpos* as *animalis homo* to affirm a human relation to a soul. Aquinas thought that all living things had a soul: nutritive, for plants; sensitive, for animals; intellectual, for humans. Yet he insisted that in humans all three powers composed one soul.[38] As he commented on that Corinthian letter, "A human is called *animalis* from the soul (*anima*), which is the form of the body,"[39] a relationship his *Summa theologiae* also established.[40] Thus, Aquinas continued to philosophize on Paul's letter that human animality referred to those powers of the soul that were the act of the bodily organs; namely, the sensitive powers of apprehension and appetite. By the sensory power of apprehension the animate human judged God by bodily fantasies, or by the letter of the law, or by philosophical reason. By the sensory power of appetite the animate human pursued an unrestrained wantonness in living. Aquinas reasoned that in nonspiritual humans the intellect was dark and the will disordered about spiritual matters, so that they regarded them as foolish. Only the Holy Spirit could enlighten the mind and inflame the feelings to those realities beyond sense and reason. Aquinas appealed typically to a hierarchy of lower to higher powers on a norm of materiality versus immateriality. Although no human could judge the mind of God, those who had the mind of Christ could judge spiritual realities.[41] Not only did Aquinas develop meanings beyond Paul's message, but he also differed from Paul's sense of

Greek *nous*, "mind," as purpose. The apostle taught the Corinthians that they knew from the Spirit's revelation the purpose of Christ, meaning the mystery hidden before the creation of his coming as the second Adam.[42] Aquinas interpreted Latin *mens* as "mind," and he believed that the imparted wisdom of Christ's mind enabled the faithful to understand the Scriptures.[43] However, Aquinas approximated Paul's meaning in his letter to the Corinthians in his commentary on the attributed letter to the Ephesians. Aquinas offered the Incarnation, the Son of God made man in Jesus, as an example of the things of God that only the Spirit knew. "Therefore, the cause of the Incarnation was hidden unless God should reveal these things through the Holy Spirit."[44] That exclusivity was part of Paul's a fortiori argument to the Corinthians, which inferred the divine Spirit's knowledge of itself from the human spirit's knowledge of itself. But that inference was only a premise for the Spirit's ability to reveal.

Revelation was Aquinas's basis for his renowned *Summa theologiae*,[45] although it is doubtful that he ever actually taught that text. It was prepared as a remedial guide for Dominican beginners in theology, the "juniors" who did not qualify to attend university for formal instruction to support their pastoral ministries. What contemporary use they made of it is unknown. After Aquinas's death that *Summa* was completed by cut-and-paste from his early writing on Peter Lombard's *Sententiae*, and its parts were circulated selectively. Its first part, which was theoretical, was the least popular for Dominican practice.[46] Aquinas began it by stating that humanity was ordered for its salvation to God as its end, and that end exceeded human reason. He argued from Paul's paraphrase in his first letter to the Corinthians of the prophet Isaiah's lament. It was a memorable verse, for Aquinas's first theological teaching had been a cursory lecture on Isaiah, which he probably delivered at Paris as a biblical bachelor.[47] As he paraphrased it, "The eye does not see, O God, apart from thee, the things you have prepared for those loving thee." Aquinas interpolated the direct address to God to explicate the biblical promise as humanly unattainable "apart from thee." He thus emphasized that certain truths of salvation beyond reason, and even those within reason but subject to trial and error, were all divinely revealed.[48]

Aquinas defended the sacred science of theology as the supreme wisdom. He appealed further to Paul's argument to the Corinthians that, as a wise architect, the apostle had laid their foundation as the

Spirit's temple. And he appealed to Augustine's *De trinitate* on wisdom as the knowledge of divine affairs. For Aquinas, sacred doctrine was a wisdom because its subject was God as the highest cause. He agreed with Augustine that divine truth was doubly known, through creation and through revelation. He then considered the spiritual human. Because judgment pertained to wisdom, just as judgment was twofold so was wisdom twofold. Judgment could be by inclination. The human who had the habit of a virtue judged the virtuous by his very inclination to it. As Aristotle wrote in *Ethica Nicomachea*, the virtuous man was the measure and rule of human acts.[49] That philosophical opinion Aquinas's commentary on Corinthians rendered compatible with Paul's statement that the spiritual human judged everything.[50] As Aquinas continued *Summa theologiae*, judgment could also be by knowledge. A human instructed in morality could judge about virtuous acts even if he was not himself virtuous. The first mode of judgment on divine affairs was wisdom as a gift of the Holy Spirit. As his principal authority, Aquinas again cited Paul to the Corinthians, "The spiritual human judges all things" (1 Cor. 3:10). He added in his exposition of virtues and vices that the spiritual human was inclined to judge everything by divine rules from the habitual virtue of charity.[51]

However insightful, Aquinas was very disadvantaged as a biblical exegete by a cultural lack of its grammar. Although Latin grammar was a standard subject in medieval schools, he read neither biblical language, Hebrew nor Greek. He depended on the Vulgate translation into Latin or on its manuscripts in circulation, for it had no established text. Aquinas was probably introduced to the *textus vulgatus* as the recension that theologians at the University of Paris in 1226 granted privilege to that city's stationers to produce. Although that version was occasioned by the need of the Parisian masters and scholars for a consistent biblical text, the product was neither sponsored nor scholarly. Aquinas may also have had access to bibles that the Dominicans of the Province of France issued with corrections of the many circulating variants.[52] Aquinas advocated for theology the primacy of the literal sense of Scripture over the spiritualized senses, which were allegorical, moral, and anagogical.[53] Yet he was reading the literal sense only in Latin translation, not in the original Hebrew and Greek languages. Moreover, he depended on a text that was unreliable, being inconsistent from copy to copy. However, Aquinas's use of the available Latin bibles was not only appropriate but also necessary to his office. He was not teaching scholars but friars, who were vowed to preach the Bible and also to administer the sacraments according to the ecclesiastical ritual texts. His bible had reasonably to match theirs. Thus, there was no inconsistency in his consultation of the best Latin translation from the Greek of Aristotle, a secular philosopher, and his apparent indifference to whether the bible at hand was the best Latin translation of the Greek New Testament.

As for historical knowledge of biblical texts, some early scholastic exegetes asked appropriate contextual questions by considering authors and audiences in their particular circumstances.[54] Their questions continued classical rhetorical practice as governed by the principle of accommodation and the topics for invention. Just as the effective writer composed his text mindful of his audience, so the responsible interpreter studied its achievement with it. However, such questions, developed from the classical rhetorical topic of times, were not exercises in modern historical method; for example, the method by which scholars have determined the inauthenticity of certain "Pauline" letters or the inadmissibility of interpreting them by the rest of the New Testament because those books dated later. Historical method in biblical exegesis only developed in the fifteenth century from the science of philology. The humanist Lorenzo Valla would innovatively replace the scholastic authority of Aristotle with the humanist authority of Quintilian to reverse the privileging of dialectic over rhetoric. Valla boldly preached an *Encomium sancti Thomae* on Aquinas's very feast day, in Rome, where Aquinas had initiated his *Summa theologiae*. Valla's sermon assigned Aquinas, "the angelic doctor," to play the cymbals in the choir Paul had orchestrated to teach the Corinthians the hierarchy of their gifts. "If I speak in the tongues of men and of angels, but have not love, I am a noisy gong or a clanging cymbal" (1 Cor. 13:1 RSV).[55] Valla's sermon accused Aquinas's theological method of philosophical abstraction, rather than rhetorical accommodation.

Without historical method to learn the contexts of texts, Aquinas was necessarily an interpreter but not a scholar of Scripture. His want of linguistic access to the biblical text and its historical reality opened him to speculation. Moreover, as a scholastic, Aquinas was disinterested in the particular realities that rhetoric addressed—who, what, where, when, and why. He sought to understand a universal reality, which in the traditional distinction of the disciplines required philosophy. Aquinas applied to exegesis the new science from Latin translations of Aristotle and his commentators that were studied in medieval universities.[56] A scholastic question in his milieu was a pedagogical method prompted by a reading of a text with a problem, whether vague or controversial. Not a passive report of traditional authorities, it was an intellectual search for the truth that required a master to judge the positive and negative interpretations.[57] Aquinas's scholastic question was not a literary genre but a premise for dialectical method. Scripture, however, was composed of literary genres, which scholasticism conscripted by quotation and allusion for its own scheme. It excised verses for argumentation of a sort different from its text and context. Aquinas valued Scripture as the authoritative theological source,[58] but he did not always interpret it congruently. Beyond his boyhood study of rhetoric in the trivium at Monte Cassino, he was unschooled and unskilled in rhetorical argumentation, for rhetoric was not taught in medieval universities. Aquinas applied philosophical argumentation.

SOURCES

Aquinas's commentary on Paul's first letter to the Corinthians appealed with attribution to the *Glossa*, the standard compilation on the Vulgate used in medieval universities. It had been conceived at the school of Laon in the twelfth century as a pedagogical aid, but it developed from a classroom text to a reference work. The gloss comprised marginal and interlinear notes of patristic and Carolingian exegeses of the biblical text that was formatted in the middle of the page. Since the Pauline letters and the Psalms retained the greatest interest,[59] Aquinas's commentary on Corinthians copied the *Glossa*'s interpretation typically. He replicated its notes about the animate human's dissolute living and about his judgment of God by bodily fantasies, by the letter of the law but also by philosophical reason. Aquinas identified those judgments philosophically as the operations of the sensitive powers of the soul. He also borrowed from the *Glossa* its definition of the spiritual human as subject to the Spirit of God for an accurate and certain knowledge of spiritual matters. That citation conformed to its definition of a spiritual life as one having the Spirit of God as governor of the soul, meaning of its animal powers. The *Glossa* distinguished, however, the soul for life from the mind for understanding.⁶⁰ Aquinas contrarily argued that the soul for life and the mind for understanding were in humans one and the same soul.⁶¹

Aquinas integrated with his biblical commentary Aristotle's ethical observation that "everyone judges well what he knows and of these things he is the best judge."⁶² That observation coincided with the premise of Paul's a fortiori argument to the Corinthians that just as a human spirit definitively knew humanity, the more so the divine Spirit definitively knew the godhead.⁶³ Aquinas interpreted it differently to mean that God's wisdom was beyond human ability. However, Aquinas's conclusion was only the intermediate term of Paul's a fortiori argument toward the divine Spirit's revelation to the human spirit. Aquinas further aligned Aristotle's ethical proposal that the virtuous human was the rule and measure of all humans with Paul's theological judgment that the spiritual human judged everything. Although Aquinas claimed that their thoughts were "in the same mode,"⁶⁴ one was philosophy, the other was theology. His *Summa theologiae* later thought otherwise that judgment by habitual inclination to virtue belonged in divine matters to wisdom as the Spirit's gift.⁶⁵

Aquinas had treated the question of the animate human (*animalis homo*) since his youthful commentary on Lombard's *Sententiae*, a voluminous compilation of opinions. Medieval universities required its bachelors of theology to address it,⁶⁶ so Aquinas at Paris in 1252 compliantly began to teach and write on it to satisfy his academic requirements. The standard format was brief statements on each of its opinions, but Aquinas also developed discursive arguments.⁶⁷ He rehearsed common definitions of "spirit": "a subtlety of some nature," whether bodily or unbodily; thus "air," and its respiratory inhalation and exhalation; "the wind"; "refined vapors" diffused as powers of the soul in bodily parts; then "unbodily realities such as the God the spirit, the angel, and the soul."⁶⁸ Remarking on Paul's animate human, he considered that it shared certain realities in common with other animals that followed brutish motions. Those were the passions of the sensitive part of the soul. Aquinas decided philosophically that the sensitive soul was what Paul meant in his first letter to the Corinthians by the term *animalis homo* (*psychikos anthrōpos*). As Aquinas explained it by Aristotelian psychology, "In the first state humans needed to occupy themselves with nutritive and generative works, without which they could not conserve life;

therefore they were said to have an animal life."[69] That judgment was different from Paul's theological identification of first Adamic humans as creatures before their incorporation into Christ as second Adamic humans.

Aquinas's *Summa theologiae* organized the subject of theology by topics, in modern studies miscalled "treatises" although they were not discursive. Each topic comprised articles, each of which began with a question to be resolved yes or no. In total there were 422 questions when Aquinas quit the work. Each question posed objections, offered a traditional statement to their contrary, stated his masterful response, and explained his answers to the posed objections. It was organized for his students as a reference in three parts: on God, on the movement of the rational creature to him, and on the human Christ as the way there.[70] But there was no question in his *Summa theologiae* "whether there is a human spirit." Aquinas's mention of the concept depended almost entirely on Paul's argument to the Corinthians about spiritual knowledge and on Paul's distinction there between ensouled and spiritual humans. The first use of the comparative term "animate human" (*homo animalis*) in *Summa theologiae* stated an objection to Boethius's definition of a person as "an individual substance of a rational nature." Aquinas presented the counterargument that the word of intention should not be included in the definition of a subject. It followed that it was a bad assignment to say that in the animal human the human was a species of animal; therefore "human" was the name of the species, "animal" the name of the intention. "Since therefore person is the name of the subject (for it signifies a certain substance of a rational nature), the individual, which is the name of the intention, is unsuitably posited in his definition." Aquinas then concurred with and justified Boethius's definition. Aquinas's reasoning occurred in the first part of that *Summa*, in the question concerning the divine persons.[71] It demonstrated his use of logic.[72]

In *Summa theologiae* he also discussed Paul's message to the Corinthians about the foolishness of the ensouled human who was immersed in sensation and therefore did not perceive the spiritual things of God. Aquinas decided that that fool was a sinner, just like someone whose sense of taste was infected by a bad humor so that he could not savor sweets.[73] He also deliberated in the disputed question *De virtutibus* (On virtues) whether the habit of virtue inclined a human being to act rightly because he had correctly estimated its end. Aristotle had opined that personal inclination accorded with the perception of an end. Just as tasting judged about flavor according to a feeling of good or bad disposition, it was appropriate, according to the inherent habitual disposition of a human to good and evil, to estimate from that what was good. For if his disposition disagreed with it, the subject estimated it evil and repugnant, whence the apostle said that animate human could not perceive those things that were of the Spirit of God.[74]

What, then, in comparison with the animate human, was the spiritual human? Although Aquinas posed no formal question about the human spirit, he offered a counterpart to "animate human" (*homo animalis*) in "spiritual human" (*homo spiritualis*). His commentary on Paul's first letter to the Corinthians noted, "we are accustomed to call 'spirit' incorporeal substances." Aquinas's hierarchy of the soul's powers deemed "spiritual" only its highest part, the intellective, which comprised intellect and will. That part was spiritual because intellection was not the act of any bodily organ. That power alone of the human spirit was capable of enlightenment by the Holy Spirit because of their compatible immateriality, he argued. As intellectual, a human was doubly spiritual. The intellect was enlightened by the divine Spirit and subjected to him, and thus knew spiritual matters with maximum certitude and fidelity. The will was inflamed by the divine Spirit to live possessed by that Spirit as its governor of the lower animal powers.[75] Aquinas considered the spiritual human passive, like a brute animal. It did not act but was acted upon, because by nature it did not move but was moved to its actions. "Similarly the spiritual human is inclined toward doing something not as if principally from the movement of his own will but from the impulse of the Holy Spirit." Aquinas quoted Isaiah on how the Spirit surged like a violent river, and the gospel on how Jesus was driven by the Spirit into the wilderness. He believed that divine impulse did not negate human free and voluntary action, however, because the Spirit was its cause.[76]

Aquinas's spiritual hierarchy was thus different from Augustine's hierarchy of body, spirit, and intellect. For both theologians, spirit functioned in a facultative psychology but in different parts. For Augustine, the spiritual in humans was the intermediate part of the soul, between its corporeal and intellectual perceptions.[77] For Aquinas, the spiritual in humans was the intellective part of the soul. Both thinkers interpreted Paul philosophically. For Paul, however, the spiritual human did not designate a power or function of the human soul. Universal animation was the ensouled human, whom the apostle did not analyze philosophically but identified as Adam and his descendants. In comparison, the spiritual human was the special heir of the second Adam, Christ, who was stamped by the Spirit as a new creature. For Paul, the soulful humans and the spiritual humans were not psychological aspects of a universal human nature but theologically different creatures, first Adamic, and second Adamic, or Christian.[78]

Aquinas's notion of the human spirit was not a dedicated theological reflection on Scripture. He composed no commentary on Genesis, which might have associated the creator Spirit with his image and likeness at 1:26 as the created human spirit. He did treat creation extensively in his *Summa theologiae* in thirty questions, however. There were three initial inquiries: on the procession of creatures from God as their first cause, on the manner of emanation of things from the first principle, and on the beginning of their duration. Beings existed by participation in God as their exemplary and final cause and as the perfect being. Aquinas defined creation as the emanation of beings from God as their universal cause. He then discussed the general distinction of things, the distinction of good and evil, and the particular distinction of things. Next he deliberated fifteen questions on angels. Ten questions followed from Genesis 1 on the work of the six days of creation. But by the time Aquinas progressed to humans, he had already predetermined their meaning as a composite of the spiritual creatures, the angels, and of the bodily creatures from light to animals. In Aquinas's hierarchical scheme, "After consideration of the spiritual and the corporeal creature, there ought to be considered the human, who is composed of a spiritual and bodily substance."[79] Augustine in *De trinitate* had argued inductively from his mind to the existence of the Trinity as its active exemplar. Aquinas argued in *Summa theologiae* deductively from divine revelation to human reality. He deduced a spiritual component of humans as the intermediate of higher angels and lower beasts. Humanity was marginal, a borderline creature of both spirit and body.[80] Aquinas's norm was immateriality versus materiality. He argued a logical fallacy by association: because spirit was immaterial and soul was immaterial, spirit was soul. His discussion of the spiritual human was defined by the immateriality of the soul, which was not a biblical concept. Aquinas did not discuss vitality—existence-to-existence. But he identified the only immaterial part of a human as the soul, especially its intellect.

LIKENESS

Addressing whether any creature could be like God, Aquinas proposed the objection no, since Scripture affirmed God's incomparability. To the contrary he then cited the verse of Genesis 1:26, "let us make man in our image and likeness." Because Aquinas maintained philosophically that likeness was based on form, he distinguished its types according to form. There was likeness according to the same formality and measure, which produced equality, as in two identical white objects. That was the most perfect likeness. Other things agreed in form and to the same formality but not measure, as in the degree of whiteness in white objects. That was an imperfect likeness. Other things agreed in the same form but not according to the same formality, as in nonuniversal agents. Such agents reproduced their effects in the same formality of the species, for example, one human from another human. But there were also agents whose effects were not contained in the same species, as in those effects generated by solar power in a generic unformal likeness that was not other suns. Aquinas reasoned that the effects of an agent not contained in any genus would reproduce the agent's form only remotely. Those effects would not participate in the likeness of the agent's form by its specific or generic formality. Its participation would only be "according to some other analogy (*aliqualem analogiam*), just as being is common to everything." Aquinas concluded, "In this way those things that are from God, insofar as they are beings, are assimilated to God as they wholly exist from him as the first and universal principle."[81] He eventually reasoned that the human likeness to divine being was intellectual.[82] Aquinas did not, however, first establish the necessary middle term that God was intellectual. He may have assumed it from patristic theology.

Patristic authors had implied the factuality of the divine mind. Definitions of mind and intellect, frequently used as interchangeable terms, were almost lacking in their literature, however. They associated the created image of God in humans with the mind, whether as an identification or a presupposition. The mind as an implicit divine attribute then became explicit in their reflection on God's design of the universe. Its intelligent design coherently suggested that it was also an intelligible design. If God thought before he created, then creation was searchable for traces of his thought. Since the divine mind was supposed the origin and end of humans, the contemplation of the divine mind became circularly for humans the purpose and end of their creation. The first Christian theologian, Irenaeus, predicated the divine mind specifically to refute the heresy that creation was necessitated.[83] Augustine forcefully repeated that apologetic for a voluntary creation.[84] Thus, mind was invoked theologically not to affirm that the Creator was thoughtful, but that he was free—not intellectual but deliberate. Creation was an emanation of his goodness, not a product of his reason. That patristic emphasis on freedom corresponded well with the biblical metaphor of the Spirit soaring at creation, as effortless and elective. The Creator was a chooser, not a thinker, who gratuitously loved what he had made. As Genesis surveyed creation, "And God saw that it was good" (Gen. 1:4, 10, 12, 18, 21, 25, 31).[85]

Yet, just as Aquinas did not formally question whether God was mind, he did not formally question whether God was spirit. He assumed so. He addressed the concept of the divine spirit only indirectly in his treatment of the Holy Spirit as the third Person of the Trinity. Inquiring whether the name "Holy Spirit" was proper, he agreed with Augustine's approval of it in *De trinitate* because of the commonality of the Holy Spirit with the Father and the Son. Aquinas added another reason for its propriety. "The noun 'spirit (*spiritus*)' in bodily things seems to signify a certain impulse and movement, for we call blowing (*flatus*) and wind (*ventus*] 'spirit.'" He stated that "the noun 'spirit' conveyed a motive power." Aquinas reasoned that "spirit" was proper to love, which impelled the will of the lover to the beloved. It was therefore applied to the Holy Spirit as the divine person who proceeded "through the love by which God is loved." The name "Holy Spirit" taken as two words applied to the entire Trinity because "by the noun 'spirit' is signified the immateriality of the divine substance." In comparison, "Corporeal spirit is invisible and hardly has material; whence we attribute this noun to all substances immaterial and invisible."[86] Aquinas did not directly ask or answer, however, whether God was spirit.

After arguing for God's existence by five means, he approached his essence negatively. Because Aquinas believed that God is knowable not as he is, but only as he is not, he proceeded by subtracting inappropriate predications from his essence in order to arrive at his simplicity. Instead of asking whether God is a spirit, he asked the opposite, "whether God is a body." Aquinas proposed the objections that Scripture attributed dimensionality, figure, members, posture, and locality to

God, which suggested his embodiment. He responded confidently that "God is absolutely not a body." His reasons were that God is the prime mover, necessarily in act not potentiality, and the noblest of beings—all statements based in Aristotle's philosophy. Aquinas then explained the biblical figures as similitudes. Dimensionality attributed God's virtual quantity, for example, "depth, his power of knowing hidden things." That alluded to Paul's a fortiori argument to the Corinthians from the human spirit to the divine Spirit. Aquinas then introduced the intention of Genesis 1:26, "Let us make man to our image and likeness." It did not refer, he thought, to the human body but to "that by which a human surpasses the other animals." Aquinas identified what Scripture did not identify. "Now a human surpasses all the other animals with respect to reason and intellect. Whence, according to intellect and reason, which are incorporeal, a human is to the image of God."[87] His enthymeme assumed that God was incorporeal, as being rational and intellectual.

Aquinas positioned his topic of humans after his considerations of spiritual and corporeal creatures because "humanity is composed from a spiritual and corporeal substance."[88] He assumed that the spiritual part of humanity was the soul. The unstated commonality, recalling his treatment of the Holy Spirit, was that spirit was immaterial, as was soul. However, commonality is not identity. It was a logical fallacy of association to argue that spirit was immaterial and soul was immaterial, therefore spirit was soul. The error was particularly problematic for theology because spirit (rûaḥ) was the biblical word for the creative Spirit, while soul (psychē)[89] was a cultural import that was not synonymous. The Greek approximation to Hebrew rûaḥ was pneuma. Aquinas did not pause to ask whether spirit might differ from soul while sharing the quality of immateriality. His reduction of the human creature's immateriality to soul was governed by and orientated to a certain patristic tradition, but especially Augustine's theology, that related the human spirit to the divine Spirit mentally. Aquinas then assumed the equation of the human spirit with soul and proceeded to inquire about the nature of that soul. He thought "it is necessary to presuppose that 'soul' is said to be the first principle of life in those things that live about us, for we call living things 'animate,' indeed those things lacking life 'inanimate.'"[90]

Aquinas emphasized that a human did not possess multiple souls. He cited to the contrary *De ecclesiasticis dogmatibus* (On Church doctrines) by Gennadius, a priest at Marseilles in the late fifth century. It confuted as false the opinion that a human has two souls—"one, animal, by which the body is animated and may be mixed with the blood; the other, spiritual, which attends to reason. We say that it is one and the same soul in a human that both vivifies the body by its association and orders itself by its reason." Aquinas then expostulated against Plato's tripartite soul—nutritive, concupiscible, cognitive—as resident in separate bodily organs, although Plato's texts only generally referenced the bodily venters.⁹¹ Aquinas argued that, if the soul was united to the body as its form, its multiplication or division was impossible. The soul unified the human being, the predication of a human animal was essential not accidental, and intense operations of the soul impeded one another. Aquinas concluded that the nutritive, sensitive, and intellectual soul in a human was "one and the same soul." The explanation was easy, he proposed, by consideration of the differences of species and forms with respect to perfection. Animate creatures were more perfect than inanimate, animals than plants, and humans than beasts. The human intellectual soul thus included the lesser perfections of the sensitive soul of animals and the nutritive soul of plants.⁹²

Aquinas did not explore the human soul—or spirit—as vital, whose beginning and end related to divine life. Vitality was basic to animality, and that subject belonged in the scholastic division of the sciences to natural philosophy, not to theology as the science of revelation. Aquinas valued the human soul as the intellect from the unique distinction of humans from other animals. For Aquinas, the principle of human intellectual activity was the soul, called "intellect or mind," as incorporeal and subsistent. Aquinas expounded the powers of the soul in general, in particular, and as divided into the intellectual, the appetitive, and the sensual. He detailed the will and its free choice, then knowledge. Finally he considered the origin of the human soul. With Augustine he denounced as heresy the notion that God made the soul from himself, rather than from nothing. Aquinas traced that error to ancient notions of everything as bodily, or more progressively of the human soul as part of a universal soul. Citing Genesis 2:7, Aquinas explained that God's breath animating Adam's face was not to be understood corporeally. "For God to breathe (*inspirare*) is the same as to make a spirit (*spiritum facere*)." Aquinas proceeded to question whether the human soul was made by divine creation. He answered in the affirmative from Genesis 1:27 that "God created man to his own image." Thus did Aquinas reinforce his identification of the human image of God as the soul. He also argued that the rational soul was made immediately by God and not through the mediation of angels because Genesis attested that "God himself breathed into the face of man the breath (*spiraculum*) of life." That citation from the translation *spiraculum*, literally an "airhole," suggested God's mouth-to-mouth or nose-to-nose animation.[93]

BODY

Advancing to the production of the human body, Aquinas considered whether Scripture appropriately described its making. Objections from Genesis were the discrepancy of the shaping of the human body from dust with the creation of other things by God's simple word, God's immediate making of the human body not of the whole being, the omission of the soul as the breath of life, the residence of the soul in the whole body not the face, and the making of the male and female genders before the soul. "To the contrary," declared Aquinas, "is the authority of Scripture." Respecting that authority, he omitted his standard response sed contra and only replied to the posed objections. Aquinas agreed with Augustine's *De Genesi ad litteram* that human dignity did not inhere in his divine fashioning but in his divine image. God's creational intention "Let us make man" (Gen. 1:26) did not address angels but referenced the Trinity. The body was not made first, then infused with the soul, because both entities composed human nature, and logically the body depended on the soul, not vice versa. Aquinas acknowledged that some exegetes read "God made the human" as his production of the body with the soul, and "He breathed into his face the breath of life" (Gen. 2:7) as the Holy Spirit's activity. Aquinas did not consider Genesis 1 and 2 as variants from different traditions, as in the modern documentary hypothesis. He appealed to Paul's paraphrase to the Corinthians, "And the human was made a living soul" (1 Cor. 15:45). Aquinas interpreted the verse as "words the apostle refers not to spiritual life but to animate life." That interpretation approximated Paul's understanding of the Adamic human as ensouled by its divine creation but not yet as spiritual by the Spirit's recreation of it in Christ. Aquinas concluded that the "breath of life" meant the soul, "for the soul is the form of the body." He there interpreted Scripture philosophically, particularly from his own anti-Platonic argument for the soul as the form of the body. He then agreed with Augustine that the breath of life was directed to Adam's face because that was the site of the senses, and he added the facial manifestation of the vital activities. Aquinas ended inconclusively on whether the soul and the body were made simultaneously.[94]

He then considered the end or term of the biblical production of humans "to the image and likeness of God" (Gen. 1:26). He proposed nine questions: whether the image of God is in humanity; whether it is in irrational creatures; whether it is more in angels than in humans; whether it is in every human; whether it exists in comparison with the essence of God, or with all the divine persons, or with one of them; whether it is found in humans only in the mind; whether it is according to power, or habit, or act; whether it compares with every object; and what the difference is between image and likeness. In his response to the question about universality, he concluded from a premise that he had not yet discussed or proved. "Since a human alone is said to be the image of God according to his intellectual nature, he is the most greatly like God according as his intellectual nature can the most imitate God." Aquinas agreed with Augustine's identification in De trinitate of the divine image with human intellectuality, understanding, and love. He also agreed with Augustine that the image existed with respect to the one divine nature and the Trinity of divine Persons.[95]

Aquinas progressed from Augustine's De trinitate to his De Genesi ad litteram in treating whether the divine image was only in the human mind. He began as usual by posing objections to that question. The first objection cited Paul's verse to the Corinthians about humans as created in the divine image. Aquinas observed that a human was not only a mind. The second objection was the creation of humans as male and female, a bodily characteristic. The third objection was that an image primarily referenced a physical shape. The fourth objection cited Augustine's classification of triple visions—corporeal, spiritual or imaginary, and intellectual. Augustine thought that the Trinitarian image in humans as the divine likeness was intellectual, which power belonged to the mind. Aquinas responded and agreed with the same biblical citations about renewal "in the spirit of your mind" to which Augustine had appealed for knowledge according to the divine image. Aquinas concluded, "Therefore, to be to the image of God belongs only to the mind."[96] He borrowed the interpretation from his commentary on

Ephesians, stating, "spirit, which is mind ... that is your mind made spiritual." He thought the biblical verse distinguished spirit as mind "because there is in us another spirit, which it is clearly common to us with brute animals."[97] Aquinas did not allow, however, a divided human spirit. In his typical equation of the spirit with the soul, he argued that the soul was one, as both the animal soul mixed with the blood that vivified it and as the spiritual soul ordered by and obedient to reason. He again rejected Plato's multiple souls with their particular bodily assignments.[98] His response suppressed tacitly his revision of Augustine's attributions of spirit to the intermediary imaginative vision. Aquinas significantly elevated spirit to the supreme intellectual vision.

Aquinas amplified that all creatures bore a likeness to God by a trace, but only humans bore the likeness of an image. Since humans, as rational, surpassed other creatures by the intellect or mind, that is where the divine image resided as a human image. However, he thought that a divine trace might be in lesser human parts just as it wholly existed in lesser creatures. Aquinas clarified that an image represented by a likeness in species, whereas a trace represented by an effect of its cause that fell short of its species. A trace he likened to an animal footprint. The image of God in the human mind he likened to an impression. "Humanity is called the image of God not because it itself is essentially an image, but because the image of God is impressed on his mind." Aquinas's example was calling a denarius an image insofar as it was stamped with Caesar's image.[99] It was not a felicitous example because in medieval numismatics the face of the temporal authority stamped on a coin was not what made it what it was, money. Rather, the intrinsic value of its precious metal and its nominal value of a fixed rate made it a measure of values and an item of exchange, money. Nor was one coin impressed from another, but all coins were issued from a common die.[100]

Aquinas did acknowledge that humans, as rational creatures, seemed somehow to represent the species of the divine nature to the extent that they imitated God "not only in that they exist and live, but also in that they understand." However, he did not explore that imitation of God in existence and living for the relation of the created human spirit to the Creator divine Spirit. Aquinas did not address directly either the human spirit or the divine Spirit; he assumed their relational reality. Instead, he focused on the human imitation of God in the mind, which he tended to elide with the spirit. As he early affirmed, "The spirit, that is the mind, without a doubt has been made to the image of God."[101] A coherent reason for his intellectualism was that Aquinas was teaching theology defined as the revealed knowledge of God, who was immaterial.[102]

From his acceptance of humans as the intellectual image of God, he proceeded to inquire about the state and condition of the first human. Aquinas regarded his intellectual soul and wondered whether in paradise Adam saw God through essence. Adam was happy in the Garden of Eden, and human happiness consisted of the vision of the divine essence, the vision that was not through a medium or enigma. Aquinas cited Paul's distinction to the Corinthians, "That was not first made which is spiritual, but that which is animated" (1 Cor. 15:46). Aquinas thought the vision of God through his essence was "maximally spiritual." He concluded that Adam "in the first state of his animal life did not see God through essence." However, Paul, whom he cited, was not writing a facultative psychology about the functions of the soul. He distinguished theologically the created human, descended from first Adam, from the recreated human, baptized in second Adam, or Christ. Aquinas continued that in his ordinary state Adam did not see God through his essence, unless perhaps in a rapture when God put him to sleep so to remove his rib for Eve's making. Yet Aquinas reasoned retroactively from Adam's sin that he could not have envisioned God through his essence because that experience would have so beatified him as to render him sinless. Nevertheless, Adam knew God more perfectly than his descendants, with a knowledge halfway between the ultimate beatific vision and the present inference through creatures.[103] Aquinas had already established that the human intellect in this life could not understand immaterial created substances. Much less, he reasoned a fortiori, could it understand the essence of the uncreated substance, who was God. Aquinas declared that "absolutely God is not the first object of our knowledge." The human intellect knew God through creation as its proper object.[104]

Aquinas's argument on creation did not connect spirit-to-Spirit exclusively because he understood the production of creatures as an imitation of the Trinitarian processions. In his *Summa contra Gentiles* (Against the Gentiles) he noted that Scripture attributed to the Holy Spirit movement. Just as the Spirit proceeded from the Father and the Son as a movement by love, so he produced diverse species from created matter. Genesis 1:2 attributed that work to the Spirit carried above the waters, meaning prime matter. It was not as if the Spirit itself was moved, he explained, but it was the principle of motion. The Spirit was a principle of creation as willed by love, the love by which God loved his own goodness and was its cause. Its motion should be understood in the same way that the will was carried to the willed and love to the beloved. Aquinas noted that some interpreted Genesis 1:2 not of the Spirit but of air, which was naturally located above the water.[105] In his disputed question *De potentia Dei* (On God's power) he specified that the spirit over the waters of creation was "air" in Plato's reading of Genesis, alluding to the popular apologetic of Plato as Attic Moses. Aquinas added Basil's patristic opinion that air as the Spirit of the Lord was an unbiblical belief.[106]

CREATION

In *Summa theologiae* on the order of creation and its elements, Aquinas only incidentally considered Genesis 1:2 on the Spirit above the waters. He declared that the biblical phrase "the 'Spirit of the Lord' was not usual except for the Holy Spirit." His typological reading of Genesis supposed that the Hebrew Scriptures prophesied Christian doctrine. Aquinas continued that the Spirit of God, meaning the Holy Spirit, "is said to be borne above the waters not corporeally but as the will of an artificer is said to move above the matter that he wishes to form." In considering the propriety of biblical language about the creation, Aquinas rejected the opinion that the expression "the Spirit of God was carried over the waters" (Gen. 1:2) was unfitting because God was not movable nor did he occupy space. Aquinas interpreted the verse to understand the waters over which God moved as "formless matter." He repeated the artisanal simile that the divine activity was "just as the love of a craftsman was carried over some material so that he might shape a work from it." Aquinas acknowledged that the Jewish philosopher Moses Maimonides understood by "the Spirit of the Lord" not the Holy Spirit of Christian doctrine but "the air or the wind," as Plato supposedly had. Aquinas reported that the rabbi thus explained it because "Scripture was accustomed everywhere to attribute to God the blowing of winds."[107] The active agency of that reading varied from the stricter Talmudic reading of *rûa 'ĕlōhîm* as the created wind among other creatures.[108] However, Aquinas did not believe air to be the Creator because it was only a natural physical element, hot and wet matter.[109]

In *Summa theologiae* Aquinas appealed to the authority of Christian saints that the spirit over the waters at creation designated the Holy Spirit. He applied Augustine's exegesis that the Spirit moved over the waters as formless matter, "lest it should be thought that God loved the works he was about to make from the necessity of deprivation." Aquinas added Basil's opinion of the Spirit's carriage over the waters because it "warmed and vivified the nature of the waters, in the likeness of a brooding hen infusing vital power to those it brooded." Aquinas noted that water had a life-giving power since so many animals were born in it, and the semen of all animals was liquid. Further, the soul was given life in the waters of baptism.[110] Thus, Aquinas deemed appropriate the biblical metaphor of the Creator spirit over the waters.

Aquinas deliberated also on the Holy Spirit as the eternal Gift within the Trinity[111] and on its external mission to humans as the gift of sanctifying grace. He cited from Augustine's *De trinitate* that the Holy Spirit proceeded temporally for the sanctification of his creatures. That was a real but invisible mission as a gift of sanctifying grace, "yet the divine Person is given." Aquinas believed that the Holy Spirit was sent not only invisibly but also visibly because human nature needed to be led to the knowledge of God from the visible to the invisible. The Spirit thus did not perform by a union with bodies but by a manifestation of signs. Aquinas rehearsed in a lengthy quotation from Augustine's *De trinitate* that this visible mission differed from prophetic vision, which was not corporeal but spiritual or imaginative. The apostles at Pentecost who saw the dove and the tongues of fire saw those signs with their eyes. They appeared physically to signify the Spirit's present yet transient activity. Similar signs were the thunder and lightning on Mount Sinai that accompanied God's giving of the commandments. Aquinas agreed with Augustine that the visible mission of the Holy Spirit was not manifest in prophetic vision, because that was imaginary but not corporeal. Nor was the Spirit manifest by the biblical use of existing things to signify some reality.[112]

Aquinas's *Summa theologiae* had considered God's existence in things, whether he was everywhere by essence, presence, and power. He responded that God was in everything by his power since creatures were subject to him, by his presence since they were transparent to his knowledge, and by his essence since he caused their being. He was in things as the object of operation was in the operator, as properly in the soul just as the object known was in the knower and the object desired was in the desirer. Thus was God especially in the rational creature who knew and loved him either actually or habitually by the initiative of grace.[113] In his commentary on Paul's first letter to the Corinthians, Aquinas affirmed that the Holy Spirit indwelled faithful Christian souls as in a temple. God principally inhabited himself, as comprehensible only to himself, but he also inhabited churches dedicated to his worship. And he inhabited humans through faith worked in love. God spiritually indwelled, as in a family house, the saints whose minds were capable of God through knowledge and love. That was a true indwelling, even if the saints did not actually know and love him, for example, baptized infants who only had those virtues by habitual grace. Aquinas reasoned that his indwelling proved the Spirit to be God. Aquinas syllogized: the Spirit's indwelling made Christians a temple, but only God's indwelling made a place a temple, therefore the Spirit's indwelling in Christians proved he was God.[114] As he continued in *Summa theologiae*, that presence of the Spirit could not be perceived by the bodily eye because God was unbodily. For, although sight was the most spiritual of the five senses,[115] it happened by the contact of the organic eye with an external physical object.[116] Nor could the indwelling of the Spirit be attained by the natural power of the created intellect. God's essence was only knowable by a supernaturally graced union of himself with the created intellect to be rendered an intelligible reality.[117]

Aquinas explained that one intellect might possess a power or faculty to see God in glory more than another, but not naturally so. That variance happened by the light of glory about which Paul wrote the Corinthians, just as the brightness of stars varied. The light of glory would constitute in the intellect a certain "deiformity" proportionate to its reception. Those souls would most participate in that light "who have charity, for where charity is greater, desire is greater; and desire somehow makes the desirer apt and prepared for receiving what it desires." Aquinas concluded, "Whence the more charity he has, the more perfectly he will see God and be the more beatified." That vision of the divine essence would not be by any likeness, but by the divine essence itself united to the intellect. In this life the experience was unattainable. Aquinas considered the biblical objections of Jacob's vision of God face to face and of Moses' conversation with God mouth to mouth. Aquinas considered Paul's distinction to the Corinthians between the visions of

God translated as "now in a mirror and an enigma, then face to face" (1 Cor. 13:12). Aquinas interpreted that God had sometimes been seen through his essence face to face in this life.[118] A mirror was a very popular medieval metaphor for knowledge, as in the Dominican friar Vincent de Beauvais's *Speculum maius*, and in other writings.[119] Aquinas's judgment perpetuated Augustine's theorization of Paul's biblical metaphor. The verse did not reflect a vision of God or the difference between its obscure perception in this life and its clear perception in the next. Paul upheld the mirror for knowledge of oneself in the perception of the church. He promoted a charitable ordering of charismatic gifts for the maturation of the Corinthians beyond childish pretensions. His solution to their dissension was the universal practice of charity as the supreme spiritual gift. As Paul taught, knowledge would perish, while charity endured. His calendar of "now" and "then" was not about time versus eternity, but about what changed and what endured—both as values in time. The lesser charismata changed and faded; but faith, hope, and charity were stable and remained. Paul's message was charitable unity, not contemplative vision.[120]

Aquinas did acknowledge the value of consulting others, against clinging to personal opinion. But his counsel was about deliberating knowledge, as derived from Aristotle's ethical recommendation for attaining certitude.[121] It was not about Paul's spiritual gift of charity that regarded oneself in communal perspective. Aquinas, after Augustine, interpreted Paul's metaphor of the mirror as reflecting the eschatological vision of God. He was convinced since his first teaching at Paris that the eschatological vision was intellectual. In a *quodlibet*, an academic exercise on an impromptu topic anyone could pose, he pronounced God the end of human desire. Moreover, "We are joined to God through the act of the intellect; and therefore, that vision of God that is the act of the intellect is substantially and originally our beatitude." The modifier "originally" meant from the creation, not creatively. It was an absolutely perfect operation in agreement with its object. Aquinas thought the intellectual vision of God was decorated and perfected by the greatest delight, just as in Aristotle's *Ethica Nicomachea* beauty adorned youth.[122] Aquinas expounded in his later disputed question *De malo* (On evil) that active beatitude consisted in the intellect, to which pertained the vision of God, more so than in the will, to which pertained its enjoyment. That facultative subordination of the will was because enjoyment followed an operation as its cause, and enjoyment was added as a certain extra perfection. Again Aquinas appealed to Aristotle's example of enjoyment and beauty.[123] Aquinas distinguished in his disputed question *De veritate* (On truth) the vision of God through his essence with the vision in this life, which was a comparative likeness to, not an equality with, him. In this life the mind could not attain the vision of God through his essence because natural knowledge was through species abstracted from phantasms. In this life there was only an imperfect vision in a mirror and enigma.[124] That was different from Paul's comparison, which was not of temporal and eternal knowledge but of two types of temporal knowledge, immature and mature.[125] For Aquinas, the vision of God through species also differed from the act of faith because its object was the first truth itself.[126] It was an intellectual gift consummated in heaven but inchoate on earth.[127]

RAPTURE

Aquinas's commentary on Paul's second letter to the Corinthians, with its revelation of a personal rapture, is not extant, although there is an unattributed report of it. In *Summa theologiae* Aquinas interpreted Paul's experience in the question "about rapture." That inquiry was divided into six articles: whether the human soul was seized to divine things, whether rapture pertained to the cognitive or appetitive power, whether Paul in rapture saw the essence of God, whether he was alienated from his senses, whether the soul was totally separated from the body in that state, and what he knew or did not know about this. The topics Aquinas proposed for deliberation immediately reflected the abstraction of scholastic method from the rhetoric of Paul's biblical text. Although those questions of Aquinas referenced Scripture and were deliberated in a theological work, his treatment of them was philosophical. Specifically it was a psychological examination of the soul and its relation to the body. Aquinas's procedure also universalized about humanity from Paul's special human experience. Paul was vague in boasting to the Corinthians about his rapture because its revelation was ineffable. He had been seized, he wrote in the third person, of "a man in Christ," although "whether in the body or out of the body" (2 Cor. 12:2) he did not know. Paul stated nothing about the "human soul" of Aquinas's inquiry.

Against objections that the human soul could not be enraptured to divine things, Aquinas initially omitted Paul's qualification that he did not know whether his rapture was in the body or out of the body. Aquinas abridged the verse to "I know a man in Christ . . . seized to the third heaven." He cited the *Glossa*'s definition, "rapt, that is, elevated contrary to nature." Aquinas responded that some violence was meant, as Aristotle's *Ethica Nicomachea* defined. Violence was a movement "whose principle was external, with he who suffered the force contributing nothing." Rapture by an external agent was contrary to inclination because concurrence followed inclination, whether voluntary or natural. That could happen according to something's end, as when a stone whose inclination fell downwards was thrown upwards, or according to the means of inclination, as when a stone was thrown downwards with greater velocity than its natural movement. Therefore, the human soul was said to be enraptured to what was beyond its nature in two ways. One was according to the end, as in being snatched to punishment. Another was according to the mode connatural to humans, which was to learn the truth through sensible things. From that Aristotelian epistemology, Aquinas argued that withdrawal from apprehension by sensibles was termed "rapture," even though the motion carried the person to those things to which he was naturally ordered. Rapture did not apply to sleep, which only happened naturally. There were three causes of violent abstraction from the senses: bodily illness, demonic possession, and divine force. Aquinas defined rapture as happening when "someone was elevated by the divine spirit to some spiritual realities, with an abstraction from the senses." His example was the prophet Ezekiel's witness that the spirit raised him between heaven and earth and led him into Jerusalem for visions of God. Aquinas disqualified as rapture the inattentive wandering of the mind. He further explained that, since it was natural for humans to attain divine realities through sensible means, the mode of rapture was unnatural. It was not contrary to nature, however, but beyond nature because grace was necessary for every elevation to divine realities.[128]

Aquinas probed his psychological distinctions. Because rapture was not by a wandering mind but by a bearing "on the wings of revelation," as the *Glossa* wrote, it was intellectual since revelation was intellectual. Both the term and the cause of rapture proved it to be cognitive, rather than appetitive. Rapture was external to personal inclination, whereas appetitive power inclined to an appetitive good to which a person moved himself. However, rapture might affect the appetitive power by causing a vehement affection for the realities to which a person was rapt. Aquinas thought that possibility explained Paul's two terms "third heaven" and "paradise," with the former designating the contemplation of the intellect and the latter, the affect. Rapture was violent, whereas ecstasy was a simple excess of the proper natural order.[129]

Aquinas deliberated whether Paul in rapture saw God's essence.[130] In that question he repudiated his earlier decision that no one in this life saw God's essence. He had previously determined that separation from this mortal life was required for such intellectual vision because human knowledge was naturally based in corporeal matter. However, the divine essence was unknowable through matter. Therefore, knowledge of him through creaturely likenesses was not of his essence. Yet Aquinas reconsidered that, just as God operated in corporeal things miraculously, so he could "elevate supernaturally and above the common order the minds of some beings living in this flesh but not using fleshly senses toward the vision of his essence." He referred to Augustine's authority in *De trinitate* concerning Moses and Paul, and he promised to treat the matter further in his own question on rapture.[131]

There, despite several objections, Aquinas proposed Augustine's speculation that "possibly God's very substance was seen by some in this life," Moses and Paul. Aquinas's response relied on Augustine's determination in *De Genesi ad litteram* that Paul indeed saw God's very essence as the "ineffable things" he referenced. Aquinas interpreted Paul's phrase as "the things that pertained to the vision of the blessed, which exceeded the state of the living." He quoted Paul's revision of Isaiah's communal lament that the eye could not see the things God prepared for his lovers but qualified it. Aquinas again added the phrase "without thee" to Paul's verse to affirm the necessity of God's intervention for the human vision of God. From that supposition he concluded that it was more appropriate than not to understand that Paul saw the divine essence.[132] However, Paul's paraphrase of Isaiah did not introduce his boast of a rapture. The verses that Aquinas conflated occurred in the two distinct letters to the Corinthians, with the prophetic citation near the beginning of the first at 1 Corinthians 2:9 and the personal relation near the end of the second at 2 Corinthians 12:2–4. Paul's intention for the first citation was to support the Spirit's revelation of the secret wisdom of God from before creation, which was Christ crucified as the Lord of glory. It immediately introduced his a fortiori argument about the Spirit searching the heights of God. Paul's intention for the second citation was to exhort the contentious Corinthians toward a mature charity. Aquinas conflated different arguments from different texts and contexts.

From his contrived premise that Paul had indeed seen the divine essence, Aquinas proceeded to define the three ways in which "the human mind is rapt by the divinity for contemplating divine truth."[133] He ignored a serious lacuna between his proposal that it was more fitting than not to interpret that Paul saw the divine essence and his identification of that putative vision as contemplative. Aquinas presupposed that there was a divine essence humanly capable of apprehension by divine power and that its vision was contemplative. However, essence was not a biblical word or concept, and neither was contemplation, so those were not Paul's literal meanings. Aquinas's procedure assumed Augustine's hermeneutics of Scripture as divine baby talk that required philosophical maturation. Although Aquinas intended his dialectical method to promote and enhance an authentic understanding of Scripture, his contemplative ideal interpreted and altered the biblical verses with philosophical ideas. It was one project to promote the contemplation of God on earth as a Christian practice of faith aided by reason, or even to propose it as the correct practice for all humans as thinking creatures. It was quite another to suppose that the human relation to God in heaven would continue to be thoughtful in an eternal and perfect contemplation.

Aquinas had not established that God, as the end of contemplation, was intellect or even mind. He apparently assumed it from a patristic tradition on the intentionality of the divine act of creation as free. Although human production could be thoughtful, Aquinas did not question whether divine creation was. The biblical metaphor of the Spirit soaring at creation intimated the effortlessness of an eagle's passive flight.[134] Isaiah's oracle extended that model to promise a tireless human renewal. Aquinas agreed that God who created humans would strengthen them in their natural fatigue and conserve them in their saintly ascent.[135] His cursory lecture on Isaiah was his first venture in biblical exegesis, and that particular chapter was among those extant in his own handwriting. It displayed Aquinas's preference for the literal sense of the biblical text.[136] But he applied a natural knowledge about birds allegorically, not literally. He compared all saints to eagles because of the exceptional altitude of their flight[137] and their solicitude for their flock.[138] The evangelist John was figured "as an eagle flying above the cloud of human weakness, he sights the light of unchangeable truth by the highest and steadiest eyes of the heart."[139]

Aquinas interpreted the psalmic image of eagle's wings spread like a tent as the place in which prayerful people were protected by divine aid. It meant especially the Israelite holy of holies as God's very defense. The mystical meaning of that tent was the assumed humanity or flesh of Christ in which he hides Christians by faith and hope.[140] Aquinas interpreted the simile of the eagle circling its nest in the Song of Moses as God circling his people for protection and custody with respect to a prelate's commitment to care for his subordinates.[141] On animal protection he cited the Vulgate's fanciful interpolation of "the eagle provoking its chicks to fly and flying over them."[142] Aquinas did not note the oddity of that simile of a protective raptor, although Aristotle's *Historia animalium*, which he knew in William of Moerbecke's translation,[143] described an eagle as a ferocious predator. Aquinas's commentary on Job recounted an eagle's sharp vision to spy its needed food at a very long distance. He compared the eagle among the birds to the lion among the quadrupeds as both powerful at hunting game. He explained the image of the eaglet sucking blood as the live prey the eagle carried back to the nest. He added that the eagle consumed not only live animals such as falcons and hawks but also their carcasses. Aquinas's commentary presented all animal actions as happening by a natural instinct ordered to the divine will. "The whole natural course of things is a certain movement of the creature toward the command of God." He commented on the eagle's dwelling in lofty heights as expressive of its "nobility of nature," and its choice of a nesting site inaccessible to both animal and human predators. But Aquinas did not understand the flight mode of raptors. Although Job's image of the hawk stretching its wings to the south wind captured the attempt to catch a thermal for takeoff in flight, Aquinas thought it referenced the molting season. "He remarks on the natural intentionality of a raptor, which in the season for a change of feathers stretches out his wings to the south wind, which is a hot wind, so that with the open pores the old feathers may shed and new ones regenerate."[144]

INTELLECTION

Aquinas's comparative reasoning from a human intellect to a divine intellect projected a continuity for contemplation that was unverifiable. He believed that the divine image was in the human mind because the mind was the spiritual component of humanity, as corresponding to the Spirit as mind. That enthymeme suppressed Aquinas's exclusive identification of mind with spirit because it also suppressed his identification of the Spirit as mind. Immateriality became the common denominator of minds. Thus, his examination of altered states of consciousness, such as the experiences of Moses and Paul were believed to represent, allowed Aquinas the opportunity to justify his theory by biblical examples, taken as empirical witnesses. Although contemplation was not a biblical word or concept, Aquinas proceeded to identify it as such. He distinguished the contemplation of divine realities in three ways by biblical exemplars. Those ways were through imagined similitudes like Peter's visionary excess, through intelligible effects like David's spoken excess, and in essence like the experiences of Moses and Paul. Aquinas thought that last pair fitting choices, for Moses was the principal teacher of the Jews while Paul was of the Gentiles. For Aquinas, the divine essence could only be seen in a created intellect through the light of glory of which Paul wrote. That acted in two ways, through an abiding form for the beatified saints in heaven and as a transient passion, such as prophecy, which he identified as Paul's rapture. Aquinas thought that Paul's beatification was not habitual but transient. He then rehearsed the meanings of the apostle's destination, the "third heaven" (2 Cor. 12:2). He affirmed Augustine's opinion that Paul's rapture to the vision of the divine essence required sensory withdrawal because such vision was impossible except through the intellect. As Aquinas explained, again from Aristotelian epistemology, the intellect considered the intelligible only by the phantasms it derived through the intelligible species from sensory perception. The abstraction of the intellect from the phantasms necessarily involved its abstraction from the senses. But the human intellect in this life had to be abstracted from the senses in order to see the divine essence because that vision transcended the natural process of knowledge. It summoned and bore the intention of the mind entirely.[145]

Aquinas had a hagiographical reputation for intense concentration,[146] but mental abstractions from ordinary reality could belong to the topic of the absentminded professor. Thales was the exemplar of the philosopher so starry-eyed that he fell into a ditch in the road.[147] Aquinas excluded from the definition of rapture any such mental wandering. He defined Paul's rapture as an elevation by divine power to a state above nature. As Aquinas analyzed it epistemologically, because the soul was the form of the body, its natural disposition was to understand by regarding phantasms. Divine power did not withdraw that disposition during rapture because it suffered no alteration. Yet, while that condition remained, the actual turning to phantasms and sensible objects was withdrawn because it would prevent the transcendence of them, which the vision of God's essence required. Thus, the enraptured soul did not cease to be the form of the body during the withdrawal of the intellect from phantasms and sensible objects as its natural inclination. Aquinas acknowledged Paul's aside that he did not know whether he was in or out of the body during his rapture. Aquinas thought the apostle's words could be interpreted in two senses. His demurral could refer to his very being as enraptured, whether his soul was abstracted from his body. Or it could refer to the rapturous mode, as in not knowing whether it affected his body and his soul or his soul alone. Aquinas rehearsed a variety of opinions about Paul's ignorance, especially Augustine's lengthy speculations.[148] Aquinas then relied on Augustine's judgment that Paul had seen the essence of God.

Those deliberations in Aquinas's *Summa theologiae* compressed his earlier disputed question *De veritate* that considered rapture. Its five articles treated the definition of rapture, whether Paul in his rapture saw the divine essence, whether in this life the intellect could see God without being withdrawn from the senses, and what the apostle did and did not know about his rapture.[149] An academic disputed question was a live event initiated from the audience by impromptu questions for debate. In that exercise Aquinas posed and answered many more considerations than his *Summa theologiae* would. His definition of rapture in that disputation employed the biblical word "spirit" rather than the philosophical terms "soul" and "intellect." He declared the dependency of the created spirit on the uncreated Spirit. He considered rapture an elevation not happening to the human spirit naturally. He defined the soul self-existing before its union with the body as the meaning of spirit, a departure from his usual equivalence of spirit and soul. Yet he thought that spirit could not be the human spirit because to be human was precisely to be a composite of soul and body. Aquinas further determined "the act of the soul insofar as spirit is to know God and the other separated substances."[150] That disputation evidenced both Aquinas's biblical foundation of a spirit-to-Spirit relationship and his soulful transformation of it as mind-to-Mind. It early indicated Aquinas's function of the spirit for knowledge.[151]

Aquinas later engaged in a relevant disputed question, *De creaturis spiritualibus* (On spiritual creatures). There he identified them as either separated substances, or angels, and composite substances, or humans, with the body as normative. Aquinas defended his theory of the union of a spiritual substance as the form of a body to compose a human being.[152] He also varied the spiritual human (*homo spiritualis*) with the term "the spirit of the human" (*spiritus hominis*). His initial reflection on the spirit commented that "spirit is joined to the body doubly." In one way spirit was the form of the matter to compose a simple unity. As joined to the body, the spirit vivified it but conversely was burdened by it. However, the spirit of a human (*spiritus hominis*) or a daemon was not joined to physical fire. In the other way spirit was joined to the body as an unbodily thing that existed in a definite place.[153]

Aquinas's logical fallacy from association was that because spirit was immaterial and soul was immaterial, therefore spirit was soul. However, biblical spirit was not soul, whether in the imagination for Augustine or in the intellect for Aquinas. Paul had understood the human spirit as a creature of the divine Spirit from the Hebrew Scriptures, which as a Pharisaic Jew he devoutly studied. Genesis 1:2 had introduced the Spirit as the creator of humans "in our image, after our likeness" (v. 26 RSV). Paul's conversion to Jesus the Christ confirmed that belief. As he wrote to the Corinthians, Jesus was the secret hidden from all ages but now revealed to them by the Spirit to their spirits. "For who of humans knows humanity if not the spirit of the human that is in him; so the godhood of God no one perceives if not the Spirit of God" (1 Cor. 2:11). Aquinas's preface to his commentaries on Paul's letters revered that apostle as the New Testament's supreme systematic theologian. Aquinas thought all fourteen canonical letters were authentic and that all had the identical theme of grace. The letters to the Gentiles, such as the two to the Corinthians, treated grace in the mystical body of Christ, the Church. Aquinas ignored the diverse historical situations that Paul contextually addressed, so as to present a coherent epistolary unity. He also thought that Paul wrote syllogistically as a thinker trained in Aristotelian logic.[154]

Aquinas thus deliberated scholastically the premise of Paul's argument to the Corinthians about the Spirit's revelation of Jesus as the mystery intended from before the creation.

Aquinas's *Summa contra Gentiles* cited Paul's letter to amplify an identification of those realities that existed only in the divine will. Such were predestination, election, justification, and other matters pertaining to creaturely sanctification. Aquinas reported Paul's verses as "those things that are of a man no one knows except the spirit of the man, which is in him. Thus also, those things that are of God no one knows except the Spirit of God" (1 Cor. 2:11).[155] Aquinas's treatment of the Holy Spirit also cited Paul's argument to the Corinthians about the human and divine spirits. After establishing that creation was solely God's work, Aquinas added that "creation pertains to the Holy Spirit." He ignored Augustine's semantic interpretation of Genesis about the Spirit over the waters at creation. Augustine had argued that the invocation of plurality, "let *us* make man in *our* image and likeness," meant the Trinity. Aquinas appealed differently to other verses from the Old Testament. The psalmist prayed, "Send forth thy Spirit and they will be created" (Ps. 104:30). Job testified, "The Spirit of God created me" (Job 33:4). And Scripture wrote of Wisdom, "He himself created her by the Holy Spirit" (Sir. 1:9). Aquinas concluded, "Therefore, the Holy Spirit is of a divine nature." The suppressed premise of his enthymeme was that only God could create. Aquinas proceeded to prove that the Holy Spirit was not a creature by citing Paul to the Corinthians as "The Spirit searches everything, even the depths of God. For who of humans knows the things that are of the human except the spirit of the human, which is in himself. Thus no one knows the things that are of God except the Spirit of God" (1 Cor. 2:11).[156] Aquinas only incidentally identified the Spirit as Creator in that proof of his divinity.

From the beginning Aquinas treated creation as a Trinitarian operation. As he affirmed in his writing on Lombard's *Sententiae*, "The processions of the eternal Persons are the cause and reason of the production of creatures." Creation was the temporal version of that eternal activity as its origin, principle, and exemplar.[157] Aquinas's belief was a particular Christian understanding of creation that did not isolate the activity of the Spirit over the waters at creation in Genesis 1:2 from that Trinitarian order. For Aquinas, there was scant theological occasion to reflect on the relation of the divine Creator Spirit to the human created spirit. Given his Trinitarian interpretation of creation, he could neither isolate the Holy Spirit from the Father and the Son nor aggregate the three Persons as one Spirit without their relations. He was thus not theologically inclined toward articulating a Spirit-to-spirit creation. However, Aquinas did amplify from Paul's argument to the Corinthians that there was a comparison of the divine and human spirits. "The Holy Spirit is constituted God just as the human spirit is constituted humanity. Moreover, the human spirit is not extrinsic to the human and is not of a foreign nature to him, but is something of his." Aquinas concluded that the Spirit of God was not extrinsic to God. He inferred the Spirit of God from the human spirit, much as Paul did, and he acknowledged a comparison, not a contrast. Yet Aquinas's task was not an exploration of the Spirit-to-spirit relationship in creation but a demonstration of the divinity of the Holy Spirit in the Trinity. He again conflated Paul's comparative verses in the second letter to the Corinthians with his paraphrase in the first letter of Isaiah's oracle about the divine promise exceeding human vision. Aquinas determined, differently from Paul, that those were the depths that the Spirit searched. He concluded that, if no one could see them beyond God, then obviously the Spirit was God.[158]

KNOWLEDGE

But exactly what was the "something of his" that constituted the human spirit? Aquinas's identification of the spirit as the soul before its union with the body could not produce the human spirit because he defined a human as a composite of soul and body. Aquinas commonly equated the human spirit with the human soul. He emphasized the spirit as the keeper of secrets, as in his interpretation of Paul's verse about "the things that are of a man" (1 Cor. 2:11).[159] Aquinas reflected that other humans and angels could discover those secrets by their effects of either an external act or a changed aspect. Physicians could diagnose some passions of the soul by taking the bodily pulse. But God alone discerned the secrets that resided in a creature's intellect and will. Aquinas thought it was because of the role of the will in considering everything that Paul wrote, as interpreted, "For what man knows the things of a man except the spirit of the man that is in him" (v. 11). Aquinas also applied the argument about secrecy to angelic knowledge. Just as one angel could not know another angel's thoughts because they depended on the other's will, a fortiori so much less could angels know the mysteries of grace because they depended on the divine will. He then cited and interpreted Paul's argument as "For no one knows the things that are of a man except the spirit of the man that is in him. And thus the things that are of God no one knows except the Spirit of God" (v. 11).[160] That was Aquinas's closest approximation to Paul's argument as distinct from a simple "comparison" or "likeness."

In his disputed question *De malo* Aquinas offered that a person knew his own thoughts comparatively "better" than another's, a revision of the exclusivity he had argued on that verse from the Latin *nisi* as "only."[161] He also transferred from his *Summa theologiae* his own afortiori argument, "much less," from angelic to demonic psychology. Reflecting on whether demons could know the thoughts of the human heart, he reaffirmed that God alone could search them. The premise of his syllogism was again his interpretation of Paul's verse as "no one can know the things of a man except the spirit of the man that is in him" (1 Cor. 2:11). Aquinas stated the minor premise that human thoughts were intrinsically in the interior. Therefore, he concluded, the demons could not know them. He then composed another lesser a fortiori argument based on Paul's greater a fortiori argument, albeit unrecognized. As Aquinas argued, much less could the intelligible species, which were in the spiritual mind, inspect human thoughts because those things that were of a man no one knew except the spirit of the man that was in him. And whatever there might be from the intellectual knowledge of the human soul, it was certain that its imaginary vision could no way elevate it to seeing the incorporeal substance and the species existing in it, which did not exist unless they were intelligible.[162] In *Summa theologiae* he argued that God alone could perceive that if it were hidden, as he interpreted Paul's verse "what man knows the things of a man except the spirit of the man that is in him."[163] Aquinas thus strengthened his quodlibetic argument that no one could be "certain" of another's state, again interpreting Paul's a fortiori argument to reference the exclusivity of one's thoughts.[164] Aquinas's writing on Job repeated the interpretation of that verse as the unknowability of hidden things.[165]

Aquinas defined theology by the revealed knowledge of God. "The principal intention of this sacred teaching is to transmit the knowledge of God, and not only according to what he is in himself but also according to the fact that he is the principle of things and their end, and especially of the rational creature." Aquinas assumed that knowledge for the end of theology was also the end of human life. Its terminal knowledge was for the created intellect to see God's essence because the intellect was the highest human image of him. As he stated, God was supremely knowable because he was perfectly actual. Aquinas acknowledged that some thinkers held that God was humanly unknowable because he transcended the human intellect, just as a bat could not by its nature see the sun. But Aquinas disagreed. "Since the ultimate beatitude of humanity consists in its highest operation, which is the operation of the intellect, if the created intellect can never see the essence of God, then it will never obtain beatitude, or its beatitude will consist in something else other than God." That frustration was contrary to faith. "For that is the ultimate perfection of the created reason since its origin of being is from him, insofar as something is perfect insofar as it attains its origin." Frustration was also contrary to reason because human nature desired to know the cause of an effect, ultimately its own first cause. That desire produced the wonder that initiated philosophy,[166] as Aristotle's *Metaphysica* asserted.[167] Aquinas drew a perfect circle from the origin of humanity in God to its return to him as its blessed perfection. The motive and the method were knowledge.[168]

That knowledge was the human end of happiness. Aquinas assumed that the divine Spirit was mind, by projecting the human mind, as the noblest human part, upward to God's mind as its cause. He understood that Christian faith did not treat knowledge by human reason but by revealed mysteries, however useful reason might be to their articulation. Yet he forthrightly asserted a human creature whose fulfillment in happiness was knowledge. In his treatment of charity, however, Aquinas initiated a possible, although tentative, alternative line of argumentation toward a spiritual vitality. Arguing for charity as united to the soul, Aquinas identified that "formally charity is the life of the soul, even as the soul is the life of the body."[169] He also proposed that no one could know with certainty his own charity because its object and end was unknowable, being God, the supreme good, to whom charity united him.[170] Further, Aquinas attributed life to the Holy Spirit because life was especially manifest in motion, and motion was attributed to that Spirit as divine love. "Thus life was also fittingly attributed to him." Aquinas cited from Scripture, "It is the Spirit who vivifies" (John 6:64 Vulg.) and

"Behold I shall send my spirit into you and you shall live" (Ezek. 37:5). He recalled that the Nicene Creed professed Christian belief in the Holy Spirit as "the giver of life." Aquinas also thought that the usage of the word "spirit" agreed even with the bodily life of animals. Those attributions of life to the person of the Holy Spirit were congruent with the name "Spirit" because "even the bodily life of animals is through the vital spirit diffused from the principle into the other members."[171] Although Aquinas believed that vitality related to charity, not to knowledge, his attention to the human spirit was invested in intellectuality. In general he did not expound life but mind. He did not separate them because he fundamentally defended one and the same human soul against its division in Platonic philosophy. Aquinas's reflection on Job's question "did he not give breath?" (Job 26:4) avoided the simple acknowledgment of the Creator that the rhetorical question expected. Instead, Aquinas interpreted Job's verse scholastically as "that is, who created the human soul through which a man both understands and breathes." Aquinas referred to his argument for the unity of soul. "For the one and the same soul it is that through the intellect discerns knowledge and through other powers vivifies the body."[172]

For Aquinas, it was the human intellect that circled back to its divine origin for eternal contemplation of its Creator. He believed that "circular movement among all movements is absolutely perfect because it returns in these to the beginning. To this point that the universe of creatures may attain to ultimate perfection, it is necessary that creatures return to their beginning." The plan of his *Summa theologiae* intended to trace such a circle from the issue of humans from God to their return to him, with Christ as the way back.[173] However, Aquinas abruptly terminated his theological project to complete that circle. He quit it in the third part, in the questions about penance. According to the fifth-hand anecdote in the process for his canonization, he protested, "I cannot because of the things that I have seen and have been revealed to me."[174] His unfinished *Summa theologiae* was not generally successful with his Dominican contemporaries or heirs. The friars preferred his writing on Lombard's *Sententiae* because of the academic requirement for bachelors of theology to treat that text. The questions of Aquinas's *Summa theologiae* that treated morality were much more popular, as pastorally useful, than its doctrinal or speculative questions. His religious order was papally delegated to preach and to hear confessions.

Aquinas's assignments had principally been to teach theology in established Dominican houses of study, beginning at the University of Paris. Finally he founded and supervised a new house of study at Rome for the junior friars, the beginners who lacked a university education but who needed a doctrinal foundation for pastoral ministry. Aquinas intended his *Summa theologiae* as a reference for them.[175] Thus, his companion Reginald of Piperno's distress that he quit it[176] was not in anticipation of a speculative monument of systematic theology. It was because Aquinas quit in the questions on penance, a subject that Dominican confessors needed to learn for their ministry of that sacrament.

Aquinas's decisive experience, whether historical or hagiographical, indicated a soulful event that stunned his body and caused him to terminate theology. Reginald's reported word for it was "change (*mutatio*)."[177] Aquinas consistently used "change (*mutatio*)" as a term of physics, often in conjunction with "motion (*motus*)." And he attributed motion to the Spirit as the agent of Trinitarian love to creatures. Aquinas's treatment of the passions of the soul in *De veritate* defined an "alteration (*alteratio*)" based in human nature as a composite of body and soul. Such an alteration was a surplus, a superabundance in one part that overflowed into the other with certain definite effects.[178] The definite effect on Aquinas of his experience was reportedly stupefaction. The process for his canonization associated the prospective St. Thomas with the beloved St. Nicholas by the topic of nourishment, both educational and eucharistic.[179] However, another tradition preserved in two sources allied Aquinas's quitting of theology with St. Paul and his extraordinary rapture. That variant presupposed that Aquinas lectured on Paul at Naples in his final months, before his departure for a council in Lyons toward an ecumenical reconciliation with the Greek Church. A fellow friar of his Neapolitan priory dreamed of Aquinas presiding in his magisterial chair, commenting on those Pauline letters to a crowd of notable dignitaries and scholars. The apostle himself suddenly entered the lecture hall. Aquinas interrupted his teaching to acknowledge Paul respectfully and to inquire whether his exegesis captured the apostle's intended meanings. Paul assured Aquinas yes, insofar as understanding them was possible in this life. Paul predicted that in time, in the other life, Aquinas would understand them better in their entire truth. Paul then took the belt of Aquinas's gown and led him away. In his dream the Neapolitan friar cried, "Help, dearest, help!" then awoke. Three days later news reached Naples of Aquinas's death.[180] The friar's dream depended on Augustine's interpretation of Paul's pastoral mirror about Church behavior in 1 Corinthians 13:12 to distinguish theoretically the earthly from the heavenly knowledge of God.

However, Paul as Aquinas's model for spiritual rapture was not deterred by his rapture from continuing his apostolate. As Erasmus, whose humanism would in the sixteenth century flourish as a renaissance of biblical learning, observed, "Although Paul was rapt to the third heaven, he still requested his manuscripts when he returned to earth."[181] By that example Erasmus meant to justify his own labors as the editor, translator, annotator, and paraphraser of the first published Greek edition of the New Testament.[182] He was inspired to its scholarship by his discovery in an abbey library of Valla's philological *Adnotationes in Novum Testamentum*, which he then edited and defended against obscurantism.[183] Against scholastic method, Erasmus dedicated himself as a biblical scholar to building Christ's library as the human heart.[184] In his last writing, on preaching, he identified that heart as the human spirit renewed by the divine Spirit, as the religious conversions of Paul and Augustine had exemplified.[185] Erasmus defined theology as the Bible made metamorphic by a seizure and transformation of its readers to "inflame spirits to heavenly things." Aquinas, whom Erasmus considered "the most diligent of all the neoterics,"[186] had begun *Summa theologiae* by quoting a revered pope. "We resound the highest things of God by stuttering."[187] The silencing of Aquinas's scholastic voice escapes modern knowledge because only a hagiographical report, not a historical record, remains about his experience. There are distinct kinds of human unknowing about God: in response to a mystery that transcends the mind, or to an experience that is not mental but spiritual.[188] If Aquinas's conclusive experience was spiritual, his compulsion to quit theology indicated that the obstacle was specifically his material at hand for theology. He did not quit a life of service. He responsibly accepted the role of consultant at the ecumenical council in Lyons, and he was actively en route there when an accident made him terminally ill. Aquinas defined the aim of theology and the purpose of life identically, as the knowledge of God toward happiness. The conjunction may have finally proved untrue in an extraordinary experience. In any case, others would revise his intellectualism to redefine the human spirit.

Part III

EARLY MODERN DISCOVERIES

CHAPTER 5

Calvin

"And the Spirit of God was driving itself on the surface of the waters." Jean Calvin's commentary on Genesis 1:2 differed from the sublimity of Hebrew "soaring" to assert the divine majesty energetically.[1] His preaching to the reformed church at Geneva reinforced his Latin diction, *se agitabat*, with the violent French verb *se demenoit*, "thrash about, struggle." Its exercise meant to "exert oneself, make tremendous effort, go to great lengths."[2] The biblical simile of aquiline soaring in Genesis 1:2 had distinguished the God of the Israelites as effortless, supreme over the foreign gods who witnessed his creation of humans. The Vulgate translation and vernacular bibles in its tradition employed a passive verb, "was carried," with a vague agency.[3] But Calvin emphasized God's absolute action as creator, sustainer, or destroyer of the universe. That divine sovereignty established his providence of all creatures both generally and particularly in infinite detail.[4] Calvin rejected the commonplace for chance, a tree branch accidentally falling on a traveler and killing him. He disagreed, citing the biblical law about violence, whereby Yahweh allowed a man to fall into the hands of his killer. Calvin thought Scripture taught that nothing in the remotest depths of the world was generated except by divine decision, so that events that seemed absolutely fortuitous were subject to his nod.[5] When Aquinas, en route to Lyons, failed to notice a tree fallen in the road and hit his head on a branch with a stunning blow,[6] his imminent demise a month later did not happen in Calvin's theology by natural accident but by divine choice.

LABYRINTH

Calvin was thus born deliberately at the Creator's nod on July 10, 1509 (d. 1564), in the town of Noyon, France, into a family of boys.[7] A rare personal narrative, introduced with polished rhetorical modesty,[8] detailed the divine plot. That preface to his commentary on the Psalms was not an odd place for self-examination. Calvin thought its prayers were "an *anathomia* of all parts of the soul, for there is no affect in oneself that anyone can find that does not reflect in this mirror."[9] Anatomy was the medical practice of dissecting the body for demonstration and examination,[10] a practice Calvin advocated for the soul. Calvin's mirror was not Augustine's mirror of his mind and its psychological operations but Scripture with its reflections of divinely inspired writers. He divulged his own divine election by regarding the psalmist David, a shepherd turned king, as an exemplary mirror for God's lesser turning of himself from scholar to minister. As Calvin wrote, from "dark and slight beginnings, he has deemed me worthy of this so honorable an office that I am a herald and minister of the gospel."[11] Calvin preached for decades, even being carried to the pulpit because of arthritic knees,[12] while secretaries transcribed his French sermons into many volumes.[13] His ecclesiastical office was only attained circuitously, however. As he continued his story, "My father destined me as a very delicate boy to theology. But, when he saw that the expertise of law heaped riches everywhere on its practitioners, that hope suddenly impelled him to change his mind. Thus it happened that, recalled from the study of philosophy, I was dragged off to learning the laws." Calvin endeavored to obey his father's will[14] by studies at Orléans and Bourges under the preeminent lawyers.[15] "Nevertheless, God with the hidden curb of his providence at length turned my course back in the other direction,"[16] an acute bend in the labyrinth.

The labyrinth was a model of Calvin's thought that has since become confused and contentious for want of semantic and graphic research.[17] The labyrinth comprised a pattern and a topic that were often at odds, for *labyrinthus* denoted both the architectural design of a labyrinth and the literary motif of a maze, which were two distinct concepts. An architectural labyrinth was a circular design with an identical entrance and egress. One path only wound through it concentrically, folding back and forth circuitously, progressing inevitably to the center of the circle. In the ecclesiastical type that central point could be cut with the saving cross. The walking of a labyrinth demanded mental perseverance and physical stamina. A maze was a very different design of multiple apertures and multiple paths. A twisting, tricky plot, it could lead or lose the walker in a blind alley or dead end as he progressed toward or regressed from an uncertain center. Cleverness, both mental ingenuity and physical agility, was needed for extrication from a maze. Its artistic depiction was a Renaissance invention, whereas a labyrinth was an ancient and common design. A literary maze, whose many chances for error confused to despair, was often miscalled a "labyrinth."[18]

The labyrinth moralized culturally about good and evil, spirit and flesh, from religious processional to amorous tryst.[19] Calvin learned of the model as a schoolboy studying Vergil's *Aeneid*. Its "game of Troy" was an initiation rite of youths on horseback in a military dance to extricate themselves from a labyrinthine design. The epic also introduced Calvin to the prototypical Cretan labyrinth through its ekphrastic design on the gate to the underworld.[20] Calvin took his example of the labryinthine mind not only from literature but also from life. His native town, Noyon, was a station on the major Roman road to Picardy's capital, Amiens,[21] which featured a splendid labyrinth. Noyon was an episcopal see, and his father, Gérard Cauvin, was its bishop's secretary. He also served as a promoter in the local ecclesiastical court, and as a fiscal prosecutor and promoter in the cathedral chapter.[22] The distance from Noyon to Amiens is only about 40 miles / 64 kilometers, so very likely Calvin visited that city. Amiens boasted the greatest of all medieval Gothic cathedrals and within it a splendid labyrinth. Its multipatterned floor was inlaid with an octagonal labyrinth of alternating white and black tiles measuring forty-two feet in diameter. The dark paths could be traced surely to its center. There four angels guarded the four ends of a victorious cross, within which arms were inlaid the four figures of the founding bishop and his architects.[23]

For Calvin, each human genius sketched within a labyrinth centered on an idol or specter.[24] With his labyrinthine metaphor Calvin did not deny the ability of the human mind to arrive eventually at some central notion of existent divinity. Indeed, he believed that a sense of the numinous was profoundly created in humanity. Although since Adam's fall in the original sin it was inefficacious for salvation, it was not obliterated for secularity. However, a mental notion was not in

Calvin's theology the correct end. A cardiac affection was, and that was uniquely the Spirit's gift. His magisterial *Institutio christianae religionis* depicted a labyrinth of papist superstition and scholastic thought that he later personalized in his confession about his extrication from that labyrinth to a biblical faith. Calvin feared and deplored the human tendency to distractions and corruptions along the labyrinth's arduous winding paths. A native deficiency deterred humanity from arrival at a pure understanding of God. The defect was culpable, as conscience accused, because every sensory perception proclaimed him and all irrational creatures were erudite about him. Humans had no excuse to "go about as ramblers and wanderers, since everything demonstrates the right way." Calvin imputed vice to humans because "the seed of the knowledge of God, sown in their minds from the wonderful artifice of nature, they soon corrupt lest a good and sound fruit develop." The bare, simple witness of creation to the glory of God was insufficient to teach them. From worldly speculation they substituted the dreams and specters of their own brains. Indulgence in curiosity was the entrance to a labyrinth where the unwary became involved in convoluted disputations. Calvin feared that everyone would be wandering in multiple scholastic labyrinths unless they were straightforwardly intent on Christ. The human heart, which "fluctuates in perpetual hesitation" about the path to God, could only be firmed by his word, could only lean on him.[25]

Calvin desired a theological shortcut through philosophical intricacies to the saving cross at the center of the worldly labyrinth. He believed that God was manifest in Christ, by "this secret and hidden philosophy that cannot be educed out by syllogisms." That shortcut was divine revelation, from the patriarchs to their posterity. Revelation "undoubtedly sculpted on their hearts the firm certitude of doctrine" by which they were persuaded of and so understood its divine origin. That doctrine was recorded in Scripture, the origin of wisdom as the studious and reverent embrace of its divine testimony. Its instruction rescued and gathered humans, who were "scattered like sheep, dispersed through the labyrinth of the world." Worldly paths were set with snares for the conscience by superstitions and scruples that portended a lengthy labyrinth with dead ends that were difficult to exit. Calvin's personal labyrinth was his youthful addiction to papist superstitions, from which God drew him by twists and turns to exit into the light. He came to understand that the divine countenance was inaccessible unless humans were guided through the intricate labyrinth "by the rope of the word." Calvin alluded to the Greek myth of the archetypal Cretan labyrinth, which housed the devouring Minotaur, through which design the goddess Ariadne guided the hero Theseus with her slender thread. Scripture became Calvin's religious version of her mythological thread. The only sure guide through the mental labyrinth was the sturdier biblical lifeline, "for errors will never be eradicated from human hearts until the true knowledge of God is implanted there."[26]

CONVERSION

Calvin confessed how as a young man he "very firmly assented to papist superstitions."[27] He characterized himself with the legal term *addictus*, for one "given up or made over to his creditor." Such a "bondman" was not a slave, as in Martin Luther's reformatory *De servo arbitrio* on the enslaved will. A bondman retained the rights to his name, surname, and tribe, and he could obtain his liberty as a freeborn man by canceling the demand against him.[28] Calvin's *Institutio christianae religionis* concluded emphatically with the same word *addictus* for the human tendency to impiety. He strengthened the resolve of believers with a reminder of Paul's incentive to the Corinthians about slaves under civil law who were spiritually freemen in Christ. As the apostle admonished, obedience was owed to God above society. "You were bought with a price; do not become the slaves of men." In legal terms Calvin enjoined believers to remember their costly redemption by Christ's crucifixion "lest we deliver ourselves over (*mancipemus*) in compliance with human cupidities, truly much less are given up (*addicti*) to impiety."[29] That bondage, which finalized Calvin's scheme, had been his own initial state (*addictus*), from which God drew him out. Calvin admitted that, in contrast to his delicate malleability as a boy, as a youth he had become "excessively hardened for my age (*pro aetate*)." The denotation of youth also connoted an excessive hardening "for the time,"[30] which was in ferment with the questions and protests about religious doctrine and practice later called the Protestant Reformation.[31] Calvin confessed that he was too firmly and deeply stuck in papist mire (*luteum*) for easy extraction.[32] He typified humanity by the synecdoche of crippled feet stuck in the deep and dangerous muck of unspiritual devotions, in which fastness it could only perish.³³ He compared himself to Adam, whose body at the creation God pulled from clay (*luteum*) as a lesson in humility. Calvin reflected that it was "a particular dignity" that God formed Adam gradually to prominence over other creatures since he could have ordered him to emerge from the dirt instantly alive.³⁴ For Calvin's own hardness, God "by that unexpected change of mind (*subita conversio*) trained it toward docility."³⁵

Calvinist biography has understood that "sudden conversion" on the model of Paul's conversion on the road to Damascus in the Acts of the Apostles. Yet it has struggled to reconcile Calvin's "sudden conversion" with the apparent lack of his explanation of what it was. Moreover, a precipitous event did not agree with his teaching of religious conversion as a gradual lifelong process, or with his belief that his dissident church did not repudiate the original Catholic faith.³⁶ Calvin did uphold Paul's conversion as noble, memorable, and consoling. But he described that persecutor of the Christians as a ferocious wild beast whose cruelty needed to be stunned and tamed by God's violent thunder and lightning.³⁷ Calvin marveled at those meteorological phenomena as a divine summons from his royal tent by "power, when by very clear evidences he seizes us to regard him."³⁸ He contrasted with Paul's character his own disposition as mild, private, even cowardly, and only frightened into the ministry by human imprecation, not divine revelation.³⁹ Calvin maintained that self-portrait to his farewell discourses in 1564, noting how every person had faults to consider and combat. He began with his own temperament, how "some are cold, given to their affairs, hardly socializing with the public." Short of breath, he confessed himself "a poor scholar, timid as I am, and as I always have been."⁴⁰ Calvin did explain his *subita conversio*—but it was not a religious conversion. Although *subita conversione* can mean "by a sudden conversion," in Calvin's personal context it meant "by an unexpected turn" of events. That change was his father's redirection of him to law from theology, in which papist subject he would only have become more deeply mired.

It was that educational diversion that allowed Calvin's hard mind to soften to God through Scripture. It did not immediately convert him, but it cultivated his mind to "docility," he explained. As he wrote, with some knowledge and experience of true piety, he eagerly pursued and progressed in legal studies, while his interest in papist theology cooled.⁴¹ That true piety was his obedience to his father's redirection. And his pious new studies were not the secret religious devotions of Calvinist biography but his public legal studies. The word *pietas* has been said to be only an occasional and situational term in Calvin's writings for reverence of God and fearful submission to his power, with a devotion manifest in communal worship and individual prayer.[42] Yet *pietas* was not reducible to "godliness." It meant "dutiful conduct" or "a sense of duty" applied not only to the gods but also to parents.[43] Calvin would have learned the term as a schoolboy in the exemplar of *pius Aeneas*, who shouldered his father from burning Troy.[44] His *Institutio christianae religionis* from its very beginning defined even religious piety as filial. "I call piety joined with the love of God the reverence that a knowledge of his benefits procures." Humans were totally indebted to their Creator's "paternal care."[45] Calvin's filial comparison cohered with his soteriology of adopted sonship, which he cited from Paul's letters and amplified by the Roman civil law of property. That law he learned piously at his father's behest.[46] But piety, for Calvin, was merely the dutiful disposition "from which religion is born." Piety was not religion but its "teacher (*magister*)." Calvin's filial obedience to his father's decision for legal studies was the "pious" submission that unexpectedly softened him for Scripture from hardened papist superstitions. It was not a natural but a graced act of obedience to the biblical commandment to honor one's parents. As he affirmed, "The search for the faculty in us of satisfying the law is in vain because God commands us to obey it, since it is established that the grace of the lawgiver is necessary for us to fulfill all precepts of God and is promised to us." Calvin defined the true knowledge of God as living "as his formation bonded (*addictum*) and bound to his rule by right of creation."[47] The recurrent term *addictus* classified his own transfer from a youthful bondsman to papist superstitions to a mature bondsman of his Creator.

Calvin's first major writing commented on the Roman philosopher Seneca's *De clementia* (On clemency),[48] where *subita* depicted Nero's character from his talents. Calvin presented the topic as "to what his noble inborn ability would lend itself, that is, to what studies his mind would apply, what method of teaching he would follow." He explained, "*subita* not only 'sudden' but also 'thoughtless.' For that reason *subitum* is accepted for 'unadvised.'" Calvin immediately discussed how greed for money spawned all vices.[49] His comment on Nero's educational prospects rehearsed the issue of his own direction in life, how he should best apply his youthful talents at study, and how his father unadvisedly and avariciously redirected him from theology to law. Calvin characterized youth or adolescence as a position "at the crossroads" where a man pondered ordering his life and chose a certain course for himself. However, he did not elect his own way. His personal story told how, within a year of his father's change of course for him from theology to law, other students came to him for purer teaching, although he was only a beginner. Despite his "somewhat countrified nature" and his love of seclusion and leisure for study, his lodgings soon became "public schools." Despite his wish for "leisure without renown" for quiet study, "thus God through various bends turned me around full circle, so that notwithstanding he never allowed me to rest until, having opposed my native talent, I was drawn anew into the light."[50]

Calvin further recorded how not by wit but by grace he was led full circle in the labyrinth to its exit. As an evangelical humanist in peril, in retreat from his native France, he decided to hide in some dark corner for the scholarly quiet he was denied. News reached him in Basle of the burning alive of many pious French dissidents, which martyrdom provoked local anger against tyranny. Contrarily, the event incited defamatory pamphlets alleging that those martyrs were actually heretics and traitors intent on the overthrow of church and state. Urged by the need to oppose those lies, Calvin composed the first version of his *Institutio christianae religionis*, which he dedicated to François I, the French king. Its purpose was to expose and justify in a brief manual the faith of the defamed martyrs. Calvin was then on the move again, seeking anonymity and refuge for his studies. A detour occasioned an overnight stopover in Geneva, a religiously factitious city, where his presence was betrayed. Guillaume Farel, whom he typed a zealot in promoting the gospel, eagerly strained every nerve to detain him in that city. When Farel's arguments against Calvin's private scholarly career failed, he resorted to cursing his retreat to leisure. Calvin was so terrified that he abruptly ended his journey. When commotions in Geneva later forced his banishment, the reformer Martin Bucer also cursed Calvin's withdrawal to leisure, terrifying him with the end of the prophet Jonah in the belly of the whale.[51]

Calvin was thus seized for ministry, but not rapturously so like Paul's disclosure to the Corinthians as it was probed by Aquinas's scholastic questions. Calvin disdained such inquiries about the relation of soul to body during Paul's rapture. He thought the apostle simply expressed the magnitude of his revelation, and he respected him for the modest acknowledgment that he did not understand how God had acted on his spirit. Calvin condemned the innate curiosity that neglected edification and audaciously established unknown and hidden realities without a doubt. He thought that much of scholastic theology owed to those faults.⁵² Against such speculations he upheld Paul's example of reticence about his revelation, and he interpreted his word *exesesti* to mean that it was unlawful, rather than impossible, to divulge it.⁵³ Although Calvin was only seized by a man, he attributed that intervention to divine hands as a metonym for power.⁵⁴ As he wrote, God's grasp stopped him in his scholarly tracks, not so much by Farel's counsel and exhortation as by his "frightful obligation, calling God to witness it, as if God from heaven had taken hold of me with a forcible hand."⁵⁵ Calvin believed divine intervention was so pervasive in the world that it could act through human agents. In the biblical type Jacob sought his father's blessing as a deposit of divine grace into his paternal hand. That transfer of power happened because God observed humans prone on earth like quadrupeds or worms, and he raised them upright by other human hands. Calvin's dedication of his commentary on Genesis to Henri, duke of Vendôme and future king of France, was inscribed "so that God, as if by taking hold of you with his hands in a re-creation, made claim on you for himself." That desire repeated the idiom *inicere manum*, by which Calvin had identified God's claim on him for a Genevan ministry through Farel's cursing. Calvin's commentary on Seneca's *De clementia* had interpreted the line "lay a restraining hand upon himself." It meant classically an immediate claim on what was owed, without recourse to juridical authority. The idiom *manus iniectio* was specifically a legal term for seizure by violence, or "main force." Calvin thought humans so vehemently given to fleshly pride that they never submitted to God "unless subjected violently." Calvin corroborated his forcible detention at Geneva in a letter to a fellow student of law, evidence that his choice of that legal term was deliberate and understandable. He believed that divine intervention by main force especially affected ministers, who were tempted to quit in failure.⁵⁶

CREATION

Calvin's translation of Genesis 1:2 thus honored from personal experience the divine majesty as supremely active in the world. He began his commentary on that verse by deliberating the identity of *'ĕlōhîm*, noting that from its Hebrew plural form the three Persons of God had been inferred. However, Calvin resisted Augustine's influential interpretation of the Creator as the Trinity. "But because the proof of such a great matter seems to me to be hardly solid, I will not insist on the word." He preferred to warn readers against such "violent glosses," for they allowed Sabellius's heresy that the Spirit alone at creation spoke the commands or incubated the waters. Calvin taught that there was no distinction of the divine Persons in that verse, and he forbade subtle distortion of the godhead into separate Persons. "For me it is sufficient that the plural number of God articulates the powers he exercised in creating the world." He determined about *'ĕlōhîm* that "the title was attributed to God as expressive of his power, which was somehow previously included in the eternal essence."[57] Calvin's criticism thus rejected the creational basis for Augustine's introspection of the divine Trinity as mirrored in the human mind.[58] Calvin, too, flashed mirrors at creation to reflect God's glorious majesty. But he directed human vision outwardly, for he believed that Adam's fall shattered the interior glass of the mind. Calvin donned a modern invention, eyeglasses, to survey creation. His spectacles were a Scriptural prescription. "If you set before the elderly or the purblind or some weak-eyed persons the most beautiful volume, even if they recognize some sort of script, nevertheless they will hardly be able to connect two syllables. But they can begin to read distinctly with the intervening aid of glasses. So Scripture, collecting the confused notion in our minds of some god, manifests to us the true God, having dispelled blindness with clarity." He added, "For just as eyes discern nothing distinctly, whether dulled by old age or dimmed by another defect, unless aided by spectacles, in our weakness unless Scripture directs us in seeking God we immediately fade out."[59]

Calvin's commentary on the full phrase *rûaḥ 'ĕlōhîm* as "the Spirit of God" (Gen. 1:2) criticized interpreters who distorted it. Their "twisting" of the text[60] was consistent with his characterization of fallen humanity as crooked from a depravity deep within its skeletal marrow. Since Adam's fall, humans were cripples unable to walk in dignity over the other animals, until Christ should re-create their primordial integrity.[61] Their distorted nature necessarily distorted Scripture. Just as Calvin's exegesis of Genesis criticized tortured interpretations, so his preaching on Genesis began by proclaiming not the Creator's glory but the creature's depravity. He announced, "It is certain how humans by their malice work to obscure the glory of God, since they are unable to open their eyes to look either here or there because they have no witness that would conduct them to his knowledge."[62] Certitude about Scripture, which was above human argument and even ecclesiastical consensus, he pronounced "wonderful" for the beautiful disposition of its parts that solidly confirmed hearts. Surpassing the exemplary orators and philosophers, Scripture "attracts, delights, moves, and enraptures. It affects you, so that it will penetrate your heart and possess your marrow."[63]

Calvin was educated to interpret the grammatical meaning of Genesis by a scholarly knowledge of its Hebrew language. Unlike the first generation of Christian Hebraists, who were taught by rabbis, Calvin belonged among the students in schools. Although he never detailed his formal education in Hebrew, he very probably began its study under Sebastian Münster in Basel, where he also acquired his Latin translation of the Hebrew Bible. After possible formal education in Strasbourg, Calvin continued with personal studies. He did not perfectly master biblical Hebrew, but he knew it well enough to render relatively faithful translations. The constraint of preaching at six or seven in the morning did not allow him the leisure for review and revision as his commentaries did. For example, at Genesis 15:11–14 he translated the birds of prey descending on Abraham's sacrifice better in his commentary as *un volée*, "a flock," than in his sermon as *les oyseaulx*, "the birds."[64] With humanist conviction Calvin established a trilingual college at Geneva to educate future leaders of church and state in Scripture from its original languages.[65] He was greatly advantaged historically over patristic and medieval theologians, such as Augustine and Aquinas, by the Renaissance discipline of philology. It established critical editions of the Bible, and it developed methods of historical and literary criticism that traditional exegesis had lacked.[66] Calvin's commentary observed that many exegetes understood *rûaḥ 'ĕlōhîm* as "the wind," but he dismissed that natural explanation as so "frigid" as to need no refutation.[67] His diagnosis of frigidity as a human malady owed to the medical theory of the phlegmatic humor as cold. Calvin knew that sluggish temperament well, for all of the diseases that afflicted him were phlegmatic.[68]

Calvin wrote that the interpretations of *rûaḥ 'ĕlōhîm* as "the eternal Spirit of God" were correct. But he added that not everyone understood its meaning in the context of Moses's discourse. Multiple interpretations of the participle *mĕraḥepet* had developed, even within the consensus about the *rûaḥ 'ĕlōhîm* as its subject. In Calvin's judgment Moses intended to introduce the world as an unordered heap before God's provision of it. Genesis thus established the Spirit's power as necessary to sustain and stabilize that mass by his secret efficacy. Calvin offered that the Hebrew participle *mĕraḥepet* had two meanings appropriate to the text. Either the Spirit moved and drove itself over the waters for stretching, or it incubated over them for hatching.[69] His first verb, *exsero*, connoted the stretching of a bodily part. Since the hand was Calvin's traditional metonym for power and will, he imagined the Spirit extending itself over the inchoate mass with a divine straightness that rectified human crookedness.[70] His second verb, *incubo*, repeated a traditional metaphor of the Spirit brooding the world egg.[71] It was very popular in sixteenth-century literature,[72] thus familiar to his readers. Calvin knew its exegetical history from patristic sources, especially Jerome's *Hebraicarum quaestionum in Genesim* (Hebrew questions on Genesis).[73] That study referenced Basil of Caesarea's *Hexameron*, which Calvin also consulted. Even Augustine, who did not read Hebrew, mentioned the Syriac equivalent of *fovebat*.[74] Münster's Hebrew dictionary and Paul Fagius's contemporary commentary further mentioned that sense.[75] Calvin, in his respect for the original Catholic faith, more probably relied on the patristic references. His commentary finally left the interpretation of *mĕraḥepet* open to judgment, providing that it acknowledged that the Spirit of God destroyed the primordial confusion by its external strength. His *Institutio christianae religionis* affirmed that the Spirit's personal energy diffused above the waters at creation proved his divinity by upholding the celestial orbs, invigorating the earthly vegetation, and vivifying the animal life. He poured out his own vigor into everything in heaven and on earth so to inspire essence, life, and movement. Just as the Spirit was the author of human beings at creation, he was also the author of their Christian regeneration for immortality in the future.[76]

Calvin's later sermon on the creation[77] confirmed God's universal manifestation of his majesty, power, and justice as the source and support of everything. He thought that it was useful to know "the secrets of nature"[78] because Moses's words about the heavens and the earth summoned people to open their eyes to observe their theater of God's glory. But Calvin disapproved of profane philosophers who tried to destroy the doctrine of creation by asking which came first, the chicken or the egg?

God dignified his noblest creature, the human, to glorify him by discernment between good and evil, and by mastery over the animals and everything else. Yet humans were fragile, being born with great pain or dying in the womb. "We are like a wind," he reflected. No human lived without God's invigoration. Calvin invited his congregation, "See why Moses says that the Spirit of God was exerting itself (*se demenoit*) over the abyss and over the waters." That exertion against disorder established creation as an article of faith against philosophical arguments for the eternity of the world. It proved the eternity of the Spirit, he believed. Calvin instructed that the term "Spirit" was also attributed to the Father and the Son as spirits in the divine essence. He asserted God as one and triune, and he preached against pagan plural gods the simple undivided essence of the Creator God.[79] Although Calvin rejected the identification of the creative Spirit as the natural wind, he conceded that the word "wind" (*flatus*) to designate the Spirit was common, as in its descent at Pentecost upon the apostles. He explicated the noun "Spirit" as a figurative "transference" from nature. "For that hypostasis of the divine essence that is called the Spirit is in itself incomprehensible, Scripture borrows the noun for 'wind (*flatus*)' because the power of God exists when as if by breathing God pours into all creatures."[80]

Calvin noted the saying that God created while floating (*nagueres*), meaning that the Spirit moved.[81] He referred without citation to the Septuagint translation of Greek *epephereto* at Genesis 1:2 for Hebrew *měraḥepet*.[82] But he revised it by explaining that Moses's *měraḥepet* signified in that verse "to extend oneself and to exert oneself." Calvin substantiated that meaning of *měraḥepet* by its use in Deuteronomy 32:11 for "eagles and other birds who spread their wings over their chicks to nurture and warm them."[83] In preaching to a congregation in crisis he took liberty with Scripture to actualize it theologically more than translate it exactly. Variations of detail, generalizations, and hyperboles characterized his preaching on Genesis,[84] so that the erasure of the distinction in natural flight mode between soaring eagles and flapping birds was not for Calvin an issue. Calvin's interpretation of the Spirit's action in his sermon on Genesis harmonized the distinct meanings of his commentary, where *měraḥepet* meant either extension or incubation and was left undetermined. He inclined theologically to the meaning extension as a powerful expression of the Creator's sovereignty. Although Calvin did not explicate Genesis 1:2 politically, divine governance was implied by his emphasis on the Creator as the origin and the sustainer or destroyer of the universe. As he preached that dependency, "And thus when it is said that 'the Spirit of God exerts itself (*se demeine*),' it means that this mass of which he has spoken cannot exist by its very self, but that it lacks and needs God. Or, the Spirit, I say, makes it." The origin of creatures in God one and triune was a mystery to be disclosed in eternity.[85] Aristotle's natural philosophy, which Calvin knew, had confirmed the propriety of an eagle as a divine model. As he wrote, "It flies high in order to see over the greatest area; because of this men say that it is divine, alone among birds."[86]

However, Calvin did not exclusively assert the divine sovereignty over humans; he also acknowledged the divine accommodation to humans.[87] That theological tension led him to favor a bird, the hen, which contradicted the biblical and traditional symbol of majesty, the eagle. Calvin's sermon on Genesis 1:2 astutely noted that Moses employed its participle *měraḥepet* also in Deuteronomy 32:11 about the eagle. His *Harmoniam in Pentateuchem* remarked on that verse, "As an eagle that rouses its nest, lies over his chicks, spreads its wings, he took him carrying over his wings." That simile intended "to express God's love with a more than paternal solicitude." Calvin agreed with the Vulgate interpolation about flying lessons. "Then God compares himself to an eagle, which not only broods its chicks with outstretched wings but indulgently and with maternal sweetness provokes them to flying." But Calvin then demurred that "it would be inopportune now to philosophize more subtly about eagles." He was convinced that the ruling interpretation of the eagle in the Hebrew Scriptures was not majesty but nurture and that the hen of the Christian gospel served that parental lesson better. Calvin criticized Jewish fables because Moses certainly wrote "eagle" for any bird whatsoever and Christ's "hen" had the same earnest purpose. However, if someone was pleased with Aristotle's treatment of eagles, Calvin allowed its accommodation. In his own opinion, "I do not reckon that anything came to Moses's mind other than what the words bear." Calvin judged sufficient what was obvious, "this inestimable goodness and indulgence of God, when he is not hesitant to lower himself to us so that in the likeness of a tiny bird he may protect us with his wings and by flying form us to follow him." The verse attested to "a more than maternal education."[88]

EAGLES

Calvin's tolerance of Aristotle on eagles was selective. That natural philosopher recorded that of the many species of eagles only the smallest but strongest, the black eagle, reared its chicks and escorted them from the nest.[89] Calvin preached that lore,[90] although its particularity was contradicted by Aristotle's knowledge of the general practice of brood reduction. Aristotle continued that all the other species of raptors, including the Golden Eagle (*Aquila chrysaetos*), the largest and only true breed, expelled—not escorted—their chicks from the nest. "They rear the nestlings until they become able to fly; then they expel them from the nest and drive them away from the whole region around it."[91] Aristotle reported the belief that the mother also acted jealously from a voracious appetite. As the surviving chicks grew and became adept at eating her prey, they fought over their position and the food in the nest. Finding her young too much trouble to feed, and herself becoming "bad-tempered," the rapacious mother clawed and struck and finally expelled them. The prematurely ejected birds, unable to fly and hunt for sustenance, were rescued by the phene. It was the phene, not the eagle, that was "a good parent, lives well, . . . and rears not only its young but those of the eagle too."[92] Aristotle's natural philosophy did not support the Vulgate's interpolation about the eagle giving lessons to its fledglings and catching them on its back should they falter.[93] His report of the mother eagle's selective rearing further discredited it. As he wrote, she tested her chicks for the keen vision required for hunting by forcing them to look at the sun, and then she struck them and turned them around when they refused. She killed the first chick whose eyes teared from solar gazing and raised the other one.[94] Calvin alluded to that ornithology,[95] but he persisted in his interpretation of Deuteronomy 32:11 as parental nurture.

Calvin preached on Job's catalogue of the animals as "mirrors or lively images" of the divine power to humble people. At its climax in the eagle's behavior, Calvin repeated the Vulgate on the eagle's keen airborne sighting of carrion. He observed its nesting habit but not its flight mode. That sermon included the lore of the black eagle alone of that species as rearing its chicks.[96] On Isaiah's simile of the eagle, Calvin praised God's power to aid the weak, faint, and exhausted of every nature. He distinguished the parallel Hebrew words for "youths" and "select young men" to specify the elect. Their renewal like eagles spreading their wings was fitting because the eagle certainly surpassed the rest of the birds in longevity. He reported that Aristotle and Pliny taught that the eagle never died of old age but of starvation, because when its upper beak grew too large it could no longer ingest food.[97] Calvin likely had the lore from Erasmus's *Adagia* on "the aged eagle."[98] Calvin again criticized as "utterly ridiculous and fabulous" the "Jewish boldness for inventing stories." He cited the rabbi Zaadias (Saadiah Gaon), who "feigned that the eagle flew very near the sun so that its worn feathers were set on fire to allow new growth underneath." Isaiah's simile meant, rather, that those who trusted in the Lord would grow like eagles to the limit of their old age. Since the eagle's higher flight than all other birds displayed its singular agility, Calvin cited the saying "an eagle in the clouds."[99] He likely had that saying also from Erasmus's *Adagia*, which reported its origin in classical drama for a great ambition that was not easily pursued.[100] Calvin concluded that Isaiah's verse was not only about longevity but also about vigor and agility. The prophet told that, after their feathers were renewed, eagles grew to be raised aloft. That was figurative for youths who ran without fatigue, propped up for obedience to their duty.[101]

Calvin was essentially indifferent to what biblical bird served edification, and he did not scruple to transform the Spirit like an eagle into Christ like a hen. For the gospel figured the hen as a gatherer and protector, active and visible in the care of its brood. Prior to Calvin's sermon on Genesis, he preached thirteen sequential sermons on the Song of Moses (Deuteronomy 32).[102] He preached its avian simile ambiguously. "God played the role of an eagle, or a hen." He observed that eagles were frequent in Scripture "because they are much commoner in that country than here, and Moses and the prophets employed the local language." He concluded, "Therefore, let us note well that when it is here spoken of an eagle, it is also as if God said, 'I have been toward you like a hen toward its chicks.'"[103] Yet eagles were also prominent in Calvin's own local language, for the citizens of Geneva lived politically under the sign of the eagle. The coat of arms and flag for the city and the canton impaled two shields, the Roman imperial eagle of freedom and the bishop's key of St. Peter's authority.[104] The golden eagle is a common native and breeder in the Swiss Alps, ranging from the foot upwards,[105] and visible around Geneva, whether on ledges or airborne.

Calvin advanced his interpretation of the simile of the eagle in Deuteronomy 32:11 as parental nurture by a hen. He established God's arm as figurative of his majesty by language descending appropriately to human crudeness and weakness. He thought the avian counterpart of the arm, wings, "expressed the goodness and sweetness God had used toward the children of Israel because he has treated them as a hen thus gathers its little ones under its wings." For Calvin, that gesture demonstrated God's infinite power to conserve his children because "he lowers himself before them, he supports them, knowing their frailty: in sum he makes himself like a hen." In that lesson "he remains at our side, knowing our weakness, so that when we appeal to God, we hide under his wings to be kept and assured there." Calvin advised that no one should be afraid or hesitant to approach God, for "what is a little chick if it is not under its mother's wings?" Humans were similarly nothing without God's protection, although in their vices they did not take advantage of his protection. That is why Christ in reproaching Jerusalem lamented that he longed to gather its children to himself as a hen spread its wings to collect its chicks; but they refused for evil reasons. Calvin offered that in all circumstances "God serves as a hen to hide us under his wings." The preaching of his word supported believers and promised them the power of his Holy Spirit against Satan's efforts.[106]

Calvin preferred Christ's persona of the hen as beneficent. However, his harmony of the gospels interpreted that hen as a scolder. He wrote that Christ expressed indignation more than commiseration so as to revile the scribes for causing the people's crimes. Christ compared himself to a hen to "worsen the ignominy of the wicked people who rejected his gentle and more than maternal invitations." His "caresses" were a "sure and incomparable proof of love" by which he lowered himself to tame a rebellious people. Calvin cited similarly the "reproach" of Deuteronomy, that "God as if an eagle with spread wings embraced his people." He continued that, although Christ "expanded his wings in more than one way for incubating his people," he applied the comparison of the hen only to the prophets sent to gather the strays into God's bosom. For Calvin, Scripture "opens his bosom with maternal sweetness" and even "descends to the zeal of a lowly hen for incubating its chicks." The comparison of the divine majesty with the abject human condition was an astonishing miracle of divine goodness. "When he assumes a maternal persona, he descends to an immense space beneath his glory." Calvin inferred a fortiori "how much more than this when, taking the form of a hen, he deems us worthy to have the likeness of his chicks?" He warned of a "horrible vengeance unless we hide quietly under his wings, which he has prepared to lift and cover us." Christ taught that by faithful obedience everyone would enjoy his protection because "under his wings they have an incomparable refuge."[107]

For Calvin, as a refugee in Geneva's church of refugees,[108] a chick was his desired likeness. In his farewell address near his death he had final recourse to the persona of the divine hen. As he addressed the city's lesser council, "We have, then, good occasion to humble ourselves and to make our way in fear and solicitude, keeping hidden under the wings of God where all our assurance ought to be." Calvin imagined all believers as "hanging from a thread." That thread was the biblical lifeline that God had handed him in youth for extrication from the labyrinth. Calvin assured the council that God kept them safe in every circumstance. Under assault from all sides and surrounded by evils hundredfold, he admonished them that "we should not lose our assurance in him, and every time and as often as something will happen, let us know that it is God who wills it in order to humble us and hold us under his wings."[109] For pastoral consolation Calvin converted the flying eagle of the Hebrew Scriptures into the flightless hen of the gospel that gathered her brood under her wings. He situated that divine shelter "under (*sous*)" God's wings.[110] Calvin's ministry sought security in the shadow of God's wings, and he preferred pastorally the hen's wings to the eagle's wings. He commented on the psalmic imagery of extended avian wings for brooding and covering chicks as the wonderful goodness of God in transforming himself to accommodate human understanding. The shadow of God's wings, spread for fostering chicks, was a familiar invitation to his committed protection.[111] About Isaiah's oracles Calvin acknowledged the immense multiple figures for the title God the father because no simile could express his goodness. For a simple understanding of what God gently bore in his breast to carry and nourish, Calvin thought best the verse of the Song of Moses, "He took them up, and he carried them just like an eagle its chicks on its wings" (Deut. 32:11). Calvin repeated the Vulgate, explaining "he teaches that God does not carry his people otherwise than an eagle props up chicks on its wings."[112]

Despite his humanist education and his scholarly disposition, Calvin was more concerned for pastoral accommodation than philological accuracy.[113] *Institutio christianae religionis* preserved two meanings of *měraḥepet* in Genesis 1:2 for the Spirit's activity. However, Calvin did ultimately subordinate his incubation as the beautification of creation to his expansion as its animation. He taught that in Moses's story "the Spirit of God was spread over the abyss, or formless matter." The beauty of the world owed to the power of the Spirit that warmed that heap. But primarily that Spirit was the Creator, "he who diffused everywhere sustains, animates, and vivifies all things in heaven and on earth." The Spirit's outpouring of vigor, essence, life, and motion to inspire creatures was plainly divine as manifested through its works. Because the Spirit had the duties of divinity, as Paul wrote the Corinthians, "It even searches the depths of God" (1 Cor. 2:10).[114] For Calvin, the essential relation of the human spirit to that divine Spirit was vivification, not mentation.

QUICKENING

Calvin's sermon on Genesis developed from a creational psalm the dependence of all creatures on their Creator for life. "When thou hidest thy face, they are dismayed; / when thou takest away their breath, they die / and return to their dust. / When thou sendest forth thy Spirit, they are created; / and thou renewest the face of the ground" (Ps. 104:29–30 RSV).[115] By generalization, a frequent practice in his preaching on Genesis, Calvin extended to humans that withdrawal of the Spirit from animals so as to dramatize his universal quickening power.[116] His commentary on Genesis invoked that psalmic verse "Send forth thy spirit and they shall be created and you will renew the face of the earth." From its prior verse he noted that, should God withdraw his power, everything would revert to dust and "vanish."[117] His commentary expounded the daily renewal of creation by God's sending forth of his spirit, as evident in animal offspring. God issued his own spirit visibly so that as soon as he sent it all things were created. "Thus he made his [spirit], ours." However, Calvin rejected the "Manichaean madness" that Augustine had survived but the physician and philosopher Miguel Servet currently revived. Debasing him as an "impure cur," meaning of mixed breed,

Calvin complained that Servet exceeded the Manichean belief that the human soul was born as "a particle of the divine spirit." Manicheans had excused their theology by citing Genesis on humans made "to the image of God" (1:26). But Servet, a lowborn worthless man, dared to assert that oxen, asses, and dogs were also "parts of the divine essence." Calvin denounced that transfer of the divine image to pigs and cattle as "doubly detestable." For Genesis did not intend "to divide the spirit of God into parts so that some part of it would dwell essentially in single animate beings." Rather, Moses "called 'the spirit of God' that which proceeded from him." That spirit was given "for life."[118]

Calvin substantiated his own interpretation by the prior verse of that psalm, which affirmed the dependency of created existence on the divine will. Humans only stood insofar as God sustained them by his power. If he withdrew his vivifying spirit, they fell. Calvin acknowledged that even pagan Plato frequently taught the one God in whom everything subsisted. As the psalmist wrote, when God hid his face all creatures were terrified; when he withdrew his spirit they died and reverted to dust. Calvin commented, "As God's eyes regard us we are vivified, and as long as his serene face shines forth all creatures are inspired with life." It was thus inexcusable blindness for humans not to return his gaze toward the goodness that vivified the whole world. God's withdrawal of his secret vigor that enlivened creatures destroyed them. The psalmist described that withdrawal gradually so that by contrast he might better commend the continual inspiration by which creatures were enlivened. Although he could have proceeded to demonstrate the regression of everything to nothingness, he was content with the crass and popular manner of speaking that anything God did not foster decayed into rottenness. He declared it the mission of the Spirit to renew the world daily.[119]

Calvin's first theological work, *Psychopannychia* (Soul sleep),[120] had focused on the human condition of mortality and immortality to affirm vivification as the Creator's essential act. Although humans were created from the clay of the earth as a check against pride, Calvin affirmed that "God not only willed to animate a brick vessel but also for it to be the domicile of an immortal spirit." Calvin understood humanity in existential life-and-death terms. Humans were primordially created from the dust of the earth as "the abode of an immortal spirit." As he defined, "By the noun 'soul (*anima*)' I understand the immortal yet created essence that is the nobler part of him. Sometimes it is called 'spirit (*spiritus*).'" Although the words were associated, their meanings differed. However, he decided, when only the noun "spirit" was specified, it included "soul." Calvin's biblical examples were the rendering of the spirit to God in death, which freed the soul from its bodily penitentiary to its eternal custodian. Thus had Stephen in martyrdom commended his "spirit" to Jesus. Calvin remarked that some interpreters imagined that the soul was called "spirit" because it was figuratively "a breath (*flatus*), or the power by divine inspiration infused in bodies that nevertheless lacks essence." Both reality and Scripture exposed that crass silliness, he thought. Although humans, as earthbound in estrangement from the Father of lights, blindly supposed they would not survive death, they were not so totally blind as to lack "a sense of their immortality."[121]

Calvin's sermons on Genesis affirmed the human duality of a body formed from earth but dignified as "a domicile of graces and of the Spirit's gifts such that we share his image."[122] His commentary on Genesis considered the sanctification of the whole human. Its division into body and soul signified the soul as the immortal spirit that indwelled the body as if in a house. Its two principal faculties were the intellect and the will, which Scripture distinguished to express the soul's power and nature. In that case the soul meant the seat of the affects, in opposition to spirit. Calvin taught that biblical "spirit" should be understood as denoting reason and intellect, and biblical "soul" as will and affects. However, considering *rûaḥ* as "spirit" (Gen. 1:2) and *něpěsh* as "soul" (Gen. 2:7), Calvin interpreted *něpěsh* simply as the living being, not the facultative soul. He thought human integrity consisted in the mind's pure and holy thoughts, rightly and well-disposed affects, and the body's operation in good works.[123] *Institutio christianae religionis* affirmed the soul as "an incorporeal substance as if dwelling in the domicile of the body." The purpose of the soul was "to animate all its parts, and render the organs apt and useful for its actions, and further to hold the primacy in ruling human life." That hegemony not only governed earthly functions but simultaneously aroused a cherishing of God, its principal aspiration." Although Calvin rehearsed a medieval facultative psychology knowledgeably, he was indifferent to its precise classifications because Adam's fall in the original sin rendered the intellect and the will incapacitated or dysfunctional.[124] Calvin expounded "the life of animate man" (Gen. 2:7) against the older majority opinion. For *ḥayiyim*, he wrote "I interpret 'breath' what they call 'vital spirit.'"[125] Although some thought the *rûaḥ* that God breathed into Adam's face was a violent wind, and that his nostrils signified anger, Calvin thought a closer examination established a different meaning. "It denotes human fragility; certainly human life is a form of breath that dissipates."[126]

Against the objection that breath did not distinguish humans from other animals, Calvin defended Moses's expression of their commonality. Calvin argued that breath did not exclude the interior faculty of the soul that the body inhaled for liveliness and movement. Because the powers of the soul were many and varied, it was not odd if Moses mentioned only one in the second chapter, omitting the intellectual part, since he had already mentioned it in the first chapter. "Three steps in the creation of humanity ought to be noted: that a mortal body was fashioned from the earth; that a soul was given whence it would have vital movement; that to these God sculpted his image on the soul to which immortality has been added." The word *népésh* denoted "the very essence of the soul." By *népésh* Moses exposed "the quickening of the clay figure by which it happened that the man began to live." Calvin noted Paul's distinction to the Corinthians between "this living soul and the vivifying spirit that Christ confers on the faithful." He thought Paul distinguished soul and spirit only to teach that the state of humanity was not final in Adam's person because Christ's singular benefit was to renew it in a heavenly life.[127] Calvin's preaching on Genesis also affirmed that God's inspiration of "a living soul" (Gen. 2:7) to Adam imparted life to a motionless corpse. He thought Moses did not indicate the soul and all its faculties but only the vigor that humans shared with brute animals. Calvin conceded that the human soul was very different from that of an ox or an ass. To speak of the entire soul, meaning all its powers and faculties as divinely conferred, meant that "the human soul is a spirit of permanent essence," as the angels are immortal spirits.[128]

Calvin's prime proof of human immortality was moral conscience. "Certainly conscience, which discriminating between good and evil responds to God's judgment, is undoubtedly a sign of the immortal spirit (*spiritus*)." He asked rhetorically how a motion without an essence could penetrate to the divine tribunal and terrify itself with the legal status of an accused criminal. Since spiritual punishment did not affect the body, only the soul, it followed that the soul was endowed with an essence. "The knowledge of God itself sufficiently proves that souls, which transcend the world, are immortal because transitory strength does not arrive at the fountain of life." All the excellent gifts operative in the human mind by which it surpassed brute beasts cried out that "something divine is engraved in it, as just so many are witnesses of an immortal essence." The sensory perception of brute animals was confined to the body and its material objects. But the human mind was agile in science, which examined the universe for the secrets of nature, and in history, which studied and organized all periods of time to anticipate future events from past ones. Human intelligence conceived of an invisible God, a feat beyond bodily ability. It apprehended the right, just, and honorable, which were also beyond bodily sensation. Calvin dignified even "sleep itself, which stupefying a human seems to strip away life." The suggestions in dreams of nonfactual things and their presentiment of future events witnessed to immortality. Calvin concluded, "It is necessary that the spirit (*spiritus*) is the seat of this intelligence." Such evidence sufficed as his simple reminder to pious readers of an immortality that pagan authors had extolled more magnificently. Calvin secured the aspiration of humans to immortality in "the worship of God that alone renders them superior" to beasts.[129]

Calvin dismissed philosophical opinions about the human soul as devoid of any knowledge or understanding of its depravity, although Plato alone solidly affirmed its "immortal substance." Scripture taught the essential separation of the soul from the body by its habitation of "mud houses." At death humans migrated from their fleshly tent, stripping off the corruptible body. Biblical passages "not only clearly distinguished the soul from the body but, by transferring the noun to humanity, indicated it to be the principal part."[130] Calvin cited Genesis 1:26 as firm proof that humanity was created "in the image of God." And he repeated a traditional Christian interpretation. "For although the glory of God truly shines in the outer human, nevertheless it is not in doubt that the proper seat of the image is in the soul." Calvin tolerated the classical model of human erect bipedality, provided that "the image of God that is visible or sparks in the external signs is spiritual." He rebuked the indiscriminate extension of the image of God to both body and soul as a mix of earth and heaven. He also dismissed exegetical quarrels about the meaning of the words "image" and "likeness" in Genesis 1:26 as ignorant of Hebrew parallelism. Calvin asserted that the whole human was created to God's image since human nature surpassed and tacitly opposed that of all other animals.[131]

IMAGE

Calvin thought a complete definition of the divine image in humans was clarified by considering their faculties as "a mirror of the divine glory." He proposed that the subject was best understood as Christ's restoration of the human nature corrupted by Adam's original sin.[132] Calvin explained "the spiritual life of Adam was to remain united to and devoted to his Maker, so that alienation from him ruined his soul." God's curse on Adam's life, consigning him to death, transmitted his original sin to all humanity. Although the divine image was not annihilated, it was "so corrupted that whatever remains is a horrible deformity," mutilated, ugly, and susceptible to disease. Calvin appealed to Paul's first letter to the Corinthians on the second Adam, Christ, who restored the created image to its "true and firm integrity."[133] Calvin's understanding thus differed from Aquinas's identification of Adam's created state as the sensitive soul of Aristotelian psychology.[134] Calvin understood that Paul contrasted Adam's creation as a "living soul" with "the vivifying spirit the faithful are given by Christ," who reformed the original but lost image. Calvin substantiated his reading by the same verses in Ephesians that Augustine and Aquinas had cited for their interpretations of "the spirit of your mind" (Eph. 4:23). That phase meant the renewal of the new human in God's image and the putting on of the new human created by God. However, Calvin understood that renewal as primarily "recognition," then "unfeigned righteousness and sanctity." His term was not *cognitio*, knowledge, but *agnitio*, acknowledgment. It included an admission of the fallen Adamic condition as depraved and needing restoration. Acknowledgment was not a mental act like cognition but a religious act. From Christ's restoration of the divine image in humans, Calvin inferred the original creation of the enlightened mind, upright heart, and complete health. By conformity to Christ as the perfect image, humanity was restored to true religion. A glimpse of the original human nature was visible in the elect as "reborn in the Spirit," although its full splendor would be obtained only in heaven.[135]

Calvin reevaluated the influential interpretation of the faculties of the soul as the divine image. "For that speculation of Augustine is not at all sound that the soul is the mirror of the Trinity because in it reside the intellect, the will, and the memory."[136] He blamed Augustine above all others for sharp philosophical argumentation to fashion the Trinity within humanity by derivation from a facultative psychology. Calvin suggested that a leisurely reader could amuse himself with reading those speculations. He preferred the biblical bipartition of spirit and body as more appropriate to a firm piety.[137] Calvin also dismissed as groundless the opinion that God's likeness in humans consisted solely in dominion over other creatures as heirs and possessors of the earth. "Inside not outside him it should properly be sought; indeed the soul's good is within." However, that interior good was not natural. Calvin began *Institutio christianae religionis* with the coherence between the knowledge of God and of self. "No human can consider himself without God in whom 'he lives and moves'" (Acts 17:28).[138] He cited that phrase from the missionary speech attributed to Paul about the Athenians' altar "to the unknown God" (v. 23). Calvin commented that its topic, "what God might be," proceeded from nature, rather than Scripture, because it was addressed to pagans. Their construction of that altar indicated their persuasion of "some divinity; but their grossly preposterous religion needed correction." Calvin inferred that "the world wanders twisty mazes, yes indeed, it turns about in a labyrinth as long as there reigns a confused opinion about God's nature."[139] He explained that Paul's speech argued from the Athenians' belief in some numen to which they owed cult by running to its temple at Delphi to consult its oracle. The speech distinguished the true God from their figments. From Christ's identification of God as "Spirit," Paul deduced that the only allowable cult was spiritual. As Calvin interpreted it, "The first entry into the right knowledge of God is if we go outside of ourselves and do not measure him by our mental capacity. Yes indeed, if we imagine nothing about him by our fleshly sense but set him above the world and distinguish him from creatures." Yet human audacity fashioned to its own capacity figments that corrupted the sincere and limpid knowledge of God. "For whoever does not ascend above the world seizes vain shadows and specters in place of God." Humans needed to be raised to heaven "on wings of faith," without which they "vanished." Burdened by their own thoughts, they necessarily sank toward death.[140] Calvin compared fallen humanity with its bowed spine to a menaced bird that lay flat on the ground without ruffling a feather so as to avoid capture in a fowler's net.[141]

Against analogy Calvin posed antithesis. For humans to live "in" God, as he quoted Paul's speech, did not assume familiarity but expressed containment because God by his power indwelled humans. Calvin expounded that by his name Jehovah (YHWH) God separated himself from all creatures as being alone, properly speaking. Paul's verse meant "to subsist in him insofar as he animates and sustains us by his Spirit. For the power of the Spirit is diffused through all parts of the world, which maintains them in his state." The Spirit supplied movement to all living things for their vigor. Calvin clarified that did not mean, as madmen said, that God existed in everything, so that stones were gods. It meant that the Spirit by his wonderful energy and instinct conserved whatever he had created from nothing. Calvin reasoned that, since human life was more excellent than motion, and motion surpassed essence, Paul ordered humanity in the highest place. Humans had neither life nor movement, nor essence, which was inferior to both, except in God. Life excelled in them because they had life and motion, not in the common animal manner but as endowed with reason and intelligence. Yet God was importantly present to humans not only in those excellent mental gifts but also "in essence itself" because coincidentally everything subsisted in him.[142] Calvin's preaching on Genesis also interpreted Paul's citation in that speech of the poetic verse "it is in him that we live, that we are, and have our movement" (Acts 17:28). Life meant annihilation "if we do not have our hope secured in God." Movement was synonymous with life, which God conducted and governed. That was God's intention when he dictated Genesis to Moses about his creation. Although Paul's citation was the hemistich of Aratus, a pagan poet, Calvin considered it as if it were the Holy Spirit's oracle.[143]

Calvin thought such poetic sayings flowed from nature and reason about a knowledge of God imparted and engraved in human minds. He blamed the papists for reasoning very differently with testimonies from Aristotle and the pope to silence the prophets, apostles, and church fathers. Calvin supposed Aratus feigned some particle of divinity in human minds, much as the Manicheans fabricated souls as transfers from God. Calvin abbreviated Vergil's *Aeneid* to "The Spirit within nourishes, and, poured into everything through the passages, Mind agitates the heap (*mens agitat molem*)."[144] That verse had poetized the spirit inherent in the universe that Aeneas's father related to him in the underworld. Macrobius had equated that spirit with Plato's "world soul (*anima mundi*)," which the medieval philosopher Abelard adapted to Christian faith as an integument for the Holy Spirit's presence.[145] Vergil's diction rivaled Calvin's interpretation of the Spirit of God in Genesis

1:2 driving itself (*Spiritus Dei se agitabat*) over the same heap (*moles*) at creation.¹⁴⁶ Calvin criticized Vergil's verse for philosophizing more Platonically about the world than understanding that God sustained it by a mysterious inspiration. Yet he conceded that Paul's speech in Acts was allowed to cite Aratus's axiom, however corrupted by human fables. For it testified that "humans are the offspring of God because by the preeminence of nature they reproduce something divine." Calvin judged that the poetic fragment corresponded to Genesis 1:26 about the creation of humanity "to the image and likeness of God."¹⁴⁷

Calvin continued that Scripture also taught the adoption by faith of sonship in Christ's body for a rebirth by the Spirit to become "new creatures." All humans were God's children generally because they approached him in intellect and understanding. But because that image was nearly erased to faint lines, the name "sons" was restricted to the faithful. They were gifted with the Spirit of adoption to reproduce their heavenly parent by the light of reason, justification, and sanctity.¹⁴⁸ Since adoption was not practiced in Geneva, it was not a social model for Calvin's congregation. However, adoption was a biblical model for God's relation to Israel, and it was also an aspect of Paul's soteriology. Calvin judged adoption fundamental to the gospels, although they lacked the word or concept, because in the Incarnation Christ became a brother to humans. "For the key to the kingdom of heaven is the gratuitous adoption of God, which we conceive from the word." As a theologian, Calvin rigorously applied his legal education to biblical exegesis. It was a compatible disciplinary method because the Hebrew Scriptures based a religion of law, on which Paul's letters commented. Appealing to the Roman civil law of property, Calvin established the human end as the possession of an inheritance, which was God's personal fund (*peculium*). The clemency of the Father and the efficacy of the Holy Spirit segregated the elect into a participation in Christ. When Christ crucified committed his spirit into his Father's hands, he embraced the elect, bundling them in his arms. In reciprocity the Father handed back to the Son their salvation. That exchange was a legal transaction, *traditio*, the voluntary transfer of something by delivery, usually physical delivery.¹⁴⁹

Calvin thus ordered by social relations a traditional emphasis on mental operations. His meditation on humanity reordered the human end as the contemplation of God to vivification as the Spirit's creative act. He criticized the intellectualist ideal of a beatific vision, complaining that Augustine had tortured himself exquisitely over it to no benefit. He dismissed Augustine as "customarily too much the Platonist rapt to ideas." Calvin opposed curious and keen disputations about paradise. It sufficed that those believers engrafted into Christ's body were sharers in his life who after death would enjoy a happy rest until the perfect glory of heavenly life was disclosed with Christ's final coming.[150] Calvin defined the blessed end of humans in paradise by their biblical creation in God's "image and likeness" (Gen. 1:26). It was "that perpetual Sabbath, in which consists the supreme human beatitude, where there is a certain likeness between them and God, by which they will be united with him." Calvin criticized philosophical disputation about the supreme good as insipid and trivial because it defined humanity by itself, whereas the human happiness was external, in God. "Therefore the supreme human good is nothing other than union with God. It attains that when we are composed to his exemplar."[151] Against argumentation over how God might be seen, Calvin advocated the serenity and holiness without which he would not be seen. In his revision of a contemplative ideal, to behold the face of God was to believe his paternal favor. Calvin altered the explanation of the divine-human relationship by a facultative psychology by resorting to a social model. He interpreted the human purpose as familial. "And what end shall we find except that of honoring God and of allowing ourselves to be governed by him, like children of a good father, to the end that after having finished the voyage of this corruptible life we should be received into his eternal inheritance? Behold, the principal and even the entire matter."[152]

VIVIFICATION

A biblical model of vivification that Calvin cited was Job's admission of dependency on God for his very life "as long there is breath (*souffle ou halaine*) in me, and the spirit of God is in my nostrils" (Job 27:3). He preached that Job did not speak of his life as if he had it without divine grace. Calvin expounded the true and common saying that humans had from God every breath and strength. Yet he observed that they lived in a brutish manner, as if they had life and sustenance from their own power, as if they did not know, like the pagans in Acts, that they lived and moved and had their being in God. Job, however, paid homage to

God as the author of his life, despite his afflictions. Calvin believed that Christians should make the same profession. He clarified that Job's mention of the spirit of God did not mean the fantastic belief that humans had in them the very Spirit of God, which was "an abominable heresy." Biblical modes of speech occasioned such slips into error, for example, that the Spirit of God was in humans as his essence. That notion, Calvin explained, would make the Spirit of God subject to error and change, thus sullied and contaminated with human vices and sins. It was heresy that human souls participated in the divine essence. For Job did not say that God's essence was in humans but, rather, "his breath, that is to say, that which inspires us by its power." Calvin's analogy was with the power of the sun, whose rays beamed light and warmth to humans. "The Spirit of God is not placed in us, indeed according to its essence, but his power is so expanded that we live in it and are confirmed by it to know that we owe homage for our life to God as the source of all we have by the grace of his Spirit."[153]

Calvin interpreted Paul's writing to the Corinthians about the relation of the human and divine spirits by emphasizing the Spirit's necessary enlightenment about salvation. Calvin did not interpret Paul's verses as an a fortiori argument, however. Calvin deemed it the absolutely clearest verse of all Scripture for condemning the natural man (*homo animalis*) as a fool.[154] He thought that Paul's phrase "for who of humans knows" (1 Cor. 2:11) taught two lessons. The gospel could not be understood except by the witness of the Holy Spirit. And the certitude of the gospel was no less solid than if Christians touched with their hands what they believed, because the Spirit was a faithful and undoubtable witness. Calvin reverted to the dichotomous exegesis of Paul's comparison of the divine and human spirits as epistemological privacy. In Calvin's syllogism, "He proves this by a similitude of our spirit, for anyone is conscious of his thoughts. Moreover, what lies in someone's heart another does not know. Thus, what might be the counsel of God and what his will are hidden to all humans." Calvin concluded that, since no one was God's counselor, he was inaccessible. Yet, if the Spirit introduced humans to those realities otherwise hidden from their senses, it rendered them more certain. Hesitation would then be banished, for nothing escaped the Spirit that was in God. Yet Calvin interjected that Paul's simile did not seem very appropriate. Humans communicated their feelings through language expressive of the character of their minds so that others became aware of their thoughts. Why then, he reasoned, could humans not likewise comprehend God's will from his word, which was his certain truth and living image? Calvin asked to what extent Paul wished to consider his comparison. Calvin decided "the inner thoughts of a man, of which others are ignorant, are perceived by him alone. Even if afterwards he exposes them to others, that does not detract from the fact that only his spirit knows what is in it." He suggested that speech was not always expressive or persuasive. Yet even if someone spoke clearly, it did not negate the fact that "his spirit is the only true knower."[155] Calvin finally distinguished between divine and human thoughts. Humans understood one another, but the speech of God was "some mysterious wisdom" to whose sublimity the human mind did not extend. Light shone in its darkness only when the Spirit opened blind eyes.[156]

Calvin was a crisp and clear delineator, and for that talent he has been characterized as an antithetical, rather than analogical, theologian. His primary technique of argumentation in his French polemics, for example, was to polarize the doctrines of his opponents with his own. He often stated or restated his adversaries' teachings to misrepresent their truth by abstracting them from context and by ignoring any good or common truth. He diabolized his adversaries as Satan's minions. Even his native French syntax employed antithetical rhythms. Antithesis manifested Calvin's thought as elemental juxtaposition "drawn in violently contrasting tones." He defined absolute negatives and positives that distinguished the truth as "black and white."[157] Calvin portrayed humans "in the darkest colors" because of their possession by sin and opposition to grace.[158] In contrast he described God and his operations conventionally as shiny white, the artistic application of a ritual color of splendid light.[159] Calvin compared creation to a painting that depicted God's powers, and he imitated divine creativity with bold strokes of black and white. He declared that light was light and dark was dark by divine will. He thought it insane to demand God to cause light to be both light and dark, or dark to be both dark and light. At will God could change the one to the other, "but to demand that light and dark not be different, what else but a perversion of the divine wisdom?"[160] Mixing black and white created disorder.[161] Job's experience demonstrated that "during this life things are so mixed up that one will not know either black or white."[162] Only divine revelation clarified reality. Calvin believed that colors were created beautiful for enjoyment,[163] but that humans metaphorically debased them. He pejoratively applied the classical rhetorical term "color" for an outward appearance to "an artful concealment of a fault, a pretext, palliation, excuse."[164] In Calvin's exegesis Genesis proclaimed the Creator the sole embellisher of the universe.[165] Calvin judged that even persons of sublime genius in art and science feigned their opinions with "flashy colors."[166] He especially deplored the "fading colors" of false prophets and hypocrites.[167] Rejecting all "vain show of colors,"[168] he condemned as colorful the insincerity, fiction, and lying of everyone's "double heart."[169] The erasure of those colors as false was thus redemptive. "Christ by his light wipes away all colors and exposes hypocrisy."[170]

Calvin was studiously argumentative in the Aristotelian tradition of rhetoric.[171] He freely employed antithesis, such as the opposition of ink versus spirit in commenting on Paul's second Corinthian letter.[172] The contrast between divine majesty and human lowliness was tangible. Humanity was "never sufficiently touched and affected in its lowly state except by comparison with God's majesty."[173] But Calvin's usage of contrast was not abstract. It was contextual, and its context was the Creator as the absolute norm for human perspective and judgment. Humans were never autonomous. Calvin's theology was relational, an evaluation of a human part within the divine whole. And that relationship governed any juxtaposition or opposition. His argumentation also transcended classical antithesis, the positing of opposites,[174] with chiaroscuro, a contemporary method. The Italian artistic concept of *chiaroscuro* entered his native tongue as *clair-oscur* through French translations of Baldassar Castiglione's *Il cortegiano* (The courtier), the Renaissance best seller.[175] Chiaroscuro played on value, defined as "the relationship of a color to the gradations of the gray scale that equates white with high and black with low." In painting, chiaroscuro developed from Leon Battista Alberti's theoretical *Della pittura* (On painting), which advanced the technique of up-modeling, the gradation of pure colors by white. Alberti recommended down-modeling, the addition to pure colors of black pigment to create shadows that imitated the natural perception of lighted objects. Its balance of white and black intended to make a rising surface more evident by relief. An artful rendition of their opposition simulated on a flat surface a sculptural plasticity. Artists expanded the potential of Alberti's popular theory beyond his mixing of black pigment into colors, which could create a murky shade. They hatched grey or brown shadows on top of the colors. Once oil paint was available as a medium to supplement egg tempera for glazing, artists began to layer colors to control their value. By adjusting the transparency and opacity of layered colors they achieved a new clarity and depth of tones. Chiaroscuro meant generally "the use of light and shade." But particularly it was "the exploitation of the contrast for theatrical effect. The shadows are blackish, dark and deep in tone. The lights are whitish, high in value, bleaching the local color." For maximum effect the transitions between black and white were sudden and sharp, in distinction from the smoky (*sfumato*) style that blurred any contrast by soft gradations.[176]

The prototypes of chiaroscuro in the first decade of Calvin's century were prints made from multiple woodcut blocks. The design formed by the superimposition of many layers of ink created the highlight and shade of light and dark that the manual coloring of a simple imprint had previously achieved.[177] Albrecht Dürer was a master of the technique, with his *Melencolia* a notable example of transferring to paper the personification of melancholy's humoral cause, black bile.[178] Erasmus, whom he twice portrayed, praised Dürer lavishly as the consummate artist. He surpassed the ancient paragon Apelles, who glazed his paintings the better to darken or to reflect their colors. However, Dürer "could express absolutely anything in monochrome, that is with black lines only—shadows, light, reflections, emerging and receding forms, and even the different aspects of a single thing as they strike the eye of the spectator." Beyond the correctness of his harmony and proportions, he could draw the impossible, from light beams to the human mind. As Erasmus exclaimed in admiration, "All this he can do just with lines in the right place, and those lines all black!" The addition of color would cheapen and spoil the effect, he judged.[179]

Distinguished artists employed chiaroscuro for religious themes relieving human darkness by divine revelation. In paintings of the Nativity the source of light was the intensely luminous body of the naked Christ child illuminating his mother's face and the gazing angels. In their reflections the shepherds with their lanterns might glow, but the remainder of the scene was executed in deep shadows and barely visible.[180] Suggestive for understanding Calvin's own enlightening role was the Netherlandish painting *Church Sermon*, which highlighted in white the preacher's surplice, his arms leaning over the pulpit, and some congregants below.[181] It was Erasmus, admirer of Dürer's artistry, who identified chiaroscuro as a theological argument. In *Diatribē de libero arbitrio* (Discourse on freedom of choice) he compared the exaggeration of original sin to amplify merciful grace to artistic deceit. "In a certain fashion it imitates painters who, when they wish the light in a painting to lie, darken with shadows the areas next to it." Erasmus again criticized the clumsy and faulty application of chiaroscuro in his riposte to Luther's response in *De servo arbitrio* (On the enslaved will). "So that he may exceedingly exalt the magnitude of grace, he nearly makes a Satan out of a human, by no other art than that by which unskilled painters, so that they may highlight certain areas, add to the proximate one shadows."[182]

VIVIDNESS

Calvin's relation of the human and divine spirits appropriated the classical collaboration of art and rhetoric. Its revival, especially for the concept of vividness, inspired Renaissance creativity.[183] Calvin's theological rhetoric aspired to and achieved vividness by colorful techniques beyond his black-and-white antitheses. The juxtaposition of spectral colors cannot be antithetical because their values are relative, not absolute. But black and white are optical opposites as respectively the absence and presence of all colors. A rhetorical antithesis was a flat and stark comparison in one dimension. As Aristotle taught, its style was pleasant and popular because contradictions, especially juxtaposed contradictions, were easily understood. That was so because an antithesis was syllogistic since refutation joined contraries.[184] The rhetorical equivalent of artistic chiaroscuro differed from the simple black-and-white scheme of antithesis. Chiaroscuro was amplification by a hyperbolic antithesis that debased one term of the pair to exalt the other. Chiaroscuro was a plastic contrast in two dimensions to heighten the value of either the dark or the light object. It simulated that full dimensionality by hyperbole, or exaggeration.

Quintilian's *Institutio oratoria*, a classical manual in revival, identified hyperbole as a method of amplification to create an effect in either direction. He discussed it among the tropes as "an appropriate exaggeration of the truth." In epideictic argument for praise or blame, hyperbole either enhanced or diminished the character of the subject. Although it classically served various uses, its meanings were literally incredible. Quintilian conceded "hyperbole is a liar," but, as he qualified, "it does not lie to deceive." Hyperbole, he argued, conformed to a human preference for the exaggeration or diminishment of truth. Even illiterate commoners used hyperbole when the plain truth was unsatisfactory. It was a pardonable disregard of the truth, Quintilian advocated, because it did not definitely assert error.[185] The manual *Rhetorica ad C. Herrenium* agreed that hyperbole exaggerated the truth for amplification or denigration because comparisons could be about either equality or superiority.[186] Calvin understood that relativity, explaining that rhetoric in the Psalms as "hyperbolic expressions that nevertheless express truly."[187] Ultimately, continued Quintilian, "hyperbole only has positive value when the thing about which we have to speak transcends the ordinary limits of nature. We are then allowed to amplify, because the real size of the thing cannot be expressed, and it is better to go too far than not to go far enough."[188] Calvin's assertion of the divine nature as transcendent of its creation required hyperbole. As he instructed, speech about God necessitated abandonment of the "common style" appropriate to human topics. Divine topics required an elevation of the spirit to "a new and more polite style," especially to maintain for human homage God's majesty as their powerful creator, keeper, nourisher, and sustainer. What human, Calvin asked, could find the proper idiom if all the angels could not chorus his infinite glory?[189] Hyperbole further recommended itself to theology as a strong scheme that in Aristotle's rhetoric displayed "vehemence of character."[190]

Calvin's theology may have seemed literally a monochromatic black-and-white scheme. But it was not antithetical if viewed in full perspective. Again, his chiaroscuro argumentation was amplification by a hyperbolic antithesis that comparatively debased the human to exalt the divine. That technique was an emphatic ordering of divine hegemony and human subordination. It focused on divine glory, not human gloom. In the prevailing Aristotelian physics the proper object of sight, the visible, was color. Black, as the absence of color, was not visible and did not exist in nature.[191] For Calvin, only the illumination of the Spirit on the human mind cast its depravity into deep shadow. Human darkness was only discernible from the perspective of and in the pool of divine light. He established at the beginning of *Institutio christianae religionis* that self-knowledge was only attainable by regarding

God's face then by lowering that consideration to personal examination. "The eye to which nothing else appears but objects of black color judges dazzling white what is nevertheless a dull white or even quite dappled with darkness."[192] Calvin thus deliberately emphasized the negative in order to magnify the positive. It was a chiaroscuro technique of highlight for God's glorification that surpassed flat antithesis so as to project dimensionality. As Aristotle explained antithesis, the mind apprehended its truth linearly by a syllogism. For Calvin, however, only the Spirit's penetration of the heart created the full dimensionality of a human being. He thus composed from perspective to encourage the perseverance of the elect in their grace.

"What is the point of exhortations?" he asked. If the reprobate spurned them with an obstinate heart, the exhortations would still testify against them at the divine tribunal as even now they wounded their consciences. "What can a miserable manikin do when the softness of heart that is necessary to obedience is denied him? Yes indeed, what except shuffle his feet since his hardness can only be imputed to no one but himself?" Exhortations, Calvin believed, were principally useful to the faithful as instruments for the Spirit's activity. The conclusion of *Institutio christianae religionis* proved his purpose since the end of a composition was the rhetorical place of emphasis. There he wrote, "Lest our spirits waver . . ." Calvin meant to brace the faithful to persevere in adversity. He continued with a scriptural "stimulus" to fortitude. The price of Christ's redemption was so costly "that we should not shackle ourselves in submission to the depraved desires of humans; for certain, much less be handed over as servants to the impiety of our creditors." Those were legal terms—*redemptio, mancipio, addicto*—climaxing Calvin's brief for the Christian inheritance of the heavenly kingdom. He concluded as he had begun by embracing "the common case of all the pious, moreover, Christ's case itself."[193] Calvin advocated on behalf of everyone in the worldly labyrinth who was disposed by grace toward the saving cross at its center.

Calvin's chiaroscuro argumentation was also borrowed from a practice of forensic rhetoric that manifested the gravity of a crime in order to elicit the gratitude of the condemned plaintiff for a merciful acquittal. A criminal in the docks before an earthly judge was Calvin's model for the sinner at the gate before the divine judge. Calvin's tactic was necessitated by his conviction of a "natural corruption." He qualified his modifier "natural" as an extraordinary and accidental predication, not a substantive one. For that corruption did not originate in Adam's created nature, which was good, but in his sin, the inheritance of which depraved and deprived all posterity. That particular use of "natural" distinguished universal hereditary corruption from individual personal habit.[194] Calvin defined original sin as "an inherited depravity and corruption of our nature, diffused in all parts of the soul." Its effects were to accuse humans as criminals before the wrath of God and to produce their carnal works. Calvin taught that original sin was no mere privation of primordial righteousness, as most theologians supposed, but a relentless active depravity that schemed evil. Its concupiscence polluted entirely: the soul with its intellect and will, and even the body, so that "the whole man is from himself nothing but concupiscence." Sin possessed the entire soul as impiety occupying its citadel of the mind to blind it, and as pride penetrating its interior to pervert the heart. However, Calvin granted that natural cupidities, which the Creator sculpted in human nature, should not be universally damned. To eradicate them would obliterate humanity. Calvin condemned, rather, "insolent and unbridled movements that combat God's ordinance." Yet, "Since on account of the depravity of nature all faculties are so very vitiated and corrupted that prominent in all actions are perpetual disorder and intemperance, which appetites are inseparable from this incontinence, therefore we contend they are vicious." As he summarized, "All human cupidities are evil."[195]

Calvin's chiaroscuro argumentation was forthright. He was confident that his reliance on Scripture would prevent him from deluding people with "colors."[196] He believed his technique was sanctioned by God's vengeance on the reprobate by hardening their hearts so that their audacity might become more detestable. "God willed the pharaoh to resist Moses persistently, by which the redemption of the people might be more illustrious."[197] Calvin acknowledged biblical "speeches accommodated to our senses, so that we may better understand how miserable and calamitous our condition is outside of Christ." In Calvin's perspective "our humbling is his exaltation."[198] Such rhetorical accommodation to the audience's character, he thought, was not a misrepresentation but an adjustment that only those who did not understand the laws of perspective construed as a distortion.[199] Calvin thus posed a series of questions to justify his method. "For example, if someone should hear . . ." He argued that if someone were to hear about God's hatred and rejection of sinners, but of his spontaneous and gratuitous indulgence that retained him in favor, not alienating him from God but delivering him from danger, "would he not be affected and feel in some way how much he owed to the mercy of God?" Calvin pressed further. If he were told of his alienation from God by sin, his inheritance of divine wrath, eternal punishment, severed from any hope of salvation, a stranger to any blessing, a slave to Satan, a captive under the yoke of the law, destined to a horrible ending; but that Christ interceded, taking his punishment upon himself to expiate with his blood those crimes, placating the divine wrath, "will he not be more thoroughly moved the more vividly he was snatched from such a calamity?"[200]

The vividness that Calvin commended was a valued quality of Renaissance rhetoric.[201] Calvin particularly imitated its classical usage in forensic oratory to represent crime. Quintilian's manual recommended graphic depiction of the murderer assaulting, the victim quaking and crying, begging for mercy, trying to escape, and then the blow, the fall, the agony, the death gasp.[202] Cicero, whom Calvin read avidly, masterfully dramatized in an oration against corrupt Verres the condemnation and execution of the Sicilian captives.[203] Vividness was a frank appeal to pathos, the arousal of the soul's affects to persuade a judgment, decision, or action. The term *pathos* meant "suffering" or "experience," and its usage was motivational, not logical.[204] Paul's letters to the Corinthians stirred pathos effectively.[205] Among the classical types of pathos was gratitude,[206] and gratitude was what Calvin intended to elicit with his chiaroscuro argumentation. He knew Cicero's memorable definition of gratitude in *Pro Plancio*, a work his commentary on Seneca's *De beneficiis* early cited.[207] Cicero esteemed gratitude as "not only the single greatest virtue but the mother of all the rest of the virtues. . . . What is piety," he asked, "but a grateful will toward parents?" Cicero defined holy persons as those who acquitted themselves in gratitude to the immortal gods by worship.[208] The particular gratitude Calvin solicited was the gratitude of an acquitted sinner. To that end he devised his chiaroscuro argumentation of exaggerating his evil so as to enhance his rescue. As Calvin argued, "In sum, since our spirit is unable to apprehend life in the mercy of God or to desire it sufficiently, unless with terror of the wrath of God and with horror of eternal death it is beforehand shocked and overwhelmed, thus we are formed by sacred teaching that without Christ we may discern God as somehow attacking us and his hand armed for our death, so that only in Christ we may embrace his benevolence and paternal charity."²⁰⁹ That biblical formation (*instituimur*) Calvin imitated theologically in *Institutio christianae religionis*, an arrangement on the Christian inheritance of the kingdom.²¹⁰

CHIAROSCURO

Calvin's chiaroscuro method was compatible with Paul's a fortiori argument to the Corinthians from the human spirit to the divine spirit. As the apostle pleaded with emphasis, if the human spirit essentially knew humanity, then all the more so did the divine Spirit know God. However, Calvin's commentary did not recognize Paul's argument as a fortiori. His commentary collapsed the human spirit traditionally into soul, although he had in other writings distinguished them. Calvin's commentary privatized Paul's "the spirit of humanity" as "the spirit of a man," and then psychologized it. As Calvin equated the distinct terms, "Note here that the spirit of a man is taken for the soul, in which resides the intellectual power, as they say." He thought Paul would have spoken improperly if he had said that the human intellect as a faculty of the soul "knew" because the soul was endowed with the power for understanding.²¹¹ Calvin did not deny human dignity as primordially created in the faculties of the soul, but he believed them since Adam's fall to be corrupt and dysfunctional toward salvation. Calvin's mirror for self-reflection was not dull, or merely crazed or cracked, but shattered glass. Humans were in danger of breakage from the cold "glassy" humor of their phlegmatic condition as morally dropsical.²¹² Calvin's exemplary mirror of a graced life reflected the fall into depravity. He had dedicated his commentary on Paul's letters to the Corinthians to Lord James of Burgundy because "when we look at you we know what that vigor of spirit is that ought to breathe in the gospel, as Paul testifies."²¹³ However, when Calvin discovered that his dedicatee had fallen from that good example, he buried him in oblivion by formally deleting his name from the commentary. As he remarked on that erasure, "I am sad that the man separated from the mirror in which he was placed by me."²¹⁴

Calvin's exegesis of Paul's metaphorical mirror for the Corinthians did differ somewhat from traditional readings that distinguished the knowledge of God in this life from that in the next. Calvin wrote respecting the ages of man that Paul taught figuratively that the current mode of knowledge was "imperfect and corresponds as if to childhood." Calvin thus understood the verse partly on the model of human maturation, although he rejected it as an exhortation to maturity in this life. Calvin believed traditionally that the metaphor affirmed the lack in this life of a clear discernment and admiration of the mysteries of the heavenly kingdom. "We do not see except as if in a mirror, and therefore darkly since by the noun 'enigma' he understands obscurity." Yet Calvin espied Paul's mirror as not the human mind, but the ecclesiastical ministry as the means of divine revelation. "Without a doubt he compares to a mirror the ministry of the Word and the instruments required for practicing it." Calvin thought the mirror also encompassed the entire fabrication of the world, in which the glory of God shone for humans. "The apostle calls creatures 'mirrors' in which the majesty of the invisible God appears." However, since Paul specified the spiritual gifts that served the ministry of the Church, Calvin decided, "I say the ministry of the Word is like a mirror." Although the angels did not need it, "we, who have not yet ascended unto such a height, gaze at the image of God such as it is offered us in the word, in the sacraments, and then the entire ministry of the Church." He thought Paul called this vision an "enigma" not because it was doubtful or false but because it was less conspicuous than it would be on the last day. Faith was satisfied with the likeness in the mirror through the word until its perspicuous manifestation face to face.[215] Vision of God now was in the weakness of the flesh; in the life of resurrection it would be in the power of the spirit.[216]

Calvin's eyeglasses were not upheld like Augustine's mirror to see the divine image in the human mind. They were donned not for introspection but for extrospection of the creation as a painting or a theater that displayed God's glory. Calvin advocated deliberative human self-knowledge before and after Adam's fall in complementarity to divine knowledge.[217] His understanding of self-knowledge remembered and cited the Delphic oracle "Know thyself." That pronounced the immense distinction between gods and mortals against human transgression of its proper nature. Calvin also expanded Augustine's self-knowledge beyond cognitive and intellectual apprehension to graced experience. That grace animated the inner human being. It was a "quickening," as in the basic vegetative life of the universe.

Calvin declared it "incontrovertible that there is in the human sensibility, and indeed by natural instinct, a faculty of feeling a divinity."

He had Cicero's history that not even barbarians in antiquity lacked a memory for the existence of God that was the seed of religion. "Therefore, from the initial boundary of the world, there was no city, then no household able to lack religion. In this fact there is a certain tacit confession that a feeling of the numinous is inscribed in all hearts." Wanton idolatry only proved that the absolutely powerful impression of the numinous was eradicable. Humans were "imbued with a persuasion about God, from which, as if from a seed, emerged a propensity for religion." The divinity implanted this religious seed, although experience testified that hardly one in a hundred fostered it, while no one cultivated it to maturity. All humans extinguished their natural light and deliberately stupefied themselves. Instead of serving God with sanctity and integrity, to curry his favor they devised silly trinkets and worthless scrupulous observances. Yet necessity extorted even from reprobates the confession that "an intimation of the numinous (*sensus divinitatis*) is naturally carved on human hearts."[218]

Calvin believed that since Adam's fall human participation in God was not possessed naturally but only attained through the Spirit's activity conferred in faith. "Through him we arrive at participation in God, so that we may somehow feel his vivifying power toward us. Our justification is his work." For Calvin, human nature was vitiated, indeed so vitiated that he transferred the word "nature" from divine creation to human depravity. He further rejected the equation of nature with God as improper language because nature was an order created and prescribed by God. Thus, jejune speculation about a universal mind animating and growing the world did not generate and foster belief in human hearts.[219] The primordial faculty of reason testified that humans were created not only to breathe but also to understand. However, fallen reason "does not attain, or indeed approach God, so that their entire intelligence is nothing but sheer vanity." Calvin concluded there was no human notion toward salvation.[220]

SEALING

Against rational argument Calvin cited the spiritual testimony of believers. "Those whom the Spirit has inwardly taught firmly acquiesce to Scripture, and this is *autopiston*, not to be subjected to demonstration and reasonings." He appealed to Paul's personal commission to preach to the Corinthians, "he has put his stamp [not RSV "seal"] upon us and given us his Spirit in our hearts as a guarantee" (2 Cor. 1:22). Calvin extended that authorization to all Christians. "He administers a seal for sealing those very promises on our hearts, the certainty of which he has previously impressed on our minds, and he takes the place of an earnest for confirming and constituting them."[221] Calvin's verb "to seal (*obsigno*)" altered Paul's image of the Spirit's "stamp" on humans as the artisan of them as his clay lamps.[222] Genevans knew what a trademark was. For their protection as consumers, their daily loaves of bread were stamped with a trademark that bakers were legally required to register with the Seigneurie as a guarantee of accurate weight.[223] For Calvin, however, a stamped terracotta figure was a lesson in humility, not a mark of creativity.[224]

As Calvin knew from Cicero's forensic oratory, *obsigno* designated sealing the papers and effects of an accused person, and also the sealing of a will.[225] Legal *institutio*, the title of Calvin's magisterial work, was the creation of an inheritance.[226] Calvin's doctrine of the Spirit's seal related to both the condemnation of sinners and their adoption as heirs. The seal accused them but then acquitted them. That act was Christian "institution," the human inheritance of the kingdom of God as adopted sons. Their inner seal by the Spirit was the gift of faith, a privilege not a nature. It was, for Calvin, "the kind of persuasion that requires no reasons, the kind of knowledge that agrees with the best reason."[227] The Spirit's pledge certified faith. Calvin excoriated the "diabolical infidelity" of the scholastics, who considered that certitude presumptuous and so left consciences fluctuating in constant doubt.[228] He believed that the Spirit would "spiritually create you new humans, so that purged from filth or flesh and world you will cherish him purely."[229] Calvin's doctrine depended for its import on Aristotle's definition of nature as the possession of an intrinsic movement. From his famous dissections of the chick embryo Aristotle had determined the heart as the origin of bodily movement in blooded animals.[230] But Calvin contradicted the philosophical naturalism of physical chicks with spiritual chicks swept by the Spirit beneath the sheltering wings of Christ the hen. "It is the proper work of God, by the intrinsic movement of the Spirit (*intrinseco spiritus motu*), to reverse the direction of human hearts to himself."[231]

In Ezekiel's prophecy of a new covenant God promised, "a new spirit I will put within you. . . . And I will put my spirit within you" (Ezek. 36:26–27). As Calvin explained that oracle, "Regeneration is like another species of creation." In comparison with the Spirit's first creation in Genesis 1:26, "it far surpasses it." Calvin identified the primordial formation of humans as sons in the image of God, then their superior reformation as sons in the Son's image. Since Adam's fall in original sin everyone was "born sons of wrath, we are born corrupt and degenerate." With the erasure of the divine image in Adam's fall, integrity was lost. Yet "now, where God refashions us, we are not so much born sons of Adam, but we are brothers of angels and members of Christ."[232] The Spirit's new sanctification in Christ was spiritual, a new and better creation than in Genesis.

CHAPTER 6

Science

Jean Calvin embodied his commentary on Genesis as "a fetus barely yet conceived in the womb," in writing to Guillaume Farel, who had by main force detained him in Geneva for church ministry.[1] Calvin defined a fetus as the *embruon* from conception to parturition. It was "a formless mass," in tacit comparison with the formless earth of Genesis 1:2, over which the Spirit created in or at the beginning. Calvin rehearsed the psalmist's a fortiori argument, acknowledging that if God knew him in the deepest caverns of the womb he could much less escape God's notice as a grown man.[2] The slow gestation of Calvin's commentary on Genesis was interrupted for one on the Acts of the Apostles and for ecclesiastical causes. His letter to Farel announced the "glad tidings" of the gospel's success in England, where the Reformed rite was being permitted selectively. Calvin divulged that "the king himself was so disposed toward religion that he even showed some goodwill toward me."[3] The king was Edward VI, whose brief reign orientated the Church of England to the Reformed faith. Since he was only a boy, that impetus came from his councilors and churchmen, and the Anglican reform was less rigorous than Geneva's church in both liturgy and polity.[4] Yet Calvin's writings multiplied in English translation more than in all the other vernaculars combined. They were directed to the laity, not the clergy, for use by reformatory groups. Publications included Thomas Tymme's translations of Calvin's commentaries on Genesis, Corinthians, and Acts, and Arthur Golding's translation of his sermons on Deuteronomy.[5] The director for the Authorized Version of the English Bible preached to its sponsor in Calvinist chiaroscuro about the glad tidings. As Lancelot Andrewes addressed King James on Christmas in 1610, "Sure there is no joy in the world to the joy of a man saved; no joy so great, so news so welcome, as to one ready to perish, in case of a lost man, to hear of one that will save him." As he amplified, "In danger of perishing by sickness, to hear of one will make him well again; by sentence of the law, of one with a pardon to save his life; by enemies, of one that will rescue and set him in safety. Tell any of these, assure them but of a Savior, it is the best news he ever heard in his life."[6]

DIVINITY

A cultural heir to the church reform was the English physician and natural philosopher William Harvey (1578–1657), who researched creation with a sure conviction of its divine origin. Yet he did not deduce that origin from Anglican theology. Although he professed his scientific conclusion most fittingly compatible with Christian belief in the biblical "Creator" of Genesis 1, he acknowledged other designations. As he catalogued them in *Exercitationes de generatione animalium* (Exercises on the generation of animals): "either 'the divine mind' with Aristotle, or 'the world soul' with Plato; or with others, 'Nature naturing'; or with heathens, 'Saturn' or 'Jove'; or preferably (as befits us) 'the Creator' and 'the Father' of everything in heaven and on earth, from whom animals and their origins depend, by whose will or word all things are made and generated."[7] Despite his generous inclusion of various origins, Harvey's scientific teleology was fundamentally an Aristotelian natural philosophy. Aristotle, however, did not acknowledge an animate external cause of the universe, a Creator as the Bible or as Christian creeds affirmed. Aristotle posited only an intrinsic prime mover of the universe,[8] although Thomas Aquinas's medieval *Summa theologiae*, with philosophical accommodation, notably adapted and applied that prime mover to "what everyone calls God."[9]

Harvey grafted to his scientific principles a contemporary religious culture that complemented Calvin's belief in a "sense of divinity" primordially created in all humans. Harvey, too, was an explorer of the human spirit, although through anatomical exercises, not biblical exegeses. Other writings—Genesis, Paul's letters to the Corinthians, and the theologies of Augustine, Aquinas, and Calvin—had treated the human spirit directly and religiously. Harvey approached the human spirit indirectly and scientifically through animal spirit. He included humans in the highest class of animals as blooded. His research and reason ultimately identified the human spirit theoretically with "courage," its modern meaning. However, there were fundamental distinctions between Harvey's anatomical investigations toward understanding the human spirit and theological deliberations about it. Calvin's theology, which prevailed in Harvey's church and its culture, provided a historical basis for continuity and change in the idea. Although the development of Calvinist theology formalized Calvin's *sensus divinitatis* as "the natural knowledge of God,"[10] Calvin himself had been neither so specific nor so rational.[11] His conviction of a religious seed deeply planted in humanity depended for its historical confirmation on Roman society,[12] which extended *divinitas* beyond gods to emperors and orators, such as the "divine" Cicero he favored. Calvin's "sense of divinity" was an intimation of the numinous, whose primary witness was not reason but conscience. Not only was that sense inefficacious for salvation, but also it ruined humanity after Adam's original sin as incapable of a worthy response to the numinous, indeed as culpable and damnable.[13] Nevertheless, Calvin did not sever that fallen creature's relation to the Creator. He allowed humanity a successful operation in secular affairs, from biological propagation to social civilization.[14]

Harvey's investigation of biological propagation was thus tolerable as secular science, although he further probed its nature ambitiously toward a divine cause and effect. Unlike Calvin, who forbade asking about the priority of the chicken or the egg,[15] Harvey made them his special subject. Calvin had praised childbirth as a miracle, which had been demeaned by familiarity. He marveled at the "fetus shut up in its mother's womb in filths that would suffocate the most robust male in the space of half an hour." Childbirth was a grace, he believed, for unless God's hand assisted the mother and the midwife by extracting the fetus into his bosom there was no hope of life. "Exit from the uterus would be entry to a thousand deaths."[16] Calvin's fear was personal, for all of his own children died in infancy, one of them perhaps at birth.[17] In a tender and poignant memory of his dead babes and his wife, Calvin praised the tongues of infants sucking their mothers' breasts as preachers of the divine glory surpassing all orators.[18]

Harvey's contribution on the human spirit was not theological argument but teleological research; that is, his method did not deduce from Scripture but induce from science. Whereas Paul exhorted the Corinthians to mature through the ages of man from fleshly quarrels to spiritual charity,[19] Harvey considered a maturation that was biological. "Before man emerged as an adult male he was a boy (indeed from the boy he grew into the man); before a boy he was an infant; before an infant, an embryo." Harvey endeavored to strip away the accretions to learn "what he was in the maternal uterus, before the embryo or the fetus existed." Was he "bubbles," or, quoting Ovid's *Metamorphosis*, a "rude and shapeless mass"? Or was a man the conception or coagulation of mixed semens, or something else?[20] Whereas Calvin had seated the sense of divinity not in reason but in conscience, Harvey restored reason. His *Exercitatio anatomica de motu cordis et sanguinis in animalibus* (Anatomical exercise on the movement of the heart and the blood in animals) became in 1628 the landmark book in the history of medicine as science. Its complex anatomical method coordinated ocular demonstrations with mental deliberations.[21] It resisted and rejected the medicine that Harvey judged a quasi-monastic tradition of copying authorities.[22] *De generatione animalium* in 1651 reiterated Harvey's "new and surer footpath" to science from examining subjects instead of reading books. He invited his own readers to "weigh in the exact scale of experience" his words, and to take them not on faith but on the testimony of their own eyes. Otherwise, he advised, they would conceive not true ideas but false idols and empty fantasies.[23]

Harvey's book on the generation of animals was not a biblical commentary but an anatomical examination. Yet it was compatible with Calvin's conviction that God's daily renewal of creation by his Spirit was indeed manifest in the generation of animals.[24] Calvin had warned of the dangers of the worldly labyrinth, in which humans tortured their minds striving to find God and fainted from fatigue before attaining their goal at its center. Harvey did not fear to enter and explore the bodily "labyrinth," although he admitted exhaustion in struggling to solve the mystery of its blood flow.[25] He was well educated for his labors at the University of Padua, where he took his medical degree under Girolamo Fabrici d'Acquapendente, its anatomical master. Fabrici understood that Aristotle surpassed comparative anatomy with philosophical inquiry about quiddity and causes. He determined not to study Aristotle's animal lore bookishly, or even to replicate his dissections simply, but to expand both theory and practice by his own efforts. Not only did

Fabrici supply omissions and correct errors in natural philosophy, but he also reinvestigated animal nature at firsthand and by eyewitness. In his essaying and successful program he published many monographs,[26] except on the heart, despite some research on it. Harvey's dedication to cardiovascular research in *De motu cordis et sanguinis* more than supplied the organ missing from Fabrici's publications. For in Aristotle's natural philosophy, to which they both subscribed, the heart was the principal organ. It was the first organ born in the fetus of blooded animals, visible as a pinpoint by the third day. It was the font of the vital blood supply, the seat of the soul, and the source of sensation.[27]

Harvey's cardiocentrism challenged Galen of Pergamum's cephalocentrism, the established physiology at the College of Physicians, London, where Harvey was appointed Lumleian lecturer in anatomy.[28] Harvey relegated the brain to the instrument of conception for art, analogous to generation as the instrument of the egg or uterus in nature.[29] Yet Galen was the prominent Roman physician whose medical volumes the collegiate members were sworn to uphold.[30] He honored the brain as the general seat of the soul, although its exclusion from the ventricular system avoided a strict equation of the rational soul with psychic spirit.[31] Galen was not only a physician but also a philosopher whose teleology praised a divine design to the structure and function of the human body.[32] On his authority Calvin recommended Christian meditation on humanity as divinely created in its pristine state before Adam's fall in the original sin. His *Institutio christianae religionis* encouraged the faithful to regard the body's design with keen acuity, to "weigh with Galen's skill its organism, symmetry, beauty, and use." Calvin acknowledged a universal belief that "the human body shows itself to be a composition so ingenious that on its account its Creator is deservedly judged wonderful." He declared that God was found not only in the soul but a hundred times over in the body. His "exquisite handicraft" was experienced in its individual members, not only in the senses of the dominant head but "even to their very toenails." Upon inspection, fingernails were "mirrors of God's providence, in which we see marvelous workmanship." Even the pagans were constrained to acknowledge a sovereign deity as "convinced by only a fingernail." Calvin believed the divine Creator superior to human craftsmen, who needed their work before their very eyes, for God worked in the dark and in secret within the maternal womb.[33]

Harvey became a bold adventurer by his scientific investigation in the womb. For Harvey was in search of more than particular physiological acts and ends. He was in search of the absolute end of life in its creative origin. As a mature anatomist, he endeavored to learn God's dark and secret workings in the maternal womb. His deliberative embryological studies were interrupted by the destruction of many notes when his lodgings at Whitehall were ransacked during the English Civil War.[34] His findings were at length published as *De generatione in animalibus*. But even decades earlier, as the College's anatomist, he had considered the egg and the chick in studying the heart and and the blood flow. Harvey initially confessed his puzzlement and frustration, for the mysteries of the cardiac movement and the blood flow seemed "almost known to God alone."[35]

LABYRINTH

Harvey's model for his cardiovascular exploration had been the labyrinth because it exemplified a difficult but solvable puzzle. By diligent vivisection and examination of various animals, by collation of many records, and by reasoned arguments, Harvey finally declared, "I got it, and I escaped clear and free from this labyrinth."[36] All metaphors, in Aristotle's rhetoric, implied riddles. But the labyrinth was the archetypal puzzle, by its status appropriate for comparison with Harvey's almost divine mystery of the movement of the heart and the blood. (Calvin had taught that God himself was an arduous labyrinth unless believers were guided to him by the biblical rope.) Harvey entered the bodily labyrinth with a probe through an incision in the vein of a ligated arm, and he explored its hollow. Persevering with his probe in the pathway of the venous membranes, Harvey reasoned toward a vascular system by positing a causal heart in its center, and he reasoned his way out of the labyrinth by positing a pathway circling back to his entry. The circularity of the labyrinth as a model coincided with the circulation of the blood.[37]

Harvey's discovery of the circulation of the blood eventually mattered to his understanding of the human spirit because that is where he finally situated it, in the blood. However, he was intent on the vital spirit, which circulated in human blood just as it circulated in all blooded animals. Whereas theologians had insistently distinguished human spirit from animal spirit, Harvey's project of an Aristotelian natural philosophy was comparatively inclusive. Theologians had distinguished the vital spirit, which animated the physical body, from the psychological spirit, or the soul. Augustine acknowledged that *spiritus* could mean "wind" or "breath," but he conflated it influentially with *anima*, "soul." He acknowledged that physical spirit pertained to all animals by appealing to a biblical verse about its common expulsion from the body in death. However, he defined the human spirit as the human soul. He identified its highest intellectual part as the mind, while relegating its spiritual part to the lesser imaginative faculty.[38] Aquinas defined the human spirit as a dual power, vital and mental. But he attended to the mental power, both cognitive and affective. In a tacit revision of Augustine's psychology he elevated the spiritual part from the imaginative faculty to the intellectual faculty. Aquinas did acknowledge the vital spirit that humans had in common with other animals, but he was intent on defending the unicity of the soul against its Platonic division. Equating spirit with soul, Aquinas identified one soul. It comprised both the animal soul mixed with blood, which vivified the body, and the spiritual soul rationally ordered, which distinguished humans from all other animals.[39] Calvin was more fundamentally existential than specifically psychological in his mission to emphasize the absolute dependence of all creatures on God for their very lives. He was thus more attentive than those medieval thinkers to the vegetative soul as the Creator's quickening.[40]

Although Harvey did not draw his agenda for anatomical research from Calvin's creational theology, that theology had welcomed an examination of the vital spirit common to animals as an indicator of God's powerful animation. It was not peculiar that the saying on the frontispiece of Harvey's *De generatione animalium* had been earlier cited by Peter Martyr Vermigli, an illustrious Reformed theologian, to witness "the natural knowledge of God."[41] That significant saying was *Jovis omnia plena*, "All things are full of Jove." Harvey investigated the animal commonality of the vital spirit toward its origin in the Creator as surely as medieval theologians had determined his image in the human mind. In *De motu cordis et sanguinis* he called the heart *lares, Lar familiaris, lares focumque*, the classical household god at the hearth, which supplied the vital heat.[42] The vital spirit was heat that nourished, grew, and quickened the body perfectly and vaporously. Harvey's observation that the right auricle of the heart in vivisected animals continued to beat convinced him that warm spirit imbued its blood until death. He conjectured that Eristratus's ancient opinion had erroneously concluded from dissection that the paucity or the vacuum of blood in the arteries and left ventricle argued that they contained only spirit. From his own discovery of the circulation of the blood as pulsed by the heart, Harvey proposed that at death the blood simply could no longer flow there.[43]

Harvey reserved fuller discussion of the spirit until *De generatione in animalium*. Its preface acknowledged the heart as the generator of the vital spirit in Aristotelian natural philosophy.[44] However, Harvey reexamined Aristotle on the formation of the fetus from the heart.[45] Using his anatomical master Fabrici's *De formato fetu* as a guide, Harvey began with the importance of the egg and he persevered with serial inspections of the egg until it hatched.[46] He recorded the medical consensus that generation occurred by a union of the male and the female, but he also observed that identification of its efficient cause had failed.[47] Dedicated to anatomical experiments against probable conjectures and written authorities, Harvey practiced "familiar conversation with nature itself." Although he severely criticized theoretical delusions and errors,[48] his experiments, too, failed to solve the problem of generation. Harvey found no evidence of what he sought, male semen in the female uterus after coition.[49] Conceding that the efficient cause of generation was indeed difficult to find, he considered contagion. If it caused death without contact, why not life?[50] Reflecting on the egg as the product not of the uterus but of the soul, Harvey mentioned Hippocratic writings on *to Theion*, "the Divinity." The term ascribed some diseases to poison or to contagion, "as if there were in them a certain life and divine principle by which they increased themselves and generated others like themselves, even in a foreign body." Harvey quoted Aristotle that "all things are full of soul," adding that "even in breaths inheres life, both beginning and annihilation." Harvey concluded his inquiries on the efficient cause not medically but philosophically by a deferral to divinity. "Therefore, he will correctly and piously (at least in my opinion) impute the matter who will deduce the generation of all things from that same eternal and almighty numen by whose nod the universe of those things depends."[51]

The inherence in all nature of a divine principle of life and death was Harvey's abiding conviction as an anatomist. The classical epigraph to his *Prelectiones anatomie universalis* (Lectures on the whole anatomy) of 1616 had declared his professional purpose. As its title page announced,

Stat Jove principium, Musae, Jovis omnia plena ("The beginning stands with Jove, O Muses, everything is full of Jove"). That cited a variant of Vergil's third eclogue.[52] Harvey's choice for that titular header was deliberate, as its complementary footer, which cited Aristotle's *Historia animalium*, established. Aristotle had observed that the arrangement and designation of the exterior, visible parts of the human body were universally familiar. Then he argued, as given in Latin translation on Harvey's title page, "But the interior parts are in fact the opposite, for those of humans are chiefly doubtful and unexamined. For that reason we ought to survey by reference to the parts of the rest of the animals that are similar to humans."[53] The citation has been judged a clear statement of Aristotle's "epistemological program" for anatomy.[54] The visual complementarity of the quotations on Harvey's title page, both header and footer, indicated their programmatic relationship. The Vergilian verse glossed the Aristotelian sentence. Vergil's text introduced in Harvey's anatomical lectures his lifelong commitment to animal research. Forty-five years later his *De generatione animalium* still quoted Vergil's *Jovis omnia plena*.[55]

The appropriation of Vergil's poetry for a scientific cause was not farfetched in seventeenth-century English culture. Francis Bacon's *The Advancement of Learning* employed Vergil's georgic as a metaphor for the new science.[56] The pastoral genre, which Harvey's textbook quoted, was at the zenith of its fashion as Renaissance poetics discovered and developed Vergil's art in detailed commentaries. Ever since the emperor Constantine discerned Vergil as a messianic prophet in his fourth eclogue, his bucolic poetry was honored as compatible with Christian belief.[57] Medieval religiosity was surpassed by Renaissance invention. Not only did Vergil's literary status bless that classical model for Christian imitation, but his progress through the poetic genres—from *Bucolica*, to *Georgica*, to the epic *Aeneid*—recommended that a poet aspiring to immortality should begin his program with the bucolic. Poets explored and exploited Vergil's classical landscape, from canonical monuments such as Edmund Spenser's *The Faerie Qveene* to discrete verses. At the Stuart court, where Harvey served as the king's physician, the bucolic vogue on the page would flourish for aristocrats, then royalists, in dramatic masques.[58] But if the punctuation on the title page of his initial *Prelectiones anatomie universalis* was Harvey's own, he misunderstood Vergil's literal sense. For there was no poetic invocation to the

Muses in the original text. The modern critical edition reads, without an apostrophe offset between commas, *Ab Ioue principium Musae: Iouis omnia plena* ("From Jove is the beginning of the Muse, everything is full of Jove").⁵⁹

Vergil supplied the texts for the current grammar schools, and his *Eclogae*, as his *Bucolica* came to be entitled, was the standard collection of poems that dominated the English curriculum.⁶⁰ Their study was prescribed for the third form at the King's School, Canterbury, where Harvey matriculated. Henry VIII's royal charter stipulated that the schoolboys were to make that work "perfectly familiar."⁶¹ Vergil's eclogues were dramatic poems, and they had actually been performed in ancient Roman theaters.⁶² Perhaps as a lad Harvey not only read but also recited his future epigraph on the dais erected at Canterbury in the old schoolroom in the almonry chapel, where students regularly gave plays.⁶³ It was a famous verse, and the competition of its singers would have been a good set piece for students to memorize for recital. Even at Cambridge University as a mature student, Harvey would have rehearsed Vergil's verses. Its lecturer in grammar had employed them since the Elizabethan curriculum.⁶⁴ When Harvey was later teaching anatomy under Vergil's epigraph, John Brinsley's grammatical translation of *Eclogae* recommended it for students as "the most familiar of all Virgil's workes, and fittest for childrens capacities."⁶⁵

Child's play could be adult policy. Servius's classical commentary had interpreted Vergil's *Eclogae* as his situational politics in the Roman Empire. In the Kingdom of England the verses politicized theory such as liberty, or practice such as isolationism. Quotations of it served as shorthand for arguments or ideologies. Vergilian epigraphs to seventeenth-century English books could represent the author's cultural positions or social alignments.⁶⁶ Harvey's epigraph about Jove continued in Vergil's next verse, "He makes the earth fruitful."⁶⁷ That petitioned a blessing on Harvey's investigation of animal fertility in his book.

JOVE

When Harvey was appointed in 1616 the lecturer in anatomy for the College of Physicians, he was a beginner at that subject. Although he had served since 1609 as chief physician of St. Bartholomew's Hospital,

London, for the sick poor,⁶⁸ the collegiate lectureship ushered him into a professional anatomy theater. It was in teaching medicine, rather than practicing it, that his notable early modern predecessors, from Andreas Vesalius to Fabrici d'Acquapendente, had established their authority. Like Spenser and later John Milton, who launched their stellar poetic careers with the bucolic genre, Harvey's citation of Vergil's verse may have introduced his own ambition for immortality through medical fame.⁶⁹ Vergil's third eclogue was an amoebean contest, the classical designation of "alternating verses." Two herders, Damoetas and Menalcas, so bantered and bickered about their individual integrity that a neighbor proposed a singing match to resolve their slinging insults. Damoetas began his song by claiming Jove as his patron; Menalcas retorted by claiming Apollo. Their contest ended in a draw. Harvey's citation of the beginning of Vergil's third eclogue hinted at a purpose that was not moot like the singing contest, however.⁷⁰ The eclogue opened in rustic dialect with the provocative question *cuium pecus*, "Whose herd?" The poem was predicated on a quarrel about the legitimate ownership and proper care of animals. Menalcas asked Damoetas whether the sheep he tended belonged to Meliboeus. No, to Aegon, he replied. Menalcas quickly accused Damoetas of milking the ewes every half hour to steal their milk. Such negligence deprived the lambs of their nourishment, stunted their growth, and endangered their lives. Damoetas retorted with the accusation that Menalcas had stolen a goat from the herd he tended.⁷¹ Both contestants were rascally hired hands, not the responsible owners of the flocks. Animals were also Harvey's charge as the collegiate lecturer in anatomy. He was appointed to demonstrate animal nature, as his *Prelectiones universalis anatomie* stated, by "universal anatomy." His *Exercitatio anatomica de motu cordis et sanguinis in animalibus* and his *Exercitationes de generatione animalium* continued his commitment to animal research. The universality of Jove's reign of nature supervised the universality of Harvey's investigation of animal nature. As Harvey declared, "In no other place whatsoever than the structure of animals is the almighty Creator more conspicuous or more manifest."⁷²

Vergil's verse about the beginning of everything from Jove coincided with the opening of that eclogue, which inquired "whose herd?" It implied that the human ownership and care of animals derived from and shared in Jove's divine order and benefaction of the universe.

Vergil's poem evoked the reader's judgment that animal husbandry was not well served by landowners who hired thieves like Damoetas and Menalcas—one no better than the other, even at poetry. Harvey's citation of the poem indicated to his own readers that his anatomies toward understanding the generation of animals shared in Jove's same governance. If a certain reminiscence of Harvey's colleague and confidant George Ent was accurate, Harvey believed in God's command in Genesis 1:26 of the human stewardship of animals. "Then God said, 'Let us make man in our image, after our likeness; and let them have dominion over the fish of the sea, and over the fowl of the air, and over the cattle, and over all the earth, and over every creeping thing that creepeth upon the earth'" (Gen. 1:26 AV). As an anatomist, Harvey was a latter-day Adam with that biblical dominion over the animals. That dominion was not an afterthought to the interpretation of the human image and likeness of God as an intellectual soul. In his epistle dedicatory to Harvey's *De generatione animalium* Ent recalled their conversation about its meaning. Harvey reportedly said, "The inspection of animals themselves has always pleased me. And from thence it is my judgment that we can attain not only the slighter mysteries of nature but some image (*imaginem*) of the supreme Creator himself."[73] The analogy of animals qua animals as bearing the divine image was seriously unorthodox. Christian doctrine, both Catholic and Protestant, insisted that only humans were created in the image of God. The scriptural proof text of Genesis 1:26 was God's decision to create humans last, after all the other animals, to none of which antecedents was ascribed his divine image: aquatic animals, avian animals, terrestrial animals. "And God said, 'Let us make man in our image, after our likeness . . . ' So God created man in his own image, in the image of God created he him; male and female created he them" (Gen. 1:20–25, 26, 27 AV). In a traditional Christian theology the human privilege of bearing the divine image did not extend to other animal species because by definition those lacked an intelligent soul. Aquinas, for example, distinguished between the image of God in humans and the trace of God in all other animals.[74] Calvin raged against the attribution of the divine spirit to base animals—oxen, pigs, and dogs—and he notoriously complied in the execution of the physician and philosopher Miguel Servet for that heresy.[75] The English translation two years later of Harvey's same conversation with Ent unsurprisingly revised its reported divine *imago*, "image," in animals to "Adumbration." That revision reduced animal dignity as an image of God to a mere foreshadowing.[76]

Harvey thus adopted meaningfully Vergil's celebrated verse "From Jove is the beginning of the Muse; everything is full of Jove." Augustine's *De civitate Dei* had quoted it to summarize pagan Roman belief.[77] Augustine would have despised Harvey's quotation of Vergil's verse for being pagan. However, Harvey's anatomy lectures did not divinize poetry or celebrate paganism. Vergil's verse had adapted Aratus's *Phaenomena*, a classical poem that belonged to scientific knowledge. A geologist, writing in the professional journal *Nature*, has praised *Phaenomena* as "one of the finest works of Greek science." As he amplified that judgment, "Most of *Phaenomena* is observational natural science as we know it today, not greatly different in purpose from modern textbooks." Its map of the starry constellations to predict weather and reckon time was "recognizably modern science." However, his review dismissed its proem, which Vergil adapted for his third eclogue, as a "luxury." It was only "a few wondrously introductory lines" before the "detailed observational record, testable and useful."[78]

Aratus's poem began, "Let us begin with Zeus. From Jove is the beginning." It continued, "Filled with Zeus are all highways and all meeting places of people, filled are the seas and harbours; in all circumstances we are all dependent on Zeus." Vergil simply echoed in his third eclogue, "everything is full of Jove."[79] Aratus's Dios was Zeus as the pervasive cosmic deity, who fathered humans and benefited them by appointing the celestial constellations as meteorological signs.[80] His proem announced a cosmological argument from design. By cataloguing the celestial signs, the titular phenomena, the poet invited their observation toward recognition of the beneficent providence ruling the universe. Aratus's *Phaenomena* was a catalogue of information, not a narrative of events. Since it organized material in a coherent structure and interpreted the data,[81] it was somewhat similar, as descriptive, to Harvey's *Prelectiones anatomie universalis*. Aratus's *Phaenomena* was imitated by Theocritus's *Idylls*, the primary source of Vergil's *Bucolica*. It inspired not only Vergil's *Eclogae*, which Harvey cited about Jove, but also Vergil's *Georgica*, which Harvey cited in other contexts.[82] Aratus's verse was translated fragmentarily by Cicero's *Aratea* as *Ab Ioue Musarum primordia*,[83] and it was adapted for the Augustan age by Germanicus Caesar as *Ab Ioue principium magno deduxit Aratus* ("From great Jove, Aratus draws down the beginning").[84]

Aratus's poem was repeated by Christian authors for a reason far exceeding their belief that Vergil's fourth eclogue was a messianic prophecy. Aratus had a canonization that even Vergil lacked, the New Testament. His *Phaenomena* was quoted favorably in a speech attributed to the apostle Paul, although modern biblical studies discredits his authorship. The Acts of the Apostles reported a speech on the Areopagus about the Athenians' altar "to an unknown God." It preached that the unknown God, maker of the world and its inhabitants, was close to humans, "for 'in him we live, and move, and have our being'; as certain also of your own poets have said, 'For we are also his offspring'" (Acts 17:28 AV). That quoted Aratus's *Phaenomena* on God's fatherhood.[85] The verse was prominent in Calvin's argument for a seed of religion in humanity as God's creature.[86] The verse has since been claimed as "probably the most printed citation in all scientific literature."[87] However, it was not published triumphantly because of its science, but only coincidentally because the Bible is among books the bestseller. Paul's attributed speech argued from the dignity of humans as divine progeny against the fashioning of idols as if they represented gods. His opposition to gods crafted of metal or stone implicitly privileged the human figure, a subject of Harvey's *Prelectiones anatomie universalis*. Paul summoned the Athenians to repentance before their judgment by the appointed man, whose authority was confirmed by his resurrection. That man was Jesus, although Paul refrained from naming him to his pagan audience, which quickly divided over the very notion of a resurrection of the dead.[88]

NUMEN

The conclusion of "Paul's" speech with the resurrection was matched by the conclusion of Harvey's preface to his *Prelectiones anatomie universalis* with the resurrection. The citation in Acts of Aratus's *Phaenomena* authorized biblically Harvey's citation of Vergil's verse reminiscent of that poem. The classical notion of a cosmic god, maker of the universe and pervasive in its creatures, especially as the father of humans, resonated with Christian apologists. But not all theologians agreed with a fundamental compatibility of pagan and Christian beliefs. Calvin, whose theology indoctrinated the Church of England, did not. As he commented on Acts, when Vergil wrote "all things are full of

Jove"—Harvey's epigraph—he expressed the power of God but "erroneously wrote the wrong name." However, citing the hemistich from Aratus's *Phaenomena*, Calvin thought it unsurprising that Paul's address to unbelievers ignorant of true piety employed that poet's witness. For extant in his poem was a notion of divinity naturally seeded or sculpted in human minds, as Calvin believed. However, he clarified, "This is far from the papist reasoning." Calvin expounded that Aratus no doubt spoke of Jove in that saying, and that Paul converted its meaning to the true God because humans were naturally imbued with a sense of God from the divine source of true principles. However, as Calvin characteristically argued, after Adam's original sin that sense of divinity naturally imbued in humans as creatures evaporated into depraved figments. The original pure seed of religion degenerated into corruptions, even while the primordial general notion of God remained. Calvin concluded that Vergil's verse about the fictional Jove was undoubtedly transferred to the true God, expressing his power under a false name.[89] But Harvey did not have his Vergilian epigraph from Vergil's pastoral. He repeated it from another investigator of animals who was keen for medieval science as causal knowledge, Aquinas's teacher Albert the Great.

That scholastic natural philosopher was twice named in Harvey's initial work, *Prelectiones anatomie universalis*, probably secondarily so from its source, Kaspar Bauhin's *Theatrum anatomicum*. However, Albert the Great's report in *De animalibus* of fetal responses to a pinprick suggested that Harvey compared that text firsthand with his own observations recorded in *De generatione animalium*.[90] Harvey was very probably exposed to Albert's natural philosophy as a student in arts and medicine at the University of Padua. Albert himself had been a student in arts there, and he left some observations of the local natural phenomena. His *De animalibus* was recommended at Padua as a text preparatory to medicine, and it was widely cited by later medieval physicians.[91] In embryology both Volcher Coiter and Ulysse Aldrovandi consulted Albert's text in the sixteenth century, as did Marcello Malpighi after Harvey in the seventeenth.[92] A respectful teacher-to-student chain, from Gaetano di Thiene, to Nicoletto Vernia, to Marcantonio Zimara, ensured the transmission at Padua of Albert's ideas among Averroist lay philosophers. Vernia willed his copy of the first edition of *De animalibus* to a monastery, which transferred it to the University of Padua library, while Zimara edited the text again personally.[93] Its incunabula were all

Italian printings, at Rome, Mantua, and Venice.⁹⁴ Albert's *De animalibus* was the first full Latin account of Aristotle's *Historia animalium, De partibus animalium*, and *De generatione animalium*.⁹⁵ Harvey's anatomical project was an Aristotelian examination of the parts of animals comparatively and teleologically in order to understand the quiddity of animal. Albert's text was an obvious basic resource for comparison with his own anatomies and deliberations in Aristotelian natural philosophy.

Albert followed Aristotle's program to examine those natural substances that generated. He agreed that the similarity of animals to humans promised a more perfect knowledge of humanity. After discussing the nature of animals, then the method for assigning causes, Albert proceeded to coordinate nature and causality in animals from the noble to the ignoble. As he moralized toward a knowledge of their Creator, "And, therefore, we ought to consider the forms of animals and to delight in him who is the designer who made them, because the artifice of the operator is manifest in the operation." Albert compared a craftsman's knowledge as displayed in his fashioning of statues or images. He argued for the necessity of not avoiding or rejecting base and ignoble animals because, in a scholastic distinction augmenting Aristotle's reason, their baseness was not from their designer but from their matter. A consideration of base natures should not burden an investigator, like a depraved person who from his vile nature conceived depraved affects. "For in all natural things there are wonders to be examined," he declared.⁹⁶

Albert related an anecdote about a poet, Eradytis, who sat outside Jove's temple and spoke to passersby wishing to join his discourses. When they saw him entering the temple, where they could not approach him, he invited them "to enter into the temple where the gods were and to listen there to his discourses, asserting that *everything was full of Jove* and that he was whatever was natural, both whatever was and whatever would be, and that discourses on these matters could only be undertaken by one who entered into the divine causes of them as if into a temple." Albert's insertion of Vergil's verse "everything is full of Jove" into Aristotle's anecdote has escaped his editor and translators. That philosophical citation, *Jovis esse omnia plena*, made fuller sense of Harvey's appropriation of Vergil's verse to announce his own *Prelectiones anatomie universalis*. Albert had urged his own students "to inquire into any animal natures whatsoever and to know that in all animals there is a natural cause noble and divine." No animal had a vain or purposeless nature. Each animal proceeded from an end that completed it and conferred on it "a place in natural things and a wonderful and noble rank."[97] That grand and generous teleology introduced Harvey's own lectures on the complete anatomy. Well after him the chemist Robert Boyle cited that same passage in *Of the Usefulnesse of Naturall Philosophy* to approve comprehensive research.[98]

Albert the Great's anecdote about the poet Eradytis compared with an anecdote about the pre-Socratic philosopher Heraclitus.[99] Since it appeared uniquely in Aristotle's *De partibus animalium*, that reference strengthened Harvey's quotation. Indeed, Harvey knew and approved the anecdote. In his *Exercitationes de circulatione sanguinis* (Exercises on the circulation of the blood) he advised his opponent the anatomist Jean Riolan. "Toward the inspection of the meanest animals, approach with Heraclitus according to Aristotle, to enter into the baker's hut (as I say) if you will, for the immortal gods are not absent even from there. The greatest and almighty Father is always in the least and quite striking in the meanest."[100] Both anecdotes, Albert's and Aristotle's, encouraged outsiders, as passersby or visitors, to investigate all of nature deeply. As Aristotle wrote, Heraclitus was once warming himself by the oven when visitors arrived. When they hesitated to enter, he beckoned them not to be ashamed. Come in! come in! he bid them, "for there are gods here too." He alluded to Heraclitus's doctrine of fire as the pervasive cosmic principle by offering hospitality at an oven, which in classical Greek usage was portable, not fixed. The anecdote illustrated Aristotle's teaching that the examination of no animal should be rejected in childish embarrassment or disgust, for all were noble and beautiful because all were purposeful. Nature did not compose randomly. Further, "A discussion about nature is about the composition and the being as a whole, not about parts that can never occur in separation from the being they belong to."[101] The passage has been considered a "justly famous defense of the study of animals." Its elegant expressions of pleasure, its prizing of the wonderful, and its recognition of universal good, with the anecdote about Heraclitus, made it excellent rhetoric. It argued for causal and theoretical research on animals, since they were more accessible to investigation than cosmic events and also since they had their own nobility.[102] Albert's argument repeated Aristotle's statement "For in all natural things there is something marvelous."[103]

Albert religiously relocated Aristotle's anecdote from a house to a temple. As he retold the story, it was only in the temple, "where the gods are," that the natural philosopher would learn the nature of animal. But Harvey reinstalled divinity to the common domestic hearth. From the origins of Indo-European civilization, the central household fire was the dwelling place of the ancestral deities.[104] Harvey renamed the heart, as the bodily center of the noblest, blooded animals, the hearth of the household gods, *lares, Lar familiaris, lares focumque*.[105] He has been declared "unusual in not giving a religious purpose to anatomy." For anatomists commonly prefaced their lists of bodily parts and functions with a justification for self-knowledge toward reverence of their Creator.[106] Galen, the anatomist to whose doctrines the College of Physicians, London, swore allegiance,[107] was respectfully teleological.[108] Although he rejected an immortal soul infused in the human body,[109] he praised bodily design as divinely ordained in each part for a perfect function. He even called his influential *De usu partium* (On the use of the parts) "a sacred discourse" and "a true hymn of praise to our Creator."[110] Harvey's resource for his initial anatomical lectures, Bauhin's *Theatrum anatomicum* (Anatomical theater), has been cited for a bold claim. It reputedly stated that the human body was the divine temple, where the image of God could be perceived like Caesar's effigy stamped on coins.[111] But that claim was not what Bauhin wrote. He wrote, concerning pseudo-Augustine's praise in *De spiritu et anima* (On the spirit and soul), about the "human intellect"—not the human body. Bauhin concluded intellectually, "Whence he is called a temple and a figure of the august God by theologians." Bauhin himself was not a theologian and he made no theological claim for his anatomies, which were performed on bodies, not intellects. He also repeated Aquinas's incorrect simile that the divine image was impressed on the human soul just as the emperor's engraving was stamped on a coin.[112]

Biographical evidence of Harvey's personal religious beliefs is thin and conventional. What evidence there is weighs heavily for his affiliation with the Church of England in both its sacraments and doctrines. Harvey was baptized and married in the Church of England.[113] He was educated at the King's School, Canterbury, and at the University of Cambridge, both of which stipulated compulsory attendance at Anglican worship and doctrinal instruction. At Cambridge he was a resident of Caius College, which, although known for its Roman

Catholic predilections,[114] hardly compelled them since Catholicism was illegal. Harvey later signed the oath of papal allegiance required by the University of Padua for his degrees in arts and medicine.[115] Signing the papal oath may have been simple expediency as a student in Italy, which was officially Catholic, before his return to England and a medical practice as chief of St. Bartholomew's Hospital, London. As a royal physician later still, Harvey was obligated, with all doctors of physick, to swear the *et cetera oath* to the established doctrine, discipline, and government of the Church of England. That oath was Charles I's personal imposition on them of Anglican orthodoxy.[116] As the king's physician, Harvey necessarily would have been the first of physicians in the realm to swear it.

Harvey's writings acknowledged principal articles of the common Christian creeds, in the Church of England specifically in allegiance to the Nicene Creed.[117] Those articles were the creation of everything by God the Father; the birth, life, and death of Jesus; and the resurrection of the dead. The divine creation in Christian belief was fundamental to his anatomical teleology, and he even imitated the anaphora in Genesis 1, "let there be," in expounding the formation of the fetus.[118] His "De partu" mentioned the custom of reckoning human pregnancy from "the term we believe Christ our Savior, the most perfect man, measured in his mother's uterus, no doubt from the day of the angelic annunciation in the month of March to that blessed day of the nativity which feast we celebrate in the month of December."[119] Harvey's identification of human perfection with Jesus was a confession of faith, but his interest in the term of his gestation was medical. Another biblical reference, in *Prelectiones anatomie universalis*, was to Jesus's death, "The wounds of Christ water with bloodshed."[120] Harvey's context was medical, but "bloodshed" biblically connoted a sacrificial death as atonement for sin, in the Holiness code of Leviticus and in New Testament about Jesus's death.[121] In contrast to a contemporary practice of biblical citation,[122] however, Harvey's writings rarely cited Scripture and referred only parenthetically to medicine, his professional practice as a physician.

He affirmed the Christian creed on the resurrection of the body in the conclusion of his preface to *Prelectiones anatomie universalis* with a paraphrase of Augustine about the utility and beauty of the human body. Augustine's *De civitate Dei* defended the resurrection with an appreciation of the providential formation and concord of the physical body yet a recognition of its deformity and ultimately death. As

Harvey paraphrased it on the distinction between beauty and necessity, "Nature is more solicitous about beauty than utility because appetite here is attained by the resurrection." Augustine's chapter condemned anatomy, the professional purpose and practice of Harvey's lectures. Augustine supposed that the beauty of the body would be more evident and better appreciated if its inner organs and networks beneath its superficial skin were known. But he pronounced that no one could discover its secrets. "The cruel diligence of doctors who are called anatomists has butchered the bodies of the dead or even of those dying in the flesh under the hands of the one cutting and investigating, and has inhumanely examined the whole human by this method to learn by which parts it ought to be cured." Yet no one was able to discover or to dare to learn by what extrinsic or intrinsic organ the bodily fitting together (*coaptatio*), in Greek *harmonia*, takes place. By his attention to that chapter, Harvey's title and the lectures announced that he would dare such a "whole anatomy" to seek the coordinating principle of the body. As he defined, "anatomy is the skill which by ocular observing and dissecting . . . the use and actions of the parts." That definition (*inspectione et sectione*) mimicked Augustine's description (*secantis perscrutantisque*) but corrected his inhumane diligence (*diligentia*) to rational skill (*facultas*).[123] Harvey emphasized his anatomy as teleological by coordinating it with the distinctive Christian end of the body in the perfected life of its resurrection. His trajectory from beginning to end shared a Christian pattern of circularity, as in Paul's letter to the Corinthians about their baptism into the revelation and the resurrection of the second Adam; in Augustine's *Confessiones* of his departure from God into the region of dissimilarity and his return to the divine likeness; in Aquinas's plan in *Summa theologiae* of the issue of humans from the Creator and their rest in him; and in Calvin's *Institutiones christianae religionis* as an arrangement of the inheritance from the creation to the resurrection. A difference was that for those writers the means for the journey was Christ, whereas for Harvey it was anatomy. In the end to which his *Prelectiones anatomie universalis* ventured a beginning, his *De generatione animalium* would declare that the constituting principle of the noblest animal bodies, which Augustine had declared a secret, was the blood as spirit.

Harvey's marginal notes on the first folio of Pulleyn's edition of his *De generatione animalium* registered his discontent with damage he thought churchmen inflicted on natural philosophy. After a refutation of the anatomist Fortunio Liceti on bodily heat, Harvey complained in general. "Philosophy has suffered many things passing through the hands of (transient) presbyters and theologians. To wit, the generation of the world, sun, and immortal soul, the spirit of angels and demons—to which as if a sanctuary of ignorance those fleeing for refuge lurk—mock philosophy." Further, "The elenchic disputation of the scholastics, by which they draw truth by a wrenched neck to a substitution, results in this mode: that we can prove and defend at will. Thus the sophists overwhelm philosophy, and because they are quite useful for shaping popular mores they are safe with impunity. See Bacon, *De difficultatibus, inicio*."[124] Since Bacon composed no such title, Harvey likely meant his preface to *Instauratio magna* (Great instauration), on the initial difficulty of his method. There Bacon distinguished contemplative paths. "The one, from a beginning arduous and difficult (*ab initio ardua et difficilis*), ends in open ground; the other, at first glance unimpeded on a downward slope, leads to wildernesses and precipices."[125] If so, Harvey criticized a theological method that began by sliding down from God easily only to land in deserts and dangers. He would essay the opposite method. His own difficult exercises would reason upward to a divinity. However, that reasoning was not theology but natural philosophy in the manner of Aristotle's reasoning toward final causality.

The Vergilian bucolic verse that Harvey adopted and its source in Aratus's *Phaenomena* have both been classified as Stoic,[126] a providential but materialist philosophy. Alexander of Hales, the first commentator on Peter Lombard's *Sententiae*, which became normative at the University of Paris for bachelors of theology, rejected the materialist heresy that "Jove is everything you see."[127] The teleology of Aristotle's natural philosophy, which guided Harvey's research, did not posit a Creator,[128] although medieval scholasticism converted final causality to that Christian end. However, Aquinas did not confuse or conflate anatomy and theology. His *Summa theologiae* introduced the question on the soul with a distinction. "The consideration of human nature pertains to the theologian from the soul's part, but not from the body's part, unless according to a habit the body has toward the soul."[129] That division of disciplines implied conversely that the natural philosopher considered human nature from the body's part, not the soul's part, unless according to a habit the soul had toward the body. The human soul was, therefore, not the province of the anatomist except insofar as its tripartite powers—nutritive, sensitive, and intellectual—were manifestly operative in the body. Teleology was not theology but philosophy. Harvey's omission from *Prelectiones anatomie universalis* of praise of a Creator reflected an Aristotelian scholastic understanding of its task.

Harvey's professionalism as an anatomist did not evidence that he was unaware or dismissive of teleology grounded in an ultimate design or designer. On the contrary. He introduced Vergil's bucolic verse in his *De generatione animalium* to recognize nature's purposeful ordering by providence and intelligence of all bodily faculties to some end. Harvey emphasized that nature disposed and fulfilled everything by providence, choice, and intelligence. "Indeed also, as in the greater world they tell us that 'all things are full of Jove,' thus equally in the tiny body of a chick, by its individual actions and operations, the finger of God, or the numen of nature, manifests."[130] That analogy applied the classical topic of the microcosm as an imitation of the macrocosm. As in Heraclitus's anecdotal comparison, just as the primal fire burned in the cosmos, so could a local fire burn on earth. The fire that kindled the universe equally warmed a pair of hands.[131] However, Harvey distinguished the cosmic elemental fire attributed to Jove from the ordinary utilitarian fire attributed to his brother Vulcan. Harvey argued from his anatomies that a more superior and divine maker than a human being fashioned and conserved all animals. "Without a doubt we declare God, the supreme and omnipotent Creator, to be present everywhere in the workshop of collective animals, and to display in their operations as if with a finger." The attributes of providence, choice, and election that Harvey discerned in a hen did not coalesce "except in the omnipotent principle of things." That principle shared various names, which he catalogued as "either 'the divine mind' with Aristotle, or 'the world soul' with Plato; or with others, 'nature naturing'; or with the heathens, 'Saturn' or 'Jove'; or preferably (as befits us) 'the Creator' and 'the Father' of everything in heaven and on earth, from whom animals and their origins depend, by whose will or word all things are made and generated."[132] Harvey's final designation, "the Creator and the Father," honored the first article of the Nicene Creed, as professed in the rites of the Anglican *Book of Common Prayer*: "I believe in one God, the Father almighty, Maker of heaven and earth and of all things visible and invisible."[133]

Harvey's inference of a teleological principle of nature was very frequent in *De generatione animalium*. Harvey again cited Vergil's "All things are full of Jove" in its appended *De partu* (On childbirth), although the modern translation has suppressed that classical quotation and converted Jove to "the Creator." Harvey explicated "the numen of nature discerned as everywhere present."[134] But that staunch confession did not render his anatomies religious. Religion was belief toward worship. Harvey's anatomies were acts toward knowledge. What sort of knowledge? Not religious knowledge but natural knowledge. As an Aristotelian natural philosopher, Harvey defined nature from Aristotle as that thing possessing an intrinsic principle of motion.[135] However, Aristotle's philosophical universe was uncreated, whereas Harvey's cultural universe was created. Harvey could not have abstracted himself from the Christian religion, which prevailed in English society. It was motivational for multitudes in his century—more so than in any other age, it has been said—which impressed the lives of even the dispassionate.[136] Yet Harvey did not overtly pose the question how a nature, as moved by an intrinsic principle, related to a Creator moving it as an extrinsic principle. He had reasoned to the heart as the intrinsic principle, or mover, in blooded animals. *De motu cordis et sanguinis* recorded his designed, sensed, and deliberated anatomies toward that end, a mystery that Harvey agreed seemed "almost known to God alone."[137]

When Harvey reportedly confessed to his colleague Ent his delight in anatomy as displaying "the image of God" in animals, he was not conversing in a theological context. He neither stated nor implied that he discerned the divine image traditionally in a facultative psychology that included all animal souls as nutritive and sensitive. Rather, he spoke professionally as one physician to another. As an anatomist, his dissections and deliberations had traced a divine design in the making (*fabrica*) of the body, not the soul. Harvey's delight was in a teleological argument from motion: from functional physical movements to their ultimate designer and mover. He observed in the chick "individual actions and operations." He reasoned from those particular workings that a greater mind or soul or divinity than their human examiner made that chick. For Harvey, that functional microcosmic design displayed the macrocosmic oversight of Jove in classical religion and the finger of "the Father and Creator" in Christian belief.[138] Harvey was amazed at the physical perfection of animals; but again, teleology was not theology.

In his epistle dedicatory to *De motu cordis et sanguinis* his procedure "from the making of nature"[139] revealed the physiological purpose of his anatomies. Although his *fabrica* alluded to Vesalius's *De humani corporis fabrica*,[140] Harvey did not mean "fabric" as stuff, as if the bodily tissues were like yards of cloth. He was less intent on composition than activity, less intent on structure than movement. The primary meaning of *fabrica* was an artisanal "workshop." With its synonym *officina* Harvey concluded *De motu cordis et sanguinis* by designating the heart "a workshop," "a workshop of perfection." However, despite his site of the soul in the heart, Harvey's intention was not locational but dynamic. Harvey's focus in *De motu cordis et sanguinis* was not only on the heart as the source and supplier of the blood, as it was for Aristotle, but on the circulation of the blood, which he himself discovered and deliberated. As Harvey wrote of the heart, with the rhetorical emphasis in the classical final place, "It is the fount and treasury of the blood and a workshop of perfection."[141] The question of how the artisanal heart as the circulator of the blood related to the Artisan "of everything in heaven and on earth" motivated his later *De generatione animalium*. That final book did not simply alter Harvey's investigation from one bodily part to another—from the heart to the reproductive organs. It was a thoughtful philosophical and scientific progression from movement to origin.

The cosmic rule of Jove that Vergil's third eclogue hymned and Harvey cited was in that poet's *Georgica* explored on earth. It was a text Harvey also cited several times in *De generatione animalium*, such as on the endowment of hiving bees with a divine spark.[142] So had Calvin's *Institutio christianae religionis* quoted it, but only to criticize "that jejune speculation about the universal mind that animates and grows the world." Such speculation created "a shadowy numen" for the true God. Calvin also complained about "nature" as a substitute to deny or destroy God.[143] Vergil's *Georgica* defined the reign of Jove as inciting mortals by their cares. In Jove's era humans were forced to work hard by inventing skills to cope with their harsh environment. Not only did they develop the agriculture the poem celebrated but also the livelihoods of sailing, hunting, fishing, and tool making. It was Jove's nod that directed the invention of tools,[144] and tools became for anatomists like Harvey instruments for dissection. Harvey famously inserted and thrust a probe into a vein toward his inference of the heart as the circulator of its blood.[145]

EXERCISE

Erasmus's prior citation of Vergil's *Georgica* on the reign of Jove explained Harvey's dedication to anatomy. Its citation appeared in his *Adagia*, a massive collection of classical sayings that was very popular in English schools, libraries, and households.[146] Erasmus recorded Vergil's famous verse that climaxed in Jove's will for humans of hard but skilled labor. "Virgil in the *Georgics:* 'Toil conquers all, / Persistent toil, and need in hardships dire.'" Erasmus catalogued similar sayings from other classical authors as witness to humans overcoming difficulty by sheer determination. But Vergil's *labor vincit omnia* was the sharp and memorable quotation. Erasmus's collected sayings all glossed the adage *Exercitatio potest omnia*, "Practice can do everything." Idiomatically that was "Practice makes perfect."[147] Harvey, as a boy writing exercises at the King's School, Canterbury, would have known the saying, for "Practice makes perfect" justified those repetitive tasks. That folk wisdom—that practice surmounts all obstacles and perfects all trials—later sustained Harvey in his anatomical "labor," as he termed it. For he freely admitted his persistent vexation and frustration toward understanding the movement of the heart and the blood, which seemed "almost known to God alone."[148] His ambition was to cleanse the Augean stable of medicine and so, as a second Hercules, to win immortality with the gods.[149] It was not fortuitous that Harvey entitled *exercitatio* three of his works: *Exercitatio anatomica de motu cordis et sanguinis in animalibus*, *Exercitationes duae de circulatione sanguinis*, and *Exercitationes de generatione animalium*. They recorded his practices, both manual and mental. As a practical record, his book on the heart did not merely convey the information he acquired by "ocular demonstrations" and deliberated by "reasoned arguments."[150] It exposed and explained his processes of problem-solving. He thought that solutions ultimately devolved to understanding the divine design of nature. So did his book of exercises on the generation of animals advocate and record his methods. Its deliberate "practices" have been mistakenly simplified to "chapters" in the modern translation,[151] as if literary divisions.

The footer on the title page to Harvey's first publication, *Prelectiones anatomie universalis*, cited Aristotle's statement that the human innards were largely vague and unexplored.[152] Vergil's header on its same title page resonated with Aratus's *Phaenomena*, which confirmed that ignorance but extended a hope. "We men do not yet have knowledge of everything from Zeus, but much still is hidden, whereof Zeus, if he wishes, will give us signs anon; he certainly does benefit the human race openly, showing himself on every side, and everywhere displaying his signs."[153] Thus it was that Harvey's inaugural lectures invoked the Muses for natural knowledge from Jove, the principle of everything, for the bodily signs that would by his anatomical practice move the subject of the heart from speculation to science.

Just as it cited Vergil's "everything is full of Jove," Harvey's *De generatione animalium* was full of acknowledgments of divinity, nature, heaven, art, and foresight. Harvey's teleological conviction surfaced typically in his puzzlement about efficient causality. He introduced the divine agent or numen of nature by protesting that it was a common philosophical error to assign only a material cause, as deduced from elemental concurrence by design or by chance, and not to mention the principle in the generation and growth of animals. "Certainly they do not acknowledge that divine efficient and numen of nature (which by supreme art, providence, and wisdom operates, effecting all things to some end or for the sake of some good or other). Yet they derogate honor to the divine architect who with no less artifice made the shell the guardian of the egg than he composed the other parts." Harvey cited on the production of the egg from the soul the same verse of Vergil's *Aeneid* as had Calvin's commentary on Paul's attributed speech in Acts about the Athenians' altar to the unknown god. They both cited Anchises's response to his son Aeneas's question about the cause of the souls thronged in the underworld. As Anchises reflected on the universal cause, "A spirit within sustains, and mind, pervading its members, sways the whole mass and mingles with its mighty frame." For Calvin, that verse philosophized inadequately about the divine mystery. For Harvey, it preluded his discussion of "the excellence of the vegetative soul and of the numen to be marveled at from its works (not without providence, art, and divine intellect)." For "they outstrip the human intellect not less than the gods do humans. And by universal consensus they are so to be admired that our mind with its dimmed acuity can no way seek to penetrate the unsearchable light."[154] Harvey thus acknowledged human incomprehension of the divine cause by an a fortiori argument from its inferior intelligence. That argument portended his theory of the efficient cause of the generation of animals as numinous.

The admirable but sudden progress in generation from the male, to the female, to the egg, to the chick seemed to Harvey "as if the Almighty should say, 'Let there be offspring,' and it is done." Harvey's *fiat progenies* imitated Genesis 1, whose divine commands of creation began in Latin translation *fiat lux*, "Let there be light." God then blessed all animals to "be fruitful, and multiply" (Gen. 1:3, 22, 24, 26 AV). Exactly how generation occurred was Harvey's scientific investigation. He advised physicians to cease to wonder at the multiplication of airborne diseases when there were far greater wonders to study. "In the generation of animals is perceived the best object for regard, the eternal and almighty God, or the numen of nature." Harvey's topic held "a mystery more divine than in the simple assembly, change, and composition of the whole from the parts since the whole is constituted and discerned before the parts, the mixture before the elements." Remembering God's commands of creation by the separation of the celestial and earthly elements, Harvey imitated the progress of Genesis 1 to describe generation. God in Genesis spoke twelve commands, *fiat* ("let"), to create everything from light to humans. Harvey imitated that biblical paradigm to explain animal generation. "As if by a command or a certain exhalation of a divine worker, the whole chick is created, if you will." As he exploited the *fiat*s of Genesis, "Let there be the white similar mass, and let it be divided into parts, and increase; and meanwhile, while it increases, let there be a separation and delineation of parts, and let there be this part harder and simultaneously thicker and whiter, that softer and simultaneously more colored; and thus it was made." Despite the difficulty of understanding generation, Harvey insisted on the necessity of research. He mocked his professor Fabrici d'Acquapendente's obscure redundancy for not addressing efficient causality. "Unless by a certain *fiat*, sitting on a throne in the likeness of the Creator, with this one word *fiat*" the cock's semen orders the bones, muscles, organs, members, and innards to divide from the homologous mass.[155]

Harvey defined efficient causality from Aristotle as "the first beginning whence change or rest; as the counselor, father, and simply the maker of what is made, the transformer of the transformed." He then involved spirit by specifying that the efficient cause could be "some internal substance existing of itself, such as spirit or innate heat." Harvey admired the efficient cause of the fetus as ultimate. "By how much providence, skill, and intelligence, how, with the divine numen having blown, all things are harmonized and ingeniously composed into use for life. Not only was vacillation not allowed about who might be the efficient architect and counselor, but also truly the almighty fabricator of such work (which deserves to be inscribed with the title 'microcosm') and preserver we justly regard and venerate." Harvey's principle for research was the arrival, timing, and location of the subsistence in the egg of "that divine reality, analogue with the element of the stars, corresponding in proportion to skill and intellect, the deputy of the almighty Creator." He recalled Stoic elemental fire, which was not the ordinary fire pagans ascribed to Vulcan but the fire they devoted to Jove. It was "the animate spirit (*spiritus animalis*), divine, and maker of animals."[156]

The preface to *De generatione animalium* advocated following nature's guidance "through footprints truly full of bends, but absolutely certain." That method alluded to the exploration of the bodily labyrinth, from which he had earlier escaped with the deliberated discovery of the circulation of the blood. Harvey promised that fatigue and even fainting from difficulty in researching generation would be rewarded by sweet discoveries. "Nature itself must advise; and the footpath she shows us must be trod; for thus when we consult with our eyes and press forward the foot to proceed from the least to the greater, we shall at length penetrate its innermost secrets." Harvey again explicitly styled his investigation of the efficient cause of the chick an arduous labyrinth. As he reflected, "If we are to extricate ourselves safely from the labyrinth of variously compounded causes, there is need of Ariadne's clew." That mythological thread Harvey developed scientifically as "long drawn out from observations of all animals rightly interwoven," a matter to reserve for a "universal encircling."[157] Harvey's research was not the "hard thing" or general "investigation" of modern translation.[158] His model was precisely a "labyrinth," the intricate and lengthy but sure classical design with one and the same entrance and exit. His projected research would be its "encircling" of the universal animal evidence. Harvey's mentality was formed by classical notions of circular perfection, such as cosmic rotation. It was manifest in his recourse to the sun in its celestial course as a macrocosmic paradigm. He had already related the circulation of the blood flow in the microcosmic animal to the movement of the macrocosmic sun.[159] Again he appealed to the sun's elliptical movement within the universe's circular motion as "the common father and begetter, or at least the immediate and universal instrument of the supreme Creator in generation."[160] Harvey was convinced of the cyclical processes of the macrocosm and the microcosm.[161] He specifically meant circularity. The same circularity that his experiments and deliberations found true for the blood flow he expected to find as the explanation of generation.

However, he did not. Harvey failed to exit the bodily labyrinth exulting "I got it!" about a discovery of the efficient cause of generation as he had with the circulation of the blood. The cardiovascular system was indeed circular. The generative system was not, despite his belief that animal generation imitated in the microcosm the celestial rotation in the macrocosm. Harvey imagined that nature's spark began as if at the zenith of nighttime but that its subtlety eluded the most talented and sharp eyes. "For we cannot with less toil find the intimate secrets and dark beginnings of generation than the structure of the entire world and the manner of its creation." He thus sought to experience the sunrise from the pitch black of night. For "the eternity of matter consists in this reciprocal order of generation and decay. And as the rising and setting of the sun by its perpetual circlings around completes an age, so similarly the mortal affairs destined to die by the alternating vicissitudes of individuals always endures reintegrated in the same species."[162] However, Harvey did not discern empirically his theorized circularity of generation as an imitation of the solar rotation. He could only spiral upwards in his reason inferentially from his observations of animals in deference to an ultimate efficient cause as divine operations. He freely admitted that his intellect was too dim even to view that cause, let alone comprehend it.

While the efficient cause of generation remained mysterious, Harvey acknowledged the instrumental causes of generation in those animals he researched. They were the cock and his semen, and the hen and her egg. He thought they drew their fertility and generative powers from the approaching sun, so that the artifice and providence discernible in their operations proceeded not from themselves as animals but from God. Harvey reasoned also that in human generation "there needs to be an efficient cause superior and more excellent than the human itself." He then departed egregiously from Christian theologians such as Augustine and Aquinas who ascribed the image of God to the human mind. Harvey asserted that "the vegetative faculty, or that part of the soul that makes and conserves a human, is far more excellent and divine and more reproduces the likeness of God than his rational part." He posited humanity's bond to its Creator as existential, like that of the other animals. The essential generation and conservation of life were superior to thought. Harvey did acknowledge the importance of the human mind; but not as the mirror of divinity but as the master of animal life. He qualified human reason, "whose excellence we extoll nevertheless with marvelous praises above all faculties of all animals—to the extent that it holds right and dominion towards them and to which all created things collectively serve."[163] That statement affirmed the creation of humans in the divine image and likeness with reference to God's command in Genesis 1:26 that Adam name and govern animal life for its increase.[164] Harvey's belief was compatible with a modern biblical consensus on the image and likeness in humanity as the Creator's deputy.[165] Calvin had thought that interpretation correct but insufficient because the divine image resided in the human interior.[166]

IMAGE

Harvey declared that "the divine mind of the eternal Creator, imprinted in things, begets its image in human conceptions." That statement did not exclude human ideas as divine imprints, but it was more generous in its inclusion. Harvey generalized about the formation somehow of everything by a univocal agent as "the same progenerating the same." That principle of like producing like included construction in the arts, ideas in the mind, and the begetting of children in the body.[167] Harvey argued "at least it must be confessed that in the operations of nature neither prudence, nor artifice, nor understanding is inherent. But it only seems so to our conceptualization, which, according to our skills and faculties (as exemplars to them derived by us ourselves), we judge divine things from natural things." As he explained, "It is as if the active principles of nature produced their effects in the way we are used to our own artificial works, indeed by determination and discipline acquired by the intellect or mind." Nature differed from human artifice, however, as "the principle of motion and rest in all things in which it exists, and the vegetative soul, the first efficient cause of any generation." Unlike humanity, nature did not have an acquired faculty called art or prudence but acted by some mandate according to laws. Harvey evidenced birds building their nests and incubating and guarding their eggs. They acted "naturally and by an inborn genius, moreover not by providence, discipline or determinations." In nature animal operations were "self-taught (*autodidaktos*) and educated by no one, inborn and instilled," in contrast to what humans had to acquire by art, intellect, or providence. Judgment of the natural by the artificial was thus hardly just because the reverse was true. Nature was the exemplar for artifice. "For all arts are prepared by some imitation of nature, and our reason or intellect has flowed from the divine intellect in acting in its operations." Correct thinking deduced the generation of all things from that "same eternal and almighty numen from whose nod the universe of those realities depends."[168]

The frontispieces of the publications of *De generatione animalium* featured Harvey's example of instinctive birds: in London by Octavian Pulleyn in a quarto edition, then in Amsterdam by Elzevir, Jansson, and Ravestyn in duodecimos.[169] Ravestyn's edition depicts in the foreground a hen and a duck brooding eggs in baskets, while above them chicks hatch from jagged eggshells. Elzevir's edition depicts a brooding hen and fowl in nests, while the arch above is decorated with hatching chicks. All four frontispieces illustrate Jove as the Roman version of Greek Zeus, crowned as king of the classical Olympiad or pantheon. He is attended by his avian attribute, the eagle. Its exaggerated talons end in arrowheads symbolic of another attribute, lightning shafts for his role as the thunderer. Classical vases had depicted him with lightning bolts, especially in scenes of his rapacious pursuit of females for offspring.[170] Although in Harvey's frontispieces Jove's loins are draped, he holds in his hands, a metonym for power,[171] a symbol of his famed sexual potency,[172] the neatly split halves of an egg. In the frontispieces by Pulleyn and by Elzevir with a Pulleyn imprint, the split egg is inscribed on its bottom half *ex ovo omnia*, "everything from the egg." From Jove's illustrated eggs in all four frontispieces animals escape. Pullyen's edition, which was the first, depicts the fliers upward—highest a bird, below an insect, then a naked human with outspread arms and kicking legs. Headed downward are a sea serpent and a snake dangling a spider. Ravestyn's edition illustrates crawlers and creepers on the ground, a tortoise, a snake, and a worm.

The standard modern history of embryology has praised Harvey's *De generatione animalium* as "clearly a work of very great importance." In particular, "There can be no doubt that the doctrine *ex ovo omnia* was an advance on all preceding thought."[173] Harvey has also been criticized, however, for the error that everything alive issued from an egg.[174] But that error was not Harvey's science. Harvey specified that his usage of the word "egg" copied his anatomy professor's definition. "For we judge (with Fabrici) that any primordial principle whatsoever that is living in potency ought to be called *ovum*, an 'egg.'" That was a term for a principle of potency that was universal—not the identification of an actual physical egg. Harvey added that he did not distinguish Aristotle's worm from the egg because both were observably and reasonably the same. More important to Harvey, both were only "potential." The worm and the egg shared the commonality that they did not issue in "living, but in potential animals." Although Harvey's book began with oviparous animals, the cock and hen, it advanced to viviparous animals, the hind and doe, a generative model for humans, whom he deemed the highest animal.[175] He promised in concluding the appended "De conceptione" to investigate the generation of all animals, including by metamorphosis and by spontaneity. In that future work he planned also to treat the soul and its affects.[176] Harvey certainly did not believe that all animals issued from a physical egg. Jove's egg on the frontispieces of *De generatione animalium* cradled potential animals until that god split the egg for their issue into real life.

Although Harvey revered the numen of nature as the efficient cause of generation, their potency, he designated live animals as the instrumental cause of generation, their actuality. The Greek god Zeus was the primitive numen of the sky and became the Roman Jupiter/Jove or Harvey's numen, as the celestial source of generation. The egg on Harvey's frontispieces referred only mythologically. The illustration in Pulleyn's first edition clarifies that the animals liberated from the egg are not merely types, however. Among the species is a hind, identifiable as male by its antlers, whose deliberated anatomies Harvey reported in the book as the model of viviparous animals. The book also studied other animals depicted on its several frontispieces: birds, insects, spiders, fish, ducks, tortoises, snakes, and worms. Of birds he observed their digestive and respiratory systems as different from earthbound animals. Of the eagle in particular he noted that stones grated nosily in its empty gizzard and that it never drank.[177]

Harvey's notable avian account in that book concerned his wife Elizabeth's parrot and offered a rare glimpse of their domestic life.[178] He reported an extraordinary talking parrot that was her pet. At liberty in the house, it would seek her out in her absence and fly to her at her call. Grabbing her clothes with its claws and beak, it would climb to her shoulder and then descend her arm to perch on her hand. "Often wanton and lustful, it used to go to sit on her lap to have its head fondled, and it used to gesture passionately to have its back stroked down; and with fluttering wings and a mild cry it would testify to the supreme joy of its spirit." Although Harvey's anecdote was personal, his observation of that bird was professional. The parrot's behavior exemplified his record on the lust of birds, how they would respond sexually to the stroking of a human finger by baring and thrusting the opening to the uterus, and by fluttering their wings and emitting a low tone. Harvey agreed with Aristotle that birds could even conceive in that way. And indeed, after Elizabeth's parrot died in its mistress's lap, from its dissection Harvey reported, "I found in the uterus an almost perfect egg but, for the lack of a male, spoiled." He thought such corruption was frequent in females caged without a cock, although he had originally assumed from the parrot's song and talk that Eve's pet was male.[179]

Harvey's anecdote of the parrot lusty in his wife's lap was poignant because the couple was childless.[180] Although he researched generation professionally, his personal progeny were, in a popular topic, only his books.[181] A colleague, Martin Llewelyn, prefaced the translation of Harvey's *Disputations Concerning the Generation of Animals* with a poem on Harvey's books as issues of his brain although his loins had none.[182] *History of the Worthies of England* posthumously awarded Harvey his children by naming his books. "The Doctor, though living a bachelor, may be said to have left three hopeful sons to posterity."[183] Yet Harvey's anecdote about Eve's lusty parrot was notable for its citation of Vergil's *Georgica* on the conception of birds in the spring. That poem traced the impetus for animal generation to Jove, who descended to earth in spring showers, as if landing in his wife's lap to create offspring. Harvey's appended "De conceptione" also revealed his purpose in tracing the animals of its frontispieces to a numen of nature. He remarked there "how the mere spider, without either a model or a brain, by fantasy alone weaves its webs." Harvey admired the natural ability of even caged birds to recall their seasonal songs, and of the smallest free birds to build their nests artfully not from memory or habit but fantasy.[184]

Significantly, one species on the frontispieces of *De generatione animalium* was not studied in that book. It is the only illustrated animal that bounds toward Jove, rather than away from him. That is a crocodile, which regards him with parted jaws as if ready to bite back its creator. The crocodile appears in the first edition, by Pulleyn, and is copied in Jansson's edition. In both illustrations Jove's eagle gazes directly at him. In the editions by Elzevir and Ravestyn, which lack the crocodile, Jove's eagle looks away from him either to an incubating bird or to the side of the frame. A text that associated the eagle and the crocodile at the turn of the seventeenth century was Giordano Bruno's *Spaccio de la bestia trionfante* (Expulsion of the triumphant beast). He wrote, "Those wise men knew God to be in things, and Divinity to be latent in Nature, working and glowing differently in different subjects and succeeding through diverse physical forms, in certain arrangements, in making them participants in her, I say, in her life and intellect." Toward victory those ancients libated to magnanimous Jove in the eagle, and against betrayal to menacing Jove in the crocodile.[185] Although the Roman Inquisition condemned Bruno to be burned as a heretic,[186] esoteric writings circulated among Harvey's colleagues, such as Robert Fludd, who was the first to accept his treatise on the circulation of the blood.[187] Harvey's frontispieces to *De generatione animalium* may have symbolized that the crocodile menaced Jove's creation while the eagle ensured its victory. Harvey's creative egg emitting animals instantiated the principle "from the egg, everything" with reference to the mythic cosmic egg, not to a real physical egg. It illustrated nature's incubation at the origins of life by Jove, or by a principle with another name as that work catalogued them.[188]

Incubation was a Christian patristic interpretation of the Spirit's activity in Genesis 1:2 over the waters at creation. Jerome, editor and translator of the Vulgate Bible, interpreted it as "not said about the spirit of the world, as so many think, but about the Holy Spirit, and the very one said to be the vivifier of everything from the beginning." As he reasoned, "If, moreover, he is the vivifier, consequently he is the maker; and because the maker, also God.[189] Calvin later entertained incubation as a translation of the Hebrew participle *měraḥepet* in Genesis 1:2.[190] The incubation of a cosmic egg remained very popular in early modern English literature.[191] Milton's *Paradise Lost* would serenely versify "on the watery calm / His brooding wings the Spirit of God outspread."[192] Harvey's citation of Vergil's *Jovis omnia plena*, "everything full of Jove," appeared late in *De generatione animalium*, in exercise 53, and much later still in its appended "De partu."[193] The citation was thus not readily accessible to the illustrator of the frontispiece of its first edition. The artist must have been directed by someone very familiar with the entire manuscript and its purpose; if not by Harvey himself, then by Ent, its dedicator. However, the frontispiece of Ent's translation did not copy the Jove of the Latin editions but engraved a bust of Harvey.[194]

NAME

Harvey thought that the name of the generative principle should not be contested. The first Agent ought to be addressed and venerated, whether called "God or nature naturing or the world soul," for every venerable name was due. He summarized the universal consensus that "it is the principle and end of everything together; that it exists eternal and almighty; and, the author and creator of all things, through various vicissitudes of generation, conserves and perpetuates perishable realities, that is everywhere present, not less heedful in the particular works of natural things than in the entire universe; that by its numen or providence, by art and divine mind procreates all animals collectively."[195] The modern translation has personalized that *principium* "principle" by "He," as if Harvey designated the biblical God. The same translation also twice rendered classical *numen* as "spirit,"[196] although Harvey reserved *spiritus* as "spirit" for an exclusively physical entity. Acknowledging various modes of birth, he detailed natural bodies as operations and instruments of its supreme numen that were only natural or simultaneously animate. Such were heat, spirit (*spiritus*), and the fomentation or pollution of the air. The word *numen*, which was Harvey's frequent diction,[197] derived in Latin from the Greek verb *neuō*, "to nod with the head." It designated the agent whose approval instigated an action externally. Although *numen* was attributed to deity in general or to gods and goddesses in particular,[198] it was especially associated with Jove's nod as supreme in the divine pantheon. Calvin's commentary on Acts wrote *numen* for the divinity the Athenians worshipped at their altar to the unknown god. He explicated, "With Erasmus we translate *numen* Luke's *to theion* written in the neuter gender for any divinity whatsoever."[199] That was the Hippocratic *to theion* that Harvey cited as the universal vital force.[200]

Harvey concluded that "to the prior, superior, and more present cause there must be recourse, to whose service are attributed providence, intelligence, art, and goodness." The effect of its operation was a fortiori more excellent to the same extent that an architect surpassed his work, or a king his ministers, or a craftsman his hands. "Therefore, it will be that both male and female are instrumental to the Creator of all things, or subservient to the supreme progenitor." In comparison with the cock and the hen as efficient causes of animal generation, "the sun, or the sky, or nature, or the soul of the world, or almighty God (for these render the same reality) are a superior and more divine cause in generation." Harvey thought that the art of medicine he practiced required the faculty of reasoning as much as mechanical and manual skills required the use of designed instruments. By his own reasoning he posited an ultimate efficient cause of generation. Resorting to Vergil's verse, he argued, "Wherefore and even in the greater world they say to us, 'All things are full of Jove,' thus equally in the tiny body of a chick and its individual actions and operations the finger of God or the numen of nature shines forth." If it was legitimate to judge faculties by operations, Harvey proposed an a fortiori argument from the quickening vegetative operations, which were arranged by art, choice, and providence. "Then the more so," he inferred, "were the mental actions of the rational soul, for that was most perfect in humans, whose knowledge and understanding were the highest perfection." From that perfection Harvey inferred the Delphic oracle. "In this chiefly consists (in Apollo's judgment) that one should 'know thyself.'"[201]

Harvey reasoned from the human mental faculty of self-knowledge that "a more divine worker than a human is apparent to fabricate and make a man, and a nobler artisan than a cock to produce a chick from an egg." As he amplified that, "Certainly we acknowledge a god, the supreme and almighty Creator, to be present everywhere in the working of animals collectively and to display as if with his finger their operations, in whose procreation of the chick the cock and the hen are the instrumental causes." He further stated, "It surely agrees that in the generation of the chick from the egg everything is constructed and fashioned out by a singular providence, by divine wisdom, and by admirable and incomprehensible craftsmanship." Such works were only attributable to the "omnipotent principle of things." Harvey thought that principle could be named freely, "whether divine mind with Aristotle, or with Plato the world-soul, or with others nature naturing, or with the pagans Saturn or Jove, or preferably (as befits us) the Creator and Father of all things that are in the heavens and on earth, by whom animals and their origins depend, by whose nod or exhalation all things are made and generated."[202] Harvey's familiar "us" assumed Christian readers but especially the College of Physicians, London, to whom their fellow member Ent presented that volume.[203] Harvey further referred to the efficient cause of generation as "nature itself or the first and supreme begetter," and "nature, or a more divine worker,"[204] and "nature whose every work is admirable and divine."[205]

Harvey related the human spirit to the divine cause of existence. He discoursed about spirit in *De generatione animalium* most extensively on innate bodily heat. He criticized the contemporary notion of spirit, specifying Julius Caesar Scaliger and Jean Fernel, as devoid of any understanding.[206] Harvey supposed that, if he proposed the blood as the riddle of the philosopher's stone, it would be esteemed. And, if Fernel were an Oedipus, he would solve that riddle. Harvey was aware that his opponents derived their fictitious aerial and ethereal spirits from Albert the Great's speculations,[207] although Harvey did not acknowledge Avicenna's light as their prior fundamental source. Albert's *De animalibus*, a paraphrase of Aristotle's animal books, stated that the heart was fully spiritous. It supposed that cardiac contraction sent an airy spirit from the heart through the arteries, as if through pipelines, while cardiac relaxation returned it to the heart. Albert explicitly agreed with Avicenna that the substance of spirit was light as a fifth body midway between the soul and elemental matter. It was necessary to posit that fifth body because the spiritous substance sometimes waxed or waned conversely with the diminishment or growth of an elemental body. Albert reasoned that could not happen if the spiritous substance was one of the physical elements or one of the bodily elements.[208]

Harvey dismissed their speculations and resorted to his own deliberated discovery of the circulation of the blood to define the origin and function of physiological spirit. He had already rehearsed his arguments in *Exercitationes duae anatomicae de circulatione sanguinis*, to Riolan, another opponent. Harvey rehearsed the numerous conflicting opinions on spirits, their definition, their bodily quality and constitution, whether they were separate and distinct from the blood and solid matter or whether mingled. He called ambiguity on the subject "a subterfuge of common ignorance" that permitted the attribution of spirits to any unknown cause. "Thus they introduce spirit as the creator of everything, and like bad poets they summon on stage 'the god from the machine' to explain the turning point of a narrative." Harvey rejected the aerial spirits and invisible substances that Fernel and others argued from nature's abhorrence of a vacuum. He further reported the Galenic medical consensus of three kinds of inflowing spirits and three kinds of fixed spirits—natural in and through the veins, vital in and through the arteries, and animal in and through the nerves. Harvey stated that his dissections had never found them. He further reported the division of spirits into incorporeal and corporeal, with the corporeal spirit being in the blood or in its thinnest part as the link to the soul. Sometimes, he added, spirit was supposed in the blood like a flame of a vapor and sustained by its continuous flow. Sometimes, contradictorily, spirit was supposed distinct from the blood. Harvey thought all declarations of incorporeal spirits were baseless, although he acknowledged that their advocates admitted the corporeal potencies of spirits in corporeal faculties or parts.[209]

As he continued his criticism, the scholastics reckoned among "spirits" fortitude, prudence, patience, and every virtue, with wisdom as the holiest one, and indeed every divine gift. Harvey reckoned that the good God did not endow those wicked critics with wisdom, his most excellent gift. For the scholastics suspected that evil and good spirits aided, possessed, debased, and wandered about. They believed that evil demons and imbalanced humors caused illnesses. Harvey complained that, although nothing was more uncertain and dubious than the traditional teaching about spirits, the majority of doctors seemed to agree with Hippocrates's tripartite division of the body into containers, contents, and drivers—the last an impetus they ascribed to spirit. Harvey objected that the designation rendered all bodily impulses a spirit, and he added that not all spirits were aery or incorporeal. Against the opinion of spirit in the blood like a flame of a vapor, he maintained that spirit coursing through the arteries or veins was no more inseparable from the blood than a flame was from its vapor. "Blood and spirit signified one and the same thing," he stated, like a noble wine and its bouquet. Just as spiritless wine palled into vinegar, so spiritless blood was mere bloodshed. "Blood without the vital spirit was not blood, but ought to be decreed immediately spoiled if it is rendered destitute of spirit." Therefore, he insisted that the spirit was the act of the blood, as in the examples of wine or a flicker. Although imbued with very many spirits, the blood was not sluggish either to spoil or to swell. Like wine, its spirit should be understood as prevailing to effect and act with greater powers and impetus, in Hippocratic fashion. Although arterial blood in the arteries was more spirituous and vital than venous blood in the veins, the same blood coursed in both. It did not change to something airier or more vaporous, as if nothing was a spirit unless airy, or nothing was a driving force except breath and flatulence. Nor were the animal, natural, and vital spirits inhabiting the solidly bodily parts and contained in blind meanderings to be thought different aerial forms or vaporous types.[210]

Harvey addressed those who taught that the heart produced spirit, as mixed from the vapors or exhalations of blood and inhalations of air. Since both components were much colder than blood, would not the spirit be much colder than the blood? he asked. The spirit would then owe its heating to the blood, rather than the reverse. Moreover, he thought such spirits should be evaluated more as sooty issues from the body than as its natural creator. Those spirits would then more probably be exhalations of the lungs, by which those issues ventilated and purified the blood in that cold environment. The process would prevent the overheating and swelling of the heart, which would distend the lungs to suffocate the animal, a danger Harvey had observed in asthmatic patients. He supposed "these things are perhaps enough and more than enough about the spirit in this place. We ought to define and teach what they are and of what nature in a physiological treatise." He added that some thinkers treated of innate heat as nature's common instrument for everything, and of its necessity for warming all parts of the body and keeping it alive. He criticized them because, although they acknowledged that innate heat could not exist without a subject, they did not find a moving body commensurate with its rapid inflow and outflow. "They introduce spirits just as if bodies absolutely subtle, perfectly penetrating and mobile, hardly other than they see a marvelous divinity of natural operations appearing from that common instrument (to wit, innate heat). They contrive those sublime, lucid, ethereal, divine spirits of a heavenly nature to be the identical bonds of the soul." Harvey compared their philosophical invention of such spirits to the speculations of ignorant commoners, "just as the crowd of uneducated people, who do not understand the causes of works, opines and thinks gods are the direct authors." Thus, he wrote, they determined that heat flowed to the bodily parts through the inflowing spirit arriving through the arteries. Harvey criticized their failure to consider that the blood itself could move that quickly, penetrate that deeply, and warm so greatly.[211]

BLOOD

Harvey did not write his proposed physiological treatise on the definition and nature of the spirit. Those deliberations on the circulation of the blood in response to the anatomist Riolan he considered sufficient "in this place." However, Harvey's later *De generatione animalium* decided and developed importantly the coincidence of spirit in blood as the source of innate bodily heat. "It is surely unnecessary to seek for any spirit distinct from the blood, or to introduce heat from another entity, or to summon the gods to the stage, or to burden philosophy with imagined opinions."[212] His reference to theatrical *deus ex machina* devices objected to René Descartes's mechanistic philosophy of the heart.[213] What the crowd sought from the stars Harvey found "born at home." He thus transferred to the blood his initial Aristotelian allegiance to the heart as the caloric source of bodily animation. From his observations of generation he argued that "surely only the blood is innate heat, or firstborn animal heat," so that it was needless to multiply entities. Applying Ockham's razor, Harvey affirmed that nothing was found in animal bodies prior to or superior to the blood, nor were there spirits distinct and separated from it.[214]

Harvey did not posit the blood essentially. For without spirit or heat it was only bloodshed (*cruor*). Bloodshed, he noted, was what issued from Jesus's side when pierced by the lance as the biblical proof of his death. That note tacitly acknowledged Jesus's bloodshed as a religious sacrifice, as in the Levitical holiness codes of the biblical Priestly tradition. However, as an anatomist, Harvey treated the physiological significance of blood, and, as a natural philosopher, he did not infer from it that the Creator or the numen of nature was itself bloody. Harvey defined blood, insofar as it was a living component of the body, as dual in nature. Materially and in itself, blood was called nutriment. Formally, to the extent that it existed with heat and spirits as the instruments of the immediate soul and with that very soul, "it ought to be determined the household god (*lar*) of the body or the conserver, the principal part, the primogenital and genital part."²¹⁵ Blood thus displaced the heart of his *De motu cordis et sanguinis in animalibus* as the household god (*lar*).²¹⁶ Harvey introduced its new identity in defining the "prime genital particle," in which "the soul inheres as the author and beginning of sense, motion, and all life." As he asserted, "The principal particle is whence the vital spirit and native heat reaches all the others; in which the innate or infixed heat of doctors first ignites; and hosts the household god (*lar familiaris*) or everlasting hearth; whence life perpetually spreads through the whole body and its singular parts; whence nutrition, growth, support, and relief originate; whence life first begins in infants and finally ends in the dying." Harvey's assertion that the soul first and principally resided in the blood did not allow the conclusion that bloodletting was dangerous, however. With a rare citation of Scripture, he argued against the popular belief that drawing blood withdrew an equal amount of life "because the sacred page [the Bible] deposited life in the blood." Harvey referred to the holiness code, "For the life of the flesh is in the blood" (Lev. 17:11 AV).²¹⁷ However, that priestly law was not a physiological statement. It forbade human consumption of the bloodshed of animals sacrificed to God on the altar.²¹⁸ Harvey thought bloodletting was not only healthful and useful in illness but also was "the chief of universal remedies" since either plethora or anemia of blood caused the most diseases. Bloodletting rescued bodies from disease and death, and it was sanctioned naturally by menstruation, hemorrhoids, and nosebleeds.²¹⁹ His identification of spirit with blood was not with blood as abstract material but as vital animation.

Harvey stated the universal discernment that "the common instrument of vegetative operations was internal heat, or innate warmth, or spirit diffused through the whole, and in that spirit was the soul or the faculty of the soul." He again cited biblical Leviticus to support his theory of the spirit inhering as the blood, although he derived that from his own reasoned anatomies. Harvey named blood the "first principal part and the principle not only because in it arises from it the beginning of movement and pulsation but also because in it animal heat is born first, and the vital spirit is generated, and the soul itself dwells." The location of the immediate and principal instrument of the vegetative faculty, which quickened life, was where the soul probably inhered and originated. He reasoned that probability "because it cannot be separated from the spirit and innate heat." Although in works of art the artist and the instrument were separate, in workings of nature they were identical. The spirit was both maker and instrument of the soul. Thus, where motion and heat originated in the body, "in the same also life first arose and in the end is extinguished." Harvey referred to the *penates* of ancient Roman religion to complement his household god (*lar*). "And in the same place the inmost guardian deities (*penates*) and the very soul possess their seat, no one will doubt." Harvey then appealed again to Scripture on the blood. "Life, therefore, consists in the blood (as moreover we read in our scriptures), indeed in it life and spirit first struggle forth and ultimately fail" (Lev. 17:11). He stated that he himself had proved that fact by numerous vivisections of dying animals whose hearts continued to beat even after they had ceased breathing. Their blood, he inferred, conserved their spirit.[220]

Harvey cited Aristotle's ambiguity on the blood as the body's innate heat, whether or not it coincided with animal spirit. He claimed again that his own anatomies had proved their coincidence. For physicians, he admitted, spirit was Hippocrates's impetus (*impetum faciens*). That entity was whatever by its own effort exerted something, and with agility and violence excited movement, or undertook some action. The term extended to wine and vitriol. Because of its generous definition "among doctors there were as many spirits as their were bodily parts or operations; to wit, animal, vital, natural, visionary, auditory, digestive, and generative, infixed, flowing, etc." Harvey insisted that the blood, meaning the firstborn and principle of the blood, was endowed with all those powers. Indeed it possessed an exceptional power of acting, so that blood preeminently deserved the name "spirit." Harvey criticized those who failed to ponder its excellent gifts but fantasized instead about airy or ethereal spirits, or their combination as the soul's proximate and omnicompetent instrument. For they based their argument on blood as a substance derived from the elements, which intrinsically could not act beyond elemental powers. Advocates of a spirit of innate heat outside the blood defined "an ether and a participant in the fifth essence, being of celestial origin and nature, indeed a body absolutely simple, subtle, fine, mobile, swift, and lucid." Harvey complained that they had never demonstrated either the gift of such spirit or its activity beyond elemental powers surpassing the blood. He added that anatomical investigators who were guided by observations had never been able to find such a spirit or even bodily cavities for its generation or conservation.[221]

Harvey affirmed an innate spirit and nature in the blood corresponding to the element of the stars. There was "a spirit or some power acting above the elemental powers and nature; yes indeed, a soul in this spirit and blood corresponding to the starry element."[222] He paused to define spirit with a historical review. Fire was claimed to be spirit by the religious virgins who guarded Apollo's temple at Delphi as sacred. It was "as if God were most grandly conspicuous in fire, and from fire speaks to us (as in times past to Moses)." Harvey referred to the biblical voice of God to Moses from the burning bush. As he continued, the element of air was also called spirit by its name from *spiro*, "to breathe." Aristotle clearly wrote of "a certain life and origin, and destruction of breaths." Harvey reported that the pagans seemed to number those elements of fire and air among the gods (*dives*) since they possessed some life, acted above elemental powers, and participated in some divine agency. He argued, however, that blood similarly acted above elemental powers. As the firstborn part and innate heat, blood fashioned in order the remaining parts of the entire body. It acted "with supreme providence and intelligence toward a sure end, as if by some reasoning." As innate heat, blood did originate from fire but "by a gift of plastic power and of the vegetative soul, and it is made the firstborn heat and the immediate and appropriate instrument of life." Harvey quoted from *Suda*, a medieval Greek lexicon, on "the blood, the living principle of humanity," and he affirmed it true of all blooded animals.[223]

Harvey's identification of spirit with circulating blood occasioned theoretically the modern meaning of the human spirit as courageous. It did not do so singularly but collaboratively with the regnant classical theories of the elements, the qualities, and the humors. The elements were air, fire, earth, and water. The qualities were hot, dry, cold, and wet.[224] The humors were sanguine, phlegmatic, bilious, and atrabilious. In Galen's influential medical scheme one humor dominated a body to constitute a temperament. Its balanced or imbalanced mixture with the other humors disposed the body to health or to illness.[225] Humoral theory in Harvey's century was not only a medical specialty but also a cultural commonplace of philosophy and literature.[226] No explanation to his readers of the ordinary association of the elements, qualities, and humors was necessary. Harvey capitalized on the current extension of "spirit" to temperament. English "spirit" was initially a cognate of the Vulgate's *spiritus* for biblical Hebrew *rûaḥ* and Greek *pneuma*. It meant "the animating or vital principle in man (and animals); that which gives life to the physical organism, in contrast to its purely material elements; the breath of life." The Renaissance meaning of "spirit" developed through humoral theory to become "a particular character, disposition or temper existing in, pervading, or animating, a person or set of persons; a special attitude or bent of mind characterizing men individually or collectively."[227] The historical and contemporary conflations of the elements, qualities, and temperaments Harvey coalesced in the blood as spirituous, thus causative of certain affects or passions of the soul, such as courage.

The sanguine, or bloody, humor was in Galenic medicine the first humor generated in the body because the fetus originated from blood and sperm. That humor was identified with elemental air as hot and moist, and it was also associated with the season of spring and the age of childhood.[228] Harvey's citation of Vergil's verses on springtime generation[229] was coherent with his argument for blood as spirit. His identification of the human spirit as blooded occasioned its acquisition of the characteristics of the sanguine humor. It was traditionally the humor in which blood prevailed as a liquid deriving from the fiery heart and, in Harvey's innovative natural philosophy, circulating back to it for restoking. Harvey's equation of the blood with the spirit thus occasioned theoretically the modern sense of the human spirit as courageous. Blood partook of all the positive qualities and virtues that both Aristotelian and Stoic psychologies ascribed to heat, rather than to cold. Medieval philosophy had further explored the classical temperaments and elements in deliberations on the soul. Blood, which was moist and hot, produced positive and generous passions such as courage. The scholastic philosopher Albert the Great, for example, believed that fearless persons had "much blood and a hot heart." In contrast, pusillanimous persons, who were dry and cold, had "little spirit and little heat in their heart."[230] A human was spirited as vitally blooded; the bloody temperament produced courage. By a generalization the human spirit, as vitally blooded, became characterized as courageous.

The history of the classical affects, then the medieval passions, such as courage, had deliberated their cause: whether they originated from sensory apprehension in a movement of the heart, by systole or diastole, then affected the mind; whether a mental, even locally cerebral, impression reverberated in the body; or whether body and soul simultaneously acted or were acted upon.[231] In the prevailing Aristotelian tradition the spirits were diffused from the heart throughout the body. As Harvey phrased the Aristotelian belief medically, the heart was "the fount and laboratory of the vital spirits by which it gives life to all the parts." The heart expelled its indwelling spirits through the arteries, which were believed to be not blood vessels but air ducts.[232] That error derived from the formidable double authority of Aristotle in philosophy and Galen in medicine. Although Harvey altered the distributor of the spirit from the heart to the blood, he personally had deliberated and discovered the heart as the organ that circulated the blood. Because in the human body the lungs flanked and surrounded the heart, those organs were traditionally interrelated. The heart was designated the hearth of animate heat, while the lungs cooled the heart lest it explode in combustion. The vital spirits were believed to be the concoction of blood and air on the hearth of the heart. For refreshment and stability the heart inhaled cold air and exhaled sooty vapors, the residue of its concoctions.[233]

Harvey's identification of life with the blood lacked knowledge of the respiratory function of the lungs to oxygenate the blood. That would only be discovered in the eighteenth century,[234] because scientific research on the function of the lungs was obscured and delayed by belief in their subservience to the heart. Harvey considered the role of the lungs traditionally, as coolants, even in the blood flow, lest the heart combust.[235] However, he was the first to describe the air sacs in birds, the system by which they breathed distinctively from other animals and not by the expansion and contraction of their lungs. He quoted his professor Fabrici d'Acquapendente on birds pecking their way to birth through the eggshell, but he wondered whether the air they sought really was for cooling the heart or the blood.[236] Elemental air was undifferentiated before the experiments in the eighteenth century of the Dissident theologian Joseph Priestley to relate metaphysics and physics. Pondering the dualism of matter and spirit, he rejected their distinction. Priestley discovered "dephlogisticated air" from mercuric oxide heated with his burning lens—technically oxygen. It was his contemporary the chemist Antoine-Laurent Lavoisier who, rejecting the theory of phlogiston, named *oxygen* and identified its properties as an atmospheric component. Priestley's explorations of theology and science did not confirm Genesis on creation. He dismissed what he believed to be Moses's personal account as unnecessary for Christian faith because it was not divinely inspired. Definitive for his Unitarianism, he denied the Trinity as "absurd," dismissing its Holy Spirit as Creator.[237]

Historical affects and passions were not emotions, despite the common modern translation "emotion" for Greek *pathos*, classical Latin *adfectus*, and medieval Latin *passio*. The psychological category "emotion" was the invention of Thomas Brown, a Scottish philosopher and physician in the late nineteenth century. Emotion displaced, not derived from, ancient and medieval ideas of a soulful motion to or from ends sensed and/or judged good or evil. Emotion particularly collapsed a traditional Christian distinction between sensory passions and volitional affections.[238] Psychology has challenged the value and even the validity of the various types of "emotion" inherited from historical texts.[239]

Harvey the physician agreed with the medieval philosophical consensus that the affects of the soul (*animi pathema*) caused the bodily consumption that caused disease and death. "For every mental affect, whence sadness and joy, hope and fear, arouses human minds and spreads all the way to the heart. And there it effects a change from the natural constitution, in temperature, and the pulse, and the rest." It should not seem "marvelous," he reasoned, that the pollution of the nourishment of the entire body at its cardiac source and that the weakening of cardiac powers should beget all sorts of incurable diseases.[240] Harvey characterized his medical contemporaries as debilitated, as sluggish for their doubt or denial of the circulation of the blood. "Very many, prone to idleness, prefer to wander with the crowd." Content with ancient medicine, they assumed that nothing more could be discovered. "And this is negligence (*socordia*) in us."[241] His *socordia* classically meant "dull- or weak-mindedness," with connotations of "silliness, folly, stupidity," and resultant "carelessness, negligence, sloth, laziness, indolence, inactivity." But etymologically *socordia* did not reference the mind. The noun derived from *se* for *sine*, "without," and *cor*, "heart."[242] Harvey's diction criticized the majority of his colleagues as if they lacked hearts, for denying that the heart's supply of the hot moist blood created spirit. His conclusion of *De generatione animalium* promised to treat the physical elements and the physiological temperaments.[243] "De conceptione" further promised to treat the affects in a "complete encircling" of animals by following Ariadne's clew through the bodily labyrinth.[244] However, Harvey never wrote that promised treatise on the physical elements and physiological temperaments. And he never wrote his promised continuation on the generation of animals that would include "the soul and its affects."[245] Harvey acknowledged the finger of God or the numen of nature in the operations of the vegetative animal soul, especially in generation, the topic of that book. Then he argued a fortiori, "Then the more so were the mental actions of the rational soul, for that was most perfect in humans, whose knowledge and understanding were the highest perfection."[246] However, he did not treat the human rational soul, whose mental actions he stated were the highest perfection of the finger of God or the numen of nature in animals. As Harvey rested the topic, the human spirit apparently exhibited courage just as an animal (the exemplary lion) exhibited courage, that is, because of their circulating hot blood.

At the turn of the seventeenth century Ben Jonson dramatized a character: "O brave and spirited! He's a right Jovialist,"[247] equating courage with spirit and deriving spirit from Jove. Harvey's contemporary understanding of the human spirit was not yet secular either. He inferred its origin in the biblical Creator or the numen of nature through the principle of animal generation. He believed that the universal efficient cause Jove, or any name, imprinted its divine image supremely in the generation of animals. The biblical Creator commanded humans in Genesis 1:26 to be his stewards by their dominion over all animals. That care became Harvey's role as an anatomist who strove to research and analyze the causes by which animals generated, for had not God mandated animals in Genesis 1:22 to be "be fruitful and multiply"? *The Human Spirit: Beginnings from Genesis to Science* has treated important ideas on that subject from biblical creation to physiological denotation. The modern sense of a spirited human as courageous derived in theory from a spirituous animal, which Harvey traced to its universal cause in a natural sense of divinity. His anatomical focus was on the human as an animal, and distinctly so as a blooded animal, which species he valued as the highest. That scientific investigation of animal quiddity for vitality differed from a theological tradition in Augustine and Aquinas that distinguished human spirit from animal spirit by strict emphasis on human mental faculties as unique. Mentation was the historical idea with the longest duration and it is still the best known. However, Paul's biblical letters to the Corinthians about the human spirit were faithful to its creation in Genesis in imitation of the divine Spirit for a relationship that was vital and social. Calvin's writings and sermons to the reformed church at Geneva endeavored to recover from a philosophical psychology the biblical human spirit.

Generation was a commonality of the human spirit from a beginning in biblical revelation to a beginning in Harvey's scientific research. It extended from the Priestly *tôledôt* formula about the generations of the Israelite tribes to Harvey's anatomical exercises toward the efficient cause of the generation of animals. The methods of the ancient priests and of that innovative early modern anatomist differed, of course. The priests looked up at the sky to observe a soaring eagle as a metaphor for the Spirit marking its own territory as Israel, and they looked around themselves to observe the increasing and multiplying Israelite assembly. Harvey looked down at the dissecting table and inside the body displayed on it to trace its divine design. Both the priests and the anatomist taught the significance of being humanly spirited. Those bookends of *The Human Spirit: Beginnings from Genesis to Science* shared a conviction of the human spirit as vital. That existential vitality was endowed by or derived from a supreme source of everything animate. The human spirit related to a divine spirit called by whatever name, *rûaḥ 'ĕlōhîm*, or Father. This book has stretched up in the air to catch some spirit and ground it in the multiform reality of human experience and reflection. Its story in politics, philosophy, and physiology has proved to be, as in that sprite Ariel's song, once again "something rich and strange."[248]

NOTES

CHAPTER 1

1. Translations of the Bible in this chapter are from the Revised Standard Version except as otherwise stated. For this verse, see also Marjorie O'Rourke Boyle, "The Beginning of Chaos for Genesis," forthcoming in the *Journal for the Study of the Old Testament*.

2. *Biblia hebraica stuttgartensia*, 5th rev. ed., ed. Adrian Schenker (Stuttgart: Deutsche Bibelgesellschaft, 1997). See also Ronald S. Hendel, *The Text of Genesis 1–11: Textual Studies and Critical Edition* (New York: Oxford University Press, 1998), 116–18; Claus Westermann, *Genesis 1–11: A Commentary*, trans. John J. Scullion (Minneapolis: Augsburg, 1984), 106–8.

3. Nahum M. Sarna, *Genesis: The Traditional Hebrew Text with the New JPS Translation* (Philadelphia: Jewish Publication Society, 1989), 'Ets Ḥayim = *Etz hayim: Torah and Commentary*, ed. David Lieber et al. (Philadelphia: Jewish Publication Society for the Rabbinical Assembly of the United Synagogue of Conservative Judaism, 2001), 4.

4. Hagiga 12a, in *The Hebrew-English Edition of the Babylonian Talmud: Ḥagigah*, trans. Israel Abrahams, ed. I. Epstein (London: Soncino, 1984), ad loc. For its status, see Jeffrey L. Rubenstein, *The Culture of the Babylonian Talmud* (Baltimore: Johns Hopkins University Press, 2003), 1, 31–35.

5. See Hyam Maccoby, *The Philosophy of the Talmud* (London: RoutledgeCurzon, 2002), 5–7.

6. Jacob Neusner, *The Reader's Guide to the Talmud* (Leiden: E. J. Brill, 2001), 205–10, 254–57; idem, *The Babylonian Talmud: A Translation and Commentary*, 22 vols. (Peabody, Mass.: Hendrickson, 2005), 7:45–46.

7. Tuvia Freedman, "And a Wind from God: Genesis 1:2," trans. Aviva Wolfers-Borazoni, *Jewish Bible Quarterly* 24 (1996): 9.

8. E. A. Speiser, *Genesis: Introduction, Translation, and Notes* (Garden City, N.Y.: Doubleday, 1964), 5; Gerhard von Rad, *Genesis: A Commentary*, rev. ed. (Philadelphia: Westminster, 1972), 49. See also Richard E. Friedman, *Commentary on the Torah* (San Francisco: Harper, 2001), 9.

9. Westermann, *Genesis*, 107–8. See especially Harry M. Orlinsky, "The Plain Meaning of Rûaḥ in Gen. 1.2," *Jewish Quarterly Review* 48 (1957–58): 174–82. For rabbinical "wind" because it approximates Babylonian texts, see Lieber, ed., *'Ets Ḥayim*, 4.

10. Deut. 32:21; Is. 4:39, 41:29.

11. Ps. 135:17.

12. Is. 66:1, 68:34.

13. Amos 4:13.

14. 2 Sam. 22:11 = Ps. 18:10; Deut. 33:26; Ps. 104:3; cf. Is. 19:1, 68:4, 33. See Sigmund Mowinckel, "Drive and/or Ride in O.T.," *Vetus Testamentum* 12 (1962): 278–99.

15. Ezek. 1, 10; cf. Ps. 104:3.

16. Ex. 15:8 and numerous texts. For the sirocco, see Aloysius Fitzgerald, *The Lord of the East Wind* (Washington, D.C.: The Catholic Biblical Association of America, 2004).

17. Gen. 3:8. Jeffrey Niehaus, "In the Wind of the Storm: Another Look at Genesis iii8," *Vetus Testamentum* 44 (1994): 263–67.

18. P. J. Smith, "A Semotactical Approach to the Meaning of the Term *rûaḥ 'ĕlōhîm* in Genesis 1:2," *Journal of Northwest Semitic Languages* 8 (1980): 100–10; Mark Smith, *The Priestly Vision of Genesis 1* (Minneapolis: Augsburg Fortress, 2010), 53–56.

19. Freedman, "Wind from God," 9–13.

20. Umberto Cassuto, *A Commentary on the Book of Genesis*, trans. Israel Abrahams, 2 vols. (Jerusalem: Magnes Press, Hebrew University, 1978), 1:24.

21. For a survey of meanings, see Paul van Imschoot, "L'Esprit de Jahvé, source de vie dans l'Ancien Testament," *Revue biblique* 44 (1935): 481–501.

22. Jerome, *Hebraicarum quaestionum in Genesim*, praef., 1.1, in *Patrologiae cursus completus, series latina*, ed. J.-P. Migne, 221 vols. (Paris, 1800–75), 23:936, 937, 939. See also C. T. R. Hayward, *St. Jerome's "Hebrew Questions on Genesis"* (Oxford: Clarendon, 1995), 103–5; Adam Kamesar, *Jerome, Greek Scholarship, and the Hebrew Bible: A Study of the "Quaestiones hebraicae in Genesim"* (Oxford: Clarendon, 1993), 129–32, but as "hovering," 131.

23. Without reference to my argument, see B. K. Waltke and Michael O'Connor, *An Introduction to Biblical Hebrew Syntax* (Winona Lake, Ind.: Eisenbrauns, 1990), 414–16; Ernst Jenni, *Das hebräische Pi'el: Syntaktisch-semasiologische Untersuchungen einer Verbalform im Alten Testament* (Zurich: EVZ, 1967), 156–64.

24. *Septuaginta*, ed. Alfred Rahlfs, 9th ed. (Stuttgart: Württembergische Bibelanstalt, 1935); Susan Brayford, *Genesis* (Leiden: E. J. Brill, 2007), 33 and see 205–6, 208; William P. Brown, *Structure, Role, and Ideology in the Hebrew and Greek Texts of Genesis 1:1–2:3* (Atlanta: Scholars, 1993), 24.

25. Is. 57:13.

26. Ps. 94:9, 11.

27. Rashi's medieval translation and commentary has been misconstrued as referring to "breath" and "hovering" for *acoveter* (Old French). Rashi, *Torah*, trans. Herczeg, 5. Old French *acoveter* meant "cover." For a bird brooding, see Deut. 26:3. For the interpretation of a bird brooding in the Hagigah of the *Talmud Bavli*, see Hayward, *Jerome's "Hebrew Questions,"* 104.

28. *Vetus Latina: Die Reste der altlateinischen Bible*, ed. Pierre Sabatier, rev. Erzabtei Beuron [Bonifatius Fischer]; *Verzeichnis der Sigel für Handschriften und Kirchenschriftsteller*, ed. Bonifatius Fischer (Freiburg: Herder, 1949–), 1:3–6.

29. *Biblia sacra iuxta Vulgatam versionem*, ed. Robert Weber, rev. ed. (Stuttgart: Württembergische Bibelanstalt, 1975).

30. *The Holy Bible from the Latin Vulgate by John Wycliffe and His Followers*, ed. Josiah Forshall and Frederic Madden, 4 vols. (Oxford: Oxford University Press, 1850).

31. *The Holy Scriptures Faithfully Translated by Myles Coverdale 1535* (rpt.; London: Samuel Bagster, 1838; rpt., Frome a Copy in the Library of the Duke of Sussex); *The Geneva Bible: A Facsimile of the 1560 Edition* (Madison: University of Wisconsin Press, 1969); *The Holy Bible: Douay 1609, Rheims 1582* (London: R. and T. Washbourne, 1914).

32. See "sweeping" in Speiser, *Genesis*, 5; Plaut, *Torah*, 18; Sarna, *Genesis*, p. 6, but cf. "hovering" for Deut. and Ugaritic; Lieber, ed., *'Ets Ḥayim*, 4.

33. For "hovering" of "spirit," see Cassuto, *Genesis*, 1:24–25; "God's spirit was hovering," Friedman, *Commentary on the Torah*, 6; "rushing-spirit of God hovering," Everett Fox, *The Five Books of Moses: Genesis, Exodus, Leviticus, Numbers, and Deuteronomy: A New Translation with Introductions, Commentary, and Notes* (New York: Schocken Books, 1995), 13; "hovering," Bill T. Arnold, *Genesis* (Cambridge: Cambridge University Press, 2009), 39; for hovering of breath, Robert Alter, *The Five Books of Moses* (New York: W. W. Norton, 2004), 17. See also "'And the wind of God was fluttering over the face of the waters' like the vibrating, trembling wing movements of a bird over its nest without forward motion." Benno Jacob, *The First Book of the Bible*, trans. E. I. Jacob and Walter Jacob (New York: KTAV, 1974), 2.

34. Speiser, *Genesis*, 5, 12; Lieber, ed., *'Ets Ḥayim*, 4; Sarna, *Genesis*, 7, adding "vibration."
35. See, without reference to this argument, J. N. D. Kelly, *Jerome: His Life, Writings, and Controversies* (London: Duckworth, 1975), 46–47, 50. The early Islamic settlement on the ruins of nearby classical Chalcis ad Belum was Qinnasrin, "Eagle's Nest."
36. See William M. Schniedewind and Joel H. Hunt, *A Primer on Ugaritic: Language, Culture, and Literature* (Cambridge: Cambridge University Press, 2007).
37. Speiser, *Genesis*, 5; Sarna, *Genesis*, 4. See also Cassuto, *Genesis*, 25. For Cassuto's reordering of the first edition of the tablets, see "La leggenda fenicia di Daniel e Aqhat," *Rendiconti dell'Accademia Nazionale dei Lincei*, Rome, 6th ser., 14, nos. 3–4 (1939): 264–68.
38. Ps. 78:27.
39. Job 39:13.
40. Richard E. Whitaker, *A Concordance of the Ugaritic Literature* (Cambridge, Mass.: Harvard University Press, 1972), 572–73.
41. *The Dictionary of Classical Hebrew*, ed. David J. A. Clines, 9 vols. (Sheffield: Sheffield Academic Press, 1993–2011), s.v. *nešer*.
42. E.g., T. Kronholm, "*nešer*," in *Theological Dictionary of the Old Testament*, ed. G. H. Johannes Botterweck, Helmer Ringgren, and Heinz-Josef Fabry, 15 vols. (Grand Rapids, Mich.: Eerdmans, 1974–95), 10:79–80.
43. G. R. Driver, "Birds in the Old Testament," *Palestine Exploration Quarterly* 87 (1955): 8–9, 20. Without reference to Driver, for the corrections made here, see Hadoram Shirihai, *The Birds of Israel: A Complete Avifauna and Bird Atlas of Israel*, ed. Ehud Dovrat and David A. Christie (London: Academic Press, 1996); Jeff Watson, *The Golden Eagle* (London: T and AD Poyser, 1997), 27, and topics below. For the preference for vulture based on Egyptian and Mesopotamian royal cults, see Othmar Keel, *Jahwes Entgegnung an Ijob* (Göttingen: Vandenhoeck & Ruprecht, 1978), 69 n. 234.

44. Keel, *Ijob*, and see F. S. Bodenheimer, *Animal and Man in Bible Lands*, 2 vols. (Leiden: E. J. Brill, 1972), 1:53–54.
45. Dick Forsman, *The Raptors of Europe and the Middle East: A Handbook of Field Identification* (London: T and AD Poyser, 1999), 126–37, 141; 13, 390–403, 369, 371, 121–22, 10, with color plates; Shirihai, *Birds of Israel*, 97–98.
46. Watson, *Golden Eagle*, 8–9.
47. Forsman, *Raptors*, 391, 393 and fully 390–403 with color plates nos. 487–506. Its wingspan is given as 73.6–86.2 inches /187–219 cm, 391; Watson, *Golden Eagle*, 9.
48. L. Brown and D. Amadon, *Eagles, Hawks, and Falcons of the World*, 2 vols. (Middlesex: Hamlyn for Country Life, 1968), 1:19, 22, 26; *Cambridge Encyclopedia of Ornithology*, ed. Michael Brooke and Tim Birkhead (Cambridge: Cambridge University Press, 1991), 96–97.
49. Watson, *Golden Eagle*, 20–21, 203–4, 13–16, 21. See Shirihai, *Birds of Israel*, 123–24. Cf. 119–21, 124–25, 127–28.
50. Seton Gordon, *The Golden Eagle, King of Birds* (London: Collins, 1955), 1; Watson, *Golden Eagle*, 18; Norman Elkins, *Weather and Bird Behavior*, 3rd ed. (London: T and AD Poyser, 2004), 52; Gordon, *Golden Eagle*, 1, 133.
51. Caspar J. Labuschange, *The Incomparability of Yahweh in the Old Testament* (Leiden: E. J. Brill, 1966), 31–63. For Deut. 32:12, 39, see especially 14, 70–72, 76, 114–16, and further studies on the emergence of monotheism, e.g., David Noel Freedman, "'Who Is Like Thee Among the Gods?' The Religion of Early Israel," in *Ancient Israelite Religion: Essays in Honor of Frank Moore Cross*, ed. Patrick D. Miller Jr., Paul D. Hanson, and S. Dean McBride (Philadelphia: Fortress, 1987), 315–35.
52. For the Griffon Vulture, see Brown and Amadon, *Eagles, Hawks, Falcons*, 1:325 and pl. 3. See also Forsman, *Raptors*, 126–37 with color plates nos. 127–42; Shirihai, *Birds of Israel*, 93–94.
53. See Brown and Amadon, *Eagles, Hawks, Falcons*, 1:50, 236, 48.
54. Gen. 15:11. See also Is. 46:11.
55. *Die keilalphabetischen Texte aus Ugarit*, vol. 1, *Transkription*, ed. M. Dietrich, O. Loretz, and J. Sanmartin

(Kevelaer/Neukirchen-Vluyn: Butzon und Bercker / Neukirchener Verlag, 1976). For convenience, the pages are cited in the most recent translations, although my translations below may differ from them. The Story of Aqhat 1.17 vi 10–40, pp. 271–76; 1.18 iv 5–18, pp. 282–86; 1.18 iv 18, pp. 284, 286; 1.18 iv 35, p. 286; 1.19 i 30, p. 294; 1. 19 ii 50, p. 303; 1.19 iii 35, p. 305; 1.19 iii 40–45, pp. 305–7, in Nicolas Wyatt, trans., *Religious Texts from Ugarit: The Words of Ilimilku and His Colleagues* (Sheffield: Sheffield Academic Press, 1998).

56. *The Baal Cycle* 1.2 iv 20, in Wyatt, *Religious Texts*, 67. Translations of *nsr* in this tale also vary: an "eagle," Cyrus H. Gordon, *Ugaritic Literature: A Comprehensive Translation of the Poetic and Prose Texts* (Rome: Pontificum Institutum Biblicum, 1949), 16, cf. Fragment 6:8, p. 51; and John L. Gibson, ed. *Canaanite Myths and Legends*, 2nd ed. (Edinburgh: Clark, 1978), 44; "vulture," Michael D. Coogan, ed. and trans., *Stories from Ancient Canaan* (Philadelphia: Westminster, 1978), 88, 89; "raptor," *Ugaritic Narrative Poetry*, ed. Simon B. Parker, trans. Mark Smith (Atlanta: Scholars, 1997), 103–4.

57. Watson, *Golden Eagle*, 9.

58. See Tom J. Cade, *The Falcons of the World* (London: Collins, 1982), 61–63. Maximum speed requires a strictly vertical, rather than slanted, descent to gain maximum advantage from the force of gravity.

59. See below, pp. 30–31.

60. See Cade, *Falcons*, 62.

61. *Story of Aqhat* 1.19 i 32–33, p. 294; 1.19 ii 56–57, p. 303; 1.19 iii 14–15, p. 304; 1.19 iii 29, p. 305.

62. Watson, *Golden Eagle*, 18.

63. *Story of Aqhat* 1.19 i 9–11, pp. 290–91.

64. Gordon, *Ugaritic Literature*, 85, 93, 94, 96, 97, 98; idem, *Ugaritic Handbook: Revised Grammar, Paradigms, Texts in Transliteration, Comprehensive Glossary* (Rome: Pontificum Institutum Biblicum, 1947), 183. See also Gibson, *Canaanite Myths and Legends*, 111, 112, 113 117, 118, 119; Kenneth T. Aitken, *The Aqhat Narrative: A Study in the Narrative Structure and Composition of an Ugaritic Tale* (Manchester: Manchester University Press, 1990), 55, 59, 67, 69, 71.

65. Baruch Margalit, *The Ugaritic Poem of AQHT: Text, Translation, Commentary* (Berlin: W. de Gruyter, 1989), 341, 135.

66. For the predators, see "birds," Smith, in *Ugaritic Narrative Poetry*, 65, 66, 68. For "raptors" and "birds of prey," see Mark Smith, *The Ugaritic Baal Cycle*, vol. 1, *Introduction with Text, Translation, and Commentary of KTU 1.1–1.2* (Leiden: E. J. Brill, 1994), 103–4; Simon B. Parker, *The Pre-biblical Narrative Tradition: Essays on the Ugaritic Poems "Keret" and "Aqhat"* (Atlanta: Scholars, 1989), 118, 122, 124, 125, 138. For "vulture," see H. L. Ginsberg, trans., "Ugaritic Myths, Epics, and Legends," in *Ancient Near Eastern Texts Relating to the Old Testament*, ed. James B. Pritchard, 2nd ed. (Princeton: Princeton University Press, 1955), 152, 153; Parker, *Pre-biblical Narrative Tradition*, 136; David P. Wright, *Ritual in Narrative: The Dynamics of Feasting, Mourning, and Retaliation Rites in the Ugaritic Tale of Aqhat* (Winona Lake, Ind.: Eisenbrauns, 2001), 173, 175, 176, 177; Coogan, *Stories from Ancient Canaan*, 39, 40, 43, 44, 88, 89; Aitkin, *Aqhat*, 55 and paralleled with "eagle," see also 67, 69, 71. For "falcon" see Margalit, *Ugaritic Poem of AQHT*, 155, 156, cf. "killer hawk," 333; Wyatt, *Religious Tales from Ugarit*, mixing "falcon" and "hawk," 284, 285, 286, 294, 303, 304, 305, 306; for the observers, "birds," "swift fliers," "birds of prey," "hawks," "vultures," both "hawks" and "vultures," and "kites" that "hover" or "soar," or "swoop" or "soar," or "coast." For "hover," see Wright, *Ritual in Narrative*, 128; Parker, *Pre-biblical Tradition*, 124–25, 136; "hover" or "soar," see Parker, in *Ugaritic Narrative Poetry*, 66, 68; "swoop" or "soar," see Coogan, *Stories from Ancient Canaan*, 40; for "coast," see Ginsberg, "Ugaritic Myths," 152, 153.

67. Wyatt, *Religious Tales from Ugarit*, 284 n. 151.

68. Jean-Marie Huser, "La mort d'Aqhat: Chasse et rites de passage à Ugarit," *Revue de l'histoire des religions* 225 (2008): 328.

69. Margalit, *Ugaritic Poem of AQHT*, 340–41.

70. Watson, *Golden Eagle*, 262; Gordon, *Golden Eagle*, 31–37, photo 16, between 214–15.
71. Margalit, *Ugaritic Poem of AQHT*, 340–41.
72. Watson, *Golden Eagle*, 207, 213, 214; Shirihai, *Birds of Israel*, 115, 117, 119, 121.
73. John Elphick, ed., *The Atlas of Bird Migration* (London: Natural History Museum, 2007), 7.
74. *Story of Aqhat* 1.19 i 40–44, 1.19 ii 13–23, pp. 295–96, 298–99; 1.18 iv 19, 29, pp. 285, 286; 1.19 i 19, 30, p. 294; 1.19 ii 14–25, pp. 298–99.
75. See Cade, *Falcons*, 21, 39, 58; Brown and Amadon, *Eagles, Hawks, Falcons*, 2:854; Cade, *Falcons*, 20–21, 61–62, 12, 20, 61; see also Dick Dekker, *Bolt from the Blue: Wild Peregrines on the Hunt* (Surrey, B.C.: Hancock House, 1999), 28, 33, 30.
76. *Story of Aqhat* 1.18 i 11–12, p. 278; 1.18 iv 24–25, 35, 23, 34, p. 285, 286. See also *Baal Cycle of Myths* 1.2 iv 22, 24, p. 67. Smith, *Ugaritic Baal Cycle*, chooses the neutral "raptor," 323.
77. For falcons, see Forsman, *Raptors*, 554–66, and pls. 669–720.
78. Cade, *Falcons*, 29–30, 58.
79. See Shirihai, *Birds of Israel*, 143–44; Brown and Amadon, *Eagles, Hawks, Falcons*, 2:853; Shirihai, *Birds of Israel*, 114.
80. For its hunting methods, see Watson, *Golden Eagle*, 47, 48–55, 18, 68–72, 56 (quotation), 18; Brown and Amadon, *Eagles, Hawks, Falcons*, 1:73–74, 18, 68–72, 30, 73–74; for its prey and kill, see Watson, *Golden Eagle*, 18, 21, 31, 68–72, 52, and between 26–27, photo 3; Brown and Amadon, *Eagles, Hawks, Falcons*, 144, 69, 75, 48; Watson, *Golden Eagle*, 69–70.
81. *Story of Aqhat* 1.19 i 9–10, pp. 290–91.
82. See Gordon, *Ugaritic Literature*, 85, 94; *Ugaritic Handbook*, 183. "Perfect translation is not attainable." Gordon, *Ugaritic Literature*, xi.
83. Ezek. 14:14, 20. Baruch Margalit, "The Geographical Setting of the Aqht Story and Its Ramifications," in *Ugarit in Retrospect; Fifty Years of Ugarit and Ugaritic* (Winona Lake, Ind.: Eisenbrauns, 1981), 158. For Moses's speech in Deut. 34:7, see William F.

Albright, "The 'Natural Force' of Moses in the Light of Ugaritic," *Bulletin of the American Schools of Oriental Research* 94 (1944): 32–35.
84. *Story of Aqhat* 1.17 i 1– 1.17 vi 8, pp. 250–70.
85. For the Priestly *tôledôt* headings, see Reinhard G. Kratz, *The Composition of the Narrative Books of the Old Testament*, trans. John Bowden (London: T. and T. Clark, 2005), 229–44; Arnold, *Genesis*, 2–7, 9–10; Westermann, *Genesis*, 12–18, and for the Priestly creation, 594–99. See also J. A. Emerton, "The Priestly Writer in Genesis," *Journal of Theological Studies* 39 (1988): 381–400.
86. Gordon, *Ugaritic Literature*, 85, 94; but cf. "hover," for the observant birds, 85, 94. Gordon, *Ugaritic Handbook*, 93. See also "soar" in Ginsberg, "Ugaritic Myths," but cf. "vulture," 152, 153; Coogan, *Stories*, 40, but cf. 88, 89.
87. See Margalit, *Ugaritic Poem of AQHT*, 155, 156; Gibson after Driver, *Canaanite Myths and Legends*, 111, 113; Wright, *Ritual in Narrative*, 128; Aitken, *Aqhat Narrative*, 55; Margalit, *Ugaritic Poem of AQHT*, 156; Wyatt, *Religious Texts from Ugarit*, 285, 286; Gordon, *Ugaritic Literature*, 94; Parker, *Pre-biblical Narrative Tradition*, 136. The translation "circles," 66, 68, is implicitly correct because in soaring an eagle spirals.
88. Mitchell Dahood, *Psalms 1: 1–50: Introduction, Translation, and Notes* (Garden City, N.Y.: Doubleday, 1965), 107.
89. See Brown and Amadon, *Eagles, Hawks, and Falcons*, 2:853.
90. See David E. Alexander, *Nature's Flyers: Birds, Insects, and the Biomechanics of Flight* (Baltimore: Johns Hopkins University Press, 2002), 3.
91. John J. Videler, *Avian Flight* (Oxford: Oxford University Press, 2005), 154, viii, 88.
92. For a survey, see Alexander, *Nature's Flyers*, 70–110; see also Videler, *Avian Flight*, 25, 118.
93. Videler, *Avian Flight*, 76–88, 90, 66, 89, 142–47, 154; Alexander, *Nature's Flyers*, 8–35.
94. *Cambridge Encyclopedia of Ornithology*, 53, 56–58, 62; for energy and wingbeat, see Alexander, *Nature's Flyers*, 98–103; for the hummingbird,

see Videler, *Avian Flight*, 154, 200–203, 31–33.

95. Alexander, *Nature's Flyers*, 159, and for soaring and gliding in general, 36–70.

96. Watson, *Golden Eagle*, 52, 9; Videler, *Avian Flight*, 89.

97. *Handbook of Bird Biology*, ed. Sandy Podulka, Ronald W. Rohrbaugh Jr., and Rick Bonney, 2nd ed. (Ithaca: Cornell Lab of Ornithology in Association with Princeton University Press, 2004), 5–31; Alexander, *Nature's Flyers*, 62, 64.

98. Cornell Lab, *Bird Handbook*, 5–36.

99. Shirihai, *Birds of Israel*, viii.

100. Yossi Lesham, "Israel: An International Axis of Raptor Migration," in *Conservation Studies on Raptors*, ed. I. Newton and R. D. Chancellor (Cambridge: I.C.B.P. [International Council for Bird Preservation], 1985), 243–50.

101. Ezek. 17:3; Hab. 1:8; Job 9:26; Deut. 28:49, Hab. 1:8; Jer. 49:22; Ob. 4; Jer. 48:40, 49:22.

102. Prov. 23:4–5.

103. For the archaic dating to 1000 B.C.E., see David A. Robertson, *Linguistic Evidence for Dating Early Hebrew Poetry* (Missoula, Mont.: Society of Biblical Literature, 1972), 154–55. For a review of its date, see Marvin H. Pope, *Job: Introduction, Translation, and Commentary* (Garden City, N.Y.: Doubleday, 1985), xxxii–xl, concluding at xl the early antecedence of its parts. It misidentifies *nešer* as "both eagles and vultures, including the golden eagle and the carrion vulture," 314.

104. 2 Sam. 1:23; Jer. 4:13; Lam. 4:19.

105. See Seton, *Golden Eagle*, 35.

106. Watson, *Golden Eagle*, 194–202.

107. Deut. 32:11; Jer. 48:40, 49:22; see also 1 Kings 8:7.

108. Ps. 104:2.

109. *Cambridge Ornithology*, 53.

110. Cornell Lab, *Bird Handbook*, 1–61 has 9,600; *Cambridge Ornithology*, 203 has 8,800.

111. Videler, *Avian Flight*, 25; for the types, see Cornell Lab, *Bird Handbook*, 5–37.

112. Brown and Armadon, *Eagles, Hawks, Falcons*, 50, and see 52–62. For the golden eagle, see Elkins, *Weather and Bird Behavior*, 43, 51, 52.

113. Elkins, *Weather and Bird Behavior*, 42–43, 49, 48.

114. Cornell Lab, *Bird Handbook*, 5–16.

115. Elkins, *Weather and Bird Behavior*, 43–48, 45.

116. Ibid., 44, 45, 46, and pl. 2; Videler, *Avian Flight*, 150. See also C. J. Pennycuick, "Field Observations of Thermals and Thermal Streets, and the Theory of Cross-Country Soaring Flight," *Journal of Avian Behavior* 29 (1998): 23–43.

117. See Cornell Lab, *Bird Handbook*, 5–39.

118. Videler, *Avian Flight*, 150–51. For altitude, see Cornell Lab, *Bird Handbook*, 5–41; for distance, see Elkins, *Weather and Bird Behavior*, 52.

119. For the Priestly Writing dated to the Second Temple period in Jerusalem, around 500 B.C.E., see Kratz, *Composition of the Narrative Books*, 245–46. However, for a much earlier dating, see Menahem Haran, *Temples and Temple-Service in Ancient Israel: An Inquiry into the Historical Setting of the Priestly School* (Oxford: Clarendon, 1958). For the exile, see Lester L. Grabbe, *Leading Captivity Captive: "The Exile" as History and Ideology* (Sheffield: Sheffield Academic Press, 1998). For Deut. 32, see Robertson, who proposes tentatively the eleventh to the tenth centuries, *Linguistic Evidence*, 154–55. Prominent scholars who also date Deut. 32 as early as the eleventh century are Otto Eissfeldt, *Das Lied Moses Deuterononomium 32 1–43 und das Lehrgedicht Asaphs Psalm 78 samt einer Analyse der Ungebung des Mose-Liedes* (Berlin: Akademie, 1958), 24, 42 to mid-eleventh century; Albright, "Some Remarks," 339, 346 to the eleventh century; Frank Moore Cross Jr. and David Noel Freedman, *Studies in Ancient Yahwistic Poetry* (Grand Rapids, Mich.: Wm. B. Eerdmans, 1997), 97 to eleventh century but perhaps not written until the tenth; Alter, *Five Books*, 1038, who also argues stylistic reasons for dating it as early as the eleventh century; Paul Sanders, *The Provenance of Deuteronomy 32* (Leiden: E. J. Brill, 1996), 436 to the pre-exilic to premonarchic period or the Aramean invasions. The principal argument for a later, exilic date for Deut. 32 was its affinities with the later prophetic

books. However, a reversal has established dependency of the prophets on Deut. 32 to authorize their message, thus, its earlier date. Ronald Bergey, "The Song of Moses (Deuteronomy 32.1–43) and Isaianic Prophecies: A Case of Early Intertextuality?" *Journal for the Study of the Old Testament* 28 (2003): 33–54. The most recent study dates its Deuteronomic redaction from older materials to Josiah's reign. Mark Leuchter, "Why Is the Song of Moses in the Book of Deuteronomy?" *Vetus Testamentum* 57 (2007): 275–317. Robertson dates Judges 5 (cited below) to posibly the end of the twelfth century.

120. See Marc Vervenne, "Genesis 1,1–2,4: The Compositional Texture of the Priestly Overture to the Pentateuch," in *Studies in the Book of Genesis: Literature, Redaction, and History*, ed. André Wénin (Leuven: Leuven University Press, 2001), 35–79; Casper J. Labuschagne, "The Setting of the Song of Moses in Deuteronomy," in *Deuteronomy and Deuteronomic Literature: Festschrift C. H. W. Brekelmans*, ed. Marc Vervenne and J. Lust (Leuven: Leuven University Press, 1997), 111–29.

121. Ernest W. Nicholson, *The Pentateuch in the Twentieth Century: The Legacy of Julius Wellhausen* (Oxford: Clarendon, 1998), 196–221; Kratz, *Composition of the Narrative Books*, 3, 98–114, 225–47. See also Sean E. McEvenue, *The Narrative Style of the Priestly Writer* (Rome: Biblical Institute, 1971).

122. Moshe Weinfeld, *The Place of the Law in the Religion of Ancient Israel* (Leiden: Brill, 2004); Haran, *Temples and Temple-Service*, 5–9, 146–48. For the writing of the scrolls in the late eighth to the sixth century, see William M. Schniedwind, *How the Bible Became a Book: The Textualization of Ancient Israel* (Cambridge: Cambridge University Press, 2004), 17–18, 64–117.

123. McEvenue, *Narrative Style*, 182.

124. Cross, *Canaanite Myth*, 301–21, 324.

125. Ps. 95:1–7.

126. Johannes C. de Moor, "Poetic Fragments in Deuteronomy and the Deuteronomistic History," in *Studies in Deuteronomy: In Honour of C. J. Labuschagne on the Occasion of His 65th Birthday*, ed. F. Garcia Martínez et al. (Leiden: E. J. Brill, 1994), 185, 187, 194.

127. Cassuto, *Genesis*, 9–12.

128. Deut. 31:19, 21, 22, 30; 32:44–45.

129. Deut. 31:1–32, 44–52.

130. G. Ernest Wright, "The Lawsuit of God: A Form-Critical Study of Deuteronomy 32," in *Israel's Prophetic Heritage: Essays in Honor of James Muilenburg*, ed. Bernhard W. Anderson and Walter Harrelson (New York: Harper and Brothers, 1962), 26–67; Matthew Thiessen, "The Form and Function of the Song of Moses (Deuteronomy 32:1–43)," *Journal of Biblical Literature* 123 (2004): 401–24.

131. Deut. 32:13, 15, 18–19. See also Michael P. Knowles, "'The Rock: His Work Is Perfect': Unusual Imagery for God in Deuteronomy xxxii," *Vetus Testamentum* 39 (1989): 307–22.

132. Vv. 5–6. See Marjorie O'Rourke Boyle, "The Law of the Heart: The Death of a Fool (1 Samuel 25)," *Journal of Biblical Literature* 120 (2001): 415.

133. Westermann, *Genesis*, 117–23.

134. Ellen van Wolde, "Why the Verb br' Does Not Mean 'to Create' in Genesis 1.1–2.4," *Journal for the Study of the Old Testament* 34 (2009): 3–23.

135. Marjorie O'Rourke Boyle, "'In the Heart of the Sea': Fathoming the Exodus," *Journal of Near Eastern Studies* 63 (2004): 17–27.

136. See Westermann, *Genesis*, ix, 1; and most recently, Arnold, *Genesis*, 1, 7. A variant is David W. Cotter, *Genesis* (Collegeville, Minn.: Liturgical Press, 2003). "Stories About Beginnings 1–11" and "Stories About the Troubled Family Chosen for Blessing 12–50," vii.

137. See Kratz, *Composition of the Narrative Books*, 245–46.

138. Gen. 12.

139. Jos Luytens, "Primeval and Eschatological Overtones in the Song of Moses (Dt 32, 1–43)," in *Das Deuteronomium: Entstehung, Gestalt, und Botschaft*, ed. Norbert Lohfink (Leuven: Peeters, 1985), 342–43.

140. See James W. Watts, "'This Song': Conspicuous Poetry in Hebrew Prose," in *Verse in Ancient Near Eastern Prose*, ed. Johannes C. de Moor and Wilfred G. E. Watson (Neukirchen-Vluyn: Neukirchener Verlag, 1993), 347–48,

352–54, 357; idem, *Psalm and Story Inset Hymns in Hebrew Narrative* (Sheffield: JSOT Press, 1992), 63–81. For its versification, see J. P. Fokkelman, *Major Poems of the Hebrew Bible at the Interface of Hermeneutics and Structural Analysis*, 3 vols., vol. 1, *Ex. 15, Deut. 32, and Job 3* (Assen: Van Gorcum, 1998), 54–149.

141. Ps. 59:14. *Oxford English Dictionary*, 2nd ed., s.vv. "yowl," "howl," "howling." But the definition of "howling" mistakes the biblical phrase "howling waste" as tending to "mere intensification."

142. Is. 15:8; Jer. 25:36; Zeph. 1:10; Zech. 11:3. See also Stephen A. Geller, "The Dynamics of Parallel Verse: A Poetic Analysis of Deut 32:6–11," *Harvard Theological Review* 75 (1982): 51–52.

143. Is. 13:6; 14:31; 15:2, 3; 16:7; 23: 1, 6, 14; Ezek. 30:2; and for Israel, Is. 65:14; Ezek. 30:2; Hos. 7:14; cf. Mic. 1:8.

144. Ex. 5:8, 15; 8:12; 4:15; 15:25; 17:4; 22:23.

145. P. K. McGregor, "Sound Cues to Distance: The Perception of Range," in *Perception and Motor Control in Birds: An Ecological Approach*, ed. Mark O. Davies and P. R. Green (Berlin: Springer, 1994), 74.

146. Cornell Lab, *Bird Handbook*, 4–45, 46; Brown and Armadon, *Eagles, Hawks, Falcons*, 29; S. A. McFadden, "Binocular Depth Perception," in Davies and Green, *Perception and Motor Control*, 61.

147. Cornell Lab, *Bird Handbook*, 4–46, 49.

148. McFadden, "Binocular Depth Perception," 63, 65. Cornell Lab, *Bird Handbook*, 4–51–53; McFadden, "Binocular Depth Perception," 54.

149. Watson, *Golden Eagle*, 55.

150. Ibid., 48–52.

151. Prov. 7:2; Ps. 17:8. Prov. 7:9; 20:20.

152. Robert Baldwin, "'Gates Pure and Shining and Serene': Mutual Gazing as an Amatory Motif in Western Literature and Art," *Renaissance and Reformation* 10 (1986): 23–48.

153. Michael Argyle and Mark Cook, *Gaze and Mutual Gaze* (Cambridge: Cambridge University Press, 1976), 4, 33.

154. See Brown and Amadon, *Eagles, Hawks, Falcons*, 30; Watson, *Golden Eagle*, 150.

155. G. R. Martin, "Form and Function in the Optical Structure of Bird Eyes," in Davies and Green, *Perception and Motor Control*, 19; Cornell Lab, *Bird Handbook*, 4–50.

156. Deut. 32:8–9.

157. Ex. 34:7. For the term, see Katherine Doob Sakenfeld, *The Meaning of "hesed" in the Hebrew Bible: A New Inquiry* (Missoula, Mont.: Scholars Press for Harvard Semitic Museum, 1977).

158. Deut. 32:10 RSV. See also Ps. 17:7–8.

159. 2 Sam. 7:24.

160. Is. 7:2.

161. Deut. 14; Lev. 11. For the Priestly insertion, see A. D. H. Mayes, "Deuteronomy 14 and the Deuteronomic World View," in Garcia Martínez et al., *Studies in Deuteronomy*, 181. For Lev. 11 as a supplement to and modification of Deut. 14 for compatibility with Gen. 1, see Howard Eilberg-Schwartz, *The Savage in Judaism: An Anthropology of Israelite Religion and Ancient Judaism* (Bloomington: Indiana University Press, 1990), 219.

162. Gen. 6:19–20; 7:2–3, 8, 9, 11–16; 8:17–19.

163. Prov. 6:5; 7:23; Ps. 124:6–7.

164. See Brown and Amadon, *Eagles, Hawks, Falcons*, 163–70.

165. See Walter Houston, *Purity and Monotheism: Clean and Unclean Animals in Biblical Law* (Sheffield: JSOT Press, 1993), 43–48, 143, 145, 196–97. See in general Marc Vervenne, "'The Blood Is the Life and the Life Is the Blood': Blood as Symbol of Life and Death in Biblical Tradition (Gen. 9,4)," in *Ritual and Sacrifice in the Ancient Near East*, ed. J. Quaegebeur (Leuven: Peeters, 1993), 451–52, 454–57, 462–70.

166. *Cambridge Ornithology*, 96.

167. Watson, *Golden Eagle*, 53, 68–70, 18, 21, 53.

168. Gen. 40:17.

169. 2 Sam. 21:10.

170. Ps. 79:2.

171. Vv. 50–68, with my change.

172. Eliezer Cohen, *Israel's Best Defense: The First Full Story of the Israeli Air Force*, trans. Jonathan Cordis (New York: Orion, 1993), 319, 413–14; Ehud Yonay, *No Margin for Error: The Making of the Israeli Air Force* (New York: Pantheon,

1993), 313. See also The Desert Eagle Pistol™.
173. Michael Jay Chan, "Cyrus, Yhwh's Bird of Prey (Isa.46.11): Echoes of an Ancient Near Eastern Metaphor," *Journal for the Study of the Old Testament* 35 (2010): 123–27.
174. Jer. 12:9.
175. Brown and Amadon, *Eagles, Hawks, Falcons*, 90–91.
176. See John Bright, *Jeremiah: A New Translation with Introduction and Commentary* (Garden City, N.Y.: Doubleday, 1986), 322.
177. See also Daniel Bourguet, *De métaphores de Jérémie* (Paris: J. Gabalda, 1987), 174–82; Angela Bauer-Levesque, *Gender in the Book of Jeremiah: A Feminist-Literary Reading* (New York: Peter Lang, 1999), 3, 158, 162–63 but without reference to the eagle.
178. Watson, *Golden Eagle*, 79–84, 88, 163. Cf. Raymond J. O'Connor, *The Growth and Development of Birds* (Chichester: John Wiley and Sons, 1984), 22–26.
179. James Barr considered it "odd," 158, but missed the rhetorical climax from hyperbole to adynaton. He thus argued that the verse supports *qen* not as a "nest" but generally as "abode, dwelling." James Barr, "Is Hebrew *qen* 'nest' a Metaphor?" in *Semitic Studies in Honor of Wolf Leslau on the Occasion of His Eighty-Fifth Birthday*, ed. Alvin S. Kaye, 2 vols. (Wiesbaden: Otto Harrassowitz, 1991), 1:150–61.
180. See also Is. 58:14 cf. Deut. 33:29; Ps. 18:34 = 2 Sam. 22:34; Hab. 3:19.
181. Ex. 33:18–23.
182. Ps. 91:1.
183. Is. 34:11–15.
184. Watson, *Golden Eagle*, 31, 18, 48.
185. For the rejection of the godlike *nešer* as a "vulture" that circles and ogles its prey as "an unfortunate fact which will be ignored.... The implications of such a metaphor in a desert context for the situation of God and Israel (Israel as Yahweh's prey) are unappetizing." Geller, "Poetic Analysis of Deut 32:6–11," 39, 52–53.
186. Deut. 32:15–18.
187. For "soars," see Wright, "Lawsuit of God," 29; Geller, "Dynamics of Parallel Verse," 39; cf. "gliding down,"

Lieber, ed., *'Ets Ḥayim*, 1187; Plaut, ed., *Torah*, 1557.
188. Deut. 22:6. For its traditional interpretation, see Eliezer Segal, "Justice, Mercy, and a Bird's Nest," *Journal of Jewish Studies* 42 (1991): 176–95.
189. Ps. 84:3.
190. O'Connor, *Growth and Development of Birds*, 18–28; Brown and Amadon, *Eagles, Hawks, Falcons*, 103–7.
191. Watson, *Golden Eagle*, 88, 74, 75, 88; Seton, *Golden Eagle*, 40. For the nest, see photos 2, 7, and 14. The tallest recorded nest for any bird was an eagle's nest looming at 23 feet / 7 meters. David H. Ellis et al., "Unusual Raptor Nests from Around the World," *Journal of Raptor Research* 43 (2009): fig. 15.
192. Watson, 80–84, 88. For the response of birds to sunshine, see also Elkins, *Weather and Bird Behavior*, 117–18. For the mother sheltering a chick from the sun with outspread wings, see Seton, *Golden Eagle*, photo 9a.
193. Ps. 17:8; 36:7; 57:1; 61:4; 63:7. See also Is. 25:4–5; Ruth 2:12.
194. Heinz Düttmann, H. Heiner Bergmann, and Wiltraud Engländer, "Development of Behavior," in *Avian Growth and Development: Evolution Within the Altricial-Precocial Spectrum*, ed. J. Matthias Starck and Robert E. Ricklefs (New York: Oxford University Press, 1998), 228–29. For the golden eagle's laying, incubation, and hatching of eggs, see Watson, *Golden Eagle*, 135, 143–44, 146, 149, 155, 158; Brown and Amadon, *Eagles, Hawks, Falcons*, 108–12, 114, 117, 118.
195. Brown and Amadon, *Eagles, Hawks, Falcons*, 116, 119–21; Watson, *Golden Eagle*, 152, 154–57. Alejandro Gonzalez-Voyer, Tamás Székely, and Hugh Drummond, "Why Do Some Siblings Attack Each Other? Comparative Analyses of Aggression in Avian Broods," *Evolution* 61 (2007): 1947.
196. *Cambridge Ornithology*, 247; O'Connor, *Growth and Development of Birds*, 137–38; for the skill of landing, see Alexander, *Nature's Flyers*, 144.
197. Watson, *Golden Eagle*, 154; *Cambridge Ornithology*, 97; Brown and Amadon, *Eagles, Hawks, Falcons*, 113.

198. Watson, *Golden Eagle*, 159–62, 163, 138, 139, 161; Gordon, *Golden Eagle*, 47, 51, photo 15.

199. O'Connor, *Growth and Development of Birds*, 15; A. F. Skutch, *Parent Birds and Their Young* (Austin: University of Texas Press, 1976), 287–91. For the golden eagle, see Watson, *Golden Eagle*, 159–62; Giuseppe Viggiani, "Cainism and Exceptionally Late Fledgling Flight of the Golden Eagle *Aquila chrysaetos* of the Southern Apennines," *Avocetta* 25 (2001): 260.

200. Brown and Amadon, *Eagles, Hawks, Falcons*, 113; Watson, *Golden Eagle*, 154; O'Connor, *Growth and Development of Birds*, 15–16; Gordon, *Golden Eagle*, 141–42.

201. Watson, *Golden Eagle*, 155.

202. Brown and Amadon, *Eagles, Hawks, Falcons*, 118.

203. See James R. Carey and Justin Adams, "The Preadaptive Role of Parental Care in the Evolution of Avian Flight," *Archaeopteryx* 19 (2001): 97–108.

204. Brown and Amadon, *Eagles, Hawks, Falcons*, 116.

205. Cornell Lab, *Bird Handbook*, 8–114, 5–22, and see fig. at 8–108; Watson, *Golden Eagle*, 152, 162, 165; Brown and Amadon, *Eagles, Hawks, Falcons*, 116–17, 122.

206. Deut. 1:31.

207. Vergil, *Aeneid* 2.708.

208. Cf. Coverdale "wynges." Hence "enticing" from the nest to the shoulders in the Douay-Rheims version.

209. See Cornell Lab, *Bird Handbook*, 5–10.

210. Ibid., 5–36.

211. Videler, *Avian Flight*, 43. For prey in the talons, see Seton, *Golden Eagle*, 3, and photo between 26–27.

212. Videler, *Avian Flight*, 25, 26, 29, 31, 35–37, 44.

213. Forsman, *Raptors*, xiv, xiii.

214. Watson, *Golden Eagle*, 9.

215. Menahem Haran, "Ezekiel, P, and the Priestly School," *Vetus Testamentum* 58 (2008): 211–18.

216. Ezek. 1:8–9, 5:26.

217. See also Is. 46:3–4; cf. Is. 60:4, 66:12.

218. With my change.

219. See Marjo C. A. Korpel, *A Rift in the Clouds: Ugaritic and Hebrew Descriptions of the Divine* (Münster: Ugarit, 1990), 544–53, 610–13, although "hovering" for Gen. 1:2, 551.

220. For the comparative philology, see Dahood, *Psalms I*, 107–8.

221. Gen. 1:2; Deut. 32:11.

222. *Cambridge Ornithology*, 97.

223. Elkins, *Weather and Bird Behavior*, 88, 21.

224. Watson, *Golden Eagle*, 131, 137.

225. Brown and Amadon, *Eagles, Hawks, Falcons*, 62, 94, and 95 fig. 21.

226. Elkins, *Weather and Bird Behavior*, 52.

227. Watson, *Golden Eagle*, 91, 170–71, 131–32, 137.

228. Brown and Amadon, *Eagles, Hawks, Falcons*, 99–101; Watson, *Golden Eagle*, 137.

229. Elkins, *Weather and Bird Behavior*, 88.

230. See Brown and Amadon, *Eagles, Hawks, Falcons*, 44.

231. See R. Wiltschko and W. Wiltschko, "Avian Orientation: Multiple Sensory Cues and the Advantage of Redundancy," in *Perception and Motor Control in Birds*, 95; for the compasses, see Cornell Lab, *Bird Handbook*, 5–84–92.

232. Cassuto also suggests lightning, in his *Genesis*, 1:26. Ps. 97:2–4, 77:17–18. See Vladimir A. Rakov and Martin A. Uman, *Lightning: Physics and Effects* (Cambridge: Cambridge University Press, 2003), 321–45.

233. See Korpel, *Rift in the Clouds*, 594–95, 597, 598, 605–6. Job 37:2–5, and v. 11; see also 30:22. See Rakov and Uman, *Lightning*, 374–93, 1.

234. Ps. 135:7, Jer. 10:13, 51:16. Cf. Ex. 9: 23–24, 13:21–22; 14:24. Ps. 18:7–14 = 2 Sam. 22:8–15. For the texts, see Theron Young, "Psalm 18 and 2 Samuel 22: Two Versions of the Same Song," in *Seeking Out the Wisdom of the Ancients: Essays Offered to Honor Michael V. Fox on the Occasion of His Sixty-Fifth Birthday*, ed. Ronald L. Troxel, Kelvin G. Triebel, and Dennis R. Magary (Winona Lake, Ind.: Eisenbrauns, 2005), 53–69, dating the composition to ninth century–eighth century B.C.E. Ps. 29:3–4, 7–8; see also 68:33; 104:7; 144:5–6; 1 Sam. 7:10. For storms, see R. B. Y. Scott, "Meteorological Phenomena and Terminology in the Old Testament,"

Zeitschrift für die alttestamentliche Wissenschaft 64 (1952): 14, 17, 19, 23.

235. For biblical dust, see Delbert R. Hillers, "Dust: Some Aspects of Old Testament Imagery," in *Love and Death in the Ancient Near East: Essays in Honor of Marvin H. Pope*, ed. John H. Marks and Robert M. Good (Guilford, Conn.: Four Quarters, 1987), 105–9; Westermann, *Genesis*, 203–6.

236. See Andrew Goudie and Nick J. Middleton, *Desert Dust in the Global System* (Berlin: Springer, 2006), 1.

237. Gen. 2:7; Deut. 32:10.

238. Ex. 13:21–22, 14:19, 24; Num. 14:14; Deut. 1:33; Neh. 9:12, 19. See also Scott, "Meteorological Phenomena," 22.

239. Ex. 14:24–25.

240. See Goudie and Middleton, *Desert Dust*, 62–63. For the Red Sea and its shore, see 25–26, 114. For different opinions of its historical location there (Gulf of Suez), see James K. Hoffmeier, *Israel in Egypt: The Evidence for the Authenticity of the Exodus Tradition* (New York: Oxford University Press, 1997), 199–222.

241. Troy L. Péwé, *Desert Dust: Origin, Characteristics, and Effect on Man*, Special Paper 186 (Boulder, Col.: Geological Society of America, 1981), 1–2. For the definitions of the Standard World Meteorological Association, see Goudie and Middleton, *Desert Dust*, 4–5.

242. See Elkins, *Birds and the Weather*, 46.

243. See Rakov and Uman, *Lightning*, 67, 667, 669.

244. A. K. Kamra, "Measurements of the Electrical Properties of Dust Storms," *Journal of Geophysical Research* 77 (1972): 5856–69; idem, "Visual Observations of Electric Sparks on Gypsum Dunes," *Nature* 240 (1972): 143–44.

245. See Wiltschko and Wiltschko, "Avian Orientation," 115–16.

246. Ps. 55:8.

247. Seton, *Golden Eagle*, 204–5.

248. Driver, "Birds in the Old Testament," 8.

249. Smith, *Ugaritic Baal Cycle*, 347–48. Cf. Gordon, *Golden Eagle*, 35.

250. See Rakov and Uman, *Lightning*, 4, 375, citing David J. Malan, *Physics of Lightning* (London: English Universities Press, 1963), 162–63.

251. See Watson, *Golden Eagle*, 48–49.

252. See Rakov and Uman, *Lightning*, 68.

253. See Edwin Firmage, "Genesis 1 and the Priestly Agenda," *Journal for the Study of the Old Testament* 82 (1999): 97–114. But see also Phyllis A. Bird, "'Male and Female He Created Them': Gen 1:27b in the Context of the Priestly Account of Creation," *Harvard Theological Review* 74 (1981): 129–59.

254. See Bernard F. Batto, "The Image of God in the Priestly Creation Account," in *David and Zion: Essays in Honor of J. M. Roberts*, ed. Bernard F. Batto and Kathryn L. Roberts (Winona Lake, Ind.: Eisenbrauns, 2004), 143–86.

255. See C. L. Crouch, "Genesis 1:26–7 as a Statement of Humanity's Divine Parentage," *Journal of Theological Studies* 61 (2010): 4–7.

256. See W. Randall Garr, *In His Own Image and Likeness: Humanity, Divinity, and Monotheism* (Leiden: E. J. Brill, 2003); W. Sibley Towner, "Clones of God: Genesis 1:26–28 and the Image of God in the Hebrew Bible," *Interpretation* 59 (2005): 341–56; Crouch, "Genesis 1:26–7," 1–15; Paul Niskanen, "The Poetics of Adam: The Creation of ʾādām in the Image of ʾĕlōhîm," *Journal of Biblical Literature* 128 (2009): 417–36.

257. Ali Abou-Assaf, Pierre Boudreuil, and Alan R. Millard, *La statue de Tell Fekherye et son inscription bilingue assyro-araméene* (Paris: Recherche sur les civilisations, 1982). See also Boudreuil and Millard, "A Statue from Assyria with Assyrian and Aramaic Inscriptions," *Biblical Archaeologist* 45 (1982): 135–41; W. Randall Garr, "'Image' and 'Likeness' in the Inscription from Tell Fakhariyah," *Israel Exploration Journal* 50 (2000): 229–34. See in general Gunnlauger A. Jónssen, *The Image of God: Genesis 1:26–28 in a Century of Old Testament Research* (Stockholm: Almqvist & Wiksell International, 1988).

258. See Elkins, *Birds and the Weather*, 50.

259. Ps. 33:6.

260. Baruch Margalit, "Ugaritic Contributions to Hebrew Lexicography (with Special Reference to the *Poem of Aqht*)," *Zeitschrift für die alttestamentliche Wissenschaft* 99 (1987): 394.

261. See also Daniel Lys, *"Nèpèsh": Histoire de l'ame dans la revélation d'Israël au sein des religions proche-orientales* (Paris: PUF, 1959); A. Murtonen, *The Living Soul: A Study of the Meaning of the Word "naefaeš" in the Old Testament*, Studia orientalia 23-1 (1958).
262. Translation by Mitchell Dahood, "Hebrew-Ugaritic Lexicography, VII," *Biblica* 50 (1969): 339, but changing "my" to "his."
263. Job 39:20, 41:20.
264. Walter R. Wifall, "The Breath of His Nostrils: Gen. 2:7b," *Catholic Biblical Quarterly* 36 (1974): 237–40.
265. See Walter Brueggemann, "From Dust to Kingship," *Zeitschrift für die alttestamentliche Wissenschaft* 84 (1972): 1–16.
266. Bird, "Male and Female," 138–44.
267. 2 Kings 19:28; Job 40:24; 41:2.
268. Is. 3:21.
269. Ezek. 23:25.
270. Ps. 62:9–10.
271. Job 4:9.
272. Ex. 15:8.
273. 2 Sam. 22:16 = Ps. 18:15.
274. Ps. 115:6.
275. Is. 65:5.
276. Is. 2:22; see also Ez. 8:17. For that obscure reference, see Jack R. Lundbom, *Jeremiah 37–52: A New Translation with Interpretation and Commentary* (New York: Doubleday, 2004), 172–73.
277. Num. 11:16–20.
278. Prov. 30:33.
279. G. R. Driver, "The Resurrection of Marine and Terrestrial Creatures," *Journal of Semitic Studies* 7 (1962): 15–16.
280. Amos 4:10.
281. For the grammar of the controversial translations of *bērē'šiyt* (Gen. 1:1) as a construct or not, see Westermann, *Genesis 1–11*, 78; Victor P. Hamilton, *The Book of Genesis: Chapters 1–17* (Grand Rapids, Mich.: W. B. Eerdmans, 1990), 103–8; Manfred Weippert, "Schöpfung am Anfang oder Anfang der Schöpfung? Nach einmal zu Syntax und Semantik von Gen 1, 1–3," *Theologische Zeitschrift* 60 (2004): 5–22; Barry Bandstra, *Genesis 1–11: A Handbook on the Hebrew Text* (Waco: Baylor University Press, 2008), 41–44; Arnold, 34–36.
282. See Hendel, *Text of Genesis 1–11*, 37.

283. Without reference to my argument, see recently Michael V. Wedin, *Aristotle's Theory of Substance: The "Categories" and "Metaphysics" Zeta* (Oxford: Oxford University Press, 2000).
284. *Gesenius' Hebrew Grammar*, ed. E. Kautzsch, rev. A. E. Cowley, 2nd ed. (Oxford: Clarendon, 1910), 423–24; Paul Joüon, trans., rev. T. Muraoka, *A Grammar of Biblical Hebrew*, 2 vols., rev. ed. (Rome: Pontifical Biblical Institute, 2006), 2:449–50.
285. 2 Sam. 7:8; Is. 39:3. 2 Sam. 3:31; Ps. 80:7. Gen. 46:3; 1:16. Without reference to my translation, for apposition, see Waltke and O'Connor, *Biblical Hebrew Syntax*, 226–34, with the citation at 232; Joüon and Muraoka, *Grammar of Biblical Hebrew*, 448–52; Gesenius, *Hebrew Grammar*, 423–27.
286. Without reference to my argument, see Y. Avishur, "Pairs of Synonymous Words in the Construct State (and in Appositional Hendiadys) in Biblical Hebrew," *Semitics* 2 (1971–72): 17–81.
287. Joel S. Burnett, *A Reassessment of Biblical "Elohim"* (Atlanta: Society of Biblical Literature, 2001), 79–152.
288. Ex. 3:13–14.
289. Gen. 3:1–13, with my translation of v. 1.
290. Without reference to my argument, for the double name, see Westermann, *Genesis*, pp. 198–99.
291. For *'eḥād*, see J. Gerald Janzen, "On the Most Important Word in the Shema (Deuteronomy VI 4–5)," *Vetus testamentum* 37 (1987): 280–300.
292. Without reference to my argument, see Robert Alter, *The Art of Biblical Poetry* (New York: Basic Books, 1985), 10–11, 13–15; Robert Alter, trans., *Genesis* (New York: W. W. Norton, 1996), xvii. However, Alter translates *rûaḥ 'ĕlōhîm* as a possessive by nounal construct, "breath of God." For biblical parallelism, see also James L. Kugel, *The Idea of Biblical Poetry: Parallelism and Its History* (New Haven: Yale University Press, 1981).
293. Cross, *Canaanite Myth*, 295–97. See also Hermann Gunkel, *Genesis übersetzt und erklärt*, 6th ed. (Göttingen: Vandenhoeck & Ruprecht, 1964), lxxxi.
294. See Jože Krašovec, "Merism—Polar Expression in Biblical Hebrew,"

Biblica 64 (1983): 231–39; idem, *Der Merismus im Biblisch-Hebräischen und Nordwestsemitischen* (Rome: Biblical Institute, 1977); A. M. Honeyman, "Merismus in Biblical Hebrew," *Journal of Biblical Literature* 71 (1952): 11–18; P. P. Boccaccio, "I termini contrari come espressione della totalità in ebraico," *Biblica* 33 (1952): 173–90; Gustave Lambert, "'Lier'–'delier,' l'expression de la totalité par l'opposition de deux contraires," *Vivre et penser* 3 [= *Revue biblique* 53] (1945): 91–101.
    295. David Novak, *The Natural Law in Judaism* (Cambridge: Cambridge University Press, 1998), 15.

CHAPTER 2

    1. 1 Cor. 13:1–13. Translations of the Bible in this chapter are from the Revised Standard Version unless otherwise stated. For Corinth and the Corinthians, see Jerome Murphy-O'Connor, *Paul: His Story* (Oxford: Oxford University Press, 2004), 78–89, 93–96, 158–73, 174–93; idem, *Paul: A Critical Life* (Oxford: Clarendon, 1996), 252–321; idem, *St. Paul's Corinth: Texts and Archaeology*, 3rd ed. (Collegeville, Minn.: Liturgical Press, 2002).
    2. Hermann Gunkel, *Die Wirkungen des heiligen Geisten nach der populären Anschauung des apostolischen Zeit und nach der Lehre Apostels Paulus* (Göttingen: Vandenhoeck & Ruprecht, 1888).
    3. 1 Cor. 2:12–13.
    4. See Timothy Michael Law, *When God Spoke Greek: The Septuagint and the Making of the Christian Bible* (Oxford: Oxford University Press, 2013), 105.
    5. See chapter 1, p. 16.
    6. Cf. Is. 64:4.
    7. Anthony C. Thiselton, *The First Epistle to the Corinthians: A Commentary on the Greek Text* (Grand Rapids, Mich.: W. B. Eerdmans, 2000), 258–59. For privacy, see George H. van Kooten, "St Paul on Soul, Spirit, and the Inner Man," in *The Afterlife of the Platonic Soul: Reflections of Platonic Psychology in the Monotheistic Religions*, ed. Maha Elkaisy-Friemuth and John M. Dillon (Leiden: E. J. Brill, 2009), 25–44; idem, *Paul's Anthropology in Context: The Image of God, Assimilation to God, and Tripartite Man in Ancient Judaism, Ancient Philosophy, and Early Christianity* (Tübingen: Mohr Siebeck, 2008), 358–70; Hans Dieter Betz, "The Concept of the 'Inner Human Being' *esō anthrōpos* in the Anthropology of Paul," *New Testament Studies* 46 (2000): 315–41, especially 327–35.
    8. E.g., Gordon D. Fee, *God's Empowering Presence: The Holy Spirit in the Letters of Paul* (Peabody, Mass.: Hendrickson, 1994), 15, citing 1 Cor. 2:11; 5:5; 7:34; 14:14; 16:18; 2 Cor. 2:13; 7:13.
    9. Hermann Lüdemann, *Die Anthropologie des Apostels Paulus und ihre Stellung innerhalb seiner Heilslehre: Nach den vier Hauptbriefen* (Kiel: Universitäts-Verlag, 1872), 49.
    10. Thiselton, *Commentary*, 257–58; Robert Jewett, *Paul's Anthropological Terms: A Study of Their Use in Conflict Settings* (Leiden: E. J. Brill, 1971), 167–200.
    11. E.g., Fee, *God's Empowering Presence*, 100–101.
    12. Aristotle, *Ethica Eudemia* 7 1235a; Cicero, *De officiis* 2.39–40.
    13. See Meyer Fortes, *Kinship and the Social Order: The Legacy of Lewis Henry Morgan* (Chicago: Aldine, 1969), 237–39, 251.
    14. See Aristotle, *Rhetorica* 2.23 1397b.
    15. Homer, *Iliad* 5.442. *A Greek-English Lexicon*, ed. Henry G. Liddell and Robert Scott, rev. Henry S. Jones with Roderick McKenzie and others (Oxford: Clarendon Press, 1968), s.v. *anthrōpos*. Homer was in the curriculum for diasporic Jewish children, and he was also read in Pharisaic circles. Murphy-O'Connor, *Paul: A Critical Life*, 48.
    16. Jean Defradas, *Les thèmes de la propagande delphique* (Paris: C. Klincksieck, 1954), 277–80, 286, 284.
    17. Jože Krašovec, *Der Merismus im Biblisch-Hebräischen und Nordwestsemitischen* (Rome: Biblical Institute Press, 1977), 47–53.
    18. Translation mine.
    19. Translation mine.
    20. Raphael Loewe, "The Medieval History of the Latin Vulgate," in *The West from the Fathers to the Reformation*, vol. 2 of *The Cambridge History of the*

NOTES TO PAGES 62–69

Bible (Cambridge: Cambridge University Press, 1975–76), 108.

21. *Biblia sacra iuxta Vulgatam versionem*, ed. Robert Weber, rev. ed. (Stuttgart: Würtembergische Bibelanstalt, 1975).

22. Liddell and Scott, *Lexicon*, s.vv. *oida* and *gignōskō*.

23. Ibid., s.v. *koilia*.

24. Ibid., s.v. *bathē*.

25. Rom. 8:38–39.

26. Prov. 25:3.

27. See also Ps. 2:4; 11:4; 33:13–14; 102:19; 123:1; 150:1.

28. See Paul's final speech in Acts 28:26–27, which quotes as justification for the salvation of the nations Isaiah's commission (Is. 6:9–10).

29. 1 Cor. 2:11. For a Corinthian context, the Corinthian speech in Thucydides's *History of the Peloponesian Wars* 1.22.4 explained *to anthrōpinon* as the principle that universal and public deliberations caused events. See Marc Cogan, *The Human Thing: The Speeches and Principles of Thucydides' "History"* (Chicago: University of Chicago Press, 1981), 233–54.

30. Is. 40:28–31.

31. 1 Cor. 1:18–31; 2 Cor. 11:16–28.

32. For allusions to other texts, see John Paul Heil, *The Rhetorical Role of Scripture in 1 Corinthians* (Atlanta: Society of Biblical Literature, 2005), 53–57. See also Christopher D. Stanley, *Paul and the Language of Scripture: Citation Technique in the Pauline Epistles and Contemporary Literature* (Cambridge: Cambridge University Press, 1992), 188–89.

33. Rodney A. Werline, *Penitential Prayer in Second Temple Judaism: The Development of a Religious Institution* (Atlanta: Scholars, 1998), 39, and for the dependency of idolatry on the Deuteronomic tradition, 1, 7, 12, 13–15. For the psalms, see Paul W. Ferris Jr., *The Genre of the Communal Lament in the Bible and the Ancient Near East* (Atlanta: Scholars, 1992).

34. Moshe Weinfeld, *Normative and Sectarian Judaism in the Second Temple Period* (London: T. and T. Clark International, 2005), 295–304.

35. Is. 63:15–64:12.

36. Dan. 4:13.

37. Is. 63:15; 64:1. Ex. 19:16–20; Judges 5:5. Joseph Blenkinsopp, *Isaiah 56–66: A New Translation with Introduction and Commentary* (New York: Doubleday, 2003), 251, 263–66.

38. For an introduction, see Paolo Sacchi, *The History of the Second Temple Period* (Sheffield: Sheffield Academic Press, 2000); Lester L. Grabbe, *Judaic Religion in the Second Temple Period: Belief and Practice from the Exile to Yavneh* (London: Routledge, 2000).

39. Blenkinsopp, *Isaiah 56–66*, 255, 256. See also *Penitential Prayer: Seeking the Favor of God*, ed. Mark J. Boda, Daniel K. Falk, and Rodney A. Werline (Atlanta: Society of Biblical Literature, 2006).

40. See Murphy-O'Connor, *Paul: A Critical Life*, 52–62. For a reconstruction of Paul's learning, see Bruce Chilton and Jacob Neusner, "Paul and Gamaliel," *Review of Rabbinic Judaism* 8 (2005): 113–62.

41. Is. 29:16; 41:25; 45:9; Jer. 1–11; cf. Gen. 2:7.

42. Rom. 9:6–29.

43. Ps. 115:5–8.

44. Is. 42:18–20; 43:8.

45. Gal. 1:13–14, 23; Phil. 3:6; 1 Cor. 15:9. For Stephen's hagiography, see François Bovon, "The Dossier on Stephen, the First Martyr," *Harvard Theological Review* 96 (2003): 279–315.

46. Joseph A. Fitzmyer, *The Acts of the Apostles: A New Translation with Introduction and Commentary* (New York: Doubleday, 1998), 49–60, 133–38. For comparative historiography of Paul, see Stanley E. Porter, *The Paul of Acts: Essays in Literary Criticism, Rhetoric, and Theology* (Tübingen: Mohr Siebeck, 1999), 186–206.

47. John Knox, *Chapters in a Life of Paul*, rev. ed. (Macon: Mercer University Press, 1987); Gregory Tatum, *New Chapters in the Life of Paul: The Relative Chronology of His Career* (Washington, D.C.: Catholic Biblical Association of America, 2006), 7–9; Murphy-O'Connor, *Paul: A Critical Life*, 260–65.

48. 1 Cor. 2:9–10.

49. Acts 9:8–9. Blindness is a medically documented effect of a lightning strike as is temporary paralysis causing a fall, transient injuries that resolve spontaneously and soon. See Anne Marie

Lewis, "Understanding the Principles of Lightning Injury," *Journal of Emergency Nursing* 23 (1997): 537, 538, 539.

50. Murphy-O'Connor, *Paul: A Critical Life*, 320 n. 798. For a reconstruction of the period, see Martin Hengel and Anna Maria Schwemer, *Paul Between Damascus and Antioch: The Unknown Years* (Louisville, Ky.: Westminster John Knox Press, 1997). For the composition of 2 Corinthians, see Harris, *Commentary*, 65–67. As a Roman citizen writing from the Roman colony of Philippi to the Roman colony of Corinth, Paul would have used the Roman calendar, which began on January 1. Harris, *Commentary*, 582–83.

51. Liddell and Scott, *Lexicon*, s.v. *pro*.

52. Phil. 1:5, 6, 10; 1 Thess. 1:9–10; Gal. 4:13.

53. Murphy-O'Connor, *Paul: A Critical Life*, 252, 130, 265; C. K. Barrett, *A Critical and Exegetical Commentary on The Acts of the Apostles*, vol. 2 (Edinburgh: T. and T. Clark, 1998), lxi; Rainer Riesner, *Paul's Early Period: Chronology, Mission Strategy, Theology*, trans. Doug Stott (Grand Rapids, Mich.: W. B. Eerdmans, 1998), 208–11. See Acts 18:11–12. See also Jerome Murphy-O'Connor, "The Corinth That Paul Saw," *Biblical Archaeologist* 47 (1984): 147–53.

54. Acts 18:1–8, cf. 17:1–2. For tentmakers, see Barrett, *Acts of the Apostles*, 2:863.

55. See Oscar Broneer, "The Apostle Paul and the Isthmian Games," *Biblical Archaeologist* 25 (1962): 11, 20, 16–17. See 1 Cor. 9:25. For athletic imagery, see Robert S. Dutch, *The Educated Elite in 1 Corinthians: Education and Community Conflict in Greco-Roman Context* (London: T. and T. Clark International, 2005), 219–48.

56. Riesner, *Paul's Early Period*, 208. For Gallio and the hearing, see Barrett, *Acts of the Apostles*, 2:870–76.

57. Douglas A. Campbell, "An Anchor for Pauline Chronology: Paul's Flight from 'the Ethnarch of King Aretas' (2 Corinthians 11:32–33)," *Journal of Biblical Literature* 121 (2002): 279–302.

58. See Broneer, "Paul and the Games," 11; Barrett, *Acts of the Apostles*, 2:870–76.

59. 2 Cor. 12:2–4.

60. 1 Cor. 1:17; 2:1–5.

61. Commonplace. E.g., Carey C. Newman, *Paul's Glory-Christology: Tradition and Rhetoric* (Leiden: E. J. Brill, 1992), 164–212. It refers numerous Pauline texts to Acts 9 (165–66), although there is no textual evidence for that association. E.g., also Fitzmyer, *Acts of the Apostles*, 420, 421, and for the conflation of three events, 141–44, 420; Hengel, *Paul Between Damascus and Antioch*, 107, and equating 1 Cor. 9:1 with the Damascus call, 38–39.

62. Gershom G. Scholem, *Jewish Gnosticism, Merkabah Mysticism, and Talmudic Tradition* (New York: Jewish Theological Seminary of America, 1965), 14–19; J. W. Bowker, "*Merkabah* Visions and the Visions of Paul," *Journal of Semitic Studies* 16 (1971): 157–73; Andrew T. Lincoln, *Paradise Now and Not Yet: Studies in the Role of the Heavenly Dimension in Paul's Thought with Special Reference to His Eschatology* (Cambridge: Cambridge University Press, 1981), 182–202; James D. Tabor, *Things Unutterable: Paul's Ascent to Paradise in Its Greco-Roman, Judaic, and Early Christian Contexts* (Lanham, Md.: University Press of America, 1986); Alan F. Segal, *Paul the Convert: The Apostolate and Apostasy of Saul the Pharisee* (New Haven: Yale University Press, 1990), 9–11, 34–71; Newman, *Paul's Glory-Christology*, 79–104; C. R. A. Murray-Jones, "Transformational Mysticism in the Apocalyptic-*Merkabah* Tradition," *Journal of Jewish Studies* 43 (1992): 1–31; idem, "Paradise Revisited (2 Cor 12:1–12): The Jewish Mystical Background of Paul's Apostolate; Part 1: The Jewish Sources," *Harvard Theological Review* 86 (1993): 177–217, "Part 2: Paul's Heavenly Ascent and Its Significance," 265–92; Jarl E. Fossum, *The Image of the Invisible God: Essays on the Influence of Jewish Mysticism on Early Christology* (Freiburg: Universitätsverlag, 1995); James M. Scott, "The Triumph of God in 2 Cor 2.14: Additional Evidence of Merkabah Mysticism in Paul," *New Testament Studies* 42 (1996): 260–81; Paula Gooder, *Only the Third Heaven? 2 Corinthians 12:1–10 and Heavenly Ascent* (London: T. and T. Clark, 2006); and in general, Timo Eskola, *Messiah and*

the Throne: Jewish Merkabah Mysticism and Early Christian Exaltation Discourse (Tübingen: Mohr Siebeck, 2001); Finny Philip, *The Origins of Pauline Pneumatology: Eschatological Bestowal of the Spirit upon Gentiles in Judaism and in the Early Development of Paul's Theology* (Tübingen: Mohr Siebeck, 2005), 176–82. Although my dissent developed independently, the literature was criticized also by Peter Schäfer, "The New Testament and Hekhalot Literature: The Journey into Heaven in Paul and in Merkavah Mysticism," *Journal of Jewish Studies* 35 (1984): 19–35.

63. Acts 9:4–5.

64. Hagigah 14b; *The Babylonian Talmud*, trans. Jacob Neusner, 22 vols. (Peabody, Mass.: Hendrickson, 2005), 7:60–66. For the rabbinic ban, see see Hyam Maccoby, *The Philosophy of the Talmud* (London: RoutledgeCurzon, 2002), 5–7.

65. *The Dictionary of Classical Hebrew*, ed. David J. A. Clines, 8 vols. (Sheffield: Sheffield Academic Press, 1993–2011), 4:488–89, s.v. *merĕkābāh*. See David J. Halperin, *The Merkabah in Rabbinic Literature* (New Haven, Conn.: American Oriental Society, 1980), 23–25.

66. *Oxford English Dictionary*, 2nd ed. (1989), s.v. "mysticism."

67. Michel de Certeau, "'Mystique' au XVIIe siécle: Le problème du langage 'mystique,'" in *L'homme devant Dieu: Mélanges offerts au père Henri de Lubac*, 3 vols. (Paris: Théologie, 1963–64), 2:268–69.

68. Representative studies are Gershom G. Scholem, *Jewish Gnosticism, Merkabah Mysticism, and Talmudic Tradition* (New York: Jewish Theological Seminary of America, 1968), which largely inaugurated the subject; Ithamar Grunewald, *Apocalyptic and Merkavah Mysticism* (Leiden: E. J. Brill, 1980); Halperin, *Merkabah in Rabbinic Literature*, whose explanation of an exegetical, not ecstatic, practice is the most plausible, 179–83; David J. Halperin, *The Faces of the Chariot: Early Jewish Responses to Ezekiel's Vision* (Tübingen: J. C. B. Mohr [Paul Siebeck], 1988); Peter Schäfer, *The Hidden and Manifest God: Some Major Themes of Early Jewish Mysticism*, trans. Aubrey Pomerance (Albany: State University of New York Press, 1992); Martha Himmelfarb, *Ascent to Heaven in Jewish and Christian Apocalypses* (New York: Oxford University Press, 1993); Nathaniel Deutsch, *The Gnostic Imagination: Gnosticism, Mandaeism, and Merkabah Mysticism* (Leiden: E. J. Brill, 1995); Michael D. Swartz, *Scholastic Magic: Ritual and Revelation in Early Jewish Mysticism* (Princeton: Princeton University Press, 1996).

69. 1 Cor. 15:12–19. For the dispute, see the survey of interpretations in Anthony C. Thiselton, *The Hermeneutics of Doctrine* (Grand Rapids, Mich.: Wm. B. Eerdmans, 2007), 555–56. For the spirit-people, see Murphy-O'Connor, *Paul: A Critical Life*, 280–84, 303–4, 311.

70. 1 Cor. 15:12–34.

71. 2 Cor. 11:23–28.

72. Engels, *Roman Corinth*, 9; Murphy-O'Connor, *Paul: A Critical Life*, 257; Lionel Casson, *Travel in the Ancient World* (Toronto: Hakkert, 1974), 68–69.

73. Ex. 3:14; 20:1–17.

74. 2 Cor. 11:22. Stephen's speech also began with the appearance of the God of glory to Abraham. Acts 7:2.

75. 1 Cor. 3:9–17.

76. Acts 9.

77. Acts 25:12–20. Barrett, *Acts of the Apostles*, 2:1158, although he considers this the third account of conversion, 1144.

78. Ps. 29:7; 77:17–18; 97:3–4; 137:5; Jer. 10:13; 51:16; Job 37:2–5, 11; 30:22.

79. Gal. 1:12, 16.

80. The phrase "because of the Holy Spirit" is after John J. Kilgallen, "'The Apostles Whom He Chose Because of the Holy Spirit': A Suggestion Regarding Acts 1, 2," *Biblica* 81 (2000): 414–17.

81. For the thorny angel, see also Murphy-O'Connor, *Paul: A Critical Life*, 321. A reference may be to Judaizers, who did not excuse Gentile Christians from Jewish observance of circumcision and diet.

82. 1 Cor. 1:17–2:14.

83. 1 Cor. 1:11–16. For the upheaval in Corinth, see Murphy-O'Connor, *Paul: A Critical Life*, 252–322.

84. Colleen Shantz, *Paul in Ecstasy: The Neurobiology of the Apostle's Life and Thought* (Cambridge: Cambridge University Press, 2009).

85. *Oxford Classical Dictionary*, s.v. "Harpies."
86. Gen. 5:24. Cf. *apothēskō*, vv. 18, 27, 31. The translation *metatithenvai* is the only use for *lāqaḥ*, "take," as in Deut. 32:11.
87. Ezek. 2:2; 3:12, 14; 8:3; cf. 10:19; 11:1, 24; cf. 12:6, 7; cf. 16:61; 43:5. For *harpazo* see Ezek. 18:7, 12, 16, 18; 19:3, 6; 22:25, 27, 29; 38:15.
88. Acts 1:2, 11; cf. Luke 24:51.
89. Liddell and Scott, *Lexicon*, s.v. *harpazo*.
90. Acts 8:26–40.
91. Acts 9.
92. Liddell and Scott, *Lexicon*, s.v. *harpazo*.
93. Deut. 1:31; 32:11.
94. See chapter 1, pp. 36–42.
95. Richard B. Hayes, *Echoes of Scripture in the Letters of Paul* (New Haven: Yale University Press, 1989), 112; David Lincium, *Paul and the Early Jewish Encounter with Deuteronomy* (Tübingen: Mohr Siebeck, 2010), 166–67, 168. For idolatry, see also Brian S. Rosner, "Deuteronomy in 1 and 2 Corinthians," in *Deuteronomy in the New Testament*, ed. Maarten J. J. Menken and Steve Moyise (London: T. and T. Clark, 2007), 130–31.
96. *Oxford English Dictionary*, 2nd ed. (1989), s.v. "paradise"; Liddell and Scott, *Lexicon*, s.v. *paradeisos*. For the philology, see also Jan N. Bremmer, "Paradise: From Persia, via Greece, into the Septuagint," in *Paradise Interpreted: Representations of Biblical Paradise in Judaism and Christianity*, ed. Gerard P. Luttikhuizen (Leiden: E. J. Brill, 1999), 1–20. Ec. 2:5; Neh. 2:8 (LXX); Luke 23:43.
97. For physical weakness as a sign of intellectual power in Pharisaic knowledge of the Torah, see Chilton and Neusner, "Paul and Gamaliel," 144, 126.
98. Engels, *Roman Corinth*, 99.
99. For building imagery, see also 1 Cor. 8:1; 10:23; 14:3–5, 12, 17, 26.
100. Albert L. A. Hogeterp, *Paul and God's Temple: A Historical Interpretation of Cultic Imagery in the Corinthian Correspondence* (Leuven: Peeters, 2006), 311–31; John R. Levison, "The Spirit and the Temple in Paul's Letters to the Corinthians," in Porter, *Paul and His Theology*, 189–215; Nijay K.

Gupta, "Which 'Body' Is a Temple (1 Corinthians 6:19)? Paul Beyond the Individual/Communal Divide," *Catholic Biblical Quarterly* 72 (2010): 518–36. See also F. W. Horn, "Paulus und die Herodianische Tempel," *New Testament Studies* 52 (2007): 184–203.
101. Engels, *Roman Corinth*, 10, 62; for the earthquake zone, see 20, 53, 63.
102. Ronald F. Hock, *The Social Context of Paul's Ministry: Tentmaking and Apostleship* (Philadelphia: Fortress, 1980); Murphy-O'Connor, *Paul: A Critical Life*, 85–89.
103. Acts 18:2–3. See Jerome Murphy-O'Connor, "Prisca and Aquila: Travelling Tentmakers and Church Builders," *Bible Review* 8 (1992): 40–51.
104. 1 Cor. 4:12; 9:19; 2 Cor. 11:7. 1 Cor. 16:19.
105. Engels, *Roman Corinth*, 8, 112, 60.
106. Ex. 31:6–18; 35:30–36:1; 36:2–39:43.
107. Menahem Haran, *Temples and Temple-Service in Ancient Israel: An Inquiry into the Character of Cult Phenomena and the Historical Setting of the Priestly School* (Oxford: Clarendon, 1978), 46, 188–94, 198–201.
108. Ibid., 149–89, 196–98, 270–75.
109. Jon D. Levenson, *Creation and the Persistence of Evil: The Jewish Drama of Divine Omnipotence* (San Francisco: Harper and Row, 1988), 81–99.
110. Is. 40:22; Ps. 104:2.
111. Haran, *Temples and Temple-Service*, 1; Grabbe, *Judaic Religion*, 316.
112. Grabbe, *Judaic Religion*, 176, 328.
113. See Donald M. Binder, *Into the Temple Courts: The Place of the Synagogues in the Second Temple Period* (Atlanta: Society of Biblical Literature, 1999), 295–97. For its substantial community of Jews, see Engels, *Roman Corinth*, 107.
114. See also John R. Lanci, *A New Temple for Corinth: Rhetorical and Archaeological Approaches to Pauline Imagery* (New York: Peter Lang, 1997). For an archaeological introduction, see Nancy Bookidis, "The Sanctuaries of Corinth," in *Corinth, the Centenary, 1896–1996*, ed. Charles K. Williams II and Nancy Bookidis, vol. 20 of *Corinth: Results of Excavations* (Cambridge, Mass.: Harvard University Press for the American School for Classical Studies at Athens, 2003), 247–59.

115. Hogeterp, *Paul and God's Temple*, 323–24. See also Horn, "Paulus und die Herodianische Tempel."

116. E. Theodore Mullen Jr., *The Assembly of the Gods: The Divine Council in Canaanite and Early Hebrew Literature* (Chico, Calif.: Scholars, 1980), 133, 136, 139.

117. See chapter 1, p. 23.

118. See Julian Morgenstern, *The Ark, the Ephod, and the "Tent of Meeting"* (Cincinnati: Hebrew Union College Press, 1945), 131–61; Mullen, *Assembly of the Gods*, 134, 168–69, 171–73.

119. Moshe Weinfeld, *Deuteronomy and the Deuteronomic School* (Oxford: Clarendon, 1972), 191–93, 199–200. See also James Barr, "Theophany and Anthropomorphism in the Old Testament," in *Vetus testamentum, Supplements: Congress Volume Oxford 1959* (Leiden: E. J. Brill, 1960), 31–38.

120. See C. G. Feilberg, *La tente noire: Contribution ethnographique à la histoire culturelle des nomades* (Copenhagen: Nationalmuseets Skrifter, 1944), 205–9. Ex. 26:7, 14; 36:14, 19.

121. Ibid., 198–99.

122. Acts 9:30; 15:41; Gal. 1:21.

123. See Feilberg, *Tente noire*, 198–99.

124. Ps. 27:5; 31:20.

125. Ps. 36:7.

126. For the standard and bearers, see Graham Webster, *The Roman Imperial Army of the First and Second Centuries A.D.*, 3rd ed. (Totowa, N.J.: Barnes and Noble Books, 1985), 133–39; for army tents, 169–70.

127. For these divisions, see Murphy-O'Connor, *Paul: His Story*, 163–68, 176–81, 184.

128. Sacchi, *History of the Second Temple Period*, 33–34.

129. John W. Yates, *The Spirit and Creation in Paul* (Tübingen: Mohr Siebeck, 2008), 85–124, examines the Spirit as "life-giving" in 1 Cor. 15 and 2 Cor. 3–5. He originates Paul's theology in the "breath of life" tradition, 22, 61, stated as being from Gen. 2:7. But see Gen. 1:2, 26, since the speech that created human life was also a spirited breath. Both versions contributed to Paul's theology.

130. Ps. 2:9.

131. Is. 45:9–11; cf. 41:25.

132. For the alternative interpretation of a wrestler caked with sand, see C. Spicq, "L'image sportive de II Corinthiens, IV, 7–9," *Ephemerides theologicae lovaniensis* 13 (1937): 216–27. Actual earthenware is the preferable interpretation because of its ordinary usage, biblical precedent, Corinthian manufacture, ritual usage, and material composition (no sand in earthenware).

133. Engels, *Roman Corinth*, 10, 33–36, 58; Cicero, *Pro Lege Manilia* 5, cited 15. For the catalogue, see Mary C. Sturgeon, *Sculpture 1: 1952–1967*, vol. 4 of *Isthmia: Excavations by the University of Chicago Under the Auspices of the American School of Classical Studies at Athens* (Princeton: The School, 1987), 2. See, more recently, Birgitta Lindros Wohl, "Lamps for the Excavations at Isthmia by UCLA," in *The Corinthia in the Roman Period*, ed. Timothy E. Gregory (Ann Arbor, Mich.: Cushing-Malloy, 1993), 130. For a catalogue, see Oscar Broneer, *Corinth IV, ii: Terracotta Lamps* (Cambridge, Mass.: Harvard University Press for the American School of Classical Studies at Athens, 1930). For the raw material, see Ian K. Whitbread, "Clays of Corinth: The Study of a Basic Resource for Ceramic Production," in Williams and Bookidis, *Corinth, the Centenary*, 1–13.

134. Broneer, "Paul and the Isthmian Games," 11–12, and 30 fig. 17.

135. Engels, *Roman Corinth*, 44.

136. 1 Cor. 9:24–26.

137. See, without reference to Paul, David Gilman Romano, "Athletic Festivals in the Northern Peloponnese and Central Greece," in *A Companion to Sport and Spectacle in Greek and Roman Antiquity*, ed. Paul Christesen and Donald G. Kyle (Chichester, UK: Wiley Blackwell, 2004), 181.

138. 1 Cor. 9:26–27.

139. For *aryballos*, see Beazley Archive, University of Oxford, www.beazley.ox.ac.uk; Andrew J. Clark, Maya Elston, and Mary Louise Hart, *Understanding Greek Vases: A Guide to Terms, Styles, and Techniques* (Los Angeles: J. Paul Getty Museum, 2002), 69; Brian A. Sparkes, *Greek Pottery: An Introduction* (Manchester: Manchester University Press, 1991), 80.

140. K. W. Arafat, "A Middle Corinthian Puzzle from Isthmia," in *Essays in Classical Archaeology for Eleni Hatzivassiliou, 1977–2007*, ed. Donna Kurtz with Casper Meyer et al. (Oxford: Archaeopress, 2008), 55–64.
141. Clark et al., *Understanding Greek Vases*, 69 and p. 76 fig. 1; Alexandra Alexandridou, *The Early Black-Figured Pottery of Attika in Context (c. 630–570 B.C.E.)* (Leiden: E. J. Brill, 2011), 28.
142. Ex. 27:20.
143. See, without reference to Paul, W. V. Harris, "Roman Terracotta Lamps: The Organization of an Industry," *Journal of Roman Studies* 70 (1980): 127–31, 142–44.
144. See Engels, *Roman Corinth*, 69.
145. Frank I. Schecter, *The Historical Foundations of the Law Relating to Trademarks* (New York: Columbia University Press, 1925), 20.
146. See, without reference to Paul, Kathleen Warner Slane, "Corinth's Roman Pottery: Quantification and Meaning," in Williams and Bookidis, *Corinth, the Centenary*, 330–31.
147. Engels, *Roman Corinth*, 33–36, 69.
148. See, without reference to Paul, Saul S. Weinberg, "Terracotta Sculpture at Corinth," *Hesperia* 26 (1957): 289, 304–5, citing at 289 Pliny, *Historia naturalis* 35.151–53.
149. See, without reference to Paul, Gloria S. Merker, "Corinthian Terracotta Figurines: The Development of an Industry," in Williams and Bookidis, *Corinth, the Centenary*, 233, 238, 243. See also Catherine de Grazia Vanderpool, "Roman Portraiture: The Many Faces of Corinth," in ibid., 373–74.
150. See above, p. 63.
151. 1 Cor. 6:11, 17.
152. Ibid., 12:3, 13.
153. Ibid., 14:3, 12, 14.
154. For the categorization, see André Munzinger, *Discerning the Spirits: Theological and Ethical Hermeneutics in Paul* (Cambridge: Cambridge University Press, 2007), 145–84.
155. 1 Cor. 2:16, 7.
156. Ibid., 14:15–16, 4, 32, 37.
157. Ibid., 5:3–5.
158. Birger A. Pearson, *The "pneumatikos"–"psychikos" Terminology in 1 Corinthians: A Study in the Theology of the Corinthian Opponents of Paul and Its Relation to Gnosticism* (Missoula, Mont.: Society of Biblical Literature, 1973). For *pneuma*, see John R. Levison, *The Spirit in First-Century Judaism* (Leiden: E. J. Brill, 1997), 217–26.
159. Richard A. Horsley, "*Pneumatikos* vs. *Psychikos:* Distinctions of Spiritual Status Among the Corinthians," *Harvard Theological Review* 69 (1976): 271, 280, 288. See Jerome Murphy-O'Connor, "Pneumatikoi in 2 Corinthians," *Proceedings of the Irish Biblical Association* 11 (1988): 59–60, who concedes "except perhaps the *pneumatikos-psychikos* contrast."
160. 1 Cor. 14:7.
161. Stanley, *Paul and the Language of Scripture*, 340–41.
162. See Yates, *Spirit and Creation in Paul*, 95–98.
163. Fee, *God's Empowering Presence*, 31, 32, 98, 263, 267.
164. 1 Cor. 5:1–2. Ps. 94:9, 11; for idols, see Deut. 32:21; Is. 4:39; 41:29.
165. Fee acknowledged the parallel, but as supporting his traditional interpretation that only the individual knows his own mind, therefore only God knows God. *God's Empowering Presence*, 101 n. 59.
166. Gen. 1:26, 2:7.
167. Luke 1:35; Matt. 3:16//; Luke 4:18, etc.
168. See Mehrdad Fatehi, *The Spirit's Relation to the Risen Lord in Paul: An Examination of Its Christological Implications* (Tübingen: Mohr Siebeck, 2000), 58–63.
169. See also T. Ryan Jackson, *New Creation in Paul's Letters: A Study of the Historical and Social Setting of a Pauline Concept* (Tübingen: Mohr Siebeck, 2010), 115–49.
170. For that citation, see Stanley, *Paul and the Language of Scripture*, 215–16.
171. For a brief survey, see Antoine Thivel, "Air, Pneuma, and Breathing from Homer to Hippocrates," in *Hippocrates in Context*, ed. Philip J. van der Eijk (Leiden: E. J. Brill, 2005), 465–91.
172. Hippocratic Corpus, *Peri physeōn* 3–4; *On Breaths*, in *Hippocrates*, ed. and trans. W. S. Jones, vol. 2 (London: William Heinemann, 1923), 228–33.

173. 1 Cor. 14:18.
174. As maintained by Hogeterp, *Paul and God's Temple*, 315–16; Thiselton, *Commentary*, 316.

CHAPTER 3

1. Augustine, *De trinitate*, ed. W. J. Mountain with Fr. Glorie, 2 vols. (Turnhout: Brepols, 1968). For recent studies, see Lewis Ayres, *Augustine and the Trinity* (Cambridge: Cambridge University Press, 2010); Luigi Gioia, *The Theological Epistemology of Augustine's "De trinitate"* (Oxford: Oxford University Press, 2008). All translations in this chapter are mine except as otherwise stated.
2. For the Spirit's role, see Franz Dünzel, *"Pneuma": Funktionen des theologischen Begriffs in frühchristlicher Literatur* (Münster: Aschendorff, 2000); Chad Tyler Gerber, *The Spirit of Augustine's Early Theology: Contextualizing Augustine's Pneumatology* (Farnham, Surrey, UK: Ashgate, 2012).
3. Marjorie O'Rourke Boyle, "Augustine in the Garden of Zeus: Lust, Love, and Language," *Harvard Theological Review* 83 (1990): 117–39. See also Augustine's much later commendation of rhetoric for Christian use in *De doctrina christiana* 4, ed. R. P. H. Green (Oxford: Clarendon, 1995), x, 196–286.
4. Augustine, *Confessions* 11.3.5, in *Confessionum libri tredecim*, ed. Lucas Verheijen (Turnhout: Brepols, 1981), 196.
5. Augustine, *De trinitate* 3 praef., 1:127. For Greek, see Pierre Courcelle, *Late Latin Writers and Their Greek Sources*, trans. Harry E. Wedeck (Cambridge, Mass.; Harvard University Press, 1969), 149–65, 207; Harald Hagendahl, *Augustine and the Latin Classics*, 2 vols. in 1 (Göteborg: Göteborg Universitet, 1967), 585–86; Berthold Altaner, "Augustinus und die griechischen Patristik: Eine Einführung und Nachlese zu dem Quellenkritischen Untersuchungen," *Revue benedictine* 62 (1952): 201–15; idem, "Augustins Methode der Quellenbenützung: Sein Studien der Väterliteratur," *Sacris erudiri* 4 (1952): 9–11.

6. *De trinitate* 6.10.11, 1:241. See Gioia, *Theological Epistemology*, 133.
7. *De doctrina christiana* 2.15.22, p. 80. See also John S. McIntosh, *A Study of Augustine's Versions of Genesis* (Chicago: University of Chicago Press, 1912).
8. H. A. G. Houghton, *Augustine's Text of John: Patristic Citations and Latin Gospel Manuscripts* (Oxford: Oxford University Press, 2008), 84, dating book 1 to about 400, the remainder to 411–22.
9. "Index locorum s. scripturae," in *De trinitate*, 2:629–719.
10. Houghton, *Augustine's Text*, 84.
11. *De trinitate* 8.9.13, 1:289. 2 Cor. 6:2–10.
12. *De trinitate* 1.1.1, 1:27–28; 1.2.4, 1:31–32.
13. Ibid., 1.2.4–3.6, 1:31–32; 2.praef.1, 1:80–81; 3.10.21, 1:149. 1.1.3, 1:30; 1.12.23, 1:62, citing 1 Cor. 2:2–3, 3:1–2; 4.1.2, 1:161, and see 2 Cor. 7–10. *De trinitate* 8.4.7, 1:275–76, and see Cor. 12:7–10.
14. *De trinitate* 8.5.8, 1:278; 8.6.9, 1:279, 280. 8.9.13, 1:289. 8.10.14, 1:290–91; 9.2.2, 1:294–95; 9.12.17, 1:308.
15. Ibid., 3.10.24, 1:153; 3.11.24, 1:153; 3.11.26, 1:156.
16. *Confessiones* 4.1.1–5.14.25, pp. 40–72; 8.12.28–29, pp. 130–31.
17. *De trinitate* 2.6.11, 1:96; 2.15.25, 1:113; 3.10.19, 1:145–46; 3.11.22–27, 1:150–58. 2.6.11, 2.7.12, 1:96.
18. See Julian Morgenstern, *The Ark, the Ephod, and the "Tent of Meeting"* (Cincinnati: Hebrew Union College Press, 1945), 131–61; E. Theodore Mullen Jr., *The Assembly of the Gods: The Divine Council in Canaanite and Early Hebrew Literature* (Chico, Calif.: Scholars, 1980), 134, 168–69, 171–73.
19. *De trinitate* 1.12.31, 1:79.
20. Ibid., 8.2.3, 1:271.
21. Marjorie O'Rourke Boyle, "Augustine's Heartbeat: From Time to Eternity," *Viator: Medieval and Renaissance Studies* 38 (2007): 19–43. *Confessiones* 7.17.23, p. 107, 7.10.16, pp. 103–4, 7.17.23, pp. 107, 103–4, 107. 8.1.1, p. 113, 7.10.16, pp. 103–4.
22. *De trinitate* 2.15.25, 1:113, citing 1 Cor. 13:12.
23. *De trinitate* 2.13.23, 1:111; 1.6.13, 1:44; 7.3.6, 1:254. For 1 Cor. 13:12, see *De trinitate* 1.8.16, 1:50; 1.13.31, 1:78; 8.4.6, 1:274, and very frequent. 5.1.1, 1:206.

24. *De trinitate* 5.13.14, 1:221–22; 3.9.18, 1:145.
25. 1 Cor. 12:8. *De trinitate* 12.14.22–25, 1:375–80.
26. Gioia, *Theological Epistemology*, 2 n. 4.
27. *De trinitate* 1.2.4, 1:31.
28. Ibid., 1.4.7, 1:34–35.
29. Ibid., 4.4.7, 1:169. See Gioia, *Theological Epistemology*, 232–97.
30. Joel S. Burnett, *A Reassessment of Biblical "Elohim"* (Atlanta: Society of Biblical Literature, 2001), 79–152.
31. *De doctrina christiana* 2.15.22, pp. 80, 81.
32. See chapter 1.
33. *De trinitate* 1.7.14, 1:46; 6.10.12, 1:242. 7.6.12, 1:266.
34. Augustine, *De Genesi ad litteram* 1.6, in *De Genesi ad litteram libri duodecim, Eiusdem libri capitula, De Genesi ad litteram imperfectus liber, Locutionum in Heptateuchum libri septem*, ed. Joseph Zycha (Vienna: F. Tempsky, 1893), 10. 3.19, p. 85. This was written 401–15 C.E.
35. See Mullen, *Assembly of the Gods*.
36. *De trinitate* 12.6.6, 1:360. 14.19, 25, 2:456.
37. Ibid., 1.12.25, 1:64.
38. *Confessiones* 13.9.10, pp. 246–47.
39. *De trinitate* 15.19.37, 2:514.
40. Ibid., 1.6.9, 1:38 and frequent. For Augustine's *verbum* as different from the tradition, which was *sermo*, see Marjorie O'Rourke Boyle, *Erasmus on Language and Method in Theology* (Toronto: University of Toronto Press, 1977), 26–29.
41. *De trinitate* 6.12, 1:242–43.
42. *De Genesi ad litteram* 1.18, pp. 26–27.
43. *De trinitate* 5.12.13, 1:220; 5.18.32–36, 1:507–13. 9.12.17, 1:308; 15.17.27, 2:501; 15.19.37, 2:513–14. 15.18.32, 2:507–8. See 1 Cor. 13:13.
44. *De trinitate* 8.3.4, 1:272. 3.8.13; 1:140. 4.praef.1, 1:159. 8.7.11, 1:285–86.
45. See Jean Defradas, *Les thèmes de la propagande delphique* (Paris: C. Klincksieck, 1954), 277–80, 286, 284.
46. Augustine, *De civitate Dei* 19.23.1, ed. Eligius Dombart and Alphonsus Kalb, 2 vols. (Turnhout: Brepols, 1955), 1:690–92. *De trinitate* 10.5.7, 1:320. For Christian interpretations, see Pierre Courcelle, *Connais-toi toi-même; de Socrate à saint Bernard*, 2 vols. (Paris: Études augustiniennes, 1974), 1:125–63.
47. Lewis Ayres, "The Discipline of Self-Knowledge in Augustine's *De trinitate* Book X," in *The Passionate Intellect: Essays on the Transformation of Classical Traditions Presented to Professor I. G. Kidd*, ed. Ayres (New Brunswick, N.J.: Transaction, 1995), 277, with reference to Cicero, *Tusculanes disputationes* 5.25.70. See also Etienne Gilson, *The Christian Philosophy of Saint Augustine*, trans. L. E. M. Lynch (New York: Random House, 1960), 66–105.
48. *De trinitate* 10.9.12, 1:325–26.
49. Gioia, *Theological Epistemology*.
50. *De trinitate* 15.7.11, 2:474.
51. Quintilian, *Institutio oratoria* 7.3.15, trans. Donald A. Russell, *The Orator's Education: Books 6–8* (Cambridge, Mass.: Harvard University Press, 2001), 225.
52. James J. Murphy, ed., *Quintilian on the Teaching of Speaking and Writing: Translations from Books One, Two, and Ten of the "Institutio oratoria"* (Carbondale: Southern Illinois University Press, 1987), xxxix.
53. *De doctrina christiana* 3.26.37, p. 168; 3.28.39, p. 170.
54. *De trinitate* 2.1.praef., 1:80.
55. Ibid., 9.12.17, 1:308. For soul, see Gerald O'Daly, *Augustine's Philosophy of Mind* (London: Duckworth, 1987), 7–79.
56. *De trinitate* 12.11.16, 1:370. 12.7.12, 1:366; 15.7.11, 2:474.
57. Augustine, *De symbolo*, in *Patrologiae cursus completus, series latina*, ed. J-P. Migne, 221 vols. (Paris, 1800–75), 40:628. Abbreviated *PL*.
58. *De trinitate* 7.6.12, 1:266; 9.11.16, 1:307. 9.12.18, 1:310.
59. Ibid., 14.16.22, 2:451–53. 1 Cor. 14:14. For the contested authorship of the letter to the Ephesians, see Bart D. Ehrmann, *The New Testament: A Historical Introduction to the Early Christian Writings*, 4th ed. (New York: Oxford University Press, 2008), 389–92.
60. *De trinitate* 9.2.2, 1:295. 3.2.8, 1:133. 6.6.8, 1:236–37. 4.3.5, 1:165–66; 4.13.16, 1:181. 4.1.3, 1:163. 1.1.1, 1:28.
61. Ibid., 6.9.10, 1:240.
62. Ibid., 1.8.18, 1:52–53; 1.12.23, 1:62. 1.8.18, 1:52. 1 Cor. 2:11.
63. *De trinitate* 9.2.2, 1:295. 9.11.16, 1:307.

64. Ibid., 15.1.1, 2:460. 5.7.11, 2:475. 2.8.14, 1:98. 15.3.5, 2:467.
65. For interpretations, see Margaret E. Thrall, *A Critical and Exegetical Commentary on the Second Epistle to the Corinthians*, 2 vols. (Edinburgh: T. and T. Clark, 1994–2000), 1:290–95.
66. See, e.g., Martin L. West, "Seventeen Distorted Mirrors in Plato," *Classical Quarterly* 59 (2002): 380–81.
67. *De trinitate* 4.20.27, 1:196–97.
68. 1 Cor. 1:19–25.
69. See chapter 2.
70. See Carol C. Mattusch, *Classical Bronzes: The Art and Craft of Greek and Roman Statuary* (Ithaca: Cornell University Press, 1996), ix, 1, 217, 2, 10, 22–24, 217.
71. Pliny, *Naturalis historia* 34.1, 6–8, 48. Carol C. Mattusch, "Corinthian Bronze: Famous but Elusive," in *Corinth, the Centenary, 1896–1996*, ed. Charles K. Williams II and Nancy Bookidis, vol. 20 of *Corinth: Results of Excavations* (Cambridge, Mass.: Harvard University Press for the American School of Classical Studies at Athens, 2003), 219; Elizabeth G. Pemberton, "The Attribution of Corinthian Bronzes," *Hesperia* 50 (1981): 101–11; Donald Engels, *Roman Corinth: An Alternative Model for the Classical City* (Chicago: University of Chicago Press, 1990), 36, 18, 54–55; Jerome Murphy-O'Connor, "Corinthian Bronze," *Revue biblique* 90 (1983): 84–85, 37.
72. Engels, *Roman Corinth*, 37, 12, 37, 70.
73. William Rostoker and Elizabeth B. Gebhard, "The Sanctuary of Poseidon at Isthmia: Techniques of Metal Manufacture," *Hesperia* 50 (1981): 347–63; Engels, *Roman Corinth*, 13.
74. See Murphy-O'Connor, "Corinthian Bronze," 93.
75. A. R. S. Kennedy, "Some Problems of Herod's Temple," *The Expository Times* 20 (1909): 270–73.
76. Acts 21:26–36.
77. See Winnifred Lamb, *Ancient Greek and Roman Bronzes*, enlarged by Leonore K. Congdon (Chicago: Argonaut, 1969), 115, 119, 241.
78. For the medium, see Mattusch, *Classical Bronzes*, 15.
79. Rom. 9:20–21; see 2 Cor. 4:7.

80. *A Greek-English*, ed. Henry George Liddell and Robert Scott, rev. Henry Stuart Jones with Roderick McKenzie, 9th ed. (Oxford: Clarendon, 1997), s.v. *ainigma*. See also Konrad Ohlert, *Rätsel und Rätselspiele der alten Griechen*, 2nd ed. (1912; rpt., New York: Olms, 1979).
81. Num. 12:8; Deut. 28:37; 3 Kings 10:1; 2 Chr. 1:6; Wis. 8:8; Sir. 39:3; 47:15; Dan. 8:23.
82. Maren Nichoff, *The Figure of Joseph in Post-biblical Jewish Literature* (Leiden: E. J. Brill, 1992), 36. For biblical riddles, see also Tom Thatcher, *The Riddles of Jesus in John: A Study in Tradition and Folklore* (Atlanta: Society of Biblical Literature, 2000), 117 n. 26, 167 n. 180.
83. 1 Cor. 13.
84. *The Apocryphal New Testament: A Collection of Apocryphal Christian Literature in an English Translation*, ed. J. K. Elliott (Oxford: Clarendon, 1993), 352–62, 380–82.
85. Jerome Murphy-O'Connor, *Paul: A Life* (Oxford: Oxford University Press, 2004), 238–39.
86. Richard M. Rothaus, *Corinth, the First City of Greece: An Urban History of Late Antique Cult and Religion* (Leiden: E. J. Brill, 2000), 17–21, 16–17.
87. Cicero, *Tusculanes disputationes* 4.14.32; cited by Mattusch, "Corinthian Bronze," 219.
88. Murphy-O'Connor, "Corinthian Bronze," 80–81, 85–86.
89. Pliny, *Historia naturalis* 34.48; Quintilian, *Institutio oratoria* 6.3.98, cited by Jerome Murphy-O'Connor, *St. Paul's Corinth: Texts and Archaeology*, 3rd ed. rev. (Collegeville, Minn.: Liturgical Press, 2002), 213, without reference to the riddle in Paul's mirror.
90. Augustine, *De magistro* 5.16, ed. K.-D. Dauer, in *Contra academicos, De beata vita, De ordine, De magistro, De libero arbitrio*, ed. W. M. Green et al. (Turnhout: Brepols, 1970), 174. The same Hortensius was an advocate for rhetoric in Cicero's *Hortensius*, which Augustine read enthusiastically about philosophy. *Confessiones* 3.3.7, p. 30. See also John H. Taylor, "St. Augustine and the *Hortensius* of Cicero," *Studies in Philology* 60 (1963): 487–98. Augustine cited the conclusion

of *Hortensius* in *De trinitate* 14.19.26, 2:457–58.

91. See, without reference to Paul's mirror, Lamb, *Ancient Bronzes*, 125–27, 160, 180. See also A. De Ridder, "Speculum," in *Dictionnaire des antiquités grecques et romaines, après les textes et les monuments*, ed. Charles Daremberg, 4-2 (Paris: Hachette, 1877), p. 1424 and fig. 6527.

92. Christiane Zivie-Coche, *Sphinx: History of a Monument*, trans. David Lorton (Ithaca: Cornell University Press, 2002), 4–12, 15, 99, 15, 10–11. For the iconography, see the exhibition catalogue *Sphinx: Les gardiens de l'Égypte*, ed. Eugène Warmenbol (Brussels: ING Belgique et Fonds Mercator, 2006).

93. For eagle's wings, see Ruth Fainlight and Robert J. Littman, trans., introduction to Sophocles, *The Theban Plays: Oedipus the King, Oedipus at Colonus, Antigone* (Baltimore: Johns Hopkins University Press, 2009), xxvii.

94. Jean-Marc Moret, *Oedipe, le sphinx, et les thébains: Essai de mythologie iconographique*, 2 vols. (Geneva: Institut suisse de Rome, 1984), 1:1, 69–75; for the plates, see vol. 2.

95. Lowell Edmunds, *Oedipus: The Ancient Legend and Its Later Analogues* (Baltimore: Johns Hopkins University Press, 1966), 12.

96. See chapter 1.

97. Moret, *Oedipe*, 1:9–20, 13, 40, and 2:pl. 23; 1:113–32.

98. Without reference to Paul, see Lowell Edmunds, *Oedipus* (London: Routledge, 2006), 20, 18–19, citing Athenaeus, *Deipnosophistai* 10.83; Edmunds, *Oedipus: Legend and Analogues*, 12, and for the ancient sources, 33, 47–57.

99. Edmunds, *Oedipus: Legend and Analogues*, 33, 34–35.

100. Moret, *Oedipe*, 1:9–20, 13, 40, and 2:pl. 23; 1:113–32. See also *Sphinx: Les gardiens de l'Égypte*, cat. 180, p. 173; cat. 196, p. 177; and Petra Baum-vom Felde, "Oedipe, la sphinge, et l'énigma," 161–71.

101. Mary C. Sturgeon, *Sculpture: The Assemblage for the Theater*, vol. 9-3 of *Corinth* (Princeton: American School of Classical Studies at Athens, 2004), 4, 52–54.

102. Sophocles, *Oedipus tyrannus*, in *Sophoclis fabulae*, ed. Hugh Lloyd-Jones and N. G. Wilson (Oxford: Clarendon, 1990), 119–80.

103. Fionna Macintosh, *Sophocles: Oedipus Tyrannus* (Cambridge: Cambridge University Press, 2009), xiii, 1–4; Fainlight and Littman, introduction to Sophocles, *Theban Play*, xxii.

104. Sophocles, *Oedipus tyrannus* lines 36–37, trans. p. 4; line 130, trans. p. 8; line 506, trans. p. 21; line 1200, trans. p. 52. For Oedipus at Delphi, see Hugh Bowden, *Classical Athens and the Delphic Oracle: Divination and Democracy* (Cambridge: Cambridge University Press, 2005), 46–55.

105. Sophocles, *Oedipus tyrannus* lines 794–99, 994–98, 744–45.

106. Fainlight and Littman, introduction to Sophocles, *Theban Plays*, xxxvi.

107. Charles Segal, *Oedipus Tyrannus: Tragic Heroism and the Limits of Knowledge*, 2nd ed. (New York: Oxford University Press, 2001), 36–37, 62–63. See also Freddie Rokem, "One Voice and Many Legs: Oedipus and the Riddle of the Sphinx," in *Untying the Knot: On Riddles and Other Enigmatic Modes*, ed. Galit Hasan-Rokem and David Shulman (New York: Oxford University Press, 1966), 263–64.

108. Sophocles, *Oedipus tyrannus* lines 787–93.

109. Defradas, *Thèmes de la propagande delphique*, 277–80, 286, 284.

110. *Oedipus tyrannus* line 1059, trans. p. 45; lines 1182–83, 1251–79.

111. Fainlight and Littman, introduction to *Theban Plays*, xxii. *Oedipus tyrannus* line 324, trans. p. 14.

112. 1 Cor. 15:3, 17, 26; 2 Cor. 5:21. See 2 Cor. 11:7. 1 Cor. 14:20.

113. See Andrew D. Clarke, *Secular and Christian Leadership in Corinth: A Socio-historical and Exegetical Study of 1 Corinthians 1–6* (Leiden: E. J. Brill, 1993), 77–88.

114. *De trinitate* 15.8.14, 2:479. For Augustine's mirror as a cracked glass, see Edward P. Nolan, *Now Through a Glass Darkly: Specular Images of Being and Knowing from Virgil to Chaucer* (Ann Arbor: University of Michigan Press, 1990), 55–81.

115. See Edmunds, *Oedipus*, 56, citing Terence, *Andria* 194; Plautus, *Poenulus* 443.

116. *Confessiones* 9.12.32, p. 151; 10.23.33, p. 173; 12.30.41, p. 240, citing Terence, *Andria*.
117. Edmunds, *Oedipus*, 57–64; Macintosh, *Oedipus tyrannus*, 36–46.
118. *De civitate Dei* 18.13, 2:604. For the sphinge falling to its death, see Segal, *Oedipus tyrannus*, 33.
119. Apollodorus, *Bibliotheca* 3.5.8.
120. *De civitate Dei* 16.8, 2:508–9, 510.
121. Ibid., 18.13, p. 604. 22.29, p. 857.
122. *De doctrina christiana* 2.16.23, p. 82; 3.11.17, p. 150; 3.29.40, p. 170.
123. Augustine, *Enarrationes in psalmos* 48.1.5, ed. Eligius Dekkers and Iohannes Fraipont, 3 vols. (Turnhout: Brepols, 1956), 1:554; 121.9, 2:1809; 138.8, p. 1995.
124. Augustine, *De spiritu et littera* 28.49, ed. Karl F. Urba and Joseph Zycha (Vienna: Tempsky, 1913), 203.
125. Norbert Hugedé, *La métaphore du miroir dans les Épîtres de saint Paul aux Corinthiens* (Neuchatel: Delachaux et Niestlé, 1957), 141–45. This mentions Oedipus in passing but incorrectly reverses the sphinx's role to him, 142. For enigma, see also Pietro Pucci, *Enigma, segreto, oraculo* (Pisa: Istituti editoriali e poligrafici internazionali, 1996), 17–105.
126. *Confessiones* 3.6.11, p. 33. Cf. 9.10.25, p. 148; 11.22.28, p. 207. See also Augustine, *In Iohannes evangelium tractatus* 97.2, ed. Radbodus Willems (Turnhout: Brepols, 1954), 574.
127. *De trinitate* 15.9.15, 2:480–81. 15.8.14, 2:479–80. 15.8.14, 2:479–80.
128. For comparative translations, see http://biblos.com/. See recently Harm W. Hollander, "Seeing God 'in a Riddle' or 'Face to Face': An Analysis of 1 Corinthians 13:12," *Journal for the Study of the New Testament* 32 (2010): 395–403.
129. Hugedé, *Métaphore du miroir*, 17, 36, 97–100.
130. V. 26.
131. See, without reference to Paul and Augustine, Dan Pagis, "Toward a Theory of the Literary Riddle," in Hasan-Rokem and Shulman, *Untying the Knot*, 81, 83.
132. *De trinitate* 10.3.5, 1:317; 10.9.12, 1:325–26. 12.1.1, 1:356.
133. Gérard Verbeke, *L'evolution de la doctrine du "pneuma" du Stoicisme à s. Augustine: Étude philosophique* (Paris: Desclée De Brouwer, 1945), 489, 498–507, 507–8.
134. Robert L. Wilken, "*Spiritus sanctus secundum scripturas sanctas*: Exegetical Considerations of Augustine on the Holy Spirit," *Augustinian Studies* 31 (2000): 1–18. See also Gioia, *Theological Epistemology*, 125–46.
135. *De Genesi ad litteram* 1.1, p. 4. 1.5, p. 8. For Augustine on intellect, see also A. N. Williams, *The Divine Sense: The Intellect in Patristic Theology* (Cambridge: Cambridge University Press, 2007), 143–87. *De Genesi ad litteram* 3.20, p. 86. See *De trinitate* 14.16.22, 2:451–55. *De Genesi ad litteram* 6.12, pp. 185, 186, 187. 6.12, p. 186.
136. Plato, *Timaeus* 91e–92a, *Cratylus* 399e; Aristotle, *De partibus animalium* 4.10 686a; Cicero, *De natura deorum* 2.140, *De legibus* 1.9.26; Sallust, *Bellum Catilinae* 1.1; Seneca, *Epistulae* 111.3, 65.20; Silius Italicus, *Punica* 15.84.87; Manilius, *Astronomicon* lines 883–87, 893–95, 897–910.
137. *De Genesi ad litteram* 7.2, pp. 201–4.
138. Ibid., 7.7, pp. 206, 207. 7.8, p. 207. 7.9–11, pp. 207–11.
139. Ibid., 7.12, pp. 211–12; 7.13, p. 212; 7.15, p. 213; 7.19, p. 215. 7.16, pp. 213–14. 7.17, p. 124. 7.21, p. 219.
140. Ibid., 7.24, pp. 222–23. 7.28, p. 228.
141. Ibid., 12.7, p. 389.
142. *A Latin Dictionary*, ed. Charlton T. Lewis and Charles Short (Oxford: Clarendon, 1969), s.v. *spiritale*; 1 Cor. 15:44.
143. *De Genesi ad litteram* 12.7, p. 389.
144. Ibid.; Ps. 148:8.
145. 1 Cor. 15:12–57.
146. *De Genesi ad litteram* 12.7, p. 389.
147. Ehrman, *New Testament*, 386–92.
148. *De trinitate* 14.16.22, 2:451–53.
149. *De Genesi ad litteram* 12.7, p. 389. Rom. 7:25. *De Genesi ad litteram* 12.7, p. 389. John 4:24.
150. *De Genesi ad litteram* 12.1–5, pp. 379–86. 12.6, pp. 386–87. 12.9, p. 391. 12.7, p. 388. 12.8, p. 390. See in general Gerard Watson, *Phantasia in Classical Thought* (Galway: Galway University Press, 1988), 135–53.
151. *De Genesi ad litteram* 12.9, pp. 391–92. For dreams, see Martine Dulaey,

Le rêve dans la vie et la pensée de saint Augustin (Paris: Études augustiniennes, 1973).

152. *De Genesi ad litteram* 12.16, pp. 401–2; Augustine, *De musica* 6.8.21, in *De musica liber VI*, ed. Martin Jacobsson (Stockholm: Almqvist and Wiksell International, 2002), 48, 50. For the extromissive theory, see David C. Lindberg, *Theories of Vision from Al-Kindi to Kepler* (Chicago: University of Chicago Press, 1976), 10–11, 90, 217–18 n. 39.

153. *De Genesi ad litteram* 12.12, pp. 395–97. 12.21, pp. 411–12. 12.17, pp. 403–6. 12.23, pp. 414–15. For imagination, see in general O'Daly, *Augustine's Philosophy of Mind*, 106–30.

154. *De Genesi ad litteram* 12.23 p. 415. 12.24, p. 416. 12.24, pp. 417–18. 12.25, pp. 417–18.

155. Ibid., 12.26, pp. 418–19. 12.27, pp. 420, 422. 12.28, pp. 422, 423.

156. Ibid., 12.31, pp. 425, 426. 12.36, p. 433. 12.10, p. 292. 12.11, pp. 393, 395.

157. *Confessiones* 4.16.28, pp. 54, 55. 3.6.10, pp. 31–32. 3.6.11, p. 33. 3.7.12 p. 33. 5.3.3–7.12, pp. 58–63. 5.10.18, 20 pp. 68, 69. 5.11.21, p. 69.

158. Ibid., 7.1.1–2, pp. 92–93. 7.5.7, p. 96. 7.7.11, p. 100. 7.9.13, p. 101. 7.10.16, pp. 103–4.

159. *De trinitate* 1.1, 1:27–28. 1.8.17, 1:51. 15.4.6, 2:467.

160. Boyle, "Augustine in the Garden of Zeus," 119.

161. *De trinitate* 1.2.2, 1:28. 1.8.17, 1:51. 15.4.6, 2:467.

162. Boyle, "Augustine in the Garden of Zeus," 117–19.

163. Ibid., 117–19, 124–30, 131, 132–33.

164. Ibid., 133–35, 147–48.

165. *De trinitate* 2.10.17–18, 1:101–4.

166. *De Genesi ad litteram* 11.33, p. 367. See also James Barr, "Theophany and Anthropomorphism in the Old Testament," *Vetus testamentum, Supplements*, vol. 7 *Congress Volume Oxford 1959* (Leiden: E. J. Brill, 1960), 31–38.

167. Especially in *De civitate Dei* 1–7.

168. *De trinitate* 2.6.11, 1:94–95. For the Holy Spirit as fire and wind, see 1.4.7, 1:35; 2.5.10, 1:93. 11.20.17, 1:354. 5.4.5, 1:209, citing Porphyry, *Isagogue* 4a.

169. *De Genesi ad litteram* 1.18, p. 27. Matt. 23:37.

170. Marjorie O'Rourke Boyle, *Divine Domesticity: Augustine of Thagaste to Teresa of Ávila* (Leiden: E. J. Brill, 1997), 62–63.

171. *De trinitate* 8.3.4, 1:272. 1.1.2, 1:29. 12.7.12, 1:366. 1.1.2, 1:29.

172. Ex. 3:13–22.

173. *Confessiones* 3.5.9, pp. 30–31.

174. Cicero, *De legibus* 1.23.61; *De republica; De legibus*, trans. William Clinton Keyes (Cambridge, Mass.: Harvard University Press, 1970), 367.

175. Marjorie O'Rourke Boyle, "The Prudential Augustine: The Virtuous Structure and Sense of His *Confessions*," *Recherches augustiniennes* 22 (1987): 129–37, 144.

176. *Confessiones* 11.3.5, p. 196.

177. Boyle, "Prudential Augustine," 143, 138.

178. *De Genesi ad litteram* 12.7, p. 388; 12.17, pp. 403–6; 12.21, pp. 411–12; 12.23, pp. 414–15; 12.24, p. 416.

179. 1 Cor. 13:12.

180. Boyle, "Prudential Augustine," 142, 144, 145, 147, 148.

181. Ibid., 149. *Confessiones* 1.6.7, p. 4.

182. *De trinitate* 8.1.1, 1:113.

183. Ibid., 15.3.5, 2:465. 6.3.4, 1:232.

184. *Confessiones* 13.7.8, p. 243.

CHAPTER 4

1. Thomas Aquinas, *Super 1 Corinthianos* chap. 2 lectio 2, in *Super epistolas sancti Pauli lectura*, ed. Raphael Cai, 8th rev. ed., 2 vols. (Turin: Marietti, 1953). A modern critical edition of his Leonine *Opera omnia* (1879) is in progress at http://www.corpusthomisticum.org/. This edition is used unless otherwise cited, e.g., above. All translations in this chapter are mine unless otherwise stated.

2. See chapter 2, pp. 60–65.

3. For his education, see Jean-Pierre Torrell, *Saint Thomas Aquinas*, vol. 1, *The Person and His Work*, trans. Robert Royal, rev. ed. (Washington, D.C.: Catholic University of America Press, 2005), 54–74.

4. Aquinas, *Summa theologiae* 1, q. 1 obj. 2 and reply.

5. Torrell, *Aquinas*, 1–5.

6. Benedict, *Regula* 1.10–12, 58.9, 17, 28; 60.9; 61.5, ed. Timothy Fry (Collegeville, Minn.: Liturgical Press, 1980).
7. Torrell, *Aquinas*, 5–12.
8. Ibid., 254–55. See also Daniel A. Keating, "Commentary on Corinthians," in *Aquinas on Scripture: An Introduction to His Biblical Commentaries*, ed. Thomas G. Weinandy, Keating, and John P. Yocum (London: T. and T. Clark, 2005), 127–28; Thomas Prügl, "Thomas Aquinas as Interpreter of Scripture," trans. Albert K. Wimmer, in *The Theology of Thomas Aquinas*, ed. Rik Van Nieuwenhove and Joseph Wawrykow (Notre Dame: University of Notre Dame Press, 2005), 390–91.
9. Roger Dragonetti, *Le mirage des sources: L'art du faux dans le roman médiéval* (Paris: Editions du Seuil with Centre national des lettres, 1987), 17–42.
10. *Super 1 Cor.*
11. *Commentaire de la première épitre aux Corinthiens (chap. 7, 10b au chap. 10, 33) de Pierre de Tarentaise*, ed. Jean Barella and Jean-Eric Stroobant de Saint-Eloy (Paris: Cerf, 2002).
12. Aquinas, *Super 2 Corinthianos*.
13. *Super 1 Cor.* proem.
14. *Summa theologiae* 2-1, q. 66 a. 5.
15. *Super 1 Cor.* proem; chap. 2, lectio 1.
16. See chapter 3, pp. 118, 125–27. See also Paul A. Macdonald Jr., *Knowledge and the Transcendent: An Inquiry into the Mind's Relationship to God* (Washington, D.C.: Catholic University of America Press, 2009), 135–71.
17. See Edward Booth, "St. Thomas Aquinas's Critique of Saint Augustine's Conceptions of the Image of God in the Human Soul," in *Gott und sein Bild: Augustins "De trinitate" im Spiegel gegenwärten Forschung* (Paderborn: Schöningh, 2000), 219–39.
18. See, in general, Anthony Kenny, *Aquinas on Mind* (London: Routledge, 1993).
19. *Super 1 Cor.* chap. 2, lectio 2.
20. See chapter 1, pp. 36.
21. Aquinas, *Expositio super Iob ad litteram*.
22. *Super 1 Cor.* chap. 2, lectio 2.
23. Ibid.
24. Ibid.
25. See chapter 2, pp. 60–65.
26. Aquinas, *Scriptum super libros Sententiarum* lib. 4, d. 14 q. 1 a. 4, qc 1 arg. 2, ed. Pierre Mandonnet and M. F. Moos, new ed., 4 vols. (Paris: P. Lethielleux, 1929–47).
27. Aristotle, *Rhetorica* 2.23 1397b.
28. See Torrell, *Aquinas*, 146.
29. *Summa theologiae* 1, q. 13 a. 5. For progress from more to less manifest truths, see *Summa contra Gentiles* 1, a. 9.
30. *Super 1 Cor.* chap. 2, lectio 2.
31. Ibid.
32. See chapter 2, pp. 60–65.
33. Augustine, *De trinitate* 10.9.12, ed. W. J. Mountain with Fr. Glorie, 2 vols. (Turnhout: Brepols, 1968), 1:325–26. See chapter 3, p. 114.
34. *Super 1 Cor.* chap. 2, lectio 2.
35. Ibid.
36. See chapter 2, pp. 88–89, 95–96.
37. *Summa theologiae* 1, q. 95 a. 1 arg. 1; 3, q. 31 a. 1 arg. 1.
38. Ibid., q. 76 a. 4.; q. 76 a. 3; *Summa contra Gentiles* 2, chap. 58.
39. *Super 1 Cor.* chap. 2, lectio 3.
40. *Summa theologiae* 1, q. 76 a. 1.
41. *Super 1 Cor.* chap. 2, lectio 3.
42. See chapter 2, pp. 64, 80, 92, 93.
43. *Super 1 Cor.* chap. 2, lectio 3.
44. Aquinas, *Super Ephesios* chap. 4, lectio 3.
45. *Summa theologiae* 1, q. 1 a. 1.
46. Leonard E. Boyle, *The Setting of the "Summa theologiae"* (Toronto: Pontifical Institute of Mediaeval Studies, 1982). Torrell, *Aquinas*, 145–46, 160–61.
47. Torrell, *Aquinas*, 27, 31, 33–34, 411.
48. *Summa theologiae* 1, q. 1 a. 1. 1, citing 1 Cor. 2:9; Is. 64:4.
49. Ibid., a. 6, citing 1 Cor. 3:10, and see 2 Cor. 10: 4–5; Aristotle, *Ethica Nicomachea* 10.5 1176a.
50. *Super 1 Cor.* chap. 2, lectio 3.
51. *Summa theologiae* 1, q. 1 a. 6, and see 2 Cor. 10: 4–5. *Summa theologiae* 2-2, q. 60 a. 1 ad 2.
52. Raphael Loewe, "The Medieval History of the Latin Vulgate," in *The West from the Fathers to the Reformation*," vol. 2 of *The Cambridge History of the Bible* (Cambridge: Cambridge University Press, 1975–76), 145–48, 149.
53. Torrell, *Aquinas*, 28, 57–59. For the scriptural senses, see Henri DeLubac,

Exégèse médiévale: Les quatre sens de l'Écriture, 4 vols. (Paris: Aubier, 1959–64).

54. Marcia L. Colish, "Authority and Interpretation in Scholastic Theology," in idem, *Studies in Scholasticism* (Aldershot: Ashgate Variorum, 2006), II-1–16; "Peter Lombard as an Exegete of Paul," IX-71–92.

55. Salvatore Camporeale, *Lorenzo Valla, Umanesimo e teologia* (Florence: Istituto Palazzo Strozzi, 1972); idem, "Lorenzo Valla tra Medioevo e Rinascimento: *Encomium s. Thomae-1457*," *Memorie domenicane* 7 (1976): 3–186; idem, "Lorenzo Valla: The Transcending of Philosophy Through Rhetoric," *Romance Notes* 30 (1990): 269–84. See also Lodi Nauta, *In Defense of Common Sense: Lorenzo Valla's Humanist Critique of Scholastic Philosophy* (Cambridge: Cambridge University Press, 2009).

56. See Leo Elders, "The Aristotelian Commentaries of St. Thomas Aquinas," *Review of Metaphysics* 63 (2009): 29–53.

57. Bernardo C. Bazàn, in idem, John W. Wippel, Gérard Fransen, and Danielle Jacquart, *Les questions disputés et les questions quodlibétiques dans les facultés de théologie, de droit, et de médicine* (Turnhout: Brepols, 1985), 27–31.

58. Wilhelmus G. B. M. Valkenberg, *Words of the Living God: Place and Function of Holy Scripture in the Theology of St. Thomas Aquinas* (Leuven: Peeters, 2000), 8–53.

59. See Lesley Smith, *The "Glossa ordinaria": The Making of a Medieval Bible Commentary* (Leiden: Brill, 2009), 1–3, 230, and for Aquinas's use, 223–25.

60. *Glossa ordinaria*, in *Patrologiae cursus completus, series latina*, ed. J.-P. Migne, 221 vols. (Paris, 1800–75), 114:522. See also *Biblia latina cum glossa ordinaria: Facsimile Reprint of the "editio princeps" by Adolph Rusch of Strassburg, 1480/81*, 4 vols. (Turnhout: Brepols, 1992).

61. *Super 1 Cor.* chap. 2, lectio 3.

62. Ibid.; Aristotle, *Ethica Nicomachea* 1.3.5 1177b.

63. See chapter 2, pp. 60–64.

64. *Super 1 Cor.* chap. 2, lectio 3.

65. *Summa theologiae* 1, q. 1 a. 6 obj. 3.

66. See Marcia Colish, "From the Sentence Collection to the Sentence Commentary and the *Summa*: Parisian Scholastic Theology, 1130–1215," in idem, *Studies in Scholasticism*, XII:16–21, 26–29.

67. Torrell, *Aquinas*, 39–45, 424–26.

68. *Super libros Sententiarum* lib. 1, d. 10 q. 1 a. 4. See also J.-M. Aubert, "'Subtil' et 'subtilité' chez saint Thomas d'Aquin," *Revue du Moyen Âge latin*, 44 (1988): 6–13.

69. *Super libros Sententiarum* lib. 2, d. 19 q. 1 a. 5 expos.

70. *Summa theologiae* 1, a. 1 q. 2 proem.

71. Ibid., q. 29 a. 1 arg. 3. See also Aquinas, *Expositio libri posteriorum* 1, lectio 1 n. 7.

72. See Ralph McInerny, ed., preface to Aquinas, *Commentary on Aristotle's "Posterior Analytics"* (Notre Dame, Ind.: Dumb Ox, 2007), xii–xxviii.

73. *Summa theologiae* 2-2, q. 46 a. 2 co.

74. Aquinas, *De virtutibus* q. 2 a. 12 co.

75. *Super 1 Cor.* chap. 2, lectio 3.

76. *Super Romanos* chap. 8, lectio 4.

77. See chapter 3, pp. 136–37.

78. See chapter 2, pp. 94–97.

79. *Summa theologiae* 1, qq. 44–74. q. 44 aa. 1, 3–4. q. 45 a. 1. qq. 44–74. q. 75.

80. See also Gerard Verbeke, "Man as a 'Frontier' According to Aquinas," in *Aquinas and Problems of His Time*, ed. idem and D. Verheist (Louvain: University Press, 1970), 195–223.

81. *Summa theologiae* 1, q. 4 a. 3. For the controversy about Aquinas's "analogy of being," see Lawrence Dewan, "St. Thomas and Analogy: The Logician and the Metaphysician," in idem, *Form and Being: Studies in Thomistic Metaphysics* (Washington, D.C.: Catholic University of America Press, 2006), 81–95. My translation here of *aliqualis* is "some other," not "some."

82. *Summa theologiae* 1.

83. A. N. Williams, *The Divine Sense: The Intellect in Patristic Theology* (Cambridge: Cambridge University Press, 2007), 2–6, 235, 237, 232, 32. This notes Aquinas's lack of attention to a divine mind but suggests the influence of Aristotle's equation of divine substance with intellect, 232.

84. See chapter 3, p. 113.

85. Gen. 1:4, 10, 12, 18, 21, 25, 31.

86. *Summa theologiae* 1, q. 36 a. 1.

87. Ibid., q. 3 a. 1 ad 2.

88. Ibid., q. 75 proem.
89. For soul from *psuyhē*, see Werner Jaeger, *Die Theologie der frühen griechischen Denker* (Stuttgart: W. Kohlhammer, 1953), 88–106.
90. *Summa theologiae* I, q. 75 a. 1.
91. Plato, *Timaeus* 69e–70d, and see 65d; 44d, 45a.
92. *Summa theologiae* I, q. 76 a. 3.
93. Ibid., q. 75 a. 2. qq. 77–86. q. 90 aa.1, 2, 3.
94. Ibid., q. 91 a. 4; and see q. 76 a. 1.
95. Ibid., q. 93 proem. a. 4. See chapter 3, pp. 111-15, 145. *Summa theologiae* I, q. 93 proem. a. 5.
96. *Summa theologiae* I, q. 93 a. 6, referring to 1 Cor. 11:7.
97. *Super Ephesios* chap. 4 lectio 7.
98. *Summa theologiae* I, q. 76 a. 3.
99. Ibid., q. 93 a. 6. Mark 12:1–14.
100. Marjorie O'Rourke Boyle, *Divine Domesticity: Augustine of Thagaste to Teresa of Ávila* (Leiden: E. J. Brill, 1997), 98–100.
101. *Summa theologiae* I, q. 93 a. 9, citing Augustine, *De diversis quaestionibus octoginta tribus* q. 51, ed. Almut Mutzenbecher (Turnhout: Brepols, 1975), 81.
102. *Summa theologiae* I, q. 1.
103. Ibid., q. 94 a .1. See also *De veritate* q. 18.
104. *Summa theologiae* I, q. 88 a 3.
105. *Summa contra Gentiles* 4, chap. 16 n. 6. chap. 20 n. 2. chap. 23 n. 7.
106. Aquinas, *Quaestio disputata de potentia Dei* q. 4 a. 1 ad 2. For Attic Moses, see James Kugel, *The Idea of Biblical Poetry: Parallelism and Its History* (New Haven: Yale University Press, 1981), 143–45; Alice Swift Riginos, *Platonica: The Anecdotes Concerning the Life and Writings of Plato* (Leiden: E. J. Brill, 1976), 64–65.
107. *Summa theologiae* I, q. 66 a. 1. q. 74 a. 3 ad 3, 4, citing Moses Maimonides, *Guide for the Perplexed* 2.30.
108. Hagiga 12a, in *The Hebrew-English Edition of the Babylonian Talmud: Ḥagigah*, trans. Israel Abrahams, ed. I. Epstein (London: Soncino, 1984). See chapter 1, 16.
109. For the elements, see Joseph Bobick, *Aquinas on Matter and Form and the Elements* (Notre Dame: University of Notre Dame Press, 1998), 171–83.

110. *Summa theologiae* I, q. 74 a. 3 ad 4.
111. Ibid., q. 38. See in general Gilles Emery, *The Trinitarian Theology of St. Thomas Aquinas*, trans. Francesca Aran Murphy (Oxford: Oxford University Press, 2007).
112. *Summa theologiae* I, q. 43 aa. 3, 7.
113. Ibid., q. 8 a. 3.
114. *Super 1 Corinthianos* chap. 3 lectio 3.
115. *Summa theologiae* I, q. 12 a. 3. q. 78 a. 3.
116. Aquinas, *In Aristotelis "De anima"* 2.7. For materialism and sensation, see Robert Pasnau, *Thomas Aquinas on Human Nature: A Philosophical Study of "Summa theologiae" 1a, 75–89* (Cambridge: Cambridge University Press, 2002), 58–60. For the extromissive theory, see David C. Lindberg, *Theories of Vision from al-Kindi to Kepler* (Chicago: University of Chicago Press, 1976).
117. *Summa theologiae* I, q. 12 a. 4.
118. Ibid., aa. 6, 9, 11.
119. Herbert Grabbes, *The Mutable Glass: Mirror-Imagery in Titles and Texts of the Middle Ages and English Renaissance* (Cambridge: Cambridge University Press 1982).
120. See chapter 3, pp. 121.
121. See Alasdair MacIntyre, "Intractable Moral Disagreements," in *Intractable Disputes About the Natural Law: Alasdair MacIntyre and Critics*, ed. Lawrence S. Cunningham (Notre Dame: University of Notre Dame Press, 2009), 15–16, citing *Summa theologiae* 2-1, q. 14 a. 3.
122. Aquinas, *Quaestiones de quodlibet* 8, q. 9 a. 1. Aristotle, *Ethica Nicomachea* 104 1174b. For those disputes, see Torell, *Aquinas*, 207–12; Kevin White, "The Quodlibeta of Thomas Aquinas in the Context of His Work," in *Theological "Quodlibeta" in the Middle Ages*, vol. 1, *The Thirteenth Century*, ed. Christopher Schabel (Leiden: Brill, 2006), 49–134; Wippel, in Bazàn et al., *Questions disputés et quodlibétiques*, 151–201; Jacqueline Hamesse, "Theological *quaestiones quodlibetales*," in *Theological "Quodlibeta,"* vol. 1, 17–48.
123. Aquinas, *De malo* q. 16 a. 6, in idem, *De malo*, ed. Brian Davies (Oxford: Oxford University Press, 2003).

124. *De veritate* q. 8 a. 2. q. 10 a. 11. q. 13 a. 3.
125. See chapter 2, pp. 101–2, 103.
126. *De veritate* q. 14 a. 8.
127. *Summa theologiae* 2-2, q. 8 a. 7.
128. Ibid., q. 175 a. 1.
129. Ibid., a. 2.
130. Ibid., a. 3.
131. *Summa theologiae* 1, q. 12 a. 11.
132. Ibid., a. 3.
133. Ibid.
134. See chapter 1.
135. Aquinas, *Super Isaiam* chap. 40. Is. 40:29–31.
136. Torrell, *Aquinas*, 27–35.
137. *Super Isaiam* chap. 40.
138. *Super Iob* chap. 39.
139. Aquinas, *Super Iohannem* proem.
140. Aquinas, *In psalmos* 26 n. 4. Ps. 91:4.
141. Ibid., and Aquinas, *Super Titum* proem. Deut. 32:11.
142. *Super Isaiam* chap. 31. Deut. 32:11.
143. For that translation, see Torrell, *Aquinas*, 431.
144. *Super Iob* chap. 39.
145. *Summa theologiae* 2-2, q. 175 aa. 1–4.
146. Torrell, *Aquinas*, 288–89.
147. "The Astronomer," in Aesop's *Fables*; Plato, *Theatetus* 174a; Diogenes Laertius, *Vitae philosophorum* 1.1.
148. *Summa theologiae* 2-2, q. 175 a. 1, aa. 5–6. 2 Cor. 12:2–3.
149. *De veritate* 13. For this work, see Torrell, *Aquinas*, 59–67.
150. *De veritate* 1.
151. See also *Super 1 Cor.* chap. 2, lectio 2.
152. Aquinas, *De creaturis spiritualibus* a. 2, in *Tractatus de spiritualibus creaturis*, ed. Leo W. Keeler (Rome: Pontifical Gregorian University, 1937).
153. *Super libros Sententiarum* lib. 4 d. 44 q. 3 a. 3 qc. 3 co.
154. Otto H. Pesch, "Paul as Professor of Theology: The Image of the Apostle in St. Thomas's Theology," *The Thomist* 38 (1974): 584–85, 589–90, 592.
155. *Summa contra Gentiles* 3, chap. 59 n. 7. For this work, see Torrell, *Aquinas*, 96–116.
156. *Summa contra Gentiles* 4, chap. 17 n. 7.
157. Gilles Emery, "Trinity and Creation," trans. Patrick I. Martin, in *Theology of Aquinas*, 58–76, citing at 59 *Super libros Sententiarum* lib. 1 d. 14 q. 1 art. 1.
158. *Summa contra Gentiles* 4, chap. 17 nn. 8–9.
159. *Super 1 Cor.*, chap. 2 lectio 2.
160. *Summa theologiae* 1, q. 57 a. 4. See *De malo* q. 16 a. 1 ad 16. *Summa theologiae* 1, q. 57 a. 5.
161. *De malo* q. 16 a. 7 s.c. 2. For the work, see Davies, ed., *De malo*, 3–53.
162. *De malo* a. 8 a. 11.
163. *Summa theologiae* 1, q. 107 a. 1 ad 1.
164. Aquinas, *Quodlibet* 9, q. 8 a. 1.
165. *Super Iob*, chap. 3.
166. *Summa theologiae* 1, q. 2 proem. q. 12 a 1.
167. Aristotle, *Metaphysica* 1 982b.
168. Torrell, *Aquinas*, 154, citing *Summa contra Gentiles* 3.25; Aquinas, *Sententiae super Metaphysicam* 1, lectio 1 n. 4.
169. *Summa theologiae* 2-2, q. 23 a. 2 ad 2.
170. *De veritate* q. 10 a. 10.
171. *Summa contra Gentiles* 4, chap. 20 n. 6.
172. *Super Iob* chap. 26.
173. Torrell, *Aquinas*, 154–55, citing *Summa contra Gentiles* 2, chap. 46.
174. *Processus canonizationis s. Thomae, Neapoli* 79, ed. M.-H. Laurent, fascicule 4 of *Fontes vitae s. Thomae Aquinatis*, ed. Dominic M. Prümmer (Toulouse, 1912–37), 376–77. See Marjorie O'Rourke Boyle, "Chaff: Thomas Aquinas's Repudiation of His *Opera omnia*," *New Literary History* 28 (1997): 383–99.
175. Boyle, *Setting of the "Summa theologiae"*; Torrell, *Aquinas*, 158–59.
176. Boyle, "Chaff," 385.
177. Ibid.
178. *De veritate* q. 26 a. 10.
179. Boyle, "Chaff."
180. *S. Thomae Aquinatis vitae fontes praecipuae*, ed. Angelico Ferrua (Alba: Edizione domenicane, 1968), 362–63. Torrell, *Aquinas*, 253.
181. Erasmus, *Antibarbari*, ed. Kazimiercz Kumaniecki, in *Opera omnia* (Amsterdam: North-Holland, 1971–), 1-1:134.
182. Erasmus, ed., *Novum testamentum*, in *Opera omnia*, ed. Jean Leclerc, 11 vols. (Leiden, 1703), vol. 6.

183. Erasmus, *Erasmi epistolae*, ed. P. S. Allen et al., 12 vols. (Oxford: Clarendon, 1906–58), 1:407–12.
184. Erasmus, *Ratio seu methodus perveniendi ad veram theologiam*, in *Ausgewählte Werke*, ed. Hajo Holborn with Annemarie Holborn (Munich: C. H. Beck, 1964), 294.
185. Erasmus, *Ecclesiastes, sive concionator evangelicus*, in *Opera omnia*, ed. Leclerc, 5:799–800.
186. Erasmus, *Ratio*, 180, 193, 183.
187. *Summa theologiae* 1, q. 4 art. 1 ad 1, citing Gregory the Great, *Moralia in Iob* 5.36.66, ed. Mark Adrian, 3 vols. (Turnhout: Brepols, 1979–85), 1:265.
188. Boyle, "Chaff."

CHAPTER 5

1. John Calvin, *Commentarius in Genesin*, in *Commentariorum in quinque libros Mosis*, in *Opera quae supersunt omnia*, ed. Eduard Reuss, Eduard Cunitz, and Johann Wilhelm Baum, 59 vols. in 26 (Brunswick: C. A. Schwetsche, 1863–1900), 23:11. All references are to this edition of Calvin's *Opera* unless otherwise cited. A critical edition of Calvin's *Opera*, ed. Helmut Feld et al., is in progress at Geneva: Droz, 1994–. For an introduction to his biblical commentaries, see *Calvin and the Bible*, ed. Donald K. McKim (Cambridge: Cambridge University Press, 2006); R. Ward Holder, *John Calvin and the Grounding of Interpretation: Calvin's First Commentaries* (Leiden: E. J. Brill, 2006). All translations in this chaper are mine unless otherwise stated.
2. Jean Calvin, *Sermons sur la Genèse: Chapitres 1,1–11,4*, ed. Max Engammare (Neukirchen-Vluyn: Neukirchener Verlag, 2000), 1.
3. See chapter 1, pp. 18, 46.
4. Calvin, *Institutio christianae religionis* 1.16–18, 2:144–74. For his theology in general, see Paul Helm, *Calvin at the Centre* (Oxford: Oxford University Press, 2010); Charles Partee, *The Theology of John Calvin* (Louisville, Ky.: Westminster John Knox, 2008); Richard A. Muller, *The Unaccommodated Calvin: Studies in the Foundation of a Theological Tradition* (New York: Oxford University Press, 2000).
5. *Institutio christianae religionis* 1.16.2, col. 145. Ex. 21:13.
6. Jean-Pierre Torrell, *Saint Thomas Aquinas*, vol. 1, *The Person and His Work*, trans. Robert Royal, rev. ed. (Washington, D.C.: Catholic University of America Press, 2005), 290.
7. For recent biographies, see Bruce Gordon, *John Calvin* (New Haven: Yale University Press, 2009); Herman J. Selderhuis, *John Calvin: A Pilgrim's Life*, trans. Albert Gootjes (Downers Grove, Ill.: Inter-Varsity Press, 2009); for a character portrayal, see William J. Bouwsma, *John Calvin: A Sixteenth-Century Portrait* (New York: Oxford University Press, 1988).
8. Calvin, *Commentarius in psalmos*, in *Opera* 31:13, 15. For rhetorical modesty, see Ernst R. Curtius, *European Literature and the Latin Middle Ages*, trans. Willard R. Trask (London: Routledge and Kegan Paul, 1953), 83–85.
9. *In psalmos*, 31:15.
10. *Oxford English Dictionary*, 2nd ed. (1989), s.v. "anatomy."
11. *In psalmos*, 31:21. For that self-portrait, see "Calvinus ad senatui Francofordiensi," in *Epistolae*, in *Opera omnia*, 15:712. See also Barbara Pitkin, "Imitation of David: David as Paradigm for Faith in Calvin's Exegesis of the Psalms," *Sixteenth Century Journal* 24 (1993): 843–63; and in general, Francis Higman, "Calvin et l'expérience," in *Expérience, coutume, tradition au temps de la Renaissance*, ed. M. T. Jones-Davies (Paris: Klincksieck, 1992), 245–56.
12. Marjorie O'Rourke Boyle, *Senses of Touch: Human Dignity and Deformity from Michelangelo to Calvin* (Leiden: Brill, 1998), 177.
13. *Opera*, 23:74–84, 641–740, 25–29; 32:451–752; 33–35; 36:235–432; 41:305–688; 42:1–174; 46:1–826, 829–968; 48:577–664; 49:577–830; 50:269–696; 51:241–862; 52:219–38; 53; 54:1–596; 58:2–206. For an introduction, see T. H. L. Parker, *Calvin's Preaching* (Louisville, Ky.: Westminster John Knox, 1992).
14. *In psalmos*, 31:21.
15. Alexandre Ganoczy, *The Young Calvin*, trans. David Foxglove and Wade

Provo (Philadelphia: Westminster, 1987), 66–70; Boyle, *Senses of Touch*, 229.

16. *In psalmos*, 31:21, 23.

17. For the argument, see Muller, *Unaccommodated Calvin*, 78–98. The discussion has ignored the distinction between a labyrinth and a maze, the actual labyrinth at Amiens, and Calvin's metaphorical complex of entry and exit, bends and turns, lameness, fatigue, the guiding rope, and circling out.

18. Marjorie O'Rourke Boyle, "Reprising Terence's Plot: William Harvey's Soliloquy to the College of Physicians," *Medical History* 52 (2008): 378–79.

19. Ibid.

20. Vergil, *Aeneid* 5.546–604.

21. See Abel Lefranc, *Histoire de la ville de Noyon et des ses institutions jusqu'à la fin du XIIIe siècle* (Paris, 1887), 1–2.

22. See Abel Lefranc, *La jeunesse de Calvin* (Paris: Fischbacher, 1888), 2–3, 7.

23. Hermann Kern, *Through the Labyrinth: Designs and Meanings over 5,000 Years*, trans. Abigail Clay (Munich: Prestel, 2000), 148–49, 191.

24. *Institutio christianae religionis* 1.5.12, col. 49.

25. Ibid., 1.5.15, col. 51; 1.13.19, col. 106; 1.13.21, col. 108; 3.25.11, col. 743; 3.2.2, col. 398; 3.2.7, cols. 402–3. See also 1.5.12, col. 49; Calvin, *Commentariorum in Acta apostolorum*, ed. Helmut Feld, 2 vols. (Geneva: Droz, 2001), 2:115–17. For the heart, see the chapter "Jean Calvin: Heart in Hand," in Marjorie O'Rourke Boyle, *Cultural Anatomies of the Heart in Aristotle, Augustine, Aquinas, Calvin, and Harvey* (New York: Palgrave Macmillan, 2018).

26. *Institutio christianae religionis* 3.20.1, col. 626; 1.6.2, col. 54; 3.2.15, col. 410; 3.6.2, col. 502; 3.19.7, col. 617; 1.6.3, col. 55.

27. *In psalmos*, 31:21.

28. *A Latin Dictionary*, ed. Charlton T. Lewis and Charles Short (Oxford: Clarendon, 1969), s.v. *addictus*. See Martin Luther, *De servo arbitrio*, in *Luthers Werke in Auswahl*, ed. Otto Clemens, 6 vols. (Berlin: Walter de Gruyter, 1950), 4:94–293.

29. *Institutio christianae religionis* 4.22.31, col. 1118. 1 Cor. 7:23.

30. *In psalmos*, 31:21.

31. Ganoczy, *Young Calvin*, 49–57, 62–63, 42–44.

32. *In psalmos*, 31:21.

33. Boyle, *Senses of Touch*, 179.

34. Calvin, *In Genesin*, 23:35. See also Calvin, *Commentarii in secundum Pauli epistolam ad Corinthios*, ed. Helmut Feld (Geneva: Droz, 1994), 76–77.

35. *In psalmos*, 31:21.

36. W. Nijenhuis, "Calvin's '*subita conversio*': Notes on a Hypothesis," in idem, *Ecclesia reformata: Studies on the Reformation*, 2 vols. (Leiden: E. J. Brill, 1994), 2:3–23; Heiko A. Oberman, "'*Subita conversio*': The Conversion of John Calvin," in *Reformiertes Erbe: Festschrift für Gottfried W. Locher zu seinem 80. Geburtstag*, ed. idem et al., 2 vols. (Zurich: Theologischer Verlag, 1993), 2:279–95, which also offers "unexpected," rather than "sudden," but still considers it a religious conversion.

37. *In Acta Apostolorum*, 1:263–68.

38. *Institutio christianae religionis* 1.5.6, col. 45.

39. *In psalmos*, 31:25, 27.

40. Calvin, "Discours d'adieu aux membres du petit conseil," in *Opera*, 9:890. "Discours d'adieu aux ministres," cols. 891, 892.

41. *In psalmos*, 31:21.

42. See Sou-Young Lee, "Calvin's Understanding of *Pietas*," in "*Calvinus sincerioris religionis vindex*": *Calvin as Protector of the Purer Religion*, ed. Wilhelm H. Neuser and Brian G. Armstrong (Kirksville, Mo.: Sixteenth Century Journal Publishers, 1997), 225–39; Joel R. Beeke, "Calvin on Piety," in *The Cambridge Companion to Calvin*, ed. Donald K. McKim (Cambridge: Cambridge University Press, 2004), 125–26.

43. *Latin Dictionary*, s.v. *pietas*.

44. Vergil, *Aeneid* 2.708. See, for example, Erasmus, *Querela pacis*, in *Opera omnia*, ed. Jean Leclerc, 11 vols. (Leiden, 1703–6), 4:627.

45. *Institutio christianae religionis* 1.2.1, col. 34.

46. Boyle, *Senses of Touch*, 227–46. In general, see I. John Hesselink, *Calvin's Concept of the Law* (Allison Park, Pa.: Pickwick, 1992); Josef Bohtec, *Calvin und das Recht* (Aalen: Scientia, 1971), 209–79.

47. *Institutio christianae religionis* 1.2.1, col. 34. 2.5.9, cols. 236–37; 1.2.2, col. 35.
48. Calvin, L. *Annaei Senecae ad Neronem Caesarem "de clementia,"* in *Calvin's Commentary on Seneca's "De clementia,"* ed. Ford Lewis Battles and André Malon Hugo (Leiden: E. J. Brill for the Renaissance Society of America, 1969); Olivier Millet, *Calvin et la dynamique de la parole: Étude de rhétorique réformee* (Geneva: Slatkine, 1992), 57–111.
49. In *"De clementia,"* 54, 56. Nijenhuis noted the semantics but out of context, and he interpreted it as Calvin's religious conversion by the Holy Spirit, "Calvin's 'subita conversio,'" 15.
50. In *psalmos*, 31:21–23; for adolescence, 32:218.
51. In *psalmos*, 31:25. See also Heiko A. Oberman, "Calvin and Farel: The Dynamics of Legitimation in Early Calvinism," *Journal of Early Modern History* 2 (1998): 32–60.
52. *Ad 2 Corinthios*, 193.
53. *Institutio christianae religionis* 1.14.4, col. 120.
54. Boyle, *Senses of Touch*, 213–16.
55. In *psalmos* intro., 31:23, 26.
56. Boyle, *Senses of Touch*, 216–18. For Calvin's perseverance, see William Naphy, *Calvin and the Consolidation of the Genevan Reformation* (Louisville, Ky.: Westminster John Knox, 1994).
57. In *Genesin*, 16, 26. For the Trinity, see Philip Walker Butin, *Revelation, Redemption, and Response: Calvin's Trinitarian Understanding of the Divine-Human Relationship* (New York: Oxford University Press, 1995); Werner Krusche, *Die Wirken des Heiligen Geist nach Calvin* (Göttingen: Vandenhoeck & Ruprecht, 1957).
58. See chapter 3, pp. 111–15.
59. *Institutio christianae religionis* 1.6.1, col. 53; 1.14.1, col. 117.
60. In *Genesin*, 16.
61. Boyle, *Senses of Touch*, 176–89.
62. *Sermons sur Genèse*, 1.
63. *Institutio christianae religionis* 1.8.1, cols. 61–62.
64. Max Engammare, *"Joannes Calvinus trium linguarum peritus? La question de l'Hébreu,"* *Bibliothèque d'humanisme et renaissance* 58 (1996): 37–60, 49. For his bibles, see Jean-François Gilmont, *John Calvin and the Printed Book*, trans. Karin Maag (Kirksville, Mo.: Truman State University Press, 2005), 143–53. Davis A. Young, *John Calvin and the Natural World* (Lanham, Md.: University Press of America, 2007), relies for avian knowledge on biblical reference works rather than on scientific ornithology, 108–16.
65. See David L. Puckett, *John Calvin's Exegesis of the Old Testament* (Louisville, Ky.: Westminster John Knox, 1995), 55–64. See also Karin Maag, *Seminary or University? The Genevan Academy and Reformed Higher Education, 1560–1620* (Brookfield, Vt.: Scolar, 1995), 13–14; Gillian Lewis, "The Genevan Academy," in *Calvinism in Europe, 1540–1620*, ed. Andrew Petegree, Alastair Duke, and Gillian Lewis (Cambridge: Cambridge University Press, 1994), 35–63.
66. For an introduction, see Jerry H. Bentley, *Humanists and Holy Writ: New Testament Scholarship in the Renaissance* (Princeton: Princeton University Press, 1983).
67. In *Genesin*, 16.
68. Boyle, *Senses of Touch*, 175–87, 250–55.
69. In *Genesin*, 16.
70. Boyle, *Senses of Touch*, 213–26, 175–83.
71. See chapter 1, p. 18.
72. Arnold Williams, *The Common Expositor: An Account of the Commentaries on Genesis, 1527–1633* (Chapel Hill: University of North Carolina Press, 1948), 52.
73. For Calvin's citation of the work, although not that particular reference, see Anthony N. S. Lane, "The Sources of the Citations in Calvin's Genesis Commentary," in idem, *John Calvin: Student of the Church Fathers* (Grand Rapids, Mich.: Baker Books, 1999), 215. See also in general Richard C. Gamble, "The Sources of Calvin's Genesis Commentary: A Preliminary Report," *Archiv für Reformationsgeschichte* 84 (1993): 206–21.
74. See chapter 3, p. 113.
75. Engammare, ed., *Sermons sur Genèse*, II n. 1.
76. *Institutio christianae religionis* 1.13.14, col. 102.
77. See in general Richard Stauffer, *Dieu, la création, et la providence dans la*

prédication de Calvin (Berne: Peter Lang, 1978), 177–259.
  78. Young, *Calvin and the Natural World*.
  79. *Sermons sur Genèse*, 1, 7–8, 9–10.
  80. *In Acta Apostolorum,*, 1:48.
  81. *Sermons sur Genèse*, 10.
  82. See chapter 1, p. 18.
  83. *Sermons sur Genèse*, 10–11.
  84. Max Engammare, "Calvin connaissait-il la Bible? Les citations de l'Écriture dans ses sermons sur la Genèse," *Bulletin de la Société d'Histoire du Protestantisme Français* 141 (1995): 163–84.
  85. *Sermons sur Genèse*, 10–11.
  86. Aristotle, *Historia Animalium* 8.32 619b; idem, *History of Animals Books 7–10*, ed. and trans. D. M. Balme (Cambridge, Mass.: Harvard University Press, 1991), 303.
  87. See Jon Balserak, *Divinity Compromised: A Study of Divine Accommodation in the Thought of John Calvin* (Dordrecht: Springer, 2006); Arnold Huijgen, "Divine Accommodation and Divine Transcendence in John Calvin's Theology," in *"Calvinus sacrarum literarum interpres": Papers of the International Congress on Calvin Research*, ed. Herman J. Selderhuis (Göttingen: Vandenhoeck & Ruprecht, 2008), 119–30; Millet, *Calvin et parole*, 247–56.
  88. Calvin, *Harmoniam in Pentateuchem*, 25:362, 363, 364. See in general Stephen G. Burnett, "Calvin's Jewish Interlocutor: Christian Hebraism and Anti-Jewish Polemics During the Reformation," *Bibliothèque d'humanisme et renaissance* 55 (1993): 113–23.
  89. Aristotle, *Historia animalium* 9.32 618b. See also J. R. T. Pollard, "The Lammergeyer: Comparative Descriptions in Aristotle and Pliny," *Greece and Rome* 16 (1947): 23–28.
  90. *Sermons sur Job*, 432. Davis, *Calvin and the Natural World*, mistranslated Calvin to read that eagles raised only their black chicks. Ibid., 110.
  91. Aristotle, *Historia animalium* 8.32 618b, 619a; trans. Balme, 301. See also 8.3 592a; 8.32 619b; and against predators 8.32 619a.
  92. Ibid. 6.6 563a; 8.34 619b–620a; trans. Balme, 303.
  93. Deut. 32:11 Vulg.
  94. Aristotle, *Historia animalium* 8.34 620a.
  95. Davis, *Calvin and Natural World*, 100, citing Calvin's commentary on Hab. 1:8 and his third sermon on Job. 39, and proposing that Calvin had it from Pliny, *Historia naturalis* 1.
  96. *Sermons sur Job*, 35:430–31, 432.
  97. *Commentarii in Isaiam prophetam*, 37:30.
  98. Erasmus, *Adagia*, ed. M. L. van Poll-van de Lisdonk et al., in *Opera omnia* (Amsterdam: North-Holland, 1969–), 2-2:378–79. For Calvin's use of medieval bestiaries, see Davis, *Calvin and the Natural World*, 111–12. However, since Calvin was there explicating proverbs, Erasmus's *Adagia* was probably his resource.
  99. *In Isaiam*, 37:30.
  100. Erasmus, *Adagia*, 2-2:342–43.
  101. *In Isaiam*, 37:30.
  102. *Sermons sur Deutéronome*, 28:658–720. See in general Raymond A. Blacketer, *The School of God: Pedagogy and Rhetoric in Calvin's Interpretation of Deuteronomy* (Dordrecht: Springer, 2006).
  103. *Sermons sur Deutéronome*, 28:695.
  104. See http://flagspot.net/flags/ch-ge.html#symb and http://en.wikipedia.org/wiki/File:Coat_of_Arms_of_Geneva.svg.
  105. See "Switzerland," in Jeff Watson, *The Golden Eagle* (London: T and AD Poyser, 1997), indexed on 373; *Verbreitungsatlas der Brutvögel der Schweiz / Atlas des oiseaux nicheurs de Suisse*, ed. Alfred Schifferli, Paul Géroudet, and Raffael Winkler (Sempach: Schweizerische Vogelwarte, 1982), 102–3. For agreement that Calvin very likely sighted the golden eagle around Geneva, see Davis, *Calvin and the Natural World*, 109.
  106. *Sermons sur Deutéronome*, 694, 696–97.
  107. *Harmoniam in evangelium*, 45:641–43.
  108. See Heiko A. Oberman, "*Europa afflicta*: The Reformation of the Refugees," *Archiv für Reformationsgeschichte* 83 (1992): 102–10.
  109. Calvin, *Discours d'adieu aux membres du petit conseil*, 889.
  110. *Sermons sur Deutéronome*, 696.

111. *In psalmos*, 31:163, 555.
112. *In Isaiam*, 37:155, 399.
113. Engammare, "Calvin connaissait-il la Bible?"; Gilmont, *Calvin and the Printed Book*, 143, 146–47.
114. *Institutio christianae religionis* 1.13.14–15, cols. 101–2. For the Spirit's dynamism in humans, see also Butin, *Revelation, Redemption, Response*, 76–94.
115. *Sermon sur Genèse*, 2–3.
116. Engammare, "Calvin connaissait-il la Bible?," 170.
117. *In Genesin*, 16.
118. *In psalmos*, 32:96. For Manichaean error, see also *Institutio christianae religionis* 1.15.5, cols. 139–40. For Servet's denial of the Trinity, see 1.13.22, col. 108.
119. *In psalmos*, 32:95.
120. Calvin, *Psychopannychia*, 5:165–232. See George H. Tavard, *The Starting Point of Calvin's Theology* (Grand Rapids, Mich.: W. B. Eerdmans, 2000), 1–112.
121. *Institutio christianae religionis* 1.15.2, col. 135.
122. *Sermons sur Genèse*, 61–62.
123. Calvin, *Commentarius in epistolam Pauli ad Thessalonicenses 1*, 52:179.
124. *Institutio christianae religionis* 1.15.6, cols. 140–42. See also 1.5.5, col. 44. *In psalmos*, 31:264, 688; 32:249; *Sermons sur Deutéronome*, 26:434; *In Philippenses*, ed. Helmut Feld, in *Opera omnia* (Geneva), 16:375. Calvin, *Institutio christianae religionis* 1.15.7, col. 142; 2.2.2, cols. 186–87; 1.16.3, cols. 146–47.
125. *In Genesin*, 35.
126. *In Isaiam*, 36:77.
127. *In Genesin*, 35–36.
128. *Sermons sur Genèse*, 97.
129. *Institutio christianae religionis* 1.15.2, cols. 135–36; 1.3.3, col. 38.
130. Ibid., 1.15.2, col. 136. For Plato and immortality, see Charles Partee, *Calvin and Classical Philosophy* (Leiden: E. J. Brill, 1977), 61–65.
131. *Institutio christianae religionis* 1.15.3, cols. 137–38. For his praise of the body, see Boyle, *Senses of Touch*, 172–75.
132. *Institutio christianae religionis* 1.15.4, col. 138. Boyle, *Senses of Touch*, 175–81. For all creatures as mirrors of God, see 1.14.21, col. 132. See also Brian A. Gerrish, "The Mirror of God's Goodness: A Key Metaphor in Calvin's View of Man," in idem, *The Old Protestantism and the New: Essays on the Reformation Heritage* (Chicago: University of Chicago Press, 1982), 150–62. However, the mirror was cracked and shattered glass. See below in this chapter, p. 232.
133. *Institutio christianae religionis* 2.1.5, col. 179; 1.15.4, col. 138.
134. See chapter 4, pp. 161–63.
135. *Institutio christianae religionis* 1.15.4, cols. 138–39.
136. Ibid., col. 139.
137. *In Genesin*, 25.
138. *Institutio christianae religionis* 1.15.4, col. 139. 1.1.1, col. 32. See also 1.5.3, col. 43; 1.5.9, cols. 47–48; 1.5.14, col. 52; 1.15.5, col. 140; 1.16.1, col. 145; 1.16.4, col. 148.
139. *In Acta Apostolorum*, 2:115–17.
140. Ibid., 117–18.
141. Boyle, *Senses of Touch*, 253.
142. *In Acta Apostolorum*, 2:124–25. Paul's a fortiori argument here is recognized by Paul Helm, *John Calvin's Ideas* (Oxford: Oxford University Press, 2004), 216, 233. However, Calvin did not interpret Paul's argument on spirits in 1 Cor. 2:11 as a fortiori. See below in this chapter, pp. 223–24.
143. *Sermons sur Genèse*, 3, 61.
144. *In Acta Apostolorum*, 2:125 citing Vergil, *Aeneid* 6.726. See also *Institutio christianae religionis* 1.5.5, col. 45.
145. Jan M. Ziolkowski and Michael C. J. Putnam, *The Virgilian Tradition: The First Fifteen Hundred Years* (New Haven: Yale University Press, 2008), 111.
146. See above, p. 195.
147. See above, n. 144.
148. *In Acta Apostolorum*, 2:125–26, citing Vergil, *Aeneid* 6.726; Gen. 1:27; Gal. 3:26. See also *Institutio christianae religionis* 1.5.5, col. 15; 1.14.1, col. 117.
149. Boyle, *Senses of Touch*, 232–33, 226–27, 234–35.
150. Ibid., 220.
151. Calvin, *In Hebraeos*, ed. T. H. L. Parker, in *Opera omnia* (Geneva), p. 63.
152. Boyle, *Senses of Touch*, 220.
153. *Sermons sur Job*, 34:454, 455, 456.
154. *Institutio christianae religionis* 2.2.20, col. 202; 3.2.34, col. 426.
155. *Commentarius in epistolam Pauli ad Corinthios 1*, 49:341. See also *Institutio christianae religionis* 3.2.34, col. 426.
156. *In 1 Corinthios*, 341–42.
157. Francis M. Higman, *The Style of John Calvin in His French Polemical Treatises* (Oxford: Oxford University

Press, 1967), 17–20, 87–88. For antithesis, see also Millet, *Calvin et parole*, 659–708.

158. Partee, *Theology of John Calvin*, 128.

159. See Moshe Barasch, "Renaissance Color Conventions: Liturgy, Humanism, Workshops," in idem, *"Imago hominis": Studies in the Language of Art* (Vienna: IRS, 1991), 174.

160. *Institutio christianae religionis* 1.5.10, col. 48. For the legitimacy and abuse of art, see 1.11.12, col. 83. 4.17.24, cols. 1023–24.

161. *In psalmos*, 31:31.

162. *Sermons sur Job*, 33:447, cited by Susan Schreiner, "Calvin as an Interpreter of Job," in *Calvin and the Bible*, 81.

163. *Institutio christianae religionis* 3.10.2, col. 530.

164. *Latin Dictionary*, s.v. *color*; see also s.v. *fuco*. For medieval usage of "color," see James J. Murphy, *Rhetoric in the Middle Ages: A History of Rhetorical Theory from Saint Augustine to the Renaissance* (Berkeley: University of California Press, 1974), 189.

165. *In Genesin*, 16.

166. *Institutio christianae religionis* 1.5.12, col. 50; 1.15.3, col. 177.

167. *Harmoniam in pentateuchem*, 24:167.

168. *In psalmos*, 31:446.

169. *In Acta Apostolorum*, 1:261; *In psalmos*, 32:167; *In Hebraeos*, 164; *Homiliae in primum librum Samuelis*, 30:167. For *couleur*, see also Higman, *Style of John Calvin*, 68–69.

170. *Harmonia in evangelias*, 45:94.

171. See Chaim Perelman and Lucie Olbrechts-Tyteca, *The New Rhetoric: A Treatise on Argumentation*, trans. John Wilkenson and Purcell Weaver (Notre Dame: Notre Dame University Press, 1969).

172. *In 2 Corinthios*, 50. See also Millet, *Calvin et parole*, 389–429.

173. *Institutio christianae religionis* 1.1.3, col. 33. Boyle, *Senses of Touch*, 218–19.

174. Aristotle, *Rhetorica* 3.9.7–8 1409b–1410a; Quintilian, *Institutio oratoria* 9.3.81.

175. René Verbraeken, *Clair-Obscur: Histoire d'un mot* (Nogent-le-Roi: Librairie des arts et métiers, 1979), 9, 83, 101–2, 118. See also Peter Burke, *The Fortunes of the "Courtier"* (Cambridge: Polity, 1995), 63–64.

176. Marcia B. Hall, *Color and Meaning: Practice and Theory in Renaissance Painting* (Cambridge: Cambridge University Press, 1992), 240, 47–48, 50, 53, 67, 94, 237. See also James Ackerman, "Alberti's Light," in *Studies in Late Medieval and Renaissance Painting in Honor of Millard Meiss*, ed. Irving Lavin and John Plummer, 2 vols. (New York: New York University Press, 1977): 1:1–27; Moshe Barasch, "The Colour Scale in Renaissance Thought," in *"Romanica et occidentialia": Études dediées à la memoire du Hiram Peri*, ed. Moshé Lazar (Jerusalem: Magnes Press, Hebrew University, 1963), 74–79.

177. Walter L. Strauss, *"Chiaroscuro": The Clair-Obscur Woodcuts by the German and Netherlandish Masters of the Sixteenth and Seventeenth Centuries: A Complete Catalogue with Commentary* (Greenwich, Conn.: New York Graphic Society, 1973). See also Dieter Graf and Hermann Mildenberger, *"Chiaroscuro": Italienische Farbholzschnitte der Renaissance und des Barock* (Berlin: G & H, 2001); Marta Cencillo Ramírez, *Das Helldunkel in der italienischen Kunsttheorie des 15. und 16. Jahrhunderts und seine Darstellungsmöglichkeiten im Notturno* (Münster: LIT, 2001).

178. See Raymond Klibansky, Erwin Panofsky, and Fritz Saxl, *Saturn and Melancholy: Studies in the History of Natural Philosophy, Religion, and Art* (London: Nelson, 1964).

179. Erasmus, *De recta latini graecique sermonis pronuntiatione*, ed. Maria Cytowska, in *Opera omnia* (Amsterdam), 1–4:40; "The Right Way of Speaking Latin and Greek: A Dialogue," trans. Maurice Pope, in *The Collected Works of Erasmus* (Toronto: University of Toronto Press, 1974), 26:399. See Pliny, *Historia naturalis* 35.97.

180. Strauss, *"Chiaroscuro,"* 159.

181. Aertgen van Leyden(?), Church Sermon, Amsterdam, Rijksmuseum. Henk van Os, Jan Piet Fildet Kok, Get Luijten, and Frits Scholten, *Netherlandish Art in the Rijksmuseum*, 4 vols., vol. 1, *1400–1600* (Zwolle: Waanders; Amsterdam: Rijksmuseum, 2000–2009), 39c, 128.

182. Erasmus, *De libero arbitrio, diatribē sive collatio*, ed. Johannes von Walter

(Leipzig, 1910), 87; idem, *Hyperaspistes diatribae adversus servum arbitrium Martini Lutheri*, in *Opera omnia* (Leiden), 10:1464–65. Marjorie O'Rourke Boyle, "Stoic Luther: Paradoxical Sin and Necessity," *Archiv für Reformationsgeschichte* 73 (1982): 78–79.

183. See Rensselaer W. Lee, "*Ut pictura poesis*": *The Humanistic Theory of Painting* (New York: W. W. Norton, 1967); John R. Spencer, "*Ut pictura poesis*," *Journal of the Warburg and Courtauld Institutes* 20 (1951): 26–44; Michael Baxandall, *Giotto and the Orators: Humanist Observers of Painting in Italy and the Discovery of Pictorial Composition, 1350–1450* (Oxford: Clarendon, 1971), 33–44; Terence Cave, "*Enargeia*: Erasmus and the Rhetoric of Presence in the 16th Century," *L'Esprit créateur* 16 (1976): 5–19; Carl Goldstein, "Rhetoric and Art History in the Italian Renaissance and Baroque," *Art Bulletin* 73 (1991): 641–48; Brian Vickers, *In Defense of Rhetoric* (Oxford: Clarendon, 1988), 340–60; David Summers, *Michelangelo and the Language of Art* (Princeton: Princeton University Press, 1981), 88–89; Moshe Barasch, *Giotto and the Language of Art* (Cambridge: Cambridge University Press, 1987); Caroline van Eck, *Classical Rhetoric and the Visual Arts in Early Modern Europe* (Cambridge: Cambridge University Press, 2007); Christopher Braider, "The Paradoxical Sisterhood: '*Ut pictura poesis*,'" in *The Cambridge History of Literary Criticism*, vol. 3, *The Renaissance*, ed. Glyn P. Norton (Cambridge: Cambridge University Press, 1999), 168–75.

184. Aristotle, *Rhetorica* 3.9.7 1409b–1410a.

185. Quintilian, *Institutio oratoria* 8.4.9, 8.6.67; Quintilian, *The Orator's Education: Books 6–8*, trans. Donald A. Russell (Cambridge, Mass.: Harvard University Press, 2001), 465.

186. *Rhetorica ad C. Herrenium* 4.4, 4.67.

187. *In psalmos*, 32:62. For hyperbole, see also Millet, *Calvin et parole*, 351–61.

188. Quintilian, *Institutio oratoria* 8.6.67; trans., p. 469. See also Cicero, *Topica* 10; *De oratore* 2.267.

189. *Sermons sur Deutéronome*, 26:600–601.

190. Aristotle, *Rhetorica* 3.11.16 1413a; *The Complete Works of Aristotle: The Revised Oxford Translation*, trans. Julian Barnes, 2 vols. (Princeton: Princeton University Press, 1984), 2:2255.

191. See David C. Lindberg, *Theories of Vision from al-Kindi to Kepler* (Chicago: University of Chicago Press, 1976), 8, cf. 116.

192. *Institutio christianae religionis* 1.1.2, cols. 32–33.

193. Ibid., 2.5.5, col. 233. 4.20.32, col. 1118. praef., col. 11.

194. Ibid., 2.1.10–11, cols. 184–85.

195. Ibid., 2.1.8–9, cols. 182–83; 3.3.12, cols. 442–43; 3.3.10, 441; cf. *Sermons sur Deutéronome*, 26:374.

196. *Institutio christianae religionis* 4.3.9, cols. 463–64.

197. *Harmoniam in Pentateuchem*, 24:86.

198. *Institutio christianae religionis* 2.16.2, col. 368; 2.2.11, col. 195.

199. Amélie Oksenberg Rorty, "Structuring Rhetoric," in *Essays on Aristotle's Rhetoric*, ed. idem (Berkeley: University of California Press, 1966), 2.

200. *Institutio christianae religionis* 2.16.2, col. 369.

201. See Leonard Barkin, "Making Pictures Speak: Renaissance Art, Elizabethan Literature, Modern Scholarship," *Renaissance Quarterly* 48 (1995): 326–51; Mary E. Hazard, "The Anatomy of 'Liveliness' as a Concept in Renaissance Aesthetics," *Journal of Aesthetics and Art Criticism* 33 (1975): 407–18. See also G. Zanker, "*Enargeia* in the Ancient Criticism of Poetry," *Rheinisches Museum für Philologie* 124 (1981): 297–311; Heinrich Lausberg, *Handbuch der literarischen Rhetorik: Eine Grundlegung der Literaturwissenschaft*, 2 vols. (Munich: Max Hueber, 1960), 1:paragraphs 810–19. D. P. Fowler, "Narrate and Describe: The Problem of Ekphrasis," *Journal of Roman Studies* 81 (1991): 25–35; James A. W. Heffernan, "*Ekphrasis* and Representation," *New Literary History* 22 (1991): 297–316.

202. Quintilian, *Institutio oratoria* 6.2.32.

203. Cicero, *In Verrem* 2.5.106–22.

204. See Jakob Wisse, *Ethos and Pathos: From Aristotle to Cicero* (Amsterdam: Hakkert, 1989), 65–76.

205. See *Paul and "Pathos,"* ed. Thomas H. Olbricht and Jerry L. Sumney (Atlanta: Society of Biblical Literature, 2001), 97–179.
206. David Konstan, *The Emotions of the Ancient Greeks: Studies in Aristotle and Classical Literature* (Toronto: University of Toronto Press, 2006), 156–68.
207. See *In "De beneficiis,"* 49.
208. Cicero, *Pro Plancio* 33.80.
209. *Institutio christianae religionis* 2.16.2, col. 369.
210. Boyle, *Senses of Touch*, 227–29.
211. *In 1 Corinthios*, 342.
212. Boyle, *Senses of Touch*, 250–55.
213. Calvin to Fallesio, January 24, 1546, in *Epistolae*, 12:258.
214. Calvin to Lord Galliazo Carracciolo, in ibid., 16:12.
215. *In 1 Corinthios*, 49:514.
216. *Institutio christianae religionis* 2.14.7, col. 358. 2.16.13, col. 380.
217. Ibid., 1.1.1, cols. 31–33; 1.15.1, cols. 134–35; 2.1.1–3, cols. 175–209.
218. Ibid., 1.3.1–3, cols. 36–38, 1.10.3, col. 74; *Homiliae in Samuelem 1*, 30:36; *Institutio christianae religionis* 1.3.2, cols. 36–37; 1.4.1, cols. 38–39; 1.4.2, col. 39; 1.4.4, cols. 40–41. For another interpretation of *sensus divinitas*, see recently Helm, *Calvin's Ideas*, 218–45.
219. *Institutio christianae religionis* 1.13.14, col. 102; 1.5.5, cols. 44–45.
220. *In Johannum*, 11–1:19–20.
221. *Institutio christianae religionis* 1.7.5, col. 60; 3.2.36, col. 428.
222. See chapter 2, pp. 90–91.
223. See William C. Innes, *Social Concern in Calvin's Geneva*, ed. Susan Cembalisty Innes (Allison Park, Pa.: Pickwick, 1983), 193.
224. *In 2 Corinthios*, pp. 76–77. Cf. chapter 2, pp. 90–91.
225. *Latin Dictionary*, s.v. *obsigno*.
226. Boyle, *Senses of Touch*, 228–29.
227. *Institutio christianae religionis* 1.7.5, col. 60.
228. Calvin, *In Galatas*, ed. Helmut Feld, in *Opera omnia* (Geneva), 16:94–95.
229. *Harmonia in Pentateuchem*, 25:54.
230. Aristotle, *Physica* 1.8 192b. *De partibus animalium* 3.4 666a, b. Calvin studied at the Collège de Monaigu in Paris, a renowned center of dynamics and kinematics. See Marcel Godet, *La congrégation de Montaigu (1490–1580)*

(Paris: H. Champion, 1912); Augustin Renaudet, *Préréforme et humanisme à Paris pendant les premières guerres d'Italie (1498–1517)*, 2nd rev. ed. (Paris: Librairie d'Argences, 1953), 267–72; Hubert Elie, "Quelques maîtres de l'Université de Paris vers l'an 1500," *Archives d'historie doctrinale et littéraire du Moyen Age*, 18–19 (1950–51): 222–24; Millet, *Calvin et parole*, 30–34. See also Christopher B. Kaiser, "Calvin's Understanding of Aristotelian Natural Philosophy: Its Extent and Possible Origins," in *Calviniana: Ideas and Influence of Jean Calvin*, ed. Robert V. Schnucker (Kirksville, Mo.: Sixteenth Century Journal Publishers, 1988), 77–92.
231. *In psalmos*, 31:725.
232. *Praelectiones in Ezechielis propheta*, 456. See also *In psalmos*, 31:518.

CHAPTER 6

1. Jean Calvin to Guillaume Farel, in *Opera quae supersunt omnia*, ed. Eduard Reuss, Eduard Cunitz, and Johann Wilhelm Baum, 59 vols. in 26 (Brunswick: C. A. Schwetsche, 1863–1900), 13:655. References are usually to this edition by the volume and column numbers. References, where available, are to the critical edition in progress of Calvin, *Opera omnia* (Geneva: Droz, 1992–) cited as Geneva by the volume and page numbers. All translations in this chapter are mine unless otherwise stated.
2. Calvin, *Commentarius in psalmos*, 32:381–82.
3. Calvin to Farel, 655.
4. Philip Benedict, *Christ's Churches Purely Reformed: A Social History of Calvinism* (New Haven: Yale University Press, 2002), 230–31, 254. See also R. T. Kendall, *Calvin and English Calvinism to 1649* (Oxford: Oxford University Press, 1981).
5. Francis Higman, "Calvin's Works in Translation," in *Calvinism in Europe, 1540–1620*, ed. Andrew Petegree, Alastair Duke, and Gillian Lewis (Cambridge: Cambridge University Press, 1994), 87–88, 96–97, 94–95, 93.
6. Lancelot Andrewes, sermon on Luke 2:10–11, cited in Benson Bobrick, *Wide as the Waters: The Story of the English Bible and the Revolution It Inspired*

(New York: Penguin Books, 2001), 219, from *Lancelot Andrewes: Selected Writings*, ed. P. E. Hewison (Manchester: Fyfield Books, 1995), 11. For chiaroscuro, see chapter 5, pp. 225–34.

7. William Harvey, *Exercitationes de generatione animalium* (London: Octavian Pulleyn, 1651), 170.

8. Aristotle, *Physica* 8; *Metaphysica* 12.6 1072a–b.

9. Aquinas, *Summa theologiae* 1, q. 2 art. 3. For the Leonine edition of his *Opera omnia*, with a critical edition in progress, see http://www.corpusthomisticum.org/.

10. Stephen J. Grabill, *Rediscovering the Natural Law in Reformed Theological Ethics* (Grand Rapids, Mich.: William B. Eerdmans, 2006).

11. Independent from but in agreement with Paul Helm, *John Calvin's Ideas* (Oxford: Oxford University Press, 2004), 220–21.

12. Calvin, *Institutio christianae religionis* 3.14.2–3, cols. 564–65.

13. Chapter 5, pp. 233–34.

14. Susan E. Schreiner, *The Theater of His Glory: Nature and the Natural Order in the Thought of John Calvin* (Durham, N.C.: Labyrinth Press, 1991), 73–95. For generation, see William J. Bouwsma, *John Calvin: A Sixteenth Century Portrait* (New York: Oxford University Press, 1988), 136–37.

15. Chapter 5, pp. 207–8.

16. Calvin, *In psalmos*, 31:655–56.

17. See Bouwsma, *Calvin*, 137, 2.

18. Calvin, *Institutio christianae religionis* 1.5.3, col. 43.

19. See chapter 2, pp. 101–2, 103.

20. Harvey, *De generatione animalium*, praef., B2.

21. William Harvey, *Exercitatio anatomica de motu cordis et sanguinis in animalibus* (Frankfurt: William Fitzer, 1628; facsimile rpt., Birmingham, Ala.: Classics of Medicine Library, 1978), 5, 58.

22. Marjorie O'Rourke Boyle, "William Harvey's Anatomy Book and Literary Culture," *Medical History* 52 (2008): 73–91.

23. Harvey, *De generatione animalium*, praef., Bv, Cv. See also Ent, epistle dedicatory.

24. See chapter 5, pp. 206, 213.

25. *De motu cordis et sanguinis*, 20.

26. Andrew Cunningham, "Fabricius and the 'Aristotle Project' in Anatomical Teaching and Research at Padua," in *The Medical Renaissance of the Sixteenth Century*, ed. Andrew Wear, Robert K. French, and Iain M. Lonie (Cambridge: Cambridge University Press, 1985), 195–222.

27. Aristotle, *Historia animalium* 6.3 561a; Aristotle, *De generatione animalium* 2.1 735a, 753b; *De partibus animalium* 3.4 665a–b, 656a, 666a.

28. *De motu cordis et sanguinis*, praef.

29. Harvey, "De conceptione," appended to *De generatione animalium*, 295–96, 300.

30. Geoffrey Keynes, *The Life of William Harvey* (Oxford: Clarendon, 1966), 53–54.

31. See Julius Rocca, *Galen on the Brain: Anatomical Knowledge and Physiological Speculation in the Second Century AD* (Leiden: Brill, 2003), 196–98; Owsei Temkin, "On Galen's Pneumatology," in idem, *The Double Face of Janus* (Baltimore: Johns Hopkins University Press, 1977), 154–61.

32. Michael Frede, "Galen's Theology," in *Galien et la philosophie*, ed. Jonathan Barnes (Geneva: Fondation Hardt, 2003), 73–129; R. J. Hankinson, "Galen and the Best of All Possible Worlds," *Classical Quarterly* 39 (1989): 206–27.

33. Marjorie O'Rourke Boyle, *Senses of Touch: Human Dignity and Deformity from Michelangelo to Calvin* (Leiden: Brill, 1998), 172–73.

34. Keynes, *Life*, 286, 291.

35. *De motu cordis et sanguinis*, 27–28, 29, 35, 62, 20. Marjorie O'Rourke Boyle, "Harvey in the Sluice: From Hydraulic Engineering to Human Physiology," *Technology and History* 24 (2008): 1–23.

36. *De motu cordis et sanguinis*, 21. Marjorie O'Rourke Boyle, "Reprising Terence's Plot: William Harvey's Soliloquy to the College of Physicians," *Medical History* 52 (2008): 379–86.

37. Boyle, "Harvey's Soliloquy," 379, 380–81.

38. See chapter 3, pp. 116–18, 133–45.

39. See chapter 4, pp. 156–57, 161–64, 168–69.

40. See chapter 5, pp. 195, 213–16, 222–23.

41. Peter Martyr Vermigli, *Most learned and fruitful commentaries upon the Epistle of S. Paul to the Romans*, trans. Sir Henry Bilingsley (London: John Daye, 1568), 22r; and *Common places*, ed. Robert Masson, trans. Anthonie Martin (London: Henri Denham, Thomas Chord, William Broom, Andrew Maunsell, 1583), 1.2.4, cited by Grabill, *Rediscovering the Natural Law*, 112 n. 96.

42. Boyle, "Harvey's Soliloquy," 385–86.

43. *De motu cordis et sanguinis*, 31, 42, 27, 45–46. For Eristratus, see Harvey, *Exercitationes de circulatione sanguinis*, in *Opera omnia*, ed. Collegium Medicorum Londinensia, 2 vols. in 1 (London: G. Bowyer, 1766), 115.

44. Harvey, *De generatione animalium*, praef., p. B.

45. Aristotle, *De partibus animalium* 3.4 665a–b, 656a, 666a.

46. Harvey, *De generatione animalium*, 1–72.

47. For the history, see Howard B. Adelmann, ed., *The Embryological Treatises of Hieronymus Fabricius ab Aquapendente, ca. 1533–1619*, 2 vols. (Ithaca: Cornell University Press, 1942), 1:36–70; idem, *Marcello Malpighi and the Evolution of Embryology*, 5 vols. (Ithaca: Cornell University Press, 1966), 2:729–81; James G. Lennox, "The Comparative Study of Animal Development: William Harvey's Aristotelianism," in *The Problem of Animal Generation in Early Modern Philosophy, 1600–1800*, ed. Justin E. H. Smith (Cambridge: Cambridge University Press, 2006), 21–46.

48. Harvey, *De generatione animalium*, 32, 120. See also Boyle, "Harvey's Anatomy Book."

49. Harvey, *De generatione animalium*, 226–29.

50. Ibid., 139. For context, see Vivian Nutton, "The Seeds of Disease: An Explanation of Contagion and Infection from the Greeks to the Renaissance," *Medical History* 27 (1983): 1–34.

51. Harvey, *De generatione animalium*, 85, 146.

52. William Harvey, *Anatomical Lectures: "Prelectiones anatomie universalis," "De musculis,"* ed. Gweneth Whitteridge (Edinburgh: E. and S. Livingstone for the Royal College of Physicians, London, 1964), 2, citing Vergil, *Eclogae* 3.60, which began *Ab Jove*.

53. *Prelectiones*, title page. Aristotle, *Historia animalium* 1.16 494b.

54. Enrico Crivellato and Domenico Ribatti, "A Portrait of Aristotle as an Anatomist," *Clinical Anatomy* 20 (2007): 478. Harvey's acknowledgment of Aristotle as the ancient master has become the epigraph and the norm for Aristotle's own anatomy, 477.

55. Harvey, *De generatione animalium*, 170; *Anatomical Exercitations concerning the Generation of Living Creatures* (London: Octavian Pulleyn, 1653), 310.

56. See Annabel Patterson, "Pastoral Versus Georgic: The Politics of Vergilian Quotation," in *Renaissance Genres: Essays on Theory, History, and Interpretation*, ed. Barbara Kiefer Lewalski (Cambridge, Mass.: Harvard University Press, 1986), 242.

57. Craig Kallendorf, "From Virgil to Vida: The *poeta theologus* in Italian Renaissance Commentary," *Journal of the History of Ideas* 56 (1995): 41–62.

58. Charles Martindale, "Green Politics: The *Eclogues*," in *The Cambridge Companion to Virgil*, ed. idem (Cambridge: Cambridge University Press, 1997), 107–8, 115. For the poetic career, see Patterson, "Pastoral Versus Georgic," 245–46; Philip Hardie, *Virgil* (Oxford: Oxford University Press for the Classical Association, 1998), 1, 61.

59. Virgil, *Bucolica* 60, in *Opera*, ed. R. A. B. Mynors (Oxford: Clarendon, 1969). See also Wendell Clausen, *A Commentary on Virgil, "Eclogues"* (Oxford: Clarendon, 1994), 106.

60. Nicholas Orme, *Medieval Schools: From Roman Britain to Renaissance England* (New Haven: Yale University Press, 2006), 42, 97, 124; Mark H. Curtis, *Oxford and Cambridge in Transition, 1558–1642: An Essay on Changing Relations Between the English Universities and English Society* (Oxford: Clarendon, 1959), 86, 94, 105, 113.

61. Arthur F. Leach, ed., *Educational Charters and Documents, 598 to 1909* (Cambridge: Cambridge University Press, 1911), 466.

62. Hardie, *Virgil*, 9.

63. For the stage, see C. E. Woodruff and H. J. Cape, "*Schola Regia*

Cantuariensis": A History of Canterbury School: Commonly Called the King's School (London: Mitchell, Hughes and Clarke, 1980), 89.

64. See William F. Costello, *The Scholastic Curriculum of Early Seventeenth-Century Cambridge* (Cambridge, Mass.: Harvard University Press, 1958), 42, 61.

65. Patterson, "Pastoral Versus Georgic," 248.

66. Ibid., 241, 248–49, 263.

67. Vergil, *Ecloga* 3.61. Virgil, *Eclogues, Georgics, Aeneid I–VI*, trans. H. Rushton Fairclough, rev. G. P. Goold (Cambridge, Mass.: Harvard University Press, 1999), 43.

68. Keynes, *Life*, 53–54.

69. For Harvey's ambition for immortality, see Marjorie O'Rourke Boyle, "Harvey, by Hercules! The Hero of the Blood's Circulation," *Medical History* 57 (2013): 6–27.

70. See Paul Alpers, *The Singer of the "Eclogues": A Study of Virgilian Pastoral* (Berkeley: University of California Press, 1979), 97–113.

71. Vergil, *Ecloga* 3.1–24.

72. Harvey, *De generatione animalium*, 136.

73. George Ent, epistle dedicatory to Harvey, *De generatione animalium*, a 1.

74. Aquinas, *Summa theologiae* 1, q. 93 a 6.

75. See chapter 5, pp. 213–14.

76. Ent, epistle dedicatory, to Harvey, *Animal Exercitations*, n.p. The translator is proposed as Ent by Keynes, *Bibliography*, 3. The Latin and English volumes may have been produced together although published in 1651 and 1653 respectively. Webster, "Harvey's *De generatione animalium*," 270. The translation also aggrandized Harvey's "it has always pleased me" to "it hath ever been the delight of my Genius," and his "inspection" of animals to "strict Inspection."

77. Augustine, *De civitate Dei* 4.9, ed. Eligius Dombart and Alphonsus Kalb, 2 vols. (Turnhout: Brepols, 1944), 105–6.

78. Euan Nisbet, "Heavenly Phenomena," *Nature* 410 (April 5, 2001): 635.

79. Aratus, *Phaenomena* 1–4, ed. and trans. Douglas Kidd (Cambridge: Cambridge University Press, 1997), 73.

Vergil, *Ecloga* 3.60, cf. *Georgica* 2.4. Ernest Maas, ed., Aratus, *Phaenomena* (Berlin: Weidmann, 1893), 3.

80. Kidd, Aratus, *Phaenomena*, 161–66; Jean Martin, ed., Aratus, *Phaenomena* (Florence: Nuova Italia, 1956), 3.

81. D. Mark Possanza, *Translating the Heavens: Aratus, Germanicus, and the Poetics of Latin Translation* (New York: Peter Lang, 2004), 96–97, 81–82.

82. Vergil, *Eclogae* 23.60; *Georgica* 2.4. See below, p. 260.

83. Cicero, *Aratea: Fragments poétiques* line 1, ed. Jean Soubiran (Paris: Belles lettres, 1972), 158 n. 1 and 197.

84. Germanicus Caesar, Aratus 1, in *The Aratus Ascribed to Germanicus Caesar*, ed. D. B. Gain (London: Athlone, 1976).

85. Joseph Fitzmyer, *The Acts of the Apostles: A New Translation with Introduction and Commentary* (New York: Doubleday, 1998), 610–11; C. K. Barrett, *A Critical and Exegetical Commentary on the Acts of the Apostles*, 2 vols. (Edinburgh: T. and T. Clark, 1994–98), 2:848–49.

86. Calvin, chapter 5, pp. 219–21, 233–34.

87. Nisbet, "Heavenly Phenomena."

88. Acts 17:29–31.

89. Jean Calvin, *Commentarius in Acta Apostolorum*, ed. Helmut Feld, 2 vols. (Geneva: Droz, 2001), 2:125–26. See also idem, *Institutio christianae religionis* 1.5.5, 2:45, 1.14.1, col. 117.

90. See Walter Pagel, "Harvey, Foetal Irritability—and Albertus Magnus," *Medical History* 10 (1966): 409–11. For Bauhin, see Whitteridge, ed., Harvey, *Anatomical Lectures*, 324, 334, xxxii–xxxiv.

91. Nancy Siraisi, "The Medical Learning of Albertus Magnus," in *Albertus Magnus and the Sciences*, ed. James A. Weisheipl (Toronto: Pontifical Institute of Medieval Studies, 1980), 380.

92. Adelmann, *Fabrici*, 1:50–51, 67, 69; idem, *Malpighi*, 5:2080–82.

93. Edward A. Mahoney, "Albert the Great and the *studio patavino* in the Late Fifteenth and Early Sixteenth Centuries," in Weisheipl, *Albertus Magnus and the Sciences*, 544–45, 561–63.

94. *Gesamtkatalog der Wiegendrucke*, ed. Kommission für den Gesamtkatalog der Wiegendrucke (Leipzig: Karl W. Hiersemann, 1925–), 1:271–73.

95. See Albert the Great, *De animalibus*, ed. Hermann Stadler, 2 vols. (Munich: Aschendorff, 1916–20).
96. Ibid., II.2.3, 1:792–93. See Aristotle, *De partibus animalium* 1.4–5 644b–645a.
97. Albert the Great, *De animalibus* II.2.3, 1:793–94.
98. See Robert Boyle, *Of the Usefulnesse of Naturall Philosophy* (1663), cited by A. L. Peck in Aristotle, *Parts of Animals*, trans. idem, 2 vols. (Cambridge, Mass.: Harvard University Press, 1965), 1: 98–99 n. a.
99. Kenneth F. Kitchell Jr. and Irven M. Resnick, *On Animals: A Medieval "Summa zoologica"* (Baltimore: Johns Hopkins University Press, 1999), 889 n. 85. *De animalibus*, 792 n. 29.
100. *De circulatione sanguinis*, 110.
101. Aristotle, *De partibus animalium* 1.5 645a; trans. D. M. Balme, *Aristotle's "De partibus animalium" I and "De generatione animalium" I (with Passages from II.1–3)* (Oxford: Clarendon, 2001), 18. See further on Aristotle's anecdote Marjorie O'Rourke Boyle, *Cultural Anatomies of the Heart in Aristotle, Augustine, Aquinas, Calvin, and Harvey* (New York: Palgrave Macmillan, 2008).
102. James G. Lennox, in *Aristotle: On the Parts of Animals*, trans. idem (Oxford: Clarendon, 2001), 172, 174.
103. Aristotle, *De partibus animalium 1*, trans. Balme, 18. See Albert the Great, *De animalibus* II.2.3, 1:794.
104. Angela Della Volpe, "From the Hearth to the Creation of Boundaries," *Journal of Indo-European Studies* 18 (1990): 158–60.
105. *De motu cordis et sanguinis*, 42, 59; Harvey, *De generatione animalium*, 54, 183, 250. Boyle, "Harvey's Soliloquy," 25.
106. Roger K. French, *William Harvey's Natural Philosophy* (Cambridge: Cambridge University Press, 1994), 4, 70, and see 190, 385.
107. George N. Clark, A. M. Cook, and Asa Briggs, *A History of the Royal College of Physicians of London*, 4 vols. (Oxford: Clarendon for the Royal College of Physicians, 1964–72), 1:101, 177. See also Boyle, "Harvey's Soliloquy," 374–75, 376–77.
108. See above, n. 32. See also Teun Tieleman, "Galen and Genesis," in *The Creation of Heaven and Earth: Re-interpretations of Genesis I in the Context of Judaism, Ancient Philosophy, Christianity, and Modern Physics*, ed. George H. van Kooten (Leiden: E. J. Brill, 2005), 125–45.
109. Rudolph M. Siegel, *Galen on Psychology, Pathology, and Function and Diseases of the Nervous System: An Analysis of His Doctrines, Observations, and Experiments* (Basel: Karger, 1973), 117; Owsei Temkin, *Galen in a World of Pagans and Christians* (Baltimore: Johns Hopkins University Press, 1991), 204.
110. Galen, *De usu partium* 3.10; trans. Margaret T. May, *On the Usefulness of the Parts of the Body*, 2 vols. (Ithaca: Cornell University Press, 1968), 1:189.
111. Kaspar Bauhin, *Theatrum anatomicum* (Frankfurt: M. Becker, 1605), dedication, as miscited by French, *Harvey's Natural Philosophy*, 43.
112. Bauhin, *Theatrum anatomicum*, 3–4 (italics mine). Aquinas, *Summa theologiae* 1, q. 93 a. 6 ad 1. See chapter 4, p. 172. *De spiritu et anima* was influentially misattributed to Augustine. Leo Norpoth, *Der pseudo-augustinische Traktat: "De spiritu et anima"* (Cologne: Institut für Geschichte der Medizin der Universität zu Köln, 1971); Gaetano Raciti, "L'autore del *De spiritu et anima*," *Rivista di filosofia neoscholastica* 53 (1961): 385–401. Aquinas cited it fifty-five times, five times naming Augustine as its author but twice denying its authenticity. Aquinas, *De veritate* q. 15 a. 1 ad 1; *Super Ioannem* chap. 10 lectio. 2.
113. Keynes, *Life*, 6, 43, 459.
114. Boyle, "Harvey's Anatomy Book," 74–77.
115. Lucia Rosetti, "La laurea di Harvey a Padova," in *Harvey e Padova*, ed. Giuseppe Ongaro, Maurizio Rippa Bonati, and Gaetano Thiene (Treviso: Antilia, 2006), 198 fig. 2, 199. See also Vivian Nutton, "Padua, Religion, and English Medicine in the Sixteenth Century," in *Libertas philosophandi in naturalibus: Libertà di ricerca e criteri di regolamentazione istiutionale tra '500 e '700*, ed. Silvia Ferretto, Pietro Gori, and Masimo Rinaldi (Padua: CLEUP, 2011), 163–76.
116. Julian Davies, *The Caroline Captivity of the Church: Charles I and the*

Remoulding of Anglicanism, 1625–1641 (Oxford: Clarendon, 1992), 82, 275–87.

117. See below, nn. 132–33.

118. See below, nn. 132–33, 155.

119. Harvey, "De partu," appendix to idem, *De generatione animalium*, 262, and see 223.

120. *Prelectiones*, 248. John 19:34. See also 1 John 5:1, 5–8.

121. Leviticus 17:11. Hebrews 9–10.

122. See recently *The Word and the World: Biblical Exegesis and Early Modern Science*, ed. Kevin J. Killeen and Peter J. Forshaw (Basingstoke: Palgrave Macmillan, 2007).

123. *Prelectiones*, 14, 4. Augustine, *De civitate Dei* 22.24, 2:849–52. *Prelectiones*, 14. Although Whitteridge's edition offers from Austin Farrar, D.D., as Harvey's source Augustine, *Sermones* 243, it seems farfetched that he would have read those sermons. Sermo 243 repeats themes of Augustine's much more popular and accessible *De civitate Dei* 22.14, which is also closer to Harvey's paraphrase. For a contemporary work addressed to the College of Physicians, London, that cites *De civitate Dei*, see Edward Jorden, *A Briefe Discourse of a Disease Called the Suffocation of the Mother* (London, 1603), 12r.

124. Harvey, *De generatione animalium* in the Pybus collection in the library of the University of Newcastle upon Tyne, f. 1; reprinted in *Disputations Touching the Generation of Animals*, trans. Gweneth Whitteridge (Oxford: Blackwell Scientific, 1981), appendix, 456.

125. Francis Bacon, *Novum organum* (Oxford: Clarendon, 1878), 154.

126. See Kidd, ed., Aratus, *Phaenomena*, 10–12, 164–66; Fakas, *Hellenistische Hesiod*, 18–39; Cyril Bailey, *Religion in Virgil* (Oxford: Clarendon, 1935), 143.

127. Alexander of Hales, *Glossa* 1 d. 36, citing Lucan, *Pharsalia* 9.580. Cited by Enzo Macagnolo, "David of Dinant and the Beginnings of Aristotelianism in Paris," in *A History of Twelfth-Century Philosophy*, ed. Peter Dronke (Cambridge: Cambridge University Press, 1988), 431–32.

128. French, *Harvey's Natural Philosophy*, 70.

129. Aquinas, *Summa theologiae* 1, q. 75 proem.

130. Harvey, *De generatione animalium*, 170.

131. See above p. 131.

132. Harvey, *De generatione animalium*, 128, 170. For the reign of Saturn, see Patricia A. Johnston, *Vergil's Agricultural Golden Age: A Study of the "Georgics"* (Leiden: E. J. Brill, 1980), 62–89.

133. *Book of Common Prayer* in the Order for the Administration of the Lord's Supper, or Holy Communion. Reception of that sacrament was mandated on the day of marriage by the Form of Solemnization of Matrimony. Harvey thus recited it at least on that occasion. See also the Apostles' Creed in the Order for Morning Prayer, and a Creed for Evening Prayer. *The Book of Common Prayer, 1559: The Elizabethan Prayer Book*, ed. John E. Booty (Charlottesville: University of Virginia Press for the Folger Shakespeare Library, 2005).

134. *De parturitone*, appendix to Harvey, *De generatione animalium*, 271; trans. Whitteridge, 411.

135. Aristotle, *Physica* 2.1 192b.

136. Douglas Bush, *English Literature in the Earlier Seventeenth Century, 1600–1660*, 2nd ed. rev. (Oxford: Clarendon, 1966), 310. See also Harold Cook, "Institutional Structures and Personal Belief in the London College of Physicians," in *"Religio medici": Medicine and Religion in Seventeenth Century England*, ed. Ole P. Grell and Andrew Cunningham (Aldershot: Scolar, 1996), 91–114; Boyle, "Harvey's Anatomy Book," 77.

137. *De motu cordis et sanguinis*, 10.

138. Harvey, *De generatione animalium*, 170.

139. *De motu cordis et sanguinis*, 8.

140. Andreas Vesalius, *De humani corporis fabrica libri septem* (Basel: I. Oporini, 1543). See also Vivian Nutton, "Vesalius Revised: His Annotations to the 1555 Fabrica," *Medical History* 56 (2012): 415–43.

141. *De motu cordis et sanguinis*, 72.

142. Harvey, *De generatione animalium*, 3, 14, 38. For the bees, see Johnston, *Vergil's Agricultural Golden Age*, 90–105.

143. *Institutio christianae religionis* 1.5.5, col. 45; 1.5.4, cols. 43–44.

144. Vergil, *Georgica* 1.118–59. See also Christopher Nappa, *Reading After*

Actium: Vergil's "Georgics," Octavian, and Rome (Ann Arbor: University of Michigan Press, 2005), 36–43; Vergil, *Georgics*, ed. R. A. B. Mynors (Oxford: Clarendon, 1990), 26–30.

145. *De motu cordis et sanguinis*, 54–58.

146. For its currency, see Erika Rummel, "The Reception of Erasmus' *Adages* in Sixteenth-Century England," *Renaissance and Reformation* 30 (1994): 19–25; Thomas W. Baldwin, *William Shakespere's Small Latine and Lesse Greeke*, 2 vols. (Urbana: University of Illinois Press, 1944), 2:749.

147. Erasmus, *Adagia*, ed. M. L. van Poll–von de Lisdonk et al., in *Opera omnia* (Amsterdam: North-Holland, 1971–), 2–3; trans. R. A. B. Mynors, *The Collected Works of Erasmus* (Toronto: University of Toronto Press, 1969–), 33:102.

148. *De motu cordis et sanguinis*, 21, 20. See André DuLaurens, *Historia anatomica*, in *Opera omnia anatomica et medica* (Frankfurt: William Fitzer, 1628), 352.

149. Boyle, "Harvey, by Hercules!"

150. *De motu cordis et sanguinis*, 5, 58.

151. Harvey, *De generatione animalium*, trans. Whitteridge.

152. See above, n. 53.

153. Aratus, *Phaenomena* 768–72, trans. Kidd, 129.

154. Harvey, *De generatione animalium*, 28–29, 83–84, citing Vergil, *Aeneid* 6.726–27; Fairclough, *Virgil*, 557. For Calvin, see chapter 5, pp. 220–221.

155. Harvey, *De generatione animalium*, 112–13, 125, 135. For *efflatus*, see also 255.

156. Ibid., 126, 127–28.

157. Ibid., praef., p. B2, 128. See also "De conceptione," 301.

158. Harvey, *De generatione animalium*, trans. Whitteridge, 211.

159. *De motu cordis et sanguinis*, 42. For the sun in medical history, see also Frede, "Galen's Theology," 111–25.

160. Harvey, *De generatione animalium*, 144–45.

161. Webster, "Harvey's *De generatione animalium*," 271; Walter Pagel, *William Harvey's Biological Ideas* (Basel: S. Karger, 1967), 82–124.

162. Harvey, *De generatione animalium*, 42.

163. Ibid., 145.

164. Genesis 1:22, 26, 28. For Christian exegesis, see Jeremy Cohen, *"Be Fertile and Increase, Fill the Earth and Master It": The Ancient and Medieval Context of a Biblical Text* (Ithaca: Cornell University Press, 1989), 221–70.

165. Gunnlaugur A. Jónsson, *The Image of God: Genesis 1:26–28 in a Century of Old Testament Research* (Stockholm: Almqvist & Wiksell, 1988).

166. See chapter 5, p. 219.

167. "De conceptione," 298–99.

168. Harvey, *De generatione animalium*, 145–46. See also "De conceptione," 296.

169. See Keynes, *Bibliography*, frontispiece (Pulleyn), between 50–51 (Ravestyn), between 74–75 (Jansson), between 86–87 (Elzevir). See also p. 52 nos. 34, 35–36; pp. 54–57 no. 37; p. 55 no. 39.

170. See K. W. Arafat, *Classical Zeus: A Study in Art and Literature* (Oxford: Oxford University Press, 1990), 82–84, 87, 116.

171. For the metonymn, see Boyle, *Senses of Touch*, 213–16.

172. See *Myth, Sexuality, and Power: Images of Jupiter in Western Art*, ed. Frances Van Keuren (Providence, R.I.: Center for Old World Archeology and Art, Brown University, 1998).

173. Joseph Needham, *A History of Embryology* (Cambridge: Cambridge University Press, 1934), 129, cited by Keynes, *Bibliography*, 48, 47.

174. Arthur W. Meyer, *An Analysis of the "De generatione animalium" of William Harvey* (Stanford: Stanford University Press, 1936), 79–81.

175. Harvey, *De generatione animalium*, 210, 214.

176. "De conceptione," 301.

177. Harvey, *De generatione animalium*, 145. 214–44. 20–22, 4–5, 22. See also *Prelectiones*, 160.

178. Keynes, *Life*, 47–48.

179. Harvey, *De generatione animalium*, 13–14. See also *Prelectiones*, 26.

180. See Keynes, *Life*, vii, 47.

181. Ernst R. Curtius, *European Literature and the Latin Middle Ages*, trans. Willard R. Trask (London: Routledge and Kegan Paul, 1953), 132–33.

182. Elizabeth Spieler, *Science, Reading, and Renaissance Literature* (Cambridge:

Cambridge University Press, 2004), 71–72.

183. Thomas Fuller, *History of the Worthies of England* (London, 1662), cited by H. P. Bayon, "William Harvey, Physician and Biologist: His Precursors, Opponents, and Successors," *Annals of Science* 3 (1938): 85.

184. Harvey, *De generatione animalium*, 14, citing Vergil, *Georgica* 2.324–29; p. 295.

185. Giordano Bruno, *Spaccio de la bestia trionfante* 3.2; *The Expulsion of the Triumphant Beast*, trans. and ed. Arthur D. Imerti (New Brunswick: Rutgers University Press, 1964), 237.

186. Ingrid Rowland, *Giordano Bruno: Philosopher/Heretic* (New York: Farrar, Straus and Giroux, 2008).

187. Boyle, "Harvey's Anatomy Book," 79.

188. For their catalogue, see Harvey, *De generatione animalium*, 170; above, n. 8.

189. Jerome, *Hebraicarum quaestionum in Genesim*, praef., 1.1, in *Patrologiae cursus completus series latina*, ed. J.-P. Migne, 221 vols. (Paris: 1800–75), 23:936, 937, 939. See also C. T. R. Hayward, *St. Jerome's "Hebrew Questions on Genesis"* (Oxford: Clarendon, 1995), 103–5; Adam Kamesar, *Jerome, Greek Scholarship, and the Hebrew Bible: A Study of the "Quaestiones hebraicae in Genesim"* (Oxford: Clarendon, 1993), 129–32, but as "hovering," p. 131. John Milton, *Paradise Lost* 7.234–35, and see 1.19–20.

190. See chapter 5, p. 206.

191. Arnold Williams, *The Common Expositor: An Account of the Commentaries on Genesis, 1527–1633* (Chapel Hill: University of North Carolina Press, 1948), 52.

192. Milton, *Paradise Lost* 1.21–22.

193. Harvey, *De generatione animalium*, 170; "De partu," 271.

194. Keynes, *Bibliography*, 58 and pl. 7.

195. Harvey, *De generatione animalium*, 146. For naming, see also praef., C3–C3v.

196. Harvey, *De generatione animalium*, trans. Whitteridge, 237.

197. Harvey, *De generatione animalium*, 147; pp. 29, 113, 136, 170; "De partu," 271.

198. *Latin Dictionary*, s.v. numen.

199. Calvin, *In Acta Apostolorum*, 2:127.

200. Harvey, *De generatione animalium*, 85, 146.

201. Ibid., 144, 145, 170.

202. Ibid., 170.

203. Ent, praefatio, ibid.

204. Harvey, *De generatione animalium*, 141, 122.

205. Harvey, "De conceptione," 296.

206. Harvey, *De generatione animalium*, 244. For Fernel, see James J. Bono, *The Word of God and the Languages of Man: Interpreting Nature in Early Modern Science and Medicine* (Madison: University of Wisconsin Press, 1995), 85–108; and for background, see idem, "Medical Spirits and the Medieval Language of Life," *Traditio* 40 (1984): 91–130. For a survey of spirit as the life force, see Marielene Putscher, *Pneuma, Spiritus, Geist: Vorstellungen von Lebensantrieb in ihren Geschichtlichen Wandlunden* (Wiesbaden: Franz Steiner, 1973). For other thinkers Harvey criticized, see Julius Caesar Scaliger, 196–97; Daniel Sennert, 207, 209.

207. Harvey, *De generatione animalium*, 251, 244–46.

208. Albert the Great, *De animalibus* 6.1.4, 1:453; 12.1.1, p. 838; 13.1.4, 2:906, 907; idem, *De motibus animalium* 1.2.4, in *Opera omnia*, ed. Augustus Borgnet (Paris: Ludovicum Vivès, 1890–99), 9:275. *De animalibus* 20.1.5, 2:1287. See Avicenna, *De anima* 5.5.8, in *Liber de anima, seu, sextus de naturalibus*, ed. Simone van Riet, 2 vols. (Louvain: Éditions orientalistes; Leiden: E. J. Brill, 1968), 2:176, 178–81. Marjorie O'Rourke Boyle, "The Wonder of the Heart: Albert the Great on the Origin of Philosophy," *Viator: Journal of Medieval and Renaissance Studies* 45 (2014): 149–72.

209. *De circulatione sanguinis*, 115, 116. For a cultural context, see *Spirits Unseen: The Representation of Subtle Bodies in Early Modern Culture*, ed. Christine Gotler and Wolfgang Neuber (Leiden: E. J. Brill, 2008).

210. *De circulatione sanguinis*, 110, 116, 117.

211. Ibid., 118, 119.

212. Harvey, *De generatione animalium*, 244.

213. See in general Marjorie Grene, "Descartes and the Heart Beat: A Conservative Innovation," in *Wrong for the Right Reasons*, ed. Jed Z. Buchwald and Allan Franklin (Dordrecht:

Springer, 2005), 91–97; Thomas Fuchs, *Mechanization of the Heart: Harvey and Descartes*, trans. Marjorie Grene (Rochester: University of Rochester Press, 2001).

214. Harvey, *De generatione animalium*, 244. For Aristotle on the heart as the source of heat, see *De partibus animalium* 3.4, 5 667b; *De generatione animalium* 2.3 737a; *De iuventute et senectute* 8 474a-b. For the vital heat and related issues, see Gad Freudenthal, *Aristotle's Theory of Material Substance: Heart and Pneuma, Form and Soul* (Oxford: Clarendon, 1995).

215. Harvey, *De generatione animalium*, 244, 248, 161.

216. See *De motu cordis et sanguinis*, 45, 59. For speculation that Harvey's shift from the heart to the blood was politically motivated by the shift in England from the monarchy to the republic, see Christopher Hill, "William Harvey and the Idea of Monarchy," *Past and Present* 27 (1964): 54–72. My articles cited in nn. 22, 35, 36, and 69 above do not support that speculation of an external political influence rather than the course of Harvey's anatomical investigations. Nor do they accept other assertions by Hill, notably that Harvey discovered the circulation of the blood in 1616.

217. Harvey, *De generatione animalium*, 148–49, 161–62.

218. See also chapter 1, pp. 38–39. Rolf Rendtorff, "Another Prolegomenon to Leviticus 17:11," in *Pomegranates and Golden Bells: Studies in Biblical, Jewish, and Near Eastern Ritual, Law, and Literature in Honor of Jacob Milgrom*, ed. David P. Wright, David Noel Freedman, and Avi Hurvitz (Winona Lake, Ind.: Eisenbrauns, 1995), 23–28. For Leviticus on contagion, see Harvey's later letter in 1653 to Giovanni Nardi, cited by Whitteridge trans., Harvey, *Disputation*, lxii–iii.

219. Harvey, *De generatione animalium*, 162. See also *De motu cordis et sanguinis*, 52. See Rudolph E. Siegel, *Galen's System of Physiology and Medicine: An Analysis of His Doctrines and Observation on Bloodflow, Respiration, Humors, and Internal Diseases* (Basel: S. Karger, 1968), 233, 352–59; Charles D. O'Malley and John B. de C. M. Saunders, introduction to Andreas Vesalius, *The Bloodletting Letter of 1539: An Annotated Translation and Study of Vesalius's Scientific Development*, ed. Saunders (New York: Henry Schuman, 1947), 5–36.

220. Harvey, *De generatione animalium*, 116; 151. *De motu cordis et sanguinis*, 26–28.

221. Harvey, *De generatione animalium*, 244, 245, 244.

222. Ibid., 247. See Aristotle, *De generatione animalium* 2.3 736b.

223. Harvey, *De generatione animalium*, 247. Ex. 3:2–5.

224. Harvey, *De generatione animalium*, 142. See G. E. R. Lloyd, "The Hot and the Cold, the Dry and the Wet in Greek Philosophy," *Journal of Hellenic Studies* 84 (1964): 92–106.

225. Siegel, *Galen's System*, 209; idem, *Galen on Psychology*, 185–97; Philip van der Eijk, "Galen on the Assessment of Bodily Mixtures," in *The Frontiers of Ancient Science: Essays in Honor of Heinrich von Staden*, ed. Brooke Holmes and Klaus-Dietrich Fischer (Berlin: De Gruyter, 2015), 675–88. See also see Richard Sorabji, *Emotion and Peace of Mind: From Stoic Agitation to Christian Temptation* (New York: Oxford University Press, 2000), 253–60; Simo Knuuttila, *Emotions in Ancient and Medieval Philosophy* (Oxford: Clarendon, 2004), 93–98; James R. Irwin, "Galen on Temperaments," *Journal of General Psychology* 36 (1947): 45–64.

226. See Susan James, *Passion and Action: The Emotions in Seventeenth-Century Philosophy* (Oxford: Oxford University Press, 1999); *Reading the Early Modern Passions: Essays in the Cultural History of the Emotions*, ed. Gail Kern Pastor, Kathryn Rowe, and Mary Floyd-Wilson (Philadelphia: University of Pennsylvania Press, 2004).

227. *Oxford English Dictionary*, 2nd ed. (1989), s.v. "spirit."

228. Siegel, *Galen's System*, 232–33, 218, 217.

229. See above, n. 184.

230. Albert the Great, *De anima* 1.1.6, ed. Clemens Stroick, in *Opera omnia*, 7-1:13, commenting on Aristotle, *De anima* 1.1 403a. See Boyle, "Wonder of the Heart."

231. Sorabji, *Emotion and Peace of Mind*; Knuuttila, *Emotions*. For some medieval authors on the central role of the heart in

the passions of the soul, particularly fear, see Marjorie O'Rourke Boyle, "Aquinas's Natural Heart," *Early Science and Medicine* 18 (2013): 266–90; idem, "Wonder of the Heart," 149–72.

232. *De motu cordis et sanguinis*, 15, 12.

233. For introductions, see C. R. S. Harris, *The Heart and the Vascular System in Ancient Greek Medicine: From Alcmaeon to Galen* (Oxford: Clarendon, 1973); Donald F. Proctor, ed., *A History of Breathing Physiology* (New York: Marcel Dekker, 1995).

234. See Proctor, ed., *History of Breathing*. For prior theories, see Daniel Piperno, *Histoire du souffle: La respiration dans l'Antiquité occidentale* (Paris: Imothep, 1998), and especially Armelle Debru, *Le corps respirant: La pensée physiologique chez Galien* (Leiden: E. J. Brill, 1996).

235. Proctor, ed., *History of Breathing*, 67–72.

236. S. Marsh Tenney, "A Brief History of Comparative Respiratory Physiology: Some Ideas and Their Proponents," in *Respiratory Physiology: People and Ideas*, ed. John B. West (New York: Oxford University Press for the American Physiological Society, 1996), 387. Harvey, *Prelectiones*, 296, 298.

237. See Robert E. Schofield, *The Enlightened Joseph Priestley: A Study of His Life and Work from 1773 to 1804* (University Park: The Pennsylvania State University Press, 2004), xiii, 91, 59–76, 93–119, 203, 217, 232–33. For context, see also Trevor H. Levere, *Transforming Matter: A History of Chemistry from Alchemy to the Buckyball* (Baltimore: Johns Hopkins University Press, 2001), 56–57, 60, 63–64, 66–79.

238. Thomas Dixon, *From Passions to Emotions: The Creation of a Secular Psychological Category* (Cambridge: Cambridge University Press, 2003).

239. Jerome Kagan, *What Is Emotion?* (New Haven: Yale University Press, 2004).

240. *De motu cordis et sanguinis*, 59–60. For his anaphoric questions, see especially proem, 10–19.

241. Harvey, *De generatione animalium* praef., Bv.

242. *Latin Dictionary*, s.v. *socordia*.

243. Harvey, *De generatione animalium*, 256.

244. "De conceptione," 301.

245. See above, n. 176.

246. Harvey, *De generatione animalium*, 144, 145.

247. Ben Jonson, *Cynthia's Revels* 5.5, cited in *Oxford English Dictionary*, 2nd ed. (1989), s.v. "spirited."

248. William Shakespeare, *The Tempest* 1.2.

INDEX

Adam, 5, 8, 10–11, 17, 32, 38, 49–56, 60–67, 87–88, 95–99, 120, 125–26, 131–34, 143–44, 157–158, 163, 165, 169–70, 173, 200, 204, 215–18, 230, 232–34, 236, 239, 241, 248, 251, 266
Albert the Great, 251–54, 273, 280
Aquinas, chapter 4, 1–3, 6–8, 195, 202, 205, 218, 238, 243, 248, 251, 254, 256–57, 265, 283
Aratus, 220–21, 249–50, 251, 257, 261–62
Aristotle/Aristotelian, 7, 10, 54, 61, 124, 140, 145, 153, 155–56, 159, 160–64, 168, 177–79, 182, 186, 191, 208–10, 218, 220, 225–29, 235, 238, 240–45, 2553–63, 268–69, 272–73, 276, 278–81
Augustine, chapter 3, 1–3, 6–7, 151, 153, 159, 164–69, 171–72, 175, 177, 180–86, 192, 196, 204, 206, 213, 218–19, 222, 233, 238, 243, 249, 254, 255–56, 265, 283

Bezalel, 81–85, 120
birds, 3–4, 18–48, 50, 52, 64–65, 79, 84–85, 122–23, 125, 130, 144–45, 153–54, 159, 181–82, 205–12, 235, 239, 242, 266–70, 281
blood, 1, 3, 9–10, 23, 25, 29, 39, 49, 75, 100, 169, 182, 231, 235, 239–42, 244, 253, 255, 259, 260–61, 264–65, 270, 272–83
breath, 3, 15–17, 23, 48, 50–54, 60, 63–68, 72, 86, 88, 92–101, 131–34, 140–41, 169–71, 200, 207, 213, 215–16, 22–25, 234, 243–44, 275, 278–80

Calvin, chapter 5, 1–3, 8–9, 238–43, 248, 250–51, 256, 260, 262, 266, 270, 284
contemplation, 6, 9, 102–3, 109–10, 122, 126, 141–45, 148–49, 166–67, 177, 180–83, 190, 221–22, 257
Corinth/Corinthians, chapter 2, 1–6, 107–25, 130, 133–38, 148, 151–81, 185–87, 191, 199, 202, 213, 218, 223, 225, 231–38, 240, 256, 283
creation, chapter 1, 1–6, 9, 11, 59–67, 72, 81–83, 87–100, 111–18, 130–36, 140–43, 146–49, 153–59, 165–75, 181, 186–87, 195, 198, 200–207, 213, 216–18, 220–24, 228, 233–34, 236, 238, 240, 243, 255, 256, 263, 265, 266, 270, 281–82, 283

Delphic oracle, 62, 113–14, 124, 146, 233, 272

English bibles, 17–19, 35, 37, 118, 237, 277

generation, 2, 4, 9–11, 26, 32–34, 143, 145, 238, 240–42, 244, 247, 256, 257, 258, 259–73, 276, 278, 280, 283–84
Genesis, chapter 1, 1–11, 59–64, 78–79, 82, 87, 94–102, 107, 111–15, 130–33, 135–36, 143–49, 165–71, 174, 185–86, 195, 203–8, 213–17, 220–21, 225, 236, 237–38, 248, 255, 263, 266, 270, 281, 283
Golden Eagle, 4, 21–26, 30–31, 36–37, 39, 42–47, 50, 52, 85, 209–10

Harvey, William, chapter 6, 1–3, 9–11

INDEX

Hebrew Bible, chapter 1, 1, 3–5, 38, 60–62, 74, 96–99, 101, 107, 111, 147, 159, 174, 185, 205–8, 217, 221

idols, 16–18, 22, 26, 33, 41, 51, 53, 65, 67, 74, 80, 97, 110, 197, 234, 240, 250
immateriality, 7–8, 129–30, 142, 157, 164, 165, 167–68, 173, 183, 185
indwelling, 5, 8, 9, 74, 80–81, 90, 98, 101, 113, 148, 176, 215, 219–20, 232
Itala/Vetus Latina, 7, 18, 62, 107

Joseph, 83, 120–21, 131

labyrinth, 2, 196–99, 202, 212, 219, 229, 240, 242, 264–65, 282

medicine, chapter 6, 63, 100
mind, 3, 6–10, 61, 80, 92–93, 102, 108, 113–18, 129–49, 153–58, 161, 165–69, 171–73, 176–92, 196–98, 200–201, 204, 213, 215, 217–18, 220, 223–24, 226, 228–30, 233–35, 238, 240, 243, 251, 258–62, 265–66, 271–72, 280–82
mirror, 6 8, 47, 102–3, 108, 110, 114, 118–29, 139, 147–49, 156, 176–78, 192, 196, 204, 209, 218, 232–33

Oedipus, 6, 103, 123–26, 273

passions, 1–10, 113, 142, 156, 162, 179–80, 183, 187, 191, 196–97, 205, 215, 225, 231, 243, 252, 268–69, 280, 283
Paul, chapter 2, 1–10, 113, 115–30, 133–39, 146, 148–49, 151–65, 168, 170–73, 176–88, 191–92, 199, 200, 202–3, 213, 216, 218–21, 223–25, 231–33, 235, 238, 240, 250–51, 256, 262, 283–84
Plato/Platonist, 109–10, 129, 141, 169–70, 172, 174, 190, 214, 217, 220–22, 238, 243, 258, 272
pottery, 67, 87–91
Priestly tradition/writing, 1–4, 9, 25–26, 31–35, 38, 45–53, 55, 57, 82, 84, 146–47, 276, 277, 248

rapture, 5, 70–73, 77–79, 97, 101–2, 135–36, 139, 173, 178–81, 183–84, 192, 202–3, 205

resurrection, 62, 73, 76, 79, 87, 89, 91, 94, 96, 134, 153, 157, 233, 250, 255–56
riddle, 6, 103, 118, 120–27, 129, 273

science, chapter 6, 1–3, 9–11, 15, 27–28, 110, 142, 151, 158, 160–61, 169, 217, 225
seal, 75, 86, 89–90, 234–35
Septuagint, 18, 20, 54, 60, 63, 78–79, 82, 84–85, 95, 100, 111, 117, 120, 207
soul, 3, 6–10, 88, 92–97, 102, 108–10, 115–18, 130–49, 156–57, 161–65, 168–73, 175–79, 184–85, 187–91, 196, 202, 214–20, 223, 230–32, 238, 241–44, 248, 254, 257–60, 266, 268, 271–73
stamp, 90–92, 123, 165, 172, 235

Talmud, 15–18, 72, 174

Ugaritic, 3, 20, 22–28, 52, 84

Vergil, 197, 220–21, 244–55, 257–62, 269, 270, 272, 280
vision, 7–8, 45–46, 50, 68, 71–75, 78, 86–87, 92, 103, 120, 126–30, 135–39, 141, 143, 148–49, 153–54, 171–73, 175–80, 183–84, 187–88, 204, 221, 233, 278
vivification, 9, 18, 133, 169, 172, 175, 185, 189–90, 206, 213–16, 218, 221–23, 243, 270–79
Vulgate, 17–19, 37, 42–45, 62, 102, 107, 117, 133, 154, 156, 159, 161, 182, 195, 208–9, 212, 270, 279

wind, 3, 15–18, 23, 28, 30–31, 35, 45, 49–55, 66–67, 78, 85–86, 100–101, 133, 162, 167, 174, 182, 205, 207, 216, 243

Yahwist tradition/writing, 32, 48–57

www.ingramcontent.com/pod-product-compliance
Lightning Source LLC
Chambersburg PA
CBHW021933290426
44108CB00012B/826